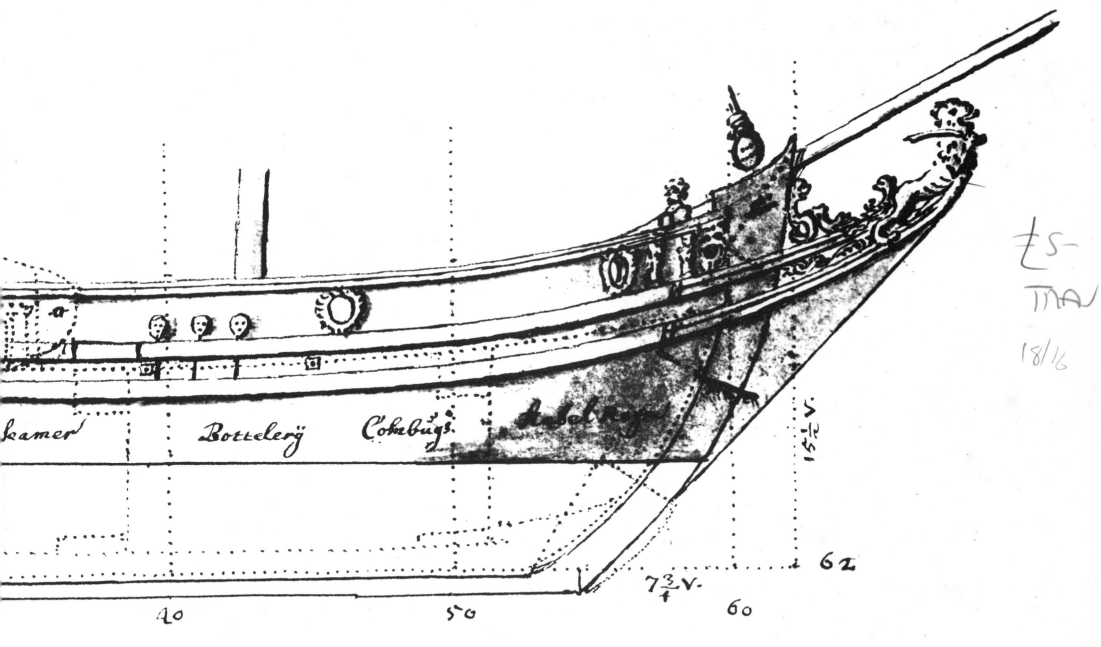

kamer   Bottelerij   Cokebuijs.   *Adelbajt*

$15\frac{1}{2}$ V.

62

$7\frac{3}{4}$ V.

40   50   60

Langh over Steven 62 . V.

Wijt binnen zijn Huijt. 18 . V.

ES-
TNA

18/16

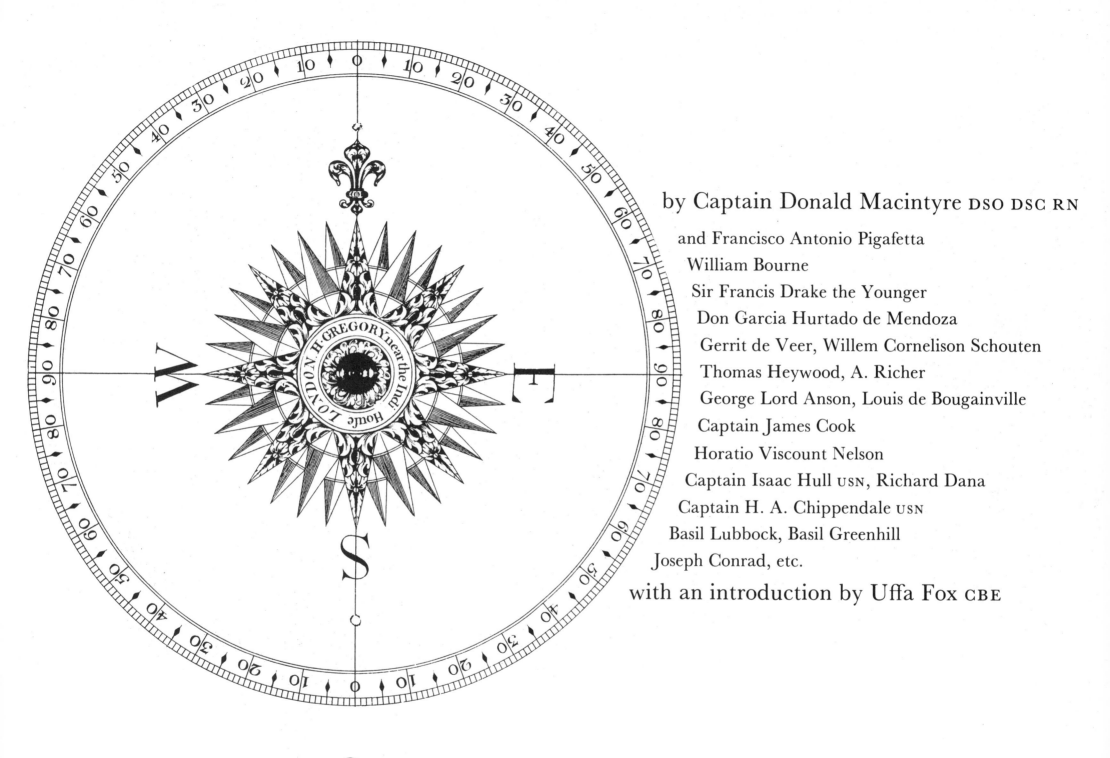

by Captain Donald Macintyre DSO DSC RN

and Francisco Antonio Pigafetta

William Bourne

Sir Francis Drake the Younger

Don Garcia Hurtado de Mendoza

Gerrit de Veer, Willem Cornelison Schouten

Thomas Heywood, A. Richer

George Lord Anson, Louis de Bougainville

Captain James Cook

Horatio Viscount Nelson

Captain Isaac Hull USN, Richard Dana

Captain H. A. Chippendale USN

Basil Lubbock, Basil Greenhill

Joseph Conrad, etc.

with an introduction by Uffa Fox CBE

 Ferndale Editions London

Advisory Editor: Captain Donald Macintyre DSO, DSC, RN
Anthology collected and edited by Julian Hall
Illustrations collected by Julian Hall and Timothy Chilvers
with the advice of
the Picture Department
National Maritime Museum, Greenwich
Glossary illustrations by Dr R. W. Horne

This edition published 1979 by Ferndale Editions
Brent House, 24-28 Friern Park, London N12,
under licence from the proprietor

The Adventure of Sail 1520-1914 © Paul Elek Productions 1970
No part of the contents of this book may be reproduced without prior
written consent of the publishers

Design and typography by Harold Bartram
Filmset in England by The Birmingham Typesetters Ltd
Printed in Italy by Amilcare Pizzi S.p.A.
Bound by Webb Son & Co. Ltd, London

Other books
by Donald Macintyre

U-Boat Killer
Jutland
Narvik
Fighting Admiral
Fighting Ships and Seamen
Fighting Under the Sea
Battle of the Atlantic
Battle of the Mediterranean
Battle for the Pacific
Admiral Rodney
Wings of Neptune
The Thunder of the Guns
The Kola Run (co-author)
The Aircraft Carrier

Front endpapers 1 and 2
Elevation from a Dutch design for a
state yacht, by Jacobus Storck, 1642.

Front endpaper 3
Three Men of War Before a Fresh
Breeze, engraving by Frans Huys
after P. Breugel (*c.* 1525 – 1569).

Half-title page
The Building of the Ark, engraving
by J. Sadeler (1550 – 1600) after
M. de Vos.

Title page
A seventeenth-century compass card.

This page
A sixteenth-century view of the port
of Amsterdam.

Contents

List of colour plates

Opposite
The Departure of an East Indiaman,
by Adam Willaerts (1577–1664).
A detail of this oil painting is shown
in colour on the front and back
jacket.

Introduction

by Uffa Fox CBE

'Roll on, thou deep and dark blue Ocean—
   roll!
Ten thousand fleets sweep over thee in vain;
Man marks the earth with ruin—his control
Stops with the shore; upon the watery plain
The wrecks are all thy deed, nor doth remain
A shadow of man's ravage, save his own,
When for a moment, like a drop of rain,
He sinks into thy depths with bubbling groan,
Without a grave, unknell'd, uncoffin'd, and unknown'

     .   .   .   .

'These are thy toys, and, as the snowy flake,
They melt into thy yeast of waves, which mar
Alike the Armada's pride or spoils of Trafalgar'

     .   .   .   .

'Unchangeable, save to thy wild waves' play,
Time writes no wrinkle on thine azure brow:
Such as creation's dawn beheld, thou rollest now.'

All my life has been closely connected with the sea and ships. The Commodore's House, in which I now live at Cowes on the Isle of Wight, was converted into a home from a warehouse where brigs laid alongside and unloaded their cargoes. With the sea round three sides of my house, whether waking or sleeping, I am surrounded by memories of square-rigged trading vessels out of the past. Square-rigged ships, in my younger days, filled the deep water bay two miles up the River Medina which meets the sea at Cowes. This was as far as they could enter the tidal river flowing to Newport, the capital of the Isle of Wight. Barges came alongside then and unloaded timber or whatever their cargo, and transported it to Newport or Cowes.

It was a wonderful sight to see these ships, which generally stayed a week while being unloaded and loaded again. If they had no cargo to take they used to drop on to the bank in the middle of Cowes harbour and load up with shingle ballast and so help to dredge the river.

These ships from the Baltic and other seas came until close on the 1914 war, so for us on the Isle of Wight the sailing ship endured longer than for most people.

I remember what a busy scene Shalfleet Quay in the Newtown River on the Isle of Wight used to be. There were many salt meadows with banks between, connected to each other by hollowed-out trees forming pipes, which enabled these meadows to be flooded or drained to the required depth of 3 inches or less; the sun evaporated the water and left the salt behind, which was then scraped up with long, flat, rake-shaped scrapers of light, thin wood. Collier brigs from the North would bring down coal for this area of the Isle of Wight, unload it on the quay and then go away loaded with a cargo of salt and corn—a very direct exchange of natural wealth.

In the south we had enough sun to make sea water into salt crystals and to grow corn easily. In the north they had the natural deposits of coal.

In some places the collier brigs laid off-shore and the coal was boated to the land by sixteen-foot long rowing boats. After the brigs had been scrubbed out they were loaded with corn in the same way. This form of trading went on all over the coast of England.

When I was young I too took part in these manifold commercial activities of the sailing ship era. I often sailed in a small spritsail rigged Thames barge, the *Rose*, for a load of shingle off the Needles, that group of sharp rocks which marks the western extremity of the Isle of Wight. She wore a cock on her mizzen mast, as she had won a race for her class on the Thames. We always left Cowes at high-water to take the south-west ebb stream down to the shingle bank abreast and north of the Needles, where the tide ran fiercely. In those far off days the shingle bank stood twelve feet above high-water mark and was shaped like a fish hook, the long shank running south-west with the barbed point curving round to the north-east. We sailed into this protected bay, and laid the barge ashore on the shingle, safe and secure from the run of tide and waves.

With the ebb at its swiftest she grounded immediately and we ran planks out to the shingle bank with a slight slope upwards from the barge's coamings. This meant that we wheeled the empty wheelbarrows slightly uphill, but when they were full, the weight of shingle pulled us where we wanted to go, to a block of wood across the bottom of our plank to stop the wheel running on into the hold; as the wheel came against this we twisted the handles and the shingle shot into the hold.

This was hard work but pretty good fun and we were always loaded before the flood made to float us off and the run of its stream to drive us north-eastward back to Cowes. The ebb stream ran south-westward and the flood flowed north-eastward, so even without wind we could always make this voyage on an ebb and flood tide—it was for all the world like being on a moving stairway.

In the early days of yachting the amateurs were not the sure navigators they are today and it was the custom for such men in their yachts to follow Thames barges who knew every shoal and exactly where they were going.

One day doing this, a deep-keeled yacht ran aground on a sand bank in the middle of the Thames Estuary, and soon after the barge also ran aground. The amateur yachtsman rowed over to the bargee in his dinghy and said: 'You have made a mistake this time.' The bargee replied: 'Well, I've come here for a load of sand—but I can't think what you've come for!'

So we see we are not far removed from days when everything was from the hand of God—the wind that drove the trading ships, and their cargoes, were all natural elements such as are met throughout the pages of this book.

I also went to sea in square-rigged ships and well remember fierce battles with sails aloft. The sails were suspended from the yards and so to reef you heaved up on the reef earings and then tied up the reef points. In doing so you had to lift the whole weight of the sail together with the wind's force in it. Meanwhile you were laid with your tummy over the yard and your feet on the foot rope, so whenever we stepped on or off the foot rope from and to the mast we gave a strong clear call, 'foot rope!' to warn those already out on the yard-arm that the foot rope would now become shorter or longer and could shoot men over the foreside of the yard.

Laying out on a yard-arm, reefing or stowing square sails was the essence of team work.

Having spent a lifetime connected with the sea, I have many, many interesting articles in my house, and among them I am fortunate in possessing the piano of the author of the lines at the beginning of this introduction, Lord Byron, which was made by Thomas Sheraton in 1790 from lovely contrasting mahoganies, then a new wood brought by our far-sailing merchantmen.

In the days gone by, the sea divided the world for a landsman, but united it for a seaman. For once on it in a well-found vessel, the mariner could travel to the uttermost ends of the earth. As his

knowledge of the world and his instruments to measure the angles of the sun and the stars improved, he was able to navigate with greater accuracy and make his charts more accurate year after year.

Today we have weather charts giving the wind directions, its strength and frequency, and also predicting the ocean currents, fogs, gales and tempests for every month of the year and for every sea and part of the world. This improved knowledge of wind and wave gives us a great advantage over the ancients and enables us to plan and carry out difficult voyages with safety and certainty. Men have now sailed round the world single-handed, and in 1969 two rowed across the Atlantic alone, and all these voyages were accomplished according to plan, thanks to this great wealth of accumulated knowledge of the sea.

So the world gradually became an open book to seamen and also a home and a meeting place. Seamen swiftly learned from each other, and thus we find similar contrivances appearing all over the world. From all over Europe men sailed across the Atlantic to fish for cod on the Grand Banks of Newfoundland, which are formed by icebergs, brought south on the Arctic current to meet the warm Gulf Stream, melting, and depositing earth and moss for the great wealth of codfish off Newfoundland. To fish for codfish the Europeans developed a fishing dory, sixteen to twenty feet long, flat bottomed with flaring topsides, so that half a dozen

1 and 2 *overleaf* Bow and stern views of *L'Invincible,* a French three-decker of the late eighteenth century.

1 This illustration, from a contemporary book on naval architecture, shows the manner of stowing the anchors at the catheads, as well as the ornamentation at the bows concealing the heads, the inadequate sanitary arrangements for the ship's crew (see p. 30). The broken off masts are a draughtsman's convention.

could nest inside one another for the voyage across the Atlantic. It was from these dories that the line fishermen worked the Grand Banks. I have heard many an American lay claim to the design of the dory, but it has been found throughout Europe and in Spain and Portugal where it originated.

For whalers too the sea was a meeting place. In that wonderful American book *Moby Dick* mention is made of meeting a British whaling ship, the *Samuel Enderby*. My great-grandfather was in charge of this ship while she was being built in Cowes by John Samuel White's, and on completion he sailed in her as mate. Enderbyland in the Antarctic takes its name from the Enderby firm of London which discovered it. I still have pictures of this ship and her whale boats and also a scale drawing of a sperm whale.

Marine drawings and paintings are full of information. Recently I studied the drawings of the old original London Bridge. I had

imagined that the schooner *America* introduced the triatic stay to this country when she came here in 1851, but in these engravings of 1834 both the triatic and the portable stays can be seen in two different schooners at Billingsgate.

As we roam through this Adventure of Sail, we must bear in mind the limiting factors in the materials the builders could lay hands on for construction, for only then can we appreciate their wondrous works. Man can only build with the materials at his disposal. I have an Eskimo kayak, built from sealskin, whalebone and driftwood, and although made of such simple materials, the only materials the Eskimos could use, it is so wonderfully made and developed that all paddling canoes today are based on it; a tribute to its perfection.

With the passing of the years and improvement in materials, vessels and their gear were improved, but even just 150 years ago there was very little metal in the construction of a ship. The frames and planking and also the deck were all of wood joined together with wooden trenails, and the size of the timber naturally controlled the size of the ship. All the early rigging was of hemp; the steel wire rigging we know today has only come into being in the last 100 years. Anchor cables were of hemp right up to Nelson's time.

The smallness of the old sailing ships enabled them to be handled by small crews and some were so handy and responsive that they were able to traverse dangerous waters. With the great weight and windage aloft the old sailing ships were, at times, blown down on their beam ends and lay at this 90 degree angle until the gale abated, sometimes remaining for two days in this uncomfortable position. Their wooden spars, once in the water, floated and so made the ships stable at this angle—provided, however, that all ports and hatches were closed and sealed to prevent the ship filling with seawater.

This Adventure of Sail, tracing some 400 years of sail in history, can be appreciated all the more if we remember the simple materials which men worked to fashion such exquisite and practical modes of transport.

2 The perfection of simple materials: a stern view of the eighteenth-century French three-decker *L'Invincible*, showing the stern windows of the great cabin and the decorations and large lanterns on which so much pride was lavished (see p. 26 *f.*). The bow view is on p. 9.

From the caravel to the clipper

by Captain Donald Macintyre RN

an observatory and school for navigation at Sagres near Cape St Vincent, ocean voyages setting out from Lisbon had gone as far afield as the Azores by 1448.

It was largely in the hope of gaining a monopoly of the spice trade that expedition after expedition set out from Lisbon. Fernando Po reached the Gold Coast in 1470; in 1482 Diego Cao discovered the mouth of the Congo River; then, in 1488, Bartholomew Diaz at last rounded the Cape of Good Hope in the *Sao Pantaleao*, proving that a sea route to the Spice Islands existed. Meanwhile before advantage of this discovery could be taken, the Genoese Christopher Columbus, under the patronage of the Spanish monarchs Ferdinand and Isabella, set out in 1492 in the *Santa Maria*, accompanied by two little caravels, the *Pinta* and *Nina*, to seek a westward route in the course of which he discovered the Bahamas, Cuba and Haiti.

Columbus went on to make three further voyages, reaching the mainland of South America and exploring the Gulf of Mexico, discoveries which were to bring the New World into existence with all that that has signified. At the time, however, it was the arrival in 1498 of the flotilla of four ships under the Portuguese Vasco da Gama at Calicut in India, the flagship *S. Raphael*, the *S. Gabriel*, the *Berio* and a small auxiliary, which made the greatest stir. The cargo of spices they brought back gave a 600 per cent profit to the voyage and heralded the final eclipse of Venice as the centre of world seaborne trade.

Two years later Pedro Alvares Cabral sailed with a squadron of twelve ships, charged not only with trading with the Indies but with establishing Portuguese sovereignty there. His square-rigged ships, beating to the south-westward across the region of the south-east trade wind, reached the coast of Brazil, and Cabral took possession of it in the name of the King before tacking back to the Cape of Good Hope.

The earliest of these voyages were made in the type of craft developed in the Mediterranean with a 'fore-and-aft' rig of lateen sails which had been introduced by the Arabs as early as the eighth century.

The main feature of the lateen sail is the very long yard it

Development of the square-rigged ship

3 Portuguese Carracks off a Rocky Coast, oil painting (*c.* 1535) attributed to Cornelis Anthoniszoon. The vessel in the bottom right corner is a galley. Portuguese navigators discovered both the eastern and western routes to the Indies; Bartholomew Diaz rounded the Cape of Good Hope in 1488 and ten years later Vasco da Gama reached India. In 1520 Ferdinand Magellan discovered the way to the Pacific through the straits which are named after him.

When the long night of the Middle Ages retreated before the dawn of the Renaissance, one of the most spectacular developments was that of the ocean-going sailing ship. The urge to find a sea route to the fabulous Indies and the wonders of Cathay which arose at that time, and the improvement in seaworthiness and mobility of the sailing ship, reacted mutually to give one another impetus.

The common incentive came from the blocking of the caravan routes from the Orient by the rise of the Ottoman Empire and the consequent cutting off of supplies of spices, a vital ingredient in the European diet of those days, and of the pain-killing drugs only obtainable in the East. Under the patronage of Prince Henry the Navigator, son of King John I of Portugal, who had established

requires. As ships increased in size this became correspondingly large and unwieldy, to overcome which the sail area was divided between first two and later three masts, the tallest of which was forward. By the end of the fourteenth century such ships had become common in the Mediterranean. They were of only moderate tonnage however, being largely limited by the size of lateen sail which could conveniently be handled. The name 'caravel', given to such ships operated by the Portuguese, is of obscure origin, but it became the generic name for such ships everywhere.

In northern waters bordering on the Atlantic and the North Sea, the square sail, a simple rectangular spread of canvas with which a ship could take advantage of a fair wind, had remained in use by seafarers since the dawn of history. During the Middle Ages the greatest number of these ships voyaged under the aegis of the Hanseatic League. The word *hansa* implies an association of merchants' guilds and the Hanseatic League was an association of North German seaports for the purposes of trade. The Baltic and North Sea were at an early date important highways of maritime trade dominated by the League, firstly from Wisby on the island of Gothland, but later from German ports on the mainland, with Lübeck and Hamburg eventually becoming supreme.

Confederacy brought political power and when Denmark became a serious and aggressive rival in the fourteenth century, the League fought and won a war with her as a result of which Denmark was subjected to its domination. The power and influence of the League began to decline during the next century, the rise of England as a major sea-trading country, the move of the profitable herring shoals from the Baltic to the North Sea and the break-up of the Holy Roman Empire being some of the chief reasons.

The type of ship in general use by the Hanse merchants was a square-sailed, single-masted vessel known as a 'cog'.

When, about this time, seaborne trade between northern and southern states of Europe began to develop, and these cogs began visiting the Mediterranean, the seamen of each region quickly appreciated the advantages of various features of the others' rig and design. The best parts of each were adopted and the result was the typical ship of the latter half of the fifteenth century in which the later voyages of discovery were made and in which, adapted for war, the struggle for supremacy at sea was to be carried on.

Northern ships, built to withstand the battering of the heavy seas in their fierce climate, had been 'clinker' (or 'clincher') built, the fore-and-aft side planking or 'strakes' each overlapping the one below it, and terminating in centre-line posts of the pointed stem and stern. Mediterranean ships from the earliest times had been

4 Man of war followed by two galleys (Fall of Phaeton), engraving after P. Breugel (*c.* 1525 – 1569). The long yard of the lateen sail is clearly seen on the galleys in the foreground.

5 A Hanseatic cog in distress by an unknown artist, *c.* 1500. The cog was the prototype of the square-rigged ship which adopted the lateen sail on the mizen.

6 Galleon before the wind (Fall of Icarus), engraving after P. Breugel (*c.* 1525–1569). Here characteristics of the northern and southern rigs are combined in a typical vessel of the sixteenth century, having square sails on the main and fore masts and a lateen sail on the mizen. Note the high fore and after castles and the shrouds secured to the chainwale on the outside of the hull.

'carvel' built, that is to say with the planking of the strakes placed edge to edge, giving a smooth ship's side and less resistance to movement through the water. The northerners copied this method of building and, with the adoption by the southerners of the centre-line rudder, as seen on the northern ships, in place of the side rudder, hulls became more or less standardized, with a rounded stern and bluff bow.

Superimposed on the hull were the fore and aft castles. Originally open platforms built on to the hull from which the ship could be navigated, the sails worked and where soldiers could be stationed when necessary, these had become integral parts of the hull, their sides pierced for gunports. The forecastle was still a single-decked structure projecting out forward of the bow. The aftercastle, however, was a towering structure of two or more decks, the one above the quarterdeck, which extended from the stern to the mainmast, being called the 'half-deck'.

Between the quarterdeck and the forecastle was the low waist, where the deck was at a level below that of the quarterdeck. To strengthen the carvel-built hull, the ends of the deck beams passed through the side planking, to which they were secured on the inside; added strength was provided by vertical battens outside the hull and by stout fore and aft planks, called rubbing strakes

13

because they also protected the hull from friction when going alongside.

The northerners had already experimented with a small second mast, the mizen, stepped abaft the mainmast, on which was spread a small square sail. The advantages of a three-masted rig to give a balanced sail plan were apparent however, and they now adopted it with a lateen sail on the mizen, while the southerners in their turn replaced the lateen sails of the fore and main by square sails. The mizen and fore sails were at first quite small and their function was rather as aids to steering than to increase propulsion. Inevitably, however, ingenuity was soon devoted to achieving greater speed by increasing the size of the sails. This called for stronger standing rigging for the masts and, in particular, for a stout fore-stay to take the strain on the foremast when the sails were taken aback by a head wind. This led to the addition of the bowsprit to which such a stay for the foremast could be attached.

At the head of the fore and main masts was a circular, enclosed platform, the 'top', in which a look-out or marksmen armed with small arms or even spears and bows could be stationed according to circumstances. Above these tops were flagstaffs on which the national flag, the banner of the commander or of some patron saint would be displayed.

The pursuit of greater sail area soon led to a small square topsail being hoisted on this staff on the main, and later on the foremast, the strengthened staffs becoming topmasts and the flagstaffs fixed above them. Topmasts were fixed firmly to the lower masts and could not be lowered or 'housed', a refinement which did not appear until the late sixteenth century. The lower sails came to be called 'courses', though colloquially the main course remained the 'mainsail' and the fore course the 'foresail'. The bowsprit was also fitted with a small yard from which a square spritsail was spread below it.

So that sail area could be reduced as the wind increased, the lower portions of the square sails, known as 'bonnets' were made detachable by means of unlacing them from the principal section. For some reason, reefing by means of reef points, though known as long ago as the era of the Viking longships, went largely out of use at this time and did not reappear in general use until the middle of the seventeenth century.

Ships having the three-masted rig with, at first, its four square sails (main course, main topsail, foresail and spritsail) and the lateen sail on the mizen and, perhaps, another small lateen mizen topsail, were known as 'holks' in northern Europe. In the Mediterranean they maintained the name 'carrack' which had been in general use by the Genoese and Venetians to describe single-masted, square-rigged merchant ships of the largest size. Soon

'caravel', originally signifying a lateen-rigged ship, came also to be applied to square-rigged ships by the Spanish and Portuguese. On the other hand there is evidence that such ships were, in fact, called simply 'nao' or 'ships' in Spain, 'carracks' or 'holks' elsewhere. Columbus's *Santa Maria* was a *nao*. The *Nina* and *Pinta* started out as lateen-rigged caravels, the former being converted to square rig during the voyage.

The rigging of carracks had become a highly complex arrangement of ropes and spars and of specialized varieties of splices, tackles and lashings bearing a multitude of technical names, a glossary of which would comprise a sizeable book on its own. Mastery of such esoteric detail is not essential to appreciation of the story of the development of the sailing ships illustrated in this volume. In tracing this development, however, and fully to appreciate the illustrations, it is necessary to understand the function of the main items of a ship's rigging.

It was of two sorts—the standing rigging by which the masts were supported and strengthened to withstand the strain imparted by the wind in the sails and the motion of the ship, and the running rigging whereby the yards and sails were manipulated and adjusted. Of the former the main items were the stays running from high up the masts forward and aft in the centre line of the ship, and the shrouds which supported the masts laterally, though these, slanting downwards towards the stern, as they must to allow the yards to be braced round, acted also in some measure as backstays.

From early times the shrouds in northern types of ship were single ropes at the lower end of which were wooden blocks called 'dead-eyes', with three holes in them, through which were rove lanyards by means of which the shrouds were set up and secured to a narrow platform on the outside of the hull, known as the 'chainwale'. Between the shrouds were stretched the 'ratlines' which formed a rope ladder for going aloft. In southern ships the shrouds were at first made up of short rope pendants to which tackles were attached and set up inside the hull. Ratlines were thus impracticable; a vertical rope ladder was therefore hung from the top for going aloft. The advantages of the northern system were quickly apparent and it soon became universally adopted.

The main items of the running rigging were halyards for hoisting and lowering the yards; braces for slewing the yards; tacks and sheets, attached to the lower corners or 'clews' of the sails to spread them, the former leading forward, the latter aft; 'bowlines' attached to 'cringles' or eyes sewn into the edges or 'leeches' of square sails and leading forward, by means of which the windward edge of the sails could be hauled flat, the better to catch the wind when sailing 'on a wind' as opposed to running before it; 'clew-lines' to haul up the lower edge or 'bunt' of the sail when furling,

7 *right* A galleon before the wind with a galley, after P. Breugel (*c*. 1525–1569). The bonnets on the mainsail are visible; these were a means of detaching part of the sail in bad weather; reef points although used by the Vikings were not rediscovered until the middle of the seventeenth century.

to which, at a later date several 'buntlines' were added; while in early square-rigged ships there was also a form of multiple leech-line called a 'martinet' to haul the leeches in under the yard when it was lowered. To hold the yard firmly against the forward side of the mast and yet allow it to move freely enough to be braced round and to be hoisted and lowered, a sort of necklace of large wooden beads known as a 'parrel' was employed. In the early days, controls for the topsails—braces, sheets and halyards—were led into the top where they were operated. Later they were led by various means down on deck. The lateen mizen sail was sheeted home to an 'outrigger' or 'outligger' projecting out over the stern. Square-rigged ships were never as good 'on a wind' as those with fore-and-aft rig; in the fifteenth and sixteenth centuries they could not steer closer than 7 points (about 79 degrees) off it; they were often forced to wait for periods of many weeks for a favourable wind to make a passage in narrow waters.

By the middle of the fifteenth century, the carrack had become established as the trading vessel of the period. It may at first sight seem strange that ships with so limited a capability of beating against a wind should have found favour; but size and carrying capacity and a rig providing a large sail area that could be economically handled was more important where routes could be found to take advantage of constant, prevailing or seasonal winds. The most important of the 'constants' were the 'trade winds' which blow from the more temperate climes towards the hot region along the equator. The rotation of the earth gives these a slant so that they blow from north-east to south-west (the N.E. trades) north of the equator, while to the south of the equator they blow from south-east to north-west (the S.E. trades).

A ship leaving a European Atlantic port for America, therefore, would use the 'prevailing' westerlies of the North Atlantic to reach southwards to the Azores where she could count on picking up the north-east trades to waft her to the West Indies. For the return journey she would work her way north up the coast of Florida and Virginia until she could make use of the prevailing westerlies to re-cross the ocean.

The best known of the seasonal winds is the monsoon. The low barometric pressure set up over the Asiatic mainland in summer results in winds from a south-westerly quarter over the Indian Ocean and the South China Sea from May to September. A reverse process takes place from October to April when the land mass is colder than the oceans to the south of it. Square-rigged ships, taking advantage of these regular winds were most suitable to undertake extensive voyages.

There had been various other developments which, for the first time, brought together all the elements necessary for such ships to

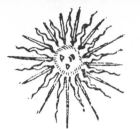

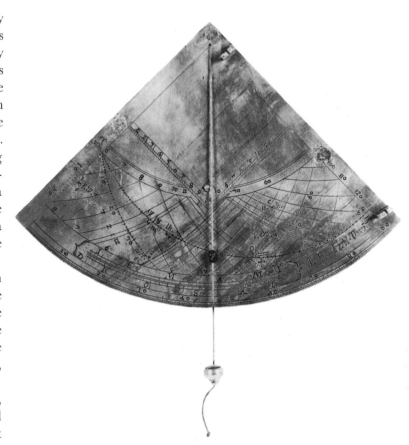

Navigational instruments (*left to right*)

8 The astrolabe was in common use in the Middle Ages and Chaucer wrote a treatise on it for his ten year old son. By measuring the height of the sun at noon, the mariner could discover his latitude.

9 Cross-staff in use, 1669. The cross-staff, an improvement over the astrolabe for accuracy, in use, was introduced early in the sixteenth century. In bright sunshine it could cause damage to the eyes.

10 Back-staff in use. The advantage of the back-staff was that the observer did not have to look directly at the sun, but measured (at noon) the angle of the shadow cast by the shadow vane on the horizon vane. This could only be done in bright sunshine.

11 Gunter's Quadrant, *c.* 1670. The height of the sun could be observed and the time of day found by reference to the engraved lines after the adjustment of the 'pearl' on the plummet line to the sun's declination.

strike out into the unknown oceans and explore them at the very moment that a powerful incentive was created. The mariner's compass had been introduced to the western world from China by the Arabs and, by 1400, every Mediterranean ship of any size was equipped with one. From the Jews and Arabs, too, had come knowledge of mathematics and astronomy and their application to navigation. Primitive charts were being made. The astrolabe had become available, making the calculation of latitude possible. The astrolabe was a metal disc, made very heavy so that it hung perpendicularly and steadily, graduated in degrees, with a diametric bar or 'alidade' pivoted on the centre, by means of which a rough altitude of the sun could be measured. Time-pieces were carried, and although not for more than 300 years yet would a reliable chronometer be produced, longitude at sea could be roughly estimated.

Other navigational instruments introduced in the early sixteenth century for measuring the angle between two objects and, more particularly, the altitude of the sun, were the cross-staff and the back-staff. The former consisted of a graduated staff with a vane at right angles. This vane could be moved along the staff until the observer saw one end touching the horizon (or one of the objects), the other the sun (or other object).

The back-staff was used by an observer with his back to the sun, one end of the staff resting on his shoulder; the angle was measured by moving a vane along the staff until the top of it shaded a sight

16

Van schiprechte,

Partio dom Vasq̃ dagama conde Almirante primeyro descobridor da Jndia por
Viso Rey della. e a noue dabril (com hũa Armada de quatorze naos) se fez
aa vella. e sendo com a frota das ditas vellas, junto da costa da Jndia se
tremeo ho mar hũ quarto dóra, e com temor esbonbardearão hũas ás
outras, das quaes estes erão os capitães

lopo vaz de sã payo
pera cochim

Do simão de meneses

Dom fernão de morroy
perdeose em Melinde
salvouse a gente; hia por
capitão degoa

Dom Vasq̃ dagama

Fco de saa

Pomas carenhas
pera malaca

Anto da siluevra

Dom Anrrique de meneses

Christovão Rosado
perdido

Francisqo de brito
perdido

Ruy glz

Gil

lopo lobo

Mossem gaspar
por ser some estrangi e madar
mayo donecessario a gente da
carauella

Afonso mexia
por veador de fazda

Partio Dom pedro mazcarenhas por Viso Rey da Jndia co seis naos
e dellas estes erão os capitães

S. cruz

felipe digno s. boa ventura

belchior de sousa

Dom pedro maz carenhas
depoys da Nao ser descarre
gada se perdeo na barra
degoa

Conçeycão

N. S. do cabo

Miquel de castanhoso

espa sancta

Fra memga

fernão gomz de sousa

Dom manoel tello
não passou, e foy ter a s ã o tomé
desbaratada

gale ainsa

Fco de guinea
invernou em mocambique

vane on the front end of the staff, through which the observer held it on the horizon.

A more complicated and more accurate form of back-staff was Davis's Quadrant. All these were eventually replaced in the eighteenth century first by the octant and then the quadrant and sextant which made use of mirrors to bring the image of the sun or star down to the horizon, the angle being then read off on a graduated arc.

By the time of the great Portuguese voyages of discovery ships had not only become large enough to bring home heavy cargoes, but they were armed with cannon on the forecastle and quarter deck and with further light pieces on the half deck. These were necessary to defend them against the fleets of the Arab traders who naturally resented competition with their long-established commerce, while King John I's orders to his ships to open fire on any strangers encountered encouraged skirmishes.

Carracks were by now often as big as 1,500 tons. Topsails were spread on fore and mainmasts and even on the mizen there might be a lateen topsail. Below the quarter deck and forecastle level were two more decks and, when the Frenchman, des Charges of Brest, experimented in 1501 with piercing ships' sides to provide gunports, allowing guns to be mounted on the lower decks, the concept quickly spread. These were the sort of ships used by the Spaniards to bring home the treasure of the New World and, by the Portuguese, the equally valuable products of the Indies.

Voyages of discovery in the sixteenth century

For their voyages to India round the Cape of Good Hope, the Portuguese were well placed to take advantage of the north-east and south-east trade winds in the Atlantic. In the Indian Ocean, however, their voyages had to coincide with the seasonal monsoons and it was the use of these winds that enabled them under the leadership of the great Albuquerque to push eastwards from India to capture Malacca in 1511, whence they advanced in the following year to establish themselves in the Moluccas, the main Spice Islands, and discover Java, Borneo, Celebes and the myriad other islands of the East Indies. By 1516 they had reached China to the north and ten years later the northern coast of New Guinea to the south-east.

In 1493, Pope Alexander VI had partitioned the unknown world between Spain and Portugal, all to the east of a line drawn from pole to pole 370 leagues west of the Cape Verde Islands being allocated to Portugal, the remainder to Spain.

In accordance with this, the Portuguese had now reached the limit of their half, though in the absence of any reliable means of determining longitude, the exact position of the dividing lines was uncertain. They were not interested therefore in pushing eastwards out into the Pacific and it was left to Spaniards, travelling in the opposite direction, to open up that ocean. It was a Portuguese, nevertheless, Ferdinand Magellan, sailing in the service of Spain, who first crossed it and discovered its vastness. Following the east coast of South America southward in 1520, he found the narrow, twisting strait that has ever since borne his name and, emerging into the legendary South Sea, which he named the Pacific, he crossed it in the trade-wind belt of the tropics to arrive, after a passage infinitely longer than expected, at the Philippine Islands. Magellan himself was killed in a fight with the natives, but one of his ships, the *Victoria*, carried on westwards to complete the first circumnavigation of the world.

Although Spain sent out other expeditions after Magellan, setting out from Peruvian ports, none were able to find steady winds to bear them back across the Pacific until 1565 when Andres de Urdaneta, the navigator of a colonizing expedition to the Philippines, sailed northwards from Manila and, picking up the south-west monsoon, arrived back on the coast of California whence he coasted south to Mexico.

Now that it had been shown that the Pacific could be crossed in both directions, there was an upsurge of interest in voyages to discover the great southern continent, *Terra Australis Incognita*, which geographers had long believed to exist, though this was generally based on no better grounds than a desire for symmetry. The southern shore of the Magellan Strait, Tierra del Fuego, was believed by them (though not by Magellan) to be the northern tip of such a continent stretching across the South Pacific to the longitude of the East Indies, where New Guinea was similarly thought to be a part of it. Covering vast areas in the tropic as well as the temperate zone, it was expected to be a continent with all the wealth of America awaiting discovery by a new Columbus.

The next expedition to seek for it left Peru in 1567 under the Spaniards Alvaro de Mendana and Pedro Sarmiento de Gamboa. Carried across the Pacific by the trade winds, they made landfall on the chain of large islands to the east of New Guinea which they named Isabella, Guadalcanal, Malaita and San Cristoval. Colourful sailors' tales on their return to Mexico, combined with the hazy, conjectural geography of the time, gave rise to the belief that they had discovered the fabled islands of King Solomon and they are known to this days as the Solomon Islands.

The peak of Spanish and Portuguese supremacy had by now been passed; both had reached the limit of their imperial expansion; something of the spirit which had animated the explorers and conquistadores of both nations had died. To replace them, the

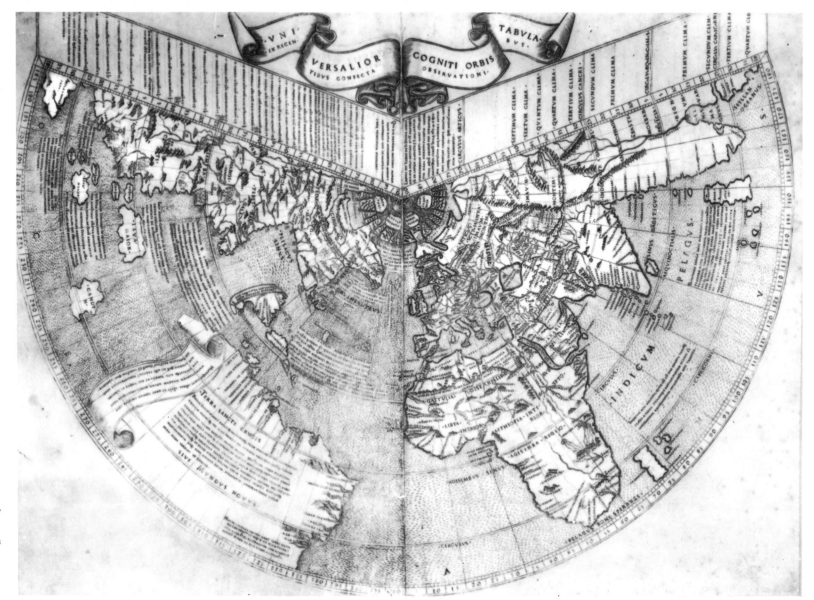

13 This map of the world by Johan Ruysch, a Dutch cartographer, is the earliest map to show the new coasts discovered by Columbus, Bartholomew Diaz and Vasco da Gama.

14 *opposite* The search for the North-west Passage was resumed sporadically right up to 1903, when the great Norwegian explorer Roald Amundsen navigated it successfully. Here is a romantic artist's impression of Sir John Franklin's ships the *Erebus* and the *Terror*. Franklin's attempt on the North-west Passage, 1845–7, was one of the great tragedies of nineteenth-century exploration. Sailing into Lancaster Sound, his ships were frozen in and were finally abandoned, but in their attempts to travel overland to civilization the crew dropped one by one from exhaustion and starvation. It was not until 1857–9 that Sir Francis Leopold McClintock on his third expedition in search of Franklin, found a message revealing the fate of the expedition.

English, the Dutch and the French were coming forward. They had, indeed, always refused to accept either the territorial partition of the world by Pope Alexander or the Spanish prohibition of trade with the colonies of the New World. As early as 1496 the Genoese John Cabot had set out under the patronage of Henry VII of England to seek a North-west Passage to Cathay; his son, Sebastian, had explored Labrador in 1509 and penetrated Hudson's Bay. For more than 60 years, however, it was in the search for a North-east Passage that English seamen were most interested, Sir Hugh Willoughby reaching Novaya Zemlya in 1553, while

Richard Chancellor, becoming separated from the expedition, pushed into the White Sea in the *Bonaventure* and visited the Czar in Moscow. The establishment of the Muscovy Trading Company followed.

A determined seeker of a North-east Passage was the Dutchman Willem Barents who piloted three expeditions between 1594 and 1596, during which he rounded the North Cape to cross the sea which now bears his name, and passed through the Vaygatz Strait between Novaya Zemlya and the mainland into the Kara Sea. On his last voyage he discovered Spitzbergen, doubled the north-

eastern cape of Novaya Zemlya, but there died (see p. 72).

The Frenchman, Jacques Cartier, landed on the Gaspe Peninsula of Quebec in 1534 and laid claim to Canada in the name of his king. The first Englishman to set out expressly to seek the North-west Passage was Martin Frobisher in 1576. He was followed in 1583 by Sir Humphrey Gilbert, who was lost at sea when returning after taking possession of Newfoundland for England. The North-west Passage, if it existed at all, had by this time been shown to be an almost hopeless quest for the sailing ships of the day. When the news of Mendana's discoveries reached England, therefore, English adventurers were fired with the idea of reaching *Terra Australis* by following Magellan's route into the Pacific.

Up to this time the British and French had contented themselves with expeditions to the West Indies and the Spanish Main which could be classified as smuggling, illegal trading or privateering according to the point of view from which they were regarded. First in the field were the French, Jean Angst of Dieppe capturing three of Cortez's treasure ships from Mexico in 1522. Another, Le Clerc, sacked Santo Domingo and Havana.

From the middle of the sixteenth century, however, the English formed the large majority, following the pioneering slave-trading voyages of John Hawkins. The treachery of the Spanish commander at San Juan de Ulloa which brought disaster to his expedition in 1568 in which the young Francis Drake took part, and the cruel treatment of English prisoners by the Inquisition provided both a spur and an excuse for subsequent privateering expeditions by Drake and others.

Drake's voyage of circumnavigation which set out in 1577 was launched ostensibly with the dual object of searching for *Terra Australis* and for the Pacific entrance of the North-west Passage. He paid little attention to either of these, however, and after raiding the Spanish colonies and sailing north as far as Oregon, he crossed the Pacific to Celebes and thence home to England round the Cape of Good Hope. The one geographical discovery of importance came about by chance and the force of weather when, after passing through the Straits of Magellan, he was driven far enough south and east to prove that Tierra del Fuego was an island as Magellan had guessed.

Open war between Spain and England and the struggle by the Netherlands to shake off Spanish rule, absorbed the energies of the leading English and Dutch seamen-adventurers during the next twenty years and it was the persistent Mendana who at last persuaded the Spanish authorities to equip a further expedition under his leadership in 1595 to colonize the Solomons. Sailing from Callao, he discovered and named the Polynesian Marquesas Islands, but got no nearer to the Solomons than a large island

15 *top right* The *Gjoa* in which the North-west Passage was finally successfully navigated by Roald Amundsen in 1903. The topsail sloop rig was assisted by an auxiliary motor.

200 miles to the eastward which he named Santa Cruz.

Fever, from which Mendana died, and trouble with the natives caused the expedition to end in failure. But ten years later his second-in-command, the Portuguese Quiros, set out again, with another Portuguese, Luis Vaez de Torres, in command of his second ship. After the discovery of the New Hebrides, Quiros was carried back to America by his mutinous crew, but Torres sailed on in search of *Terra Australis* and made the most important of the Spanish discoveries, in 1605, by passing through the shallow, reef-strewn strait amongst a maze of small islands to the south of New Guinea to explode the idea that New Guinea was part of the great southern continent. His discovery was not made public, however, and the geographers remained in ignorance of it until the eighteenth century.

Development of the ship-of-the-line

All sailing ships were armed with a few cannon and during the early sixteenth century were not only expected to be able to protect themselves against pirates or privateers but were themselves often converted to ships of war by the addition of further guns. Then the fierce rivalry between the European powers to obtain a share of the trade and treasure of ever-expanding new worlds to east and west, leading to an almost permanent state of undeclared war in the distant seas and from time to time to open warfare in European waters, led to the development of specialized men-of-war. For the next 250 years—until the end of the Napoleonic Wars—it was towards improvement of this type that the major developments of the sailing ship were directed.

The earliest examples of large fighting ships were, in fact, simply large, heavily armed and lavishly rigged carracks, one of the earliest being the Scottish *Great Michael*, built in 1511, which was 240 feet in length overall. She was followed three years later by the English *Henry Grace à Dieu* or *Great Harry*, a very ambitious design

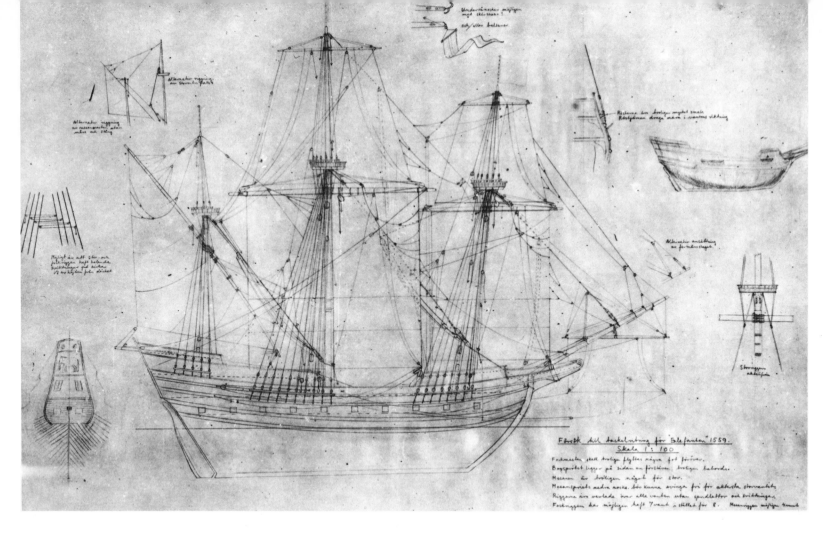

16 The rigging plan of the *Elefanten* a Swedish 'kravel' built for Gustavus Vasa in 1532.

with topgallant sails above the topsails on the fore, main and mizen masts, and a second or 'bonaventure' mizen mast carrying also two lateen sails. This rig must have been most awkward, while the towering fore and after castles, providing in all no less than eight decks must have made the *Great Harry* and other ships of her type clumsy craft. She mounted as many as 184 guns, though this included a large number of quite small pieces (see Colour Plate 4).

It is reasonable to look upon such ships as the *Great Harry* and her French rival, the five-masted *Grand François* which never actually got to sea, as prestige symbols rather than practicable fighting ships. The Swedish 'kravel' *Elefanten* built for Gustavus Vasa in 1532, was more sensibly rigged with square course and topsails on the fore and main, a square spritsail or *blinde*, and two lateen sails on the mizen.

The practice of piercing the sides to mount guns on the main deck, however, led to the emergence of the specialized fighting sailing ship or 'galleon'. Though this Spanish word connotes a ship of the galley type, the only features derived from the oar-propelled galley were a hull shape low, straight and slim in comparison with the more lofty, pot-bellied carrack, and a beak-head projecting forward from the stem below the bowsprit. The rig was the usual three or four-masted arrangement with square sails on the fore and main; but the hull shape and reduction of top hamper by cutting down the castles made for better sailing qualities.

Ships of this sort, fast-sailing, handy and armed with long-range guns of the culverin type, appealed particularly to the English. Under the direction of John Hawkins who had been made Comptroller of the Navy by Queen Elizabeth, English shipwrights produced the finest fighting galleons of the age, with which they were able successfully to engage the larger, more numerously manned Spanish ships which mounted heavier, but shorter-range cannon and relied on the tactics of close combat followed by boarding.

It was English galleons of this sort, notably Lord Howard of Effingham's flagship *Ark Royal* and Drake's *Revenge* which were thus able to harry the greatly superior Invincible Armada up the Channel in 1588. Though the English ships were too few to force

17 *below* A Spanish galleon, after P. Breugel (*c.* 1525–1569).

18 *right* One of a series of sixteenth-century maps illustrating the engagements in the English Channel between the Spanish Armada and the English fleet in 1588. Here the Spanish Armada is entering the English Channel with the English fleet going out of Plymouth to attack in the rear. The English fleet divided, some vessels beating against the wind to the west in order to encircle the Armada. The crescent formation of the Spanish fleet was a defensive manoeuvre.

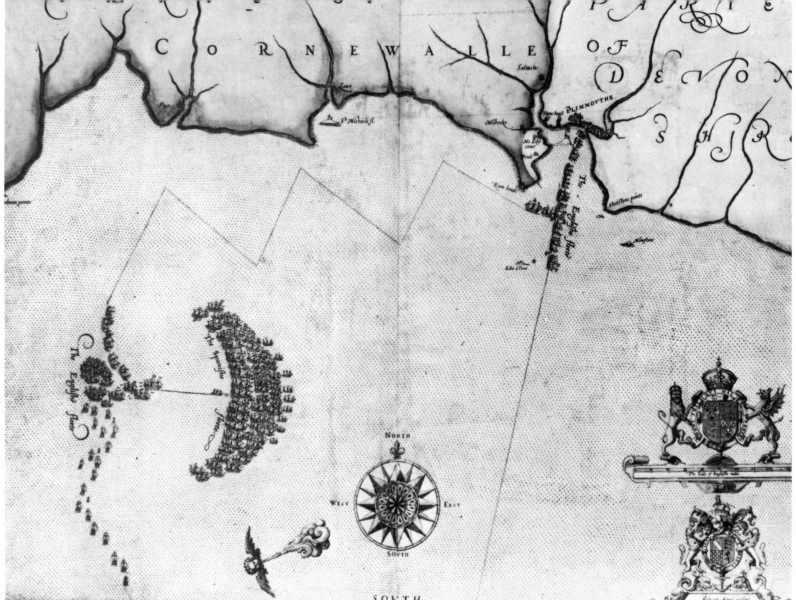

a decisive action, the Spaniards were unable to hit back effectively at the sea wolves snapping at their heels, who could choose their own distance at which to fight.

The Armada, prevented from making its planned junction with the Spanish invasion force waiting in the Netherlands, was driven into the North Sea to be overwhelmed and destroyed by storm as its scattered units tried to return to Spain by circumnavigating the British Isles.

The Spanish absorbed the lesson and laid down real fighting galleons of their own, as opposed to the clumsy-sailing armed carracks, encumbered by troops of soldiers, on which they had previously relied. It was a group of these, named after the Twelve

Apostles, that formed the hard core of the squadron into the midst of which Sir Richard Grenville contemptuously but rashly sailed the *Revenge* to her heroic end in 1591.

It was to the design of warships, indeed, that the leading naval constructors everywhere applied themselves. In England the foremost of these was Phineas Pett, descendant of a family of shipbuilders and the first to have been educated to apply mathematical calculation to the rules of practical experience. In 1610 he launched his first masterpiece, the *Prince Royal*, mounting 56 guns on three decks. Apart from this innovation she was an early example of a ship incorporating the highly elaborate decoration or 'gingerbread' which was a feature of so many during the seventeenth

of the Anglo-Dutch wars, she was an unwieldy craft and somewhat 'crank' or top-heavy; so that in 1652 she was cut down to a two-decker. Her 'royals' too were prestige features and probably rarely spread, as such sails were not adopted generally in the Navy for many years to come.

That the design of English ships had, in fact, lost its pre-eminence, was exposed when a French naval revival in mid-century under Louis XIV's great minister, Colbert, set in after a period of decline. English ships were too narrow, making them unstable gun platforms, and mounted too many guns for their size. Though this was recognized by the English and in 1672 Sir Anthony Deane, the leading English ship designer of the day, considered the French *Superbe* of 74 guns a better ship than any English three-decker and worthy of copying, the design of British men-of-war was to lag behind that of French, Spanish and, later, American ships to the end of the sail era.

The seventeenth century saw the introduction of the majority of the remaining modifications to the sailing ship leading to the standard rig of the classic period which preceded the invention of the steam engine. To the Dutch is ascribed the introduction of staysails in about 1658 though such sails, as noted earlier, had long been used in smaller craft. Starting with a main staysail, set only as a stormsail when most of the other sails had been furled, sails were later added to the main topmast stay, the mizen stay and finally to the fore-topmast stay. Curiously, the foremost of all the staysails, the jib, was not introduced for another fifty years, the awkward spritsail topsail being retained. The Dutch are also credited with the introduction during the sixteenth century of an arrangement whereby topmasts, hitherto simply lashed to the lower masts, could be lowered or 'housed' in heavy weather and this came into general use early in the seventeenth century.

Another innovation, or more accurately, a re-introduction after centuries of disuse, were reef-points with which the area of individual sails could be reduced by tying folds of the sail to the yard, the bonnet being done away with. At the same time foot-ropes were extended below the yards on which the sailors could stand while reefing or furling the sails. As the century progressed, the ships became less barrel-shaped or, put more technically, the tumble-home was reduced, and the decks lost much of their curve upwards from the waist to the stern and forecastle, becoming more or less horizontal. The long, thrusting beak-head was shortened, terminating usually in an ornamental figure-head representative of the ship's name.

A feature which persisted beyond the end of the seventeenth century was the far from ideal steering device, the 'whipstaff'. This had been introduced to enable the tiller attached to the rudder

century. The piled-up forecastle of the sixteenth century disappears at this time but a longer beakhead now projects almost horizontally forward from the bow. Phineas Pett's other famous design the *Sovereign of the Seas* built by his son Peter in 1637, marked another great advance in ship-building. Mounting 100 guns on three decks, she carried a greatly increased spread of sail with two square sails—topgallant and royal—above the topsail on the fore and main masts, a square topsail and topgallant sail above the lateen mizen and a square spritsail topsail spread on a yard above the bowsprit. The last of these was an awkward contraption introduced to redress the balance of sail area necessitated by the disappearance of the high forecastle. Nevertheless it was to be retained until the end of the century.

This was one of the spectacular prestige ships of the period and, though she was to take a conspicuous part in many of the battles

19 The *Vergulde Zon* (Gilded Sun) a warship of Dunquerque; two views by W. van de Velde the Elder, *c.* 1645.

20 Jean-Baptiste Colbert (1619–
1683), Louis XIV's great minister
and father of the French navy.

21 *top right* Battle of the Downs, 1639
by H. van Anthonissen (*c.* 1606–
1657). To the right of the painting is
the *Aemilia*, Marten Tromp's flagship
with the admiral's flag at the main
and the 'blood-flag' at the stern.

22 *right* The Battle of Agosta, 22
April 1676, after Louis Garneray.
The confusion and destruction of a
sea battle is well illustrated here.

23 *above* English Squadron Beating to Windward, by W. van de Velde the Younger (1633–1707). Ships of this time were unable to steer close to the wind, particularly as they had no fore-and-aft headsails. The lateen mizen is the only fore-and-aft sail set, while the courses are sheeted round as hard as they will go. Note also the curve of the masts in the wind, which van de Velde the Younger was one of the few artists to illustrate correctly.

24 The *Royal Sovereign* by W. van de Velde the Younger (1633–1707).

Plate 4 The *Great Harry* by Cruikshank after Holbein – an imaginative portrait. In Holbein's day accuracy in ship painting was not yet a main preoccupation but the lateen sails on the mizen and the bonaventure are typical of the period. The gun ports were a comparatively recent innovation, but the ones in the stern were dropped in later ships since these weakened the hull.

head and so several decks below the poop, to be worked from a deck or two decks higher whence the steersman could see something of the sails and be in earshot of the master on deck. The whipstaff consisted of a long pole the bottom end of which was attached by a ring to the end of the tiller and which was pivoted where it passed through the deck above the tiller in such a way that besides rotating on the pivot it could slide up and down. The whipstaff could thus be tilted to one side or the other, moving the tiller through its horizontal arc.

That such a primitive contraption which could swing the tiller through only a limited arc should have survived so long is astonishing and an indication of the lack of mechanical ingenuity of the age. It was not until the first years of the eighteenth century that the wheel began to be introduced to swing the tiller by means of a simple run of rope and pulleys. Yet another innovation at this time were 'studding-sails'. These were additions to the larger sails, for use when running before light winds, which were spread on booms hauled out as extensions of the yards.

By the end of the seventeenth century, the full-rigged ship-of-the-line had developed into the thing of beauty whose pyramid of swelling, snowy sails excited the admiration and drew forth the pictures in paint or in words of artists and writers. Lovely as they were to these beholders, they must have been less attractive to those who had to accept their accommodation and their amenities.

The captain of such a ship, occupying the 'great cabin' extending across the after end of the ship on the level of the quarter deck, enjoyed a fair degree of comfort, to be sure. Glass casement windows across the full width of the stern gave him light and fresh air. Cushioned settees lining the cabin's sides served also as lockers for his effects. In a curtained-off space would be a swinging cot and a portable wash-basin on a tripod. In the centre would be a dining table to seat perhaps eight or more at which fellow captains or notables from the shore, when in harbour, or his subordinate officers when at sea, could be entertained. For the captain, though he lived alone in god-like seclusion, was expected to 'keep a table'.

Below the great cabin was the ward-room, a narrow space running down the centre of the deck, most of which was taken up by a dining table. Down each side of this space, as well as forward of the partition (bulkhead) closing off the ward-room from the main deck, would be a row of cabins with portable wooden or canvas sides for the four senior lieutenants, the captain of marines and the master (the warrant officer responsible for navigation and pilotage). A door on each side led to the quarter galleries, narrow passages built on to the outside of the hull and providing lavatories for the officers, though this humble domestic function did not prevent their sharing the decorative carving and gilding lavished

on the outside of the whole of the ship's after part. Stern windows gave light and ventilation as in the great cabin. The junior lieutenants and marine officers and perhaps the chaplain, if one were carried, had cabins below the forward end of the ward-room on the lower deck, while abaft these was the gun-room where the gunner reigned over the youngest midshipmen, who slept, like the sailors, in hammocks.

The next deck down, the lowest true deck in the ship, (we are visualizing a so-called two-decker), below the water line, was the orlop, where daylight never and fresh air rarely penetrated. Here were the cabins of the surgeon and purser and, right aft, the after cockpit where the senior midshipmen or 'oldsters' messed and slept and where, in action, the surgeon and his mates plied their grisly butchery (see p. 97). Store-rooms also occupied space in the after part of the orlop and below it in the hold—hence the unenviable site of the purser's cabin.

The bulk of the ship's company occupied the lower deck, sleeping in hammocks slung from hooks in the overhead beams, and eating on athwartship tables lowered from their stowage overhead between the guns. A few also messed on the main deck in whatever space was not occupied by the workshops of the carpenter, blacksmith and armourer, by the pens for livestock which supplied fresh meat in the early days of a cruise and by the capstan to which the anchor cables were led from the hawse pipes at the fore end. The most conspicuous feature of the orlop deck, apart from the cylindrical bulk of the masts, would be these great hempen anchor cables, stowed in the cable tiers running fore and aft and the stout oaken beams making a double cross—the 'bitts'

Plate 5   The Defeat of the Spanish Armada, design for a tapestry by an unknown artist. The vessel in foreground is a galleas, a cross between a galleon and a galley.

25 A Snug Cabin, or Port Admiral

'Come Hurricane drink your wine
Here's to The Wind that Blows
The ship that goes
and the lass that loves a Sailor'

by Thomas Rowlandson (1756–1827).

26 *right* The English ship *Mordaunt* by W. van de Velde the Elder, *c*. 1681. The van de Veldes, father and son, were the first marine artists to be meticulously concerned with the accuracy of their representation of ships.

to which the inboard end of the cables were secured.

At the fore end of the lower deck was the brick-floored galley with its wood-fired ranges, the vast coppers for boiling oatmeal into the gruel known as 'burgoo' and the tubs in which salt beef and pork were steeped to soften them sufficiently for cooking and

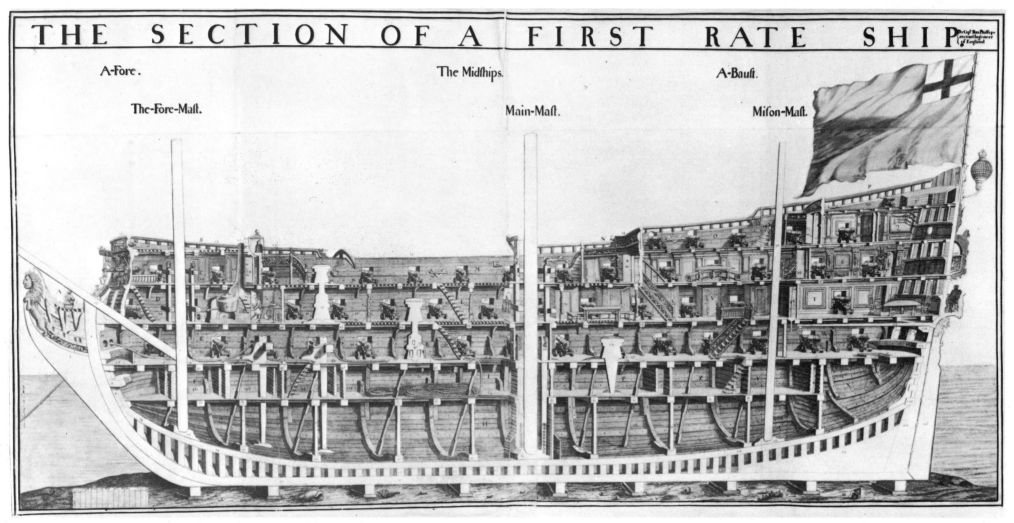

A-Fore.   The Midſhips.   A-Bauſt.

The-Fore-Maſt.   Main-Maſt.   Miſon-Maſt.

27 above This Section of a First Rate Ship, by Captain Thomas Phillips illustrates the description of the interior of a ship of the line given on this page.

28 right A French two-decker by W. van de Velde the Younger, c. 1667.

29 opposite The Dutch ship *Jaarsveld* by W. van de Velde the Elder, c. 1665, a drawing, which shows all the appeal, in both form and detail, which the wooden sailing ship had for the artist.

to extract some of the salt. Above this space, at the fore end of the main deck, warmed by the galley chimney, was the sick bay, made no more salubrious by its proximity to the few primitive lavatories overhanging the side in the beak head, the only sanitary arrangements for the ship's company of nearly 700 men, and unusable in heavy weather.

Even in an age in which hygiene was little practised or appreciated, the lack of sanitation and the consequent atmosphere below deck, overlaid though it was with the all-pervading aroma of Stockholm tar, made 'sweetening' the ship a recurrent preoccupation of her captain. Washing down with vinegar, flooding and pumping out the bilges and, during refits, replacing the shingle ballast, were methods used.

That epidemics swept through ships and fleets on extended cruises is not to be wondered at. A ship commissioning for a long

30 A naval battle off the Ile de Ré on
15 September 1625, by Ozanne.

31, 32 and 33 *opposite* These
seventeenth-century statuettes of
sailors captured by Barbary pirates
were displayed in Hamburg by the
prisoners' friends and relations in
order to collect ransom money.

voyage in distant seas would embark a much bigger crew than was necessary in expectation that a great many would die from such epidemics, which were, of course, made more probable and more severe by the resultant overcrowding. Another and even more certain scourge was the scurvy, brought on by the lack of fresh food in the seaman's diet. In spite of it, however, long voyages of discovery were successfully completed in the seventeenth and eighteenth centuries and not the least of their contributions was the discovery, after much experiment, of the means of prevention of scurvy of which the easiest to apply was the daily issue of lemon juice.

Smaller types of fighting ship

Besides the ships expressly designed for the line of battle, many smaller types of warship were developed during the seventeenth and eighteenth centuries, bearing a multiplicity of names most of which have assumed different meanings since. The 'pinnace' for instance, began as a craft of some 50 tons or less, but rigged in a similar fashion to the bigger ships, with three masts and square sails and able to be propelled also by oars or 'sweeps'. From it developed the frigate, the scouting cruiser and general handmaiden of the war fleets, though the name from the Italian 'fregata' which was an oared galley, seems to have been first applied in northern waters to the fast privateers which operated out of Dunkirk in the middle of the seventeenth century; but it came also to mean at that time any small two-decker warship.

The frigate of the type which became famous in the naval wars of the eighteenth century was a single decker ship of 28 or 32 guns, designed for speed and rigged with the most recent innovations making for handiness. They were amongst the first, for instance, to substitute a third staysail forward in place of the old, clumsy spritsail topsail. This was the jib, to spread which a jib boom was added as a prolongation of the bowsprit. Similarly they led the way in substituting a gaff-sail on the mizen for the lateen sail on that mast, though the first modification was simply the removal of the part of the lateen sail before the mast.

The next class below the frigate was the 'sloop', though here again the name was loosely used to cover small ships of various rigs. The French equivalent was the 'corvette'. Indeed when we come to consider the many types of small ships of the eighteenth and early nineteenth centuries, we come up against a confusion of names, some of which refer to the rig, some to the hull design, some to a combination of the two. At first the sloop was a two-masted ship with two square sails on each mast and one or perhaps two fore staysails, mounting about 18 guns on a single deck. During the eighteenth century the rig was improved by the addition of top-gallant sails on each mast and a jib forward, while for the main course was substituted a gaff-sail with a boom at its foot. Such ships were also called 'brigantines', though this again is a mis-application of a Mediterranean name for a lateen-rigged craft with oars.

Another two-master was the 'snow', fully rigged with three square sails on each mast but, in addition, a little separate mast close abaft the mainmast and fixed under the maintop, on which a gaff-sail was set. Later the snow and the sloop or brigantine were combined in a single type, the man-of-war brig which had the square mainsail of the former and the gaff and boom mainsail of the latter on the same mast.

In spite of convincing demonstrations of the superiority of the square-rigged man-of-war over the fighting galley during the sixteenth century, the latter survived in the Black Sea, where the Turks continued to use them; and Peter the Great, when he founded the Russian Navy in 1694, followed suit, both there as

34 *top right* 'The *United States* and *Macedonian*: extract from COMMODORE DECATUR's official letter "at sea, Oct. 30th 1812. On the 25th inst. being in latitude 39° N, longitude 20° 30 minutes W, we fell in with and after an hour and a half CAPTURED His Britannic Majesty's Ship MACEDONIAN commanded by Captain John Carden, and mounting 49 carriage guns". The *United States* had five killed and seven wounded, the *Macedonian* 36 killed and 68 wounded.' Stephen Decatur (1779–1820) went on to deal with the Barbary pirates in 1815 (see this page).

well as in the Baltic for use against the Swedes. The French also used galleys in the Mediterranean at that time. Our interest in these craft is directed to their descendants the 'xebecs' which were adaptations of the galley to enable them to mount guns on the broadside, developed originally by the Arabs of the Barbary States for their piratical operations.

They retained the lateen sail rig on three short masts and, though they were designed primarily for sailing, and, indeed could outsail most square-rigged merchantmen, benches for rowers were also sited between the guns. Such ships were greatly feared by merchantmen trading in the Mediterranean, many of whom were overwhelmed by the daring rovers who specialized in the stealthy approach under cover of fog or calm, dark nights. The fate of the Christian crews was slavery at the galley oars or in sweated labour ashore for their Moslem masters. From time to time naval expeditions would be mounted with varying success by the French and British to exact reparation and to free the captives, but it was not until the beginning of the nineteenth century that the Barbary pirates were finally put out of business.

On 30 June 1815, the American Admiral Decatur led a squadron to exact a treaty from the Dey of Algiers guaranteeing immunity for American ships from the depredations of his corsairs. He then went on to Tunis and Tripoli where similar terms were obtained, while Bainbridge with another squadron further cowed the sea rovers. A year later the British found it necessary to bombard Algiers to obtain the same security for their merchantmen. Finally the occupation of Algiers by the French in 1830 brought the era of the Barbary Pirates to an end.

The Russians also adopted similar craft retaining the Arabic name in the form of 'shebek', but they soon modified the rig, often combining lateen sails on one mast with square and gaff sails on others. The Swedes replied with their own versions of combined galley and sailing man-of-war, with a square rig of sails on fore and main and a driver mizen, while the oars were pivotted on wide outriggers like those of a galley. A type known as a 'turuma' mounted a broadside of 24 cannon below these outriggers. The 'udema', instead, mounted a few cannon on the centre-line which could be used on either side, firing over the top of the outriggers.

Merchant ships

The majority of merchant ships remained quite small, their hull design concentrating on maximum cargo capacity rather than speed or good sailing qualities and their rig limited to what could be efficiently handled by their comparatively small crews, namely the six sails—foresail and mainsail each with a topsail above, a spritsail and a lateen mizen. It was in such ships, rarely much over 300 tons, that the steady flow of immigrants to the American colonies took place.

The Dutch developed a distinctive design for their merchant ships in the European trade in which the hull curved inwards and upwards from the waterline to a narrow upper deck, the object being to circumvent the tax system based on deck area, used by the Baltic States with whom a vital trade in timber and other maritime stores was carried on. Ships with this extreme 'tumble-home' were called 'fluyt' ships, the narrow, almost pointed stern of the hull and the narrow after castle clearly distinguishing them from the broad-sterned ships of other nations.

Another invention of Dutch shipbuilders of the early seventeenth century was the 'yacht', a small craft of graceful lines and small draught with 'leeboards' acting as a drop keel for use when beating to windward, which was employed patrolling the waterways. A yacht, the *Mary*, was presented to King Charles II in 1660 on his restoration. So delighted with it were he and his sailor brother James, Duke of York, that they ordered others for sporting purposes to be built in English yards with deeper hulls and fixed keels instead of leeboards. Yachts were usually rigged with a single mast, a fore-and-aft mainsail spread along a gaff but with no boom for its foot, a square topsail, a triangular sail spread along the forestay (staysail) and another along a stay leading to the end of the bowsprit (jib). The gaff mainsail introduced at this period in various types of small vessels was basically a development from the lateen, being that part of the lateen spread abaft the mast, the fore part having been discarded. In other small ships of the period, in addition to the above rig, there might be a second mast stepped forward of the poop on which a gaff mizen would be hoisted, the whole constituting a ketch rig.

A name of Scandinavian origin, which survived into the age of steam and came to be slang for any small tramp steamer was 'hooker'. This was originally a small ship with a tall mainmast, carrying three square sails and a gaff-sail, a mizen with the usual gaff-sail sometimes called a 'spencer', a mizen topsail and, to balance the sail-plan in the absence of a foremast, a long jib-boom on which were spread large headsails in the form of a staysail, a jib and a flying jib.

Another term of Scandinavian origin for a type of small merchant sailing ship was 'cat'; but whereas 'hooker' indicated a type of rig, 'cat' or more accurately 'cat-built' indicated a broad-bellied, immensely strong and shallow-draught hull. Of such construction were the majority of the swarm of colliers plying their trade up and down the shoal-studded waters of the English east coast, the majority two-masted brigs, others with a full ship rig of three masts. It was one of the latter that the great explorer, Captain James Cook, selected, re-named *Endeavour*, for his first voyage of discovery 1768–71; two other Whitby colliers, *Resolution* and *Adventure* were taken up by the Admiralty for his second and third voyages.

Some small ships, in order to simplify sail handling, hoisted their square sails on masts made of one piece (pole-masts) which enabled the yards to be lowered to the deck when required instead of furling the sails with the yards in place. Such ships were called 'polaccas' or 'polacres' though the word strictly referred to the rig. They commonly had square-rigged fore and main masts and a small mizen with a gaff and boom sail or 'driver'.

The aristocrats amongst merchant ships were the East Indiamen, operated by the East India Companies, the two most important of which were the English and Dutch, incorporated respectively in 1600 and 1602. The two Companies operated in fierce rivalry as a result of which the Dutch succeeded in ousting the English as well as the Portuguese from the Eastern Archipelago (Dutch East Indies), when the English East India Company concentrated its energies on India where it established large trading posts. Charters granted by Charles II vested it with civil and criminal jurisdiction and permitted it to make war with non-Christian nations and to coin money. Dutch rivalry was largely removed when the Treaty of Breda brought the Anglo-Dutch war to an end in 1667. French rivalry followed and continued until the end of the Napoleonic War.

The Honourable East India Company—its sonorous official title—wielded virtually the powers of a sovereign state in India until an Act of Parliament in 1773 centralized the administration of the various provinces it had acquired in the hands of a governor-general and brought its civil and military affairs under the review of the British Government. From that time each renewal of its charter reduced its privileges until in 1831 the company had lost its commercial character and had become merely an administrative agency. Although in time of war East Indiamen were normally sailed in escorted convoy through the European war zones, they

could still encounter enemy men-of-war, privateers or armed merchantmen further afield, while in eastern waters the threat from pirates as well as the requirements of prestige ('face') called for an imposing show of strength. The majority mounted twenty-six 18-pounders on the main or middle deck; the lower deck was given over to cargo stowage, but dummy gunports would be painted along the side at that level.

Some, however, mounted a really powerful broadside with as many as 74 guns in all. In 1804, indeed, a squadron of English East Indiamen homeward bound from Canton, forced a French squadron of men-of-war which intercepted it to break off the action and flee with the merchantmen in pursuit.

At the same time roomy holds were essential for the outward cargoes of manufactured goods and cloth and the homeward loads of silk and spices and, later, tea. The next requirement was strength and reliability of hull and rigging for the long voyages away from dockyard support. Speed could be sacrificed as, until the East India Companies' monopolies were abrogated in the nineteenth century, there was no competition to face. They were thus massively built and slow. Though they could show a huge spread of canvas—they were amongst the first to have royals above the topgallants, and studding sails, and by the end of the eighteenth century often carried numerous extra sails going by such names as 'sky-sails', 'moonrakers', 'cloudscrapers' and 'star-gazers'—they would take in all their fair weather canvas before dark and reduce sail drastically at the first signs of a blow.

The majority of these East Indiamen of the English Company were built at Blackwall on the Thames and, strangely enough,

36 Dutch fluyt, mid seventeenth century. The first fluyt was built in Hoorn in 1595, and the design was greatly criticized until the ship was launched and was found to sail faster than most others. Note the narrow upper deck and the pronounced 'tumble-home'.

37 A Ship Sailing into a River (oil), by H. C. Vroom (1566–1640).

35

38 *top* The Launch of the East India Company's Ship *Edinburgh*, after W. J. Huggins (1781 – 1845). Most English East Indiamen in the late eighteenth and early nineteenth centuries were built at Blackwall on the River Thames.

39 *bottom left* A fleet of Indiamen at Sea, by N. Pocock (1741 – 1821) (oil). The ships are maneouvring into line abreast with all the precision of a fleet of men of war (see page 35).

40 *bottom right* Cat-ships on Hoorn Roads, by H. Rietschoof (1687 – 1746). One of the only two known pictures of the early catship, a cheaply constructed and full-ended trader with a large cargo capacity. According to Nicolaas Witsen (1641 – 1717), burgomaster of Amsterdam and an authoritative writer on shipbuilding, catships were mainly built of pine. They had square waterlines and a flat bottom. The rig consisted of pole-masts with short yards on halyards, and high narrow sails. The mizen however was like the mainsail of a small inland vessel. Witsen says these ships are 'slow as a donkey' and bad seaships, but take much cargo.

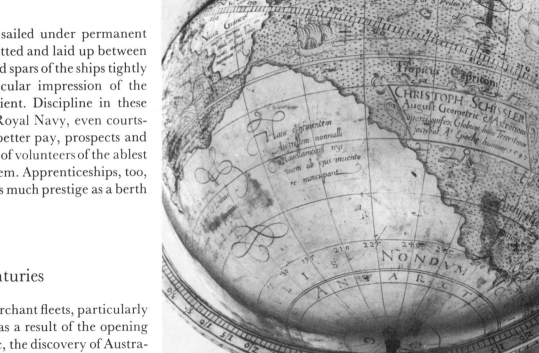

were not owned by the Company but sailed under permanent charter. At Blackwall, too, they were refitted and laid up between voyages, a veritable forest of tall masts and spars of the ships tightly berthed in the basins giving a spectacular impression of the country's sea-borne trade with the Orient. Discipline in these ships was as strictly enforced as in the Royal Navy, even courts-martial being held on board. With far better pay, prospects and food, however, the crews were composed of volunteers of the ablest seamen and discipline was less of a problem. Apprenticeships, too, were eagerly sought and carried almost as much prestige as a berth in the gunroom of a man-of-war.

Voyages of discovery—seventeenth and eighteenth centuries

The greatest expansion of the world's merchant fleets, particularly the British and American, came about as a result of the opening of the hitherto virtually unknown Pacific, the discovery of Australia and New Zealand and the innumerable islands of that vast ocean, and the establishment of the sailing ship route making use of the constant westerly winds in the far south latitudes, when the existence of *Terra Australis Incognita* was finally disproved.

During the seventeenth century, the maritime energies of the French and English were largely taken up with founding colonial empires in America and the West Indies and in preliminary steps to the same end in India. It was the Dutch, therefore, who, after ousting the Portuguese from most of the East Indies, played the major part in the continued search for the great southern continent.

Their first expedition to the East Indies set out via the Cape of Good Hope in 1595 and within ten years they were sufficiently established to begin probing southwards. Willem Janszoon, striking south from the southern shore of New Guinea entered the Gulf of Carpentaria to become the first to discover Australia. Ignorant of the existence of the Torres Strait, however, he had to assume it was a southern extension of New Guinea.

The next Dutch discovery came about through their adoption in 1616 of a southerly route to the East Indies in the belt of constant westerly winds which made them independent of the seasonal south-west monsoon. This brought them knowledge of the West Australian coast and some of the south coast; they called the country New Holland. But it was another twenty-six years before Abel Tasman sailed eastwards round the south of New Holland to prove it was no part of the fabled southern continent. Discovering what was later to be called Tasmania, which he named Van Diemen's

41 and 42 Globe by Schissler, 1597 and pocket globe after Adams, *c.* 1750. The advance in geography in the period between these two globes is clearly seen in the replacement of the vast imaginary southern continent by Australia (known as New Holland) and part of New Zealand on the later globe. However it was not until the second voyage of Captain James Cook in 1772–5 that the existence of the mythical *Terra Australis Incognita* was finally disproved.

The last voyage of any importance during the seventeenth century was again undertaken by Tasman in 1644. Its object was the dual one of determining whether there was a channel south of New Guinea and whether the waters sailed into by Janszoon comprised a huge gulf or were the entrance to a channel cutting Australia in half. The maze of islands at its western end concealed from him the existence of the Torres Strait and he sailed on down the western side of the York Peninsula following it when it turned west and then north to establish the existence of the Gulf of Carpentaria and that New Holland was connected to the land stretching south from New Guinea. Further exploration of the South Pacific now came virtually to a halt for 120 years except for a last Dutch expedition under Jacob Roggeveen in 1721 which sailed via Cape Horn, bent once again on discovering the southern continent. It discovered only mysterious Easter Island with its huge stone statues of problematical origin and a few of the Pacific's myriad small islands.

Spain and Portugal had all they could handle in the way of imperial possessions. England and France were engaged in the succession of wars for supremacy in America, the West Indies and India. The Dutch concentrated on exploitation of the East Indies. It was to strike at Spain by detaching Chile and Peru from her Empire that the British Admiralty despatched Commodore Anson in the ship-of-the-line *Centurion* and a small squadron to the Pacific in 1740. Though Anson successfully harried the Spaniards, capturing and plundering the Peruvian port of Paita and, after crossing the Pacific to the Philippine Islands, captured the so-called 'Manilla Galleon' carrying home the annual trade and treasure, before continuing home via Macao and the Cape of Good Hope route, the chief interest of the voyage is as an extreme example of the ravages of scurvy (see p. 127). Before reaching his temporary base of operations, Juan Fernandez Island, the *Centurion* had already buried 200 of her crew and had 130 sick, a number of whom died as they were being carried ashore where fresh vegetables quickly restored the remainder. In all, out of 961 men of his squadron, 626 died during the voyage, mostly from scurvy.

The most notable voyages of discovery during the first half of the eighteenth century were sponsored by Peter the Great of Russia who commissioned the Danish captain, Vitus Bering, to explore the Siberian coast in the course of which he sailed round the north-eastern tip of Asia in 1728 to establish the existence of the Strait between Asia and America which bears his name. Twelve years later he crossed the strait and explored the south coast of Alaska. It was in pursuit of that will-of-the-wisp, the North-west Passage that the next British expedition entered the Pacific in 1765 under

43 Squadron of seven warships by W. van de Velde the Elder, 1653. The ships are recognizable by their stern decorations. On the left the *Maeght van Enkhuysen*, the '*Star*' and the *Edam* (usually referred to as the *Bull*). On the extreme left is the *Gouda* and in front of her probably the *Brederode*, flagship to Tromp.

Land after the Governor of the Dutch East Indies, he sailed on into the Pacific until he found his further progress barred by a coast running north and south. His discovery was to be named New Zealand. Following the coast to its northern extremity, he went no further and returned to Batavia round the north of New Guinea. Thus he failed to discover that New Zealand was a group of islands and his assumption that it was part of the southern continent sloping away south-eastward to Cape Horn was to remain the current belief for another 127 years.

At about the same time that Dutch seamen first sighted the West Australian coast, two other Dutchmen Willem Schouten and Jacob Le Maire were entering the Pacific by sailing south of Tierra del Fuego. Before rounding Cape Horn, which they named, they passed between Tierra del Fuego and a lofty coast which, inevitably, they assumed to be part of the southern continent. It was, in fact, the island which still retains the name of Staten Land which they gave it (see pp. 91-7).

Commodore The Hon. John Byron in the frigate *Dolphin*, who was instructed to sail north to the Californian coast and search for a passage back to Hudson's Bay. Beset by scurvy amongst his crew, he ignored his orders, crossed the Pacific in the trade-wind belt and made no discoveries of importance.

The *Dolphin* sailed again in 1766 under Captain Samuel Wallis in company with the *Swallow* commanded by Philip Carteret, a smaller, slower and less well-found ship. Their instructions, this time, were expressly to search the southern latitudes for the elusive continent. Losing touch in heavy weather after getting through the Straits of Magellan, the two ships crossed in different latitudes. Wallis was soon discouraged by the contrary winds in the south and edged back into the trade-wind belt where his fame was assured by his discovery of the dream-island of Tahiti which, with its laughing, hospitable people, has been the lure of South Seas voyagers ever since. It was Carteret, however, whose dogged persistence took him more than half way across the Pacific south of the tropics, who contributed most to geographic knowledge by wiping from the maps much of the southern continent.

In the wake of Wallis in 1768 sailed the Frenchman, Louis Antoine de Bougainville in the *Boudeuse*, accompanied by a store ship the *Étoile*. He, too, found Tahiti which he viewed with rapture and named the New Cythera. Thereafter, however, he steered more southerly and, after sighting Samoa and re-discovering Quiros' Espiritu Santo in the New Hebrides, pressed on westwards until he found his way barred by the Great Barrier Reef off the east coast of Australia.

To escape from this perilous lee shore he beat northwards, sailing as close to the easterly trade wind as possible so as to weather the eastern end of New Guinea. Unable to do so, he found himself at the eastern end of Torres Strait; but rather than plunge blindly amongst the uncharted reefs, shoals and islands which strewed it and hid its existence from him, he tacked and beat his way painfully eastwards before finally turning north again and sailing through the Solomons in Carteret's wake to Batavia. Returning home round the Cape, the *Boudeuse* overtook the *Swallow* in the Atlantic and the two explorers exchanged compliments.

Still the *Terra Australis Incognita* defied discovery or disproof. Tasman, by sailing eastward to New Zealand, passing south of New Holland, had exploded the myth that part of the great southern continent lay in tropical latitudes; but his view was generally held that New Zealand was a northern extension of a land mass. All other navigators of the South Pacific had travelled from east to west; meeting the prevailing westerlies they had inevitably been edged northwards into the trade wind belt, leaving unexamined the latitudes in which the continent was believed to lie. Only by going from the Cape of Good Hope into latitude 50 degrees south or more and then sailing before the westerlies could the question be cleared up. For this a navigator was needed sufficiently dedicated to accept the hardships entailed, and experienced enough to keep his ship seaworthy and his men healthy over long periods away from land and in heavy weather.

Such a man was about to come forward and the fact that he was at the same time a brilliant and most conscientious surveyor and a born mathematician, was to make James Cook a *sans pareil* amongst the great navigators of history. The son of a Yorkshire day labourer, born in 1728, self-educated except for the elementary 'three R's' learnt at the village school, at sea from the age of 18 aboard East Coast colliers where he had risen to the rank of mate at the age of 24, he had volunteered as an Able Seaman in the Royal Navy at the outbreak of the Seven Years' War in 1755. Within seven months he had become boatswain (warrant officer) of the 60-gun ship-of-the-line *Eagle*.

The shoal-strewn, foggy North Sea had made him an expert in pilotage. He now taught himself the rest of the science of navigation and its attendant mathematics. By 1757 he had been made master (navigating officer) of the 64-gun *Pembroke* in which he took part in the expedition which captured Quebec in 1759. The success of this expedition depended largely on the survey of the River St Lawrence made by the masters of the fleet of whom Cook soon became the leader, being referred to as 'master-of-the-fleet' and 'master surveyor'.

For the next seven summers Cook was engaged in surveys of the St Lawrence estuary and the coasts of Nova Scotia and Newfoundland. During the winters, with his ship laid up in the Thames, in the intervals of drawing the resultant charts he perfected his knowledge of astronomical calculations. In August 1766 he made observations of an eclipse of the sun visible in Newfoundland which earned him the commendations of the Royal Society which referred to him as 'Mr Cook, a good mathematician, very expert in his business'.

Thus when in February 1768, at the urging of the Royal Society, George III instructed the Admiralty to provide a ship to carry a scientific expedition to the South Pacific to observe the predicted transit of Venus across the sun, Cook was selected to command it. The ship selected on Cook's recommendation, was not a man-of-war like the frigate *Dolphin*, which arrived back in May 1768, or even the smaller *Swallow* which reached England ten months later, but a little Whitby collier of the type he had got to know so well from his early days at sea—a 'cat' of the type described earlier—and re-named HMS *Endeavour*.

The advantages of such a ship were numerous. She was of light

44 Captain James Cook, 1728–79, detail from an oil painting by N. Dance (see also pp. 146–152).

draught; could be handled by a small crew for which she could carry ample provisions for a long voyage; was flat-bottomed and so would not suffer too badly if she ran aground.

Before sailing in August 1768 the *Endeavour*'s hull was sheathed against the attack of the teredo worm which in tropical waters could wreak havoc to the underwater planks in a very short time. The later practice of applying a sheath of copper was already being experimented with, but the *Endeavour* was given a layer of tarred felt over which was laid an extra skin of planking. The Admiralty was determined that some practical advantage besides the purely scientific knowledge should be achieved by the voyage. After rounding Cape Horn and crossing the Pacific to Tahiti (the knowledge of which reached England in the *Dolphin* in May 1768) for the observations of the transit of Venus, he was to sail to latitude 40 degrees south in search of the southern continent and, if he did not find it, to sail west to the eastern shore of New Zealand, the coast of which he was to explore before returning home either via Cape Horn or round the Cape of Good Hope.

Cook followed his instructions faithfully. While at Tahiti where the observations were duly made, he carefully surveyed the island coast. On leaving it he sailed to 40 south in steadily worsening weather without sighting land. On 7 October 1769 he made landfall on the east coast of the North Island of New Zealand and by 27 March 1770 had circumnavigated and surveyed both islands and the strait between them which bears his name. Several more nails had been driven into the coffin of the fabled southern continent.

This voyage possessed two features entirely new to maritime exploration. For the first time the dreaded scurvy had been eliminated and the *Endeavour* had not one man sick when she reached Tahiti, a remarkable tribute to Cook's provision of unsalted 'portable-soups', fruit and vegetable juices, his forcible methods of administering them and his insistence on cleanliness and hygiene. The other new feature was that the longitude of every place touched at was established to a much greater accuracy than ever before.

John Harrison, a carpenter and another self-taught mathematician had already constructed the first of his chronometers which were to solve the hitherto intractable problem of accurately measuring longitude at sea. Cook did not carry any such reliable time-piece on his first voyage. From Charles Green, one of the party of scientific observers, however, he learned the complicated system devised by Dr Maskelyne, the Astronomer Royal, which by means of measurements of the angular distance of the moon from a fixed star and some involved mathematics, gave the longitude with an accuracy of one degree. It was not a method which

could be used from the rolling deck of a ship, however, and the approach to land across the ocean had still to be made by sailing north or south until on the correct latitude and then east or west along the parallel, a process known as 'running down the latitude'.

Leaving New Zealand on 1 April 1770, Cook sailed west with the intention of making Van Diemen's Land but was driven north by a southerly gale. He made a landfall on the south-east corner of New Holland whence he sailed northwards up the entire coast, carefully charting as he went, though there was time only for establishing the main features and the general outline. Passing inside the Great Barrier Reef, the existence of which only became apparent when it slanted into the shore, he found himself in waters so reef-strewn that they taxed his pilotage skill to the utmost. The *Endeavour* ran on to a coral reef and was badly holed. She was got off, however, hauled up on a sandy beach and partly repaired.

The dockyard facilities of Batavia in the Dutch East Indies were needed if she was to get home to England, however. Cook resumed his northward track and on 21 August reached its northern extremity, Cape York. Torres' account of a strait between it and New Guinea was known to him and, despite the denials of Dutch explorers, the westerly swell now experienced seemed to indicate its existence and persuaded him to investigate. Skilful pilotage

45 and 46 To determine longitude by comparing local time with Greenwich time, it was essential to have an absolutely accurate chronometer. A prize of £20,000 was offered by the British Admiralty to the inventor of a chronometer accurate enough for this purpose.

45 Front view of Harrison's first chronometer, 1735.

46 Harrison's fourth chronometer, 1759, which eventually won the prize.

brought him safely through by a different route from Torres', which was close to the New Guinea shore. Cook was justified in naming his the Endeavour Strait.

Batavia provided the necessary repairs to get the ship home; but malaria and dysentery now struck down thirty amongst those whose health Cook's methods had so well preserved.

For Cook's second voyage which was to last from 13 July 1772 until 29 July 1775, two new Whitby colliers of 462 and 336 tons were commissioned to replace the worn-out *Endeavour* and were named, respectively, *Resolution* and *Adventure*, the latter being commanded by Tobias Furneaux. By this time, with the French also showing themselves keenly interested in the subject, the Admiralty was anxious once and for all to have the question of *Terra Australis* decided. The accumulated knowledge of the wind pattern made it clear that a sailing ship could only cover the relevant area from west to east; consequently Cook's orders were to make first for the Cape of Good Hope and then strike south before turning east to explore and circumnavigate the globe in the highest possible southern latitude. With the onset of winter he was to retire northwards, returning to continue the exploration in the summer season.

There was, of course, as is known now, no land for him to discover short of the ice-bound continent surrounding the South Pole. Long before he could reach that he found himself amongst icebergs and pack ice which barred further progress and subjected him and his crews to great suffering and hardship and forced him to edge northward into navigable waters. Nevertheless in January 1773 he became the first explorer to cross the Antarctic Circle and by mid-March he had reached the longitude of Eastern Australia having covered 145 degrees of longitude at latitudes never before navigated. The *Adventure* had lost touch in stormy weather in February and had made straight for the rendezvous in Queen Charlotte's Sound, New Zealand. Now, with the southern winter approaching, the *Resolution* also turned north and in mid-May the two ships were re-united.

During that winter Cook made a long cast eastwards from New Zealand in latitudes between 41 and 46 south before circling north to the Tuamotus and west again to Tahiti for rest and refreshment. Sailing on to re-discover and map the Friendly Islands, the two ships steered south again to refit in Queen Charlotte's Sound. Once again the *Adventure* was separated by gales and when Cook sailed to resume his search of Antarctica she had not yet rejoined; though she arrived a few days later, the two ships had finally parted company. Furneaux took the *Adventure* to some 60 degrees south, turned east and sailed into the South Atlantic 400 miles south of Cape Horn and after crossing the South Atlantic at that

latitude, refitted at Cape Town before returning home in July 1774, the first commander to complete a circumnavigation in an easterly direction. He had finally proved that there was no southern continent in a temperate climate.

It was a tremendous and epoch-making achievement. But Cook was not to be satisfied with less than the three years of exploration he had planned. During this second summer he quartered the ocean in the region of the Antarctic Circle, crossing it and reaching the latitude of 71 degrees south on 30 January 1774 before circling north again in a wide sweep into the trade wind belt, touching at Easter Island, the Marquesas, Tahiti, and the New Hebrides before making Queen Charlotte's Sound again for a final refit. Each place at which he touched he was able for the first time to fix accurately, for in the *Resolution* he carried a replica of Harrison's chronometer which proved amazingly reliable.

In November 1774 he left for the last stretch of his planned circumnavigation reaching Cape Horn at Christmas time, where he spent a fortnight surveying before crossing the South Atlantic in southern latitudes. Cape Town was reached in March and Portsmouth on 29 July 1775. During the three years' voyage the *Resolution* had lost three men by accident, only one by disease.

The existence of a great southern continent in habitable climes had been finally disproved. There remained that other fancy, a navigable North-west Passage, more than ever sought after since the growth of the tea trade with China which was having to take

47 The *Resolution* and *Discovery* in the northern ice, 1779, after J. Webber (1750–1793). Both ships were English east coast cat-built colliers which Cook favoured for their sturdy construction.

the long route to England round the Cape of Good Hope. Although the search for an Atlantic entrance had been abandoned since 1631 when Luke Foxe and Thomas James searched in vain for a northern exit from Hudson's Bay, the existence of such a passage was not entirely ruled out and it was with the object of seeking the Pacific end of the North-west Passage that Cook was despatched in 1776 on his third and final voyage.

In spite of her three winters in the cruel Antarctic Seas, the *Resolution* was declared sound and re-commissioned; but bad workmanship in the Royal Yard at Deptford where she was refitted was to make her a constant source of trouble during the voyage. She was accompanied by yet another cat-built collier, the *Discovery* of less than 300 tons, commanded by Charles Clerke who had taken part in both previous voyages.

Cook sailed on 30 November 1776 with orders to proceed via Cape Town and, after examining the French discoveries in the Indian Ocean—the Marion and Crozet Islands and Kerguelen—to make for Tahiti and thence to the west coast of North America. The need to refit the leaky *Resolution* at Cape Town and again at the Friendly Islands before reaching Tahiti forced him to postpone his northward exploration until the summer of 1778. Leaving Tahiti at the end of 1777 he discovered the Sandwich (now Hawaiian) Islands and made landfall on the American coast on 7 March. Coasting northward he once again had to refit at Nootka Sound before sailing on to survey the coast of Alaska, establishing it as part of the American continent and not an island or island group as had been suspected. Passing through the Bering Strait and pushing northwards until his way was barred by ice in $70\frac{1}{2}$ degrees latitude, he turned back to winter in the Sandwich Islands.

Having surveyed Hawaii, largest of the islands, Cook anchored his ships on 17 January 1779 in Kealakekua Bay. He was initially warmly, indeed lavishly welcomed by the Hawaiians whose priests proclaimed him a returning Polynesian god. The burden which this imposed in the shape of free provisions was, however, becoming resented by the time the two ships sailed after a three weeks' stay. When a storm drove them back and the sight of *Resolution*'s foremast being brought ashore for repairs indicated a prolonged stay and a renewal of burdensome tribute, discontent rose amongst the ordinary natives which led to stone-throwing, thefts and scuffles.

Going ashore with a guard of marines to take a chief hostage for the return of a stolen ship's boat, Cook was confronted by an angry crowd of some 3,000 Hawaiians. Even so, under cover of a volley from the marines, he had reached the water's edge and was about to step into his boat when the crowd rushed him, struck him down and killed him and four marines.

The basically peaceful Hawaiians soon regretted their deed and made friendly overtures. All that remained of Cook's dismembered and burnt body was delivered up and was buried in the waters of the bay. Charles Clerke assumed command of the expedition and made a second voyage into Bering Strait, visiting Petropavlovsk on the Russian side. He, too, died in the Pacific, however, from consumption and it was John Gore, a veteran of Byron's and Wallis's voyages as well as all of Cook's, who brought the two ships home in October 1780.

For the sheer volume of geographic knowledge of the oceans he gave to the world, James Cook must be reckoned without compare amongst the great company of navigators. Apart from the positive achievements of charting New Zealand, the east coast of Australia and the numerous island groups and confirming the separation of Australia from New Guinea, his dogged persistence in probing southwards to the Antarctic and circumnavigating the world in the stormy, ice-beset southern latitudes, to prove the non-existence of *Terra Australis* opened up the most important route of the last great days of the sail era along which the tea and wool clippers made their famous voyages.

All the main features of the Pacific were now disclosed. Much remained to be done, of course, by such as Vancouver, who took part in Cook's last voyage and returned to chart the Canadian west coast, and Flinders, who charted much of the coast of Australia. The myriad islands of Micronesia and Polynesia still awaited discovery and charting. But the Pacific was opened at last, the map of the world, in the main, complete.

The clipper epoch

Even before the British East India Company ceased trading activities in 1831, rivals or 'free-traders' had begun to compete in the commerce with the Far East. The best-known of these were the 'Blackwall Frigates' built by the firm of Green & Wigram of Blackwall until 1843 when the partnership was dissolved, the business becoming R. & H. Green & Co. Blackwall Frigates were also built at Sunderland and on the Tyne, where T. & W. Smith & Co. were soon well-known. Speed now became an important feature and such ships designed with faster lines, flush-decked without the large poop of the old East Indiamen, began to break records in passages to India. Green & Wigram's 818-ton *Seringapatam*, for instance, reached Bombay from England in 85 days, and the *Minden* built on the Tyne in 1848 made Calcutta in 90 days.

Meanwhile a new and rapidly expanding passenger traffic to Australia and New Zealand had also begun. Cook's exploration

48 *opposite* The launch of a Blackwall frigate, probably the *Highflyer* in 1861. Watercolour attributed to G. Rogers.

49 *opposite* The *Seringapatam* by J. Lynn (*fl.* 1826 – 1838), built at Blackwall by the famous firm of Green & Wigram, heaving to off the Downs, probably to pick up a pilot. The boat under sail in the foreground is probably the pilot boat.

50 *far right* Portsmouth, Showing the Prison Hulks (detail), by D. Turner (oil), after Louis Garneray, who was a prisoner at Portsmouth from 1806 to 1814. Note the tumble-home of the ships. This was to provide stable gun platforms when the ships were in commission. Elderly ships provided isolated floating prisons and receiving points for convicts due to be transported.

however; instead, the British Government had decided that the congestion in the prisons and prison hulks caused by the harsh penal laws of the time should be reduced by transportation of the convicts to New South Wales, and in 1788 Captain Arthur Phillip had reached Botany Bay with the first consignment.

They were soon joined by free settlers and by 1840, when transportation ceased, colonization had spread to Victoria, Tasmania and Queensland while Western Australia and South Australia were colonized directly from England. At the same time the situation in New Zealand, where the lawless behaviour of European adventurers and the combative nature of the indigenous Maoris combined to bring about constant disturbances, led to the annexation of the country by a reluctant British Government followed by a steady flow of emigrants. The construction of fast merchant ships received a great fillip from these new movements.

An important influence leading to improvement in the sailing qualities of merchant ships was the immensely profitable trade in opium between India, where it was grown under an East India Company monopoly, and South China where the drug was eagerly sought and, indeed, was virtually the only commodity other than silver that the Chinese would accept in return for their tea, silk, etc. Ships engaged in this commerce not only had to be able to beat against the monsoon on passage from India, but could earn the largest profits by then getting back to Europe or America first with the annual tea crop.

The term 'clipper' came gradually to be applied to these types of fast sailing ships, probably first by the Americans who had their share in the opium and tea trade and with whom the term had for some time been in use to describe the fast schooners built mainly in Virginia and Maryland. Rigged with two raking masts each carry-

of the east coast of New Holland (not until 1817 did it become officially known as Australia following the suggestion of Matthew Flinders) had encouraged plans of colonizing what Cook had named New South Wales. These plans had failed to mature,

ing a gaff mainsail with two square sails above it, and three trysails extended out on the long bowsprit, these Baltimore Clippers, as they were known, introduced a new design of hull, long, low and broad, with a draught deeper aft than forward. A sharp, raked stem—the true mark of the 'clipper'—and an inclined, overhanging stern, reducing the area of hull in contact with the water, combined with their fine lines and efficient rig to make them the fastest ships in the world. They had become famous during the War of 1812 with Britain when, with guns mounted on their open deck, their speed had made them highly successful and elusive blockade runners and privateers, able to cut out and destroy a ship from a convoy under the eyes of the slower enemy frigates. The narrow hulls of such ships reduced the space available for cargo to a degree not sufficiently compensated for by their good sailing qualities to make them suitable for normal trading, and after the war they were commonly used for the unsavoury role of slaver at a time when the navies of the world were endeavouring to scotch this repulsive trade. By 1850 it had virtually ceased and from this time the Baltimore Clippers were constructed on less thoroughbred lines and became commercial propositions. Nevertheless it was a combination of their long slim hulls with the three-masted, square-sailed, ship-rig that produced the famous clipper ships.

The Americans were their originators and the first clipper ship is generally considered to have been the *Rainbow* built in 1845 at New York, though as early as 1832 the *Ann McKim* of Baltimore had been built, an enlarged Baltimore Clipper with a ship rig. The discovery of gold in California in 1848 and in Australia in 1850 with the resultant demand for the fastest possible passages to each, gave a tremendous fillip to the production of clippers in which

Donald Mackay of Boston took the lead, being the first to introduce machinery into his yard. His *Flying Fish* and *Flying Cloud* were perhaps the most famous clippers of the day.

It is sad to recall, however, that American clippers, things of exquisite beauty under their pyramids of taut white sails which drove them frothing through the seas with such speed and grace, were often managed in a way that earned them the name of Yankee Hell Ships. Brutal mates, armed with belaying pins and even fire-arms imposed a savage discipline, the results of which can be read in Liverpool newspapers of the 1850s reporting trials for injuries and death inflicted. The system comprised a vicious circle in that seamen refused to volunteer to sign on in them and crews were often composed of men of bad character 'shanghaied' aboard. Brutal methods of enforcing discipline then became a necessity; but the 'bucko mates' blows fell on innocent and guilty alike.

American clippers, at this time the fastest and most successful of any, were first most regularly used on the route to San Francisco round the Horn with passengers and freight, whence they would cross the Pacific to China for a cargo of tea for America. After the repeal of the British Navigation Acts in 1849 allowed foreign ships to bring freights into British ports, they also took tea to England, the first to arrive being the *Oriental* of 1,003 tons, in 1850. The competition spurred British ship-owners and ship-builders. Up to this time they had been mainly content with improving the sailing qualities of Blackwall Frigates, but retaining their comparatively heavy frames and timbers and lacking the clippers' fine bows, they could not compete in speed with the latter.

Advance towards the clipper type by British shipbuilders had in fact been made as early as 1839 when Alexander Hall & Sons of Aberdeen had built schooner-rigged ships for the England-Scotland passenger trade such as the *Scottish Maid* which made the trip from Leith to London in 33 hours. It was the same firm which now built the first small British clippers, the *Stornoway* and *Chrysolite* for the China trade. They were followed in 1852 by R. & H. Green of Blackwall with the *Challenger*.

It was to trans-atlantic shipbuilders, however, that James Baines of Liverpool turned for ships for his Black Ball Line which, having previously been the transatlantic passenger line, now took up the carriage of immigrants to Australia. The *Marco Polo* built at St John's, New Brunswick in 1850, a clipper of 1,625 tons, in 1833 beat all records of the day for the voyage from Liverpool to Melbourne. Ships for the Black Ball Line were also bought from Donald Mackay of Boston, famous ones being the *Lightning*, *Champion of the Sea*, *James Baines* and *Donald Mackay*. All these ships were built almost entirely of wood and, of course, copper-sheathed against marine growth and the attacks of the teredo worm.

51 *above* The Baltimore schooner *Mary Felker* of Newburyport, built in 1851. A typical Baltimore schooner from whose fast hull design the clipper ships with square rigs were later developed. Oil, artist unknown.

52 A slaving ship of the mid nineteenth century. These fast topsail schooners with raking masts were designed to out-manoeuvre the naval patrols which were trying to stop the slave trade. They often managed to make their escape upwind.

Plate 6 Ships Trading in the East, detail from an oil painting by H. C. Vroom (1566–1640). The artist shows typical East Indiamen of the period. The whole painting is reproduced in black and white on p. 116.

a vessel with square rig on the foremast only, was a 'barquentine'). The four-masted rig did not come into general use for another 20 years. Another innovation was the division of the topsails into two smaller sails, each on separate yards, enabling the ship's huge spread of sail to be handled by a relatively small crew. To hoist her huge yards and to work her pumps she had a steam engine; the first ship to be so fitted. Before she could be tried out in service, however, she was severely damaged by fire and was subsequently re-built with a much reduced sail plan under which she made her maiden voyage from New York to Land's End in 13 days. It was another American clipper, *Sovereign of the Seas*, which made the all-time record for a sailing ship for the voyage from New York to Liverpool of 13 days and 14 hours and was credited with making 22 knots on occasion. Another American flyer which broke records was the *Challenge*.

Meanwhile other British yards, chiefly Scottish, were also building clippers, notably Robert Steele & Co. of Greenock who, between 1855 and 1859 completed a number which, though comparatively small ships, were very successful. Thus when in 1857 financial depression and the Civil War brought on a decline in American commercial shipbuilding, the way was clear for the revival in Britain which was to result in the golden age of the tea-clipper.

A development at this time was that of the composite ship with wooden hull but interior framework and fittings of iron, a system which was to be employed for all the famous tea-clippers. Several of the most famous were built by Robert Steele, the *Taeping, Ariel* and *Sir Lancelot*—the last-named being generally considered the most beautiful of them all—coming from his Greenock yard. The other two and the *Serica* took part in the famous Tea-Clipper Race in 1866 when all three left Foochow on the same tide on 30 May and docked in London on the same tide on 6 September.

Other famous clippers built in Scotland in 1868 were the *Thermopylae*, designed by Bernard Waymouth and built at Aberdeen by Walter Hood, and the *Cutty Sark* designed by Hercules Linton and built at Dumbarton partly by the firm of Scott and Linton and completed by Denny Brothers. The two ships took part in a famous and thrilling race home from China in 1872. The *Cutty Sark* was in the lead until she lost her rudder in a gale and was narrowly beaten by her rival.

Both these ships had a long career, remaining in the tea trade until the opening of the Suez Canal made the long trip round the Cape of Good Hope unprofitable for that specialized freight. In 1880 they transferred to the Australian wool trade, the *Thermopylae* shifting again ten years later to the carrying of rice from Rangoon to Vancouver. The *Cutty Sark* is the only tea clipper still

Plate 7 Dutch Ships Running in to a Rocky Coast, oil painting formerly attributed to Aert van Antum (*c.* 1580–1620), but now believed to be by Andries van Eertvelt (1590–1662). The sailors of the period would probably have been horrified at the artist's portrayal. In fact, the courses would probably have been furled and the ships sailing on the topsails.

53 *above* The Boston-built clipper *James Baines* of the Black Ball Line (see p. 44), after coming to an anchor off Liverpool.

54 The *Great Republic* built by Donald Mackay of Boston in 1833; she had four masts and was the biggest wooden sailing ship ever built.

Mackay's most ambitious design was the *Great Republic*, built in 1833, the biggest wooden sailing ship ever to be built, with a length of 335 feet and a beam of 53 feet. Perhaps the statistic which best illustrates her size is that of her main yard which was 120 feet long. She had a fourth or 'jigger' mast, fore-and-aft rigged, and so was a four-masted barque. (The term 'barque' at this time indicated a three- or more-masted ship fore-and-aft rigged on the mizen, while

47

in existence, having been saved from the breaker's yard and in 1957 opened as a museum ship in a dry-dock at Greenwich close to the National Maritime Museum.

The competition of the steamship and the technical advances of the industrial revolution combined, from 1860 onwards, to replace the comparatively small, composite sailing ships such as the tea-clippers which were usually less than 1,000 tons, by ever larger ships. Unable to compete in speed of passages with the steamship, though under certain conditions they were faster, economics demanded larger cargoes, smaller crews and cheaper maintenance. The result was first the iron and then the steel-hulled ship, division of topgallant sails as well as topsails into two smaller sails, provision of steel spars and wire-rope rigging, the discarding of such refinements as studding sails. As the hulls grew longer, the additional space allowed and a balanced sail plan demanded a fourth mast. This was at first square-rigged, but as had already happened with many three-masted ships built in the 1860s, it was found easier for a small crew to handle if the after mast was fore-and-aft rigged.

By the turn of the century, by which time the British had sold or scrapped the majority of theirs, large sailing ships were often more than 4,000 tons gross registered tonnage and rigged as five-masted barques. The French, Germans and Scandinavians continued to build them or to have them built in British yards. By making them highly mechanized, with hand winches for working the braces as well as for hoisting topsails and topgallant sails, and by confining them to freights requiring long, direct voyages between the ports of origin and destination, they succeeded in making them paying propositions right up to the onset of the First World War. Thus they were employed in the wool, and later grain trade from Australia and carrying coal to the west coast of South America, returning with a cargo of saltpetre or nitrates.

The German, Ferdinand Laeisz of Hamburg, whose ships' names all began with 'P', was perhaps the best-known sailing ship-owner in the last years of the nineteenth century and the early twentieth century. His *Potosi*, a five-masted barque, of 4,026 gross registered tons, made eleven consecutive voyages between Hamburg and Peru at an average speed of eleven knots. The *Preussen* of 5,081 tons and probably the largest sailing ship ever built, was ship-rigged.

Between the wars the Laeisz Company were again operating their famous P-Line, but the number of their ships diminished until, by 1938 only two barques remained, the *Padua* and *Priwall*. The majority of German sailing ships of that period were fore-and-aft rigged on the four after masts and square-rigged only on the foremast, so they were barquentines. Others had square-rig topsails and topgallants on the first and third masts only and so could be classed as topsail schooners. The French company Dom Borde Fils of Bordeaux, with the aid of government subsidies, also operated these large barquentines until the 1920s.

The ship-owner who persisted longest with sail was the Norwegian Gustav Erikson of Mariehamn, his numerous steel barques being employed chiefly in the grain trade from Australia. Competition in fastest passage times between ships on this run remained keen to the end. In the last grain race, in 1939, out of thirteen ships engaged, ten belonged to Erikson, the winner being his four-

masted barque *Moshulu*, built by William Hamilton & Co. of Port Glasgow in 1904. The voyage out and home has been vividly and entertainingly described by Eric Newby who served as an apprentice in the *Moshulu*, in his book *The Last Grain Race*. Today the last square-riggers have long vanished from the trade routes. A few have been preserved as museum pieces. The *Cutty Sark* is at Greenwich. At Chatham, moored in the River Medway, is the boys' training ship *Arethusa*, once the Laeisz Company's four-masted barque *Peking*, while the *Passat* of the same line lives on in the same capacity at Travemünde. The *Viking* is at Gothenburg, the *Pommern* at Mariehamn. The last three of these all took part in the Last Grain Race. At San Francisco there is to be found, fully restored, the steel Glasgow-built *Balclutha*.

So far we have been keeping as far as possible to the trail of the square-rigged sailing ship, though the fore-and-aft rig has from time to time intruded where its story affected that of the square rig. And it is some very large schooners that must be noted before we leave the subject of ocean-going sailing ships. These 4-, 5- and 6-masted fore-and-aft rigged ships were almost entirely American. One, indeed, there was with seven masts, the *Thomas W. Lawson* built in 1902, while the 6-masted *Wyoming*, built in 1910 was the longest wooden sailing ship (350 feet) ever built, though her displacement was less than that of the *Great Republic* mentioned earlier.

To trace the origin of the fore-and-aft rig one must go back far into antiquity when the first steps to develop the lateen sail were probably taken by the Egyptians when they turned the long, narrow square sail of their Nile river craft into a 'lug' by shifting the point of suspension of the yard from its centre and tilting it. This permitted them to sail with the wind on the beam. The next step was to make the sail triangular and dispense with the boom: the lateen sail had been born. It was carried eastwards across the Indian Ocean by Arab seamen and is still to be seen in Arab craft generically named 'dhows' and until recent times in the 'praus' of the Malay races.

Such, at least is the most generally accepted theory, though it has been suggested that the lateen may equally well have come west across the Indian Ocean from Java. The one thing certain, and of interest in tracing the further development of the fore-and-aft rig is that it was the Arabs who introduced the lateen into the Mediterranean leading, as noted earlier, to the development of the caravel. It was then incorporated into the 'holks' of Northern Europe, and the gaff mizen, it can be said, developed from doing away with the part of the lateen forward of the mast.

No doubt this process had its influence on the development of the fore-and-aft rig in Northern Europe; but its true progenitor

60 *top* The last days of the sailing ship, soon to be superseded by steam, are poignantly recalled in this large oil painting of Hamburg Harbour in 1904 by Schnars-Alquist.

61 *above* Inveterate rivals: a French lugger and an English cutter engaged in a running fight. Luggers were used for smuggling, cutters for chasing smugglers. Oil, artist unknown.

62 *below opposite* The Ferryboat Before the Wind, by Simon de Vlieger (1601–1652) (oil), showing two good examples of the spritsails so common in small Dutch craft of the period, which still survive in the few remaining Thames barges (see Uffa Fox's introduction).

63 *right* The *Bezaan*, 1661. Presented by Amsterdam to Charles II, in addition to the *Mary*, the *Bezaan* was used to sail on the Thames above London Bridge. The name *Bezaan* came to denote the type of rig seen on this vessel.

64 *below* The *Ann of Norfolk*, an example of American inventiveness in the fore-and-aft rig. Note the many reef points on the sails and the hoops for attaching the sails to the masts, while the foot of the sail is only attached to the boom by an outhaul.

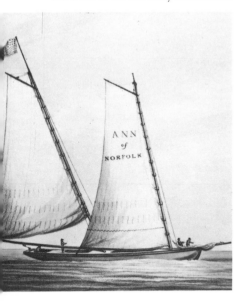

was not the lateen, but the sprit-sail. The Dutch, with their narrow off-shore channels and the maze of inland waterways constructed during and after the fifteenth century had the greatest incentive to develop a handy rig with which small craft could beat against the wind; they did so initially with the sprit-sail and were subsequently responsible for most of the innovations which were effected over the next two centuries.

The sprit-sail must not be confused with that mentioned earlier, the square sail spread beneath the bowsprit of a seventeenth-century ship. The fore-and-aft sprit-sail is a simple quadrilateral sail with one edge laced to the mast and spread by means of a spar —the sprit—placed diagonally from its foot to its peak. It is controlled by a 'vang'—a rope attached to the peak—and a sheet, both held by the steersman in a small boat. It is still to be seen in the few surviving Thames sailing barges and in several other kinds of small craft.

The next development was a triangular headsail bent on the forestay, antedating and no doubt inspiring the staysails which replaced the sprit-sail and sprit-sail topsail in square-rigged ships.

The sprit-sail, quite satisfactory as a small sail for a boat, was less so as it grew bigger and the sprit, getting longer and heavier was hard to control by means of the vang. A tackle had therefore to be led from the top of the mast to support the sprit and prevent it falling away to leeward. It was but a step from this arrangement to fit, in place of the sprit, a spar along the top edge of the sail with jaws at one end embracing the mast, the sail then being furled by brailing it into the mast. Such a spar is known as a 'gaff' and a rig comprising a gaff mainsail with no boom, but a bonnet laced to its

lower edge, and a fore staysail was the original Dutch 'sloepe'-rig anglicized as 'shallop' or 'sloop'. With the addition of a square top-sail, it was the rig carried by the yacht *Mary* mentioned earlier as being presented to Charles II of England.

Another Dutch rig, however, which was used for yachts or contributed to the 'cutter' or sloop-rig as it eventually crystallized, does seem to owe its origin to some extent to the lateen or to a sail seen in early seventeenth-century Dutch pictures. This was virtually a lateen sail whose yard was also the mast, stepped well forward and raked steeply aft. The next step was to give the sail a very small curved gaff at the top, a boom along the bottom, and greatly reducing the rake of the mast. The result was known as a 'bezaan' sail. Its contribution to the later sloop rig was the boom and the method of furling the mainsail which was by lowering it and stowing it along the boom.

When two-masted fore-and-aft craft were evolved, they were at first usually gaff-rigged 'yawls', that is to say with a large mainsail and a very small gaff-mizen right aft, or 'ketches' in which the mizen was larger and its mast stepped about a quarter of the ship's length from the stern. Sprit-rigged two-masted craft were usually 'yawls'. For a long time such craft were also rigged with a square topsail and topgallant sail on the mainmast; but these were eventually replaced by the triangular fore-and-aft topsail which filled in the space between the gaff of the mainsail and the mast. So rigged but with a sprit mainsail and sprit mizen, they were the models for the Thames sailing barge. The typical fishing smack which developed, however, was a gaff-rigged ketch.

Following these two types of rig there came that of the 'schooner' which, instead of a mainmast and mizen, had a mainmast and foremast, that is to say the mast furthest aft was the bigger and carried the larger sails. Such a rig first appeared late in the seventeenth century, and, in the same way as ketches and yawls, soon increased its sail area with topsails. Unlike those other types, however, the square topsail and topgallant sail were to be retained on the foremast of many schooners, which were therefore designated 'topsail schooners'. It was the schooner that became the most favoured fore-and-aft rig across the Atlantic and the Baltimore clippers mentioned earlier were 'two-topsail-schooners'.

The schooner, indeed, reached its finest development on the eastern seaboard of North America. In northern European waters, too, schooners fulfilled a number of functions, forming a large part of the fishing fleet, which went from Europe to fish the Newfoundland banks and they carried much of the coastal trade along the shores of the Baltic and North Sea.

Two types of fore-and-aft sailers on which interest centres in the English Channel area were the 'lugger' and the 'cutter', each a

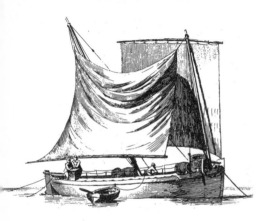

fierce rival of the other; for the former was the favourite craft of the smugglers bringing contraband, principally French brandy, into England; the latter was the type of craft in which the Revenue Service carried on a ceaseless and not too successful campaign against them during the eighteenth and nineteenth centuries.

As its name implies, the lugger was rigged with lug sails, fore-and-aft quadrilateral sails spread from a yard the point of suspension of which was about one-third of its length from the forward end. The yard was inclined upwards from forward aft by means of a topping lift on the after part in the same way as a gaff was supported.

Lug sails are of two types, one being suspended by the halliards at a point about one-third of the length of the yard from its fore end, the other much nearer to the fore end. With the former, when going about from one tack to another, a large portion of the sail is left flattened and useless against the mast unless the yard is dipped round to the other side by lowering it a short way, hauling down on the fore end then re-hoisting. This is known as a 'dipping lug'.

With the latter type, the amount of sail area lost by having the yard on the windward side is so small that it is not worthwhile to shift it. This is a 'standing lug'.

The majority of luggers had 'dipping lugs', that is to say the fore end of the yard was dipped and re-positioned on the other side of the mast on going about from one tack to another. Large luggers, of which one well-known type was the French *chasse-marée*, were used largely for fishing; but with guns replacing their fishing gear were equally suitable for smuggling or, in time of war, privateering, having hulls designed for speed and a large spread of sail on three masts. Dipping lug topsails were hoisted above the foresail and mainsail and even, at times, above the dipping-lug mizen, which was extended, yawl-fashion, over the stern on an outrigger. On the long bowsprit would be set a triangular jib.

Cutters were single-masted craft with, in their simplest form, the sloop-rig inaugurated by the Dutch. In the Revenue cutters, however, manned by a comparatively large crew, much ingenuity was brought to bear to increase the sail area spread on their already extra-long masts and spars. In addition to the fore-and-aft gaff mainsail there would be a square-sail 'course', topsail and even topgallant sail, and besides the normal jib and fore stay-sail studding sails could be added to the topsail. Such craft might be as large as 200 tons and mount 16 guns; but there were many smaller down to 18 tons.

In spite of this abundance of sail, however, and although cutters could make to windward better than luggers, the latter were faster when reaching; so much so that the Government themselves commissioned some luggers to work in co-operation with their cutters. Even when overhauled, the well-armed smugglers were sometimes known to defy the Revenue men who, with little incentive to hazard themselves in a service in which every man's hand was against them, refrained from engaging them.

When the advent of the steamship finally drove the sailing ship from the main trade routes of the world, these smaller craft remained to carry on in the coastal trade, where the sprit-sail Thames barge was until recently a conspicuous example, and in inter-island trade as in the Pacific and the West Indies, where the trading schooner was often sole means of communication with the outside world.

Today it is in the realm of sport that sail almost exclusively survives in many variations from the little dinghies for 'pottering about' or for racing, to the big racing yachts built for millionaires or syndicates of wealthy sportsmen. Early examples of the latter craft were often two-masted lugger-rigged or schooners; the single-masted cutter eventually displaced them and has held sway ever since, though the original sail plan with gaff sail and triangular topsail has given way to the graceful triangular sail of the Bermuda rig.

The stately majesty of the lofty square-rigged ship with its triple pyramid of snowy sails has gone; but in the exquisitely dainty grace of the yacht the adventure of sail lives on.

FERDINAN. MAGALA.

53

The adventure of sail

A beautiful strait

67 *on previous page* Ferdinand Magellan, 1470–1521. Engraving from an early account of his voyage.

68 Storm at Sea, oil painting by Adam Willaerts (1577–1664).

The story of sail illustrated in our book really begins with the first circumnavigation of the earth by Magellan in 1519–22 (see p. 19). His discovery in October 1520 of the straits which still bear his name opened a route to the Pacific and the west coast of South America, as well as a westward route to the East Indies. The Pacific proved much wider than expected, taking nearly four months to cross with no opportunity to take in provisions. In this piece from the account of Francisco Antonio Pigafetta, an Italian who sailed with Magellan, we find Magellan's four ships on the east coast of Patagonia . . .

Leaving that place, we found, in 51 degrees less one-third degree, toward the Antarctic Pole, a river of fresh water. There the ships almost perished because of the furious winds; but God and the holy bodies aided them. We stayed about two months in that river in order to supply the ships with water, wood and fish, the latter being two feet in length and more, and covered with scales. They were very good although small. Before leaving that river, the captain-general and all of us confessed and received communion as true Christians.

Then going to fifty-two degrees toward the same pole, we found a strait on the day of the feast of the eleven thousand virgins [October 21], whose head is called Capo de le Undici Millia Vergine [cape of the Eleven Thousand Virgins] because of that very great miracle. That strait is one hundred and ten leagues or 440 miles long, and it is one-half league broad, more or less. It leads to another sea called the Pacific Sea, and is surrounded by very lofty mountains laden with snow. There it was impossible to find bottom for anchoring, but it was necessary to fasten the moorings on land 25 or 30 fathoms away. Had it not been for the captain-general, we would not have found that strait, for we all thought and said that it was closed on all sides. But the captain-general who knew where to sail to find a well-hidden strait, which he saw depicted on a map in the treasury of the king of Portugal, which was made by that excellent man, Martin of Bohemia, sent two ships, the *Santo Anthonio* and the *Conceptione* (for thus they were called), to discover what was inside the cape de la Baia [cape of the Bay]. We, with the other two ships, namely, the flagship, called *Trinitade*, and the other the *Victoria*, stayed inside the bay to await them. A great storm struck us that night, which lasted until the middle of next day, which necessitated our lifting anchor, and letting ourselves drift hither and thither about the bay. The other two ships suffered a headwind and could not double a cape formed by the bay almost at its end, as they were trying to return to join us; so that they thought that they would have to run aground. But on approaching the end of the bay, and thinking that they were lost, they saw a small opening which did not appear to be an opening, but a sharp turn. Like desperate men they hauled into it, and thus they discovered the strait by chance. Seeing that it was not a sharp turn, but a strait with land, they proceeded farther, and found a bay. And then farther on they

found another strait and another bay larger than the first two.
Very joyful they immediately turned back to inform the captain-
general. We thought that they had been wrecked, first, by reason
of the violent storm, and second, because two days had passed
and they had not appeared, and also because of certain signals
with smoke made by two of their men who had been sent ashore
to advise us. And so, while in suspense, we saw the two ships with
sails full and banners flying to the wind, coming toward us.
When they neared us in this manner, they suddenly discharged
a number of mortars, and burst into cheers. Then all together
thanking God and the Virgin Mary, we went to seek the strait
farther on.

Had we not discovered that strait, the captain-general had
determined to go as far as seventy-five degrees toward the Antarctic
Pole. There in that latitude, during the summer season, there is
no night, or if there is any night it is but short, and so in the winter
with the day. In order that your most illustrious Lordship may
believe it, when we were in that strait, the nights were only three
hours long, and it was then the month of October. The land on
the left-hand side of that strait turned toward the south-east and
was low. We called that strait the strait of Patagonia. One finds the

safest of ports every half league in it, water, the finest of wood
(but not of cedar), fish, sardines, and missiglioni, while smallage
[celery], a sweet herb (although there is also some that is bitter)
grows around the springs. We ate of it for many days as we had
nothing else. I believe that there is not a more beautiful or better
strait in the world than that one. In that Ocean Sea one sees a
very amusing fish hunt. The fish that hunt are of three sorts, and
are two feet and more in length, and are called dorado, albicore,
and bonito. Those fish follow the flying fish called colondrini,
which are one foot and more in length and very good to eat.
When the above three kinds of fish find any of those flying fish,
the latter immediately leap from the water and fly as long as their
wings are wet—more than a crossbow's flight. While they are
flying, the others run along back of them under the water following
the shadow of the flying fish. The latter have no sooner fallen into
the water than the others immediately seize and eat them. It is in
fine a very amusing thing to watch.

from *A Brief Declaration of the Voyage of Navigation Made About the World*,
by Francisco Antonio Pigafetta.

Sixteenth-century navigation

The rise of ocean-going voyages as distinct from coasting voyages brought a demand for a sophisticated art of navigation. At a time when theory was for the learned, who read it in Latin, and the ordinary craftsman worked by rule of thumb, William Bourne (*c.* 1535–1582), an innkeeper at Gravesend on the Thames, who may never have gone to sea, wrote the first manual in the English vernacular which offered navigational theory to the ordinary sea captain and pilot, and began to supplant the 'routiers' and 'waggoners' (as the books which listed landmarks for the pilot of the coasting vessel were called). 'A Regiment for the Sea' explains the use of navigational instruments, and contains instructions for finding latitude by sun and stars. The problem of finding longitude at sea was not solved until the invention of the chronometer, a time-piece able to maintain reasonable accuracy in spite of a ship's motion in a seaway, by James Harrison in the eighteenth century (1765). These extracts are from the first edition of 1574.

What the Equinoctial circle is, being a Parallel line or circle fixed

The equinoctial is a fixed circle in the heavens equally distant from both the poles, and doth pass directly over the middle of the earth round about, and is called the equinoctial, for that if the sun be there, then through all the whole world the sun is twelve hours above the horizon, and twelve hours under the horizon saving under the two poles, and there the equinoctial is with the horizon. So they shall see half the sun and no more, till the sun be departed from the equinoctial. And also to them that do inhabit or dwell in any place under the equinoctial, the sun, moon, and all the stars be twelve hours above the horizon, and twelve hours under the horizon.

The use of the Equinoctial circle

The use of the equinoctial, is to know what declination the sun or any other star hath from it, and of which side, and by that is known the height of the equinoctial, and by the height of that is known the height of either of the two poles of the world.

What the line Ecliptic is

The line ecliptic, is a circle in the very middle of the zodiac, the which the very middle or centre of the sun doth go upon.

Declination is leaning: the use thereof

Declination is counted in the heavens, if that the sun or any other star be unto the north part, or south part of the equinoctial, then it is said, that the sun or star hath so many degrees of declination to the south or to the north parts, as it happeneth.

What Navigation is

Navigation is this, how to direct his course in the sea to any place assigned, and to consider in that direction what things may stand with him, and what things may stand against him, having consideration how to preserve the ship in all storms and changes of weather that may happen by the way, to bring the ship safe unto the port assigned, and in the shortest time.

The use of Navigation

The use thereof is this, first to know how that the place doth bear from him, by what wind or point of the compass, and also how far that the place is from him, and also to consider the stream, or tide gates, currents, which way that they do set or drive the ship, and also to consider what dangers is by the way, as rocks and sands, and such other like impediments, and also if that the wind change or shift by the way, to consider which way to stand, and direct his course unto the most advantage to attain unto the port in shortest time: and also if any storms do happen by the way, to consider how for to preserve the ship and the goods, and to bring her safe unto the port assigned. And also it is most principally to be considered and foreseen, that if they have had by occasion of a contrary tempest, for to go very much out of the course or way, to know then how that the place doth then bear, that is to say, by what point of the compass the place doth stand from you: and also how far it may be from you. Which way to be known is this: first to consider by what point that the ship hath made her way by, and how fast and swiftly that the ship hath gone, and to

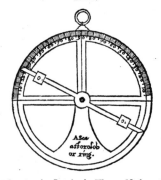

70 Title page of the first edition of William Bourne's *A Regiment for the Sea*, 1574.

71 A sixteenth-century compass.

72 *opposite* The Bristol Channel from a Dutch 'waggoner' (a book of sailing directions) *c.* 1648, which gives bearings, directions for navigation and a brief description of the land.

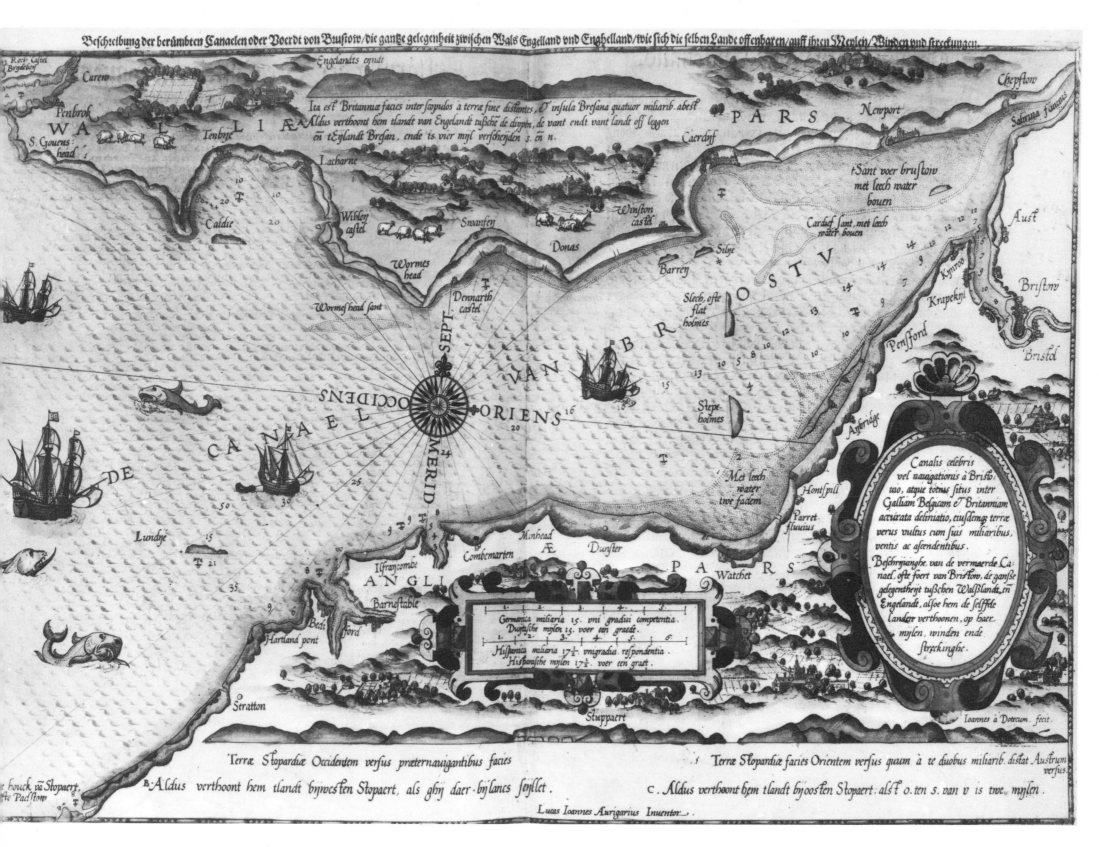

Rock Castel
Brydeben

Carew

Engelandts eyndt

Chepstow

PARS

Penbrok

Ita est Britanniæ facies inter scopulos a terræ fine distantes, T insula Bresana quatuor miliarib. abest
Aldus verthoont hem tlandt van Engelandt tusschē de diepen, de vant endt vant landt off leggen
en tEijlandt Bresan, ende is vier mijl verscheijden s. en n.

Newport

Sabrina fluuius

WA
LLIÆ
S. Gouens
head

Tenbye

Lacharne

Caerdyf

tSant voer brustow
met leech water
bouen

Aust

Caldie

Wiblei
castel

Swansey

Winston
castel

Cardief sant, met leech
water bouen

Donas

Silye

Barrey

Bristow

Wormes
head

Krapeknil

SLech, ofte
flat
holmes

Penfford

Wormes head sant

Dennarith
castel

Bristel

VAN

BROSTU

CANAEL

ORIENS

SEPT.
MERID.
OCCIDENS

Stepe
holmes

Asbridge

DE

Met leech
water
twe faciem

Hontspill

Lundye

Parret
fluuius

Beds

Minhead

Dunster

PARS

ANGLI

Combemarten

Æ

Watchet

Barnestable
Ilfrancombe
Bedisford

Canalis celebris
vel nauigationis à Bristo
uio, atque totius situs inter
Galliam Belgicam et Britanniam
accurata deliniatio, eiusdemq; terræ
verus vultus cum suis miliaribus,
ventis ac ascendentibus.

Beschrijuinghe, van de vermaerde Ca
nael, ofte foert van Bristow, de gantse
gelegentheijt tusschen Walslandt, en
Engelandt, alsoe hem de selffde
landen verthoonen, op haer
mylen, winden ende
streckinghe.

Germanica miliaria 15. vni gradui competentia.
Duijtsche mijlen 15. voer een graet.

Hispanica miliaria 17½. vni gradui respondentia.
Hispanische mijlen 17½. voer een graet.

Ioannes à Doteeum fecit.

Hartland pont

Stratton

Stuppaert

houck, vā Stopaert
te Padstow

Terræ Stopardiæ Occidentem versus præternauigantibus facies

B. Aldus verthoont hem tlandt bijwesten Stopaert, als ghij daer bijlancs seijlet.

Terræ Stopardiæ facies Orientem versus quum à te duobus miliarib. distat Austrum
versus

C. Aldus verthoont hem tlandt bijoosten Stopaert: alst o. ten s. van v is twe mylen.

Lucas Ioannes Aurigarius Inuentor.

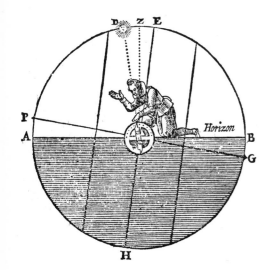

consider how often that the ship hath altered her course, and how much that she hath gone at every time, and then to consider all this in your plate or card, and so you may give a near guess, by what point or wind it beareth from you, and also how far it is thither. And also you may have a great help by the sun or stars, to take the height of the pole above the horizon, and also in some place you may guess by the sounding, both by the depth, and also by the ground. And also it is very meet and necessary to know any place, when that he doth see it.

Of instruments to use at the sea for to take the height of the sun or any stars
All instruments to take the height of the sun or any star, the original of the making thereof, it is either a circle or the part of a circle, whose division is the 360 part of a circle what form soever that it hath, as your cross staff, it is marked according unto the proportion of a circle, and every one of the degrees, is the equal part of a circle, the three hundred and sixtieth part.

The use of the Instruments
The use of the instruments, as astrolabes or common rings, or the cross staff, is to take the height of the sun or other stars, whose uses do follow hereafter in the book.

What manner of persons be meetest to take charge of Ships in Navigation
As touching those persons that are meet to take charge, that is·

to say, to be as master of ships in Navigation, he ought to be sober and wise, and not to be light or rash headed, nor to be too fumish or hasty, but such a one as can well govern himself, for else it is not possible for him to govern his company well: he ought not to be too simple, but he must be such a one as must keep his company in awe of him (by discretion) doing his company no injury or wrong, but to let them have that which men ought to have, and then to see unto them that they do their labour as men ought to do in all points. And the principal point in government is, to cause himself both to be feared and loved, and that groweth principally by this means, to cherish men in well doing, and those men that be honestly addicted, to let them have reasonable pre-eminence, so that it be not hurtful unto the merchant nor to himself, and to punish those that be malefactors and disturbers of their company, and for small faults, to give them gentle admonition to amend them: and principally these two points are to be foreseen by the masters (that is) to serve God himself, and to see that all the whole company do so in like manner, at such convenient time as it is meet to be done: the second point is, that the master use no play at the dice or cards, neither (as near as he can) to suffer any, for the sufferance thereof may do very much hurt in divers respects. And furthermore, the master ought to be such a one, as doth know the moon's course, whereby he doth know at what time it is a full sea, or a low water, knowing in what quarter or part of the sky, that the moon doth make a full sea at that place, and also the master ought to be acquainted, or know that place well, that he doth take charge to go unto (except that he have a pilot) and also he that taketh charge upon him, ought to be expert, how the tide gates or currents do set from place unto place: and also not to be ignorant of such dangers as lie by the way, as rocks, sands, or banks, and also most principally he ought to be such a one, as can very well direct his courses unto any place assigned, and to have capacity how for to handle or shift himself in foul weather or storms. And also it behoveth him to be a good coaster that is to say, to know every place by the sight thereof. And also he that taketh charge for long voyages, ought to have knowledge in plates or cards, and also in such instruments as be meet to take the height of the sun or any star, and to have capacity to correct those instruments, and also he ought to be such a one, that can calculate the sun's declination, or else to have some true regiment, and also he ought to know how to handle the sun's declination, when that he hath taken the height of the sun.

from *A Regiment for the Sea* by William Bourne, 1574

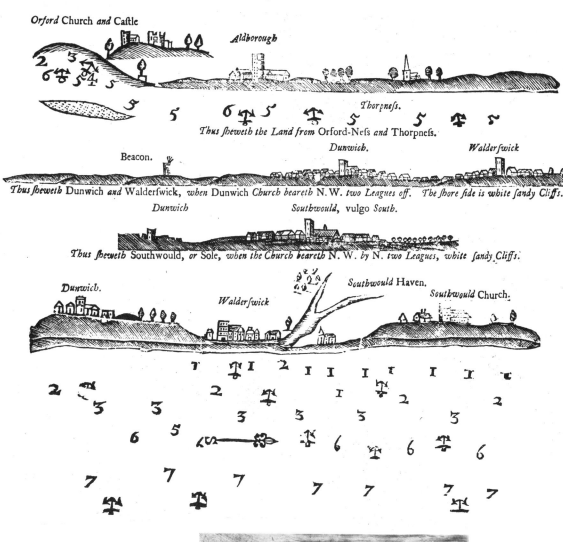

Orford Church and Caftle

Aldborough

Thus fheweth the Land from Orford-Nefs and Thorpnefs.

Beacon.
Dunwich.
Walderfwick

Thus fheweth Dunwich *and* Walderfwick, *when* Dunwich *Church beareth N.W. two Leagues off. The fhore fide is white fandy Cliffs.*

Dunwich
Southwould, vulgo South.

Thus fheweth Southwould, *or* Sole, *when the Church beareth N.W. by N. two Leagues, white fandy Cliffs.*

Dunwich.
Walderfwick
Southwould Haven.
Southwould Church.

75 Early sailing directions for the coast of East Anglia, from Orford Church to Blakeney. This shows the leading features of the coastline, and enabled the coasting navigator to proceed with some confidence. Note particularly Dunwich, which has now almost entirely been washed away.

76 Cherub using quadrant, 1674.

Plunder in the Pacific

As a result of the Papal decree in 1493, dividing the unknown world between Spain and Portugal, and Spain's veto on trade by other countries with its colonies in the New World, the British entered the Pacific as plunderers of Spanish wealth.

Holding Queen Elizabeth I's commission for his actions, Francis Drake was essentially a privateer, though looked on as a pirate by the Spaniards. When war with Spain became official, he commanded a royal expedition which successfully attacked the Spanish fleet in Cadiz; later he played a notable part in the defeat of the Spanish Armada in 1588.

Drake set out on his voyage of circumnavigation with five ships, his flagship being the *Pellican*, renamed the *Golden Hind* during the voyage. Sailing from Plymouth on 15 November 1577, he entered the Pacific via the Straits of Magellan the following September, soon afterwards losing touch with two of his ships in a storm, one of which returned safely to England. Drake arrived home laden with Spanish treasure on 26 September 1580, having 'spent two years, ten months and some few odd days beside, in seeing the wonders of the Lord in the deep'. Here we find him off the Pacific coast of South America . . .

This harbour the Spaniards call Valperizo, and the town adjoining Saint James of Chile: it stands in 35 deg. 40 min., where, albeit, we neither met with our ships nor heard of them; yet there was no good thing which the place afforded, or which our necessities indeed for the present required, but we had the same in great abundance . . .

Our necessities being thus to our content relieved, our next care was the regaining (if possible) of the company of our ships, so long severed from us: neither would anything have satisfied our General or us so well, as the happy meeting, or good news of them: this way therefore (all other thoughts for the present set apart) were all our studies and endeavours bent, how to fit it so as that no opportunity of meeting them might be passed over.

To this end, considering that we could not conveniently run in with our ship (in search of them) to every place where was likelihood of being a harbour, and that our boat was too little, and unable to carry men enough to encounter the malice or treachery of the Spaniards (if we should by any chance meet with any of them) who are used to show no mercy where they may overmaster; and therefore, meaning not to hazard ourselves to their cruel courtesy, we determined, as we coasted now towards the line, to search diligently for some convenient place where we might, in peace and safety, stay the trimming of our ship, and the erecting of a pinnace, in which we might with better security than in our boat, and without endangering our ship, by running into each creek, leave no place untried, if happily we might so

77 Sir Francis Drake, 1545–1595, by W. Marshall.

find again our friends and countrymen.

For this cause, December 19, we entered a bay, not far to the Southward of the town of Cyppo, now inhabited by the Spaniards, in 29 deg. 30 min., where, having landed certain of our men, to the number of 14, to search what conveniency the place was likely to afford for our abiding there; we were immediately descried by the Spaniards of the town of Cyppo aforesaid, who speedily made out 300 men at least, whereof 100 were Spaniards, every one well mounted upon his horse: the rest were Indians, running as dogs at their heels, all naked, and in most miserable bondage.

They could not come any way so closely, but God did open our eyes to see them, before there was any extremity of danger, whereby our men being warned, had reasonable time to shift themselves as they could: first from the main to a rock within the sea, and from thence into their boat, which being ready to receive them, conveyed them with expedition out of the reach of the Spaniards' fury without the hurt of any man.

This being not the place we looked for, nor the entertainment such as we desired, we speedily got hence again, and, December 20, the next day, fell with a more convenient harbour, in a bay somewhat to the northward of the forenamed Cyppo, lying in 27 deg. 55 min. south the line.

Within this bay, during our abode there, we had such abundance of fish, not much unlike our gurnard in England, as no place had ever afforded us the like (Cape Blanc only upon the coast of Barbary excepted) since our first setting forth of Plymouth, until this time, the plenty whereof in this place was such, that our gentlemen sporting themselves day by day with 4 or 5 hooks or lines, in 2 or 3 hours, would take sometimes 400, sometimes more at one time.

All our businesses being thus dispatched, January 19, we set sail from hence; and the next place that we fell withal, January 22, was an island standing in the same height, with the north cape of the province of Mormorena. At this island we found 4 indians with their canoes, which took upon them to bring our men to a place of fresh water on the foresaid cape; in hope whereof, our General made them great cheer (as his manner was towards all strangers), and set his course by their direction, but when we came unto the place, and had travelled up a long way into the land, we found fresh water indeed, but scarce so much as they had drunk wine in their passage thither.

As we sailed along, continually searching for fresh water, we came to a place called Tarapaca, and landing there we lighted on a Spaniard who lay asleep, and had lying by him 13 bars of silver, weighing in all about 4,000 Spanish ducats: we would not

(could we have chosen) have awaked him of his nap: but seeing we, against our wills, did him that injury, we freed him of his charge, which otherwise perhaps would have kept him waking, and so left him to take out (if it pleased him) the other part of his sleep in more security.

Our search for water still continuing, as we landed again not far from thence, we met a Spaniard with an Indian boy, driving 8 lambes [llamas] or Peruvian sheep: each sheep bore two leathern bags, and in each bag was 50 pound weight of refined silver, in the whole 800 weight: we could not endure to see a gentleman Spaniard turned carrier so, and therefore without entreaty we offered our service and became drovers, only his directions were not so perfect that we could keep the way which he intended; for almost as soon as he was parted from us, we with our new kind of carriages, were come unto our boats.

Farther beyond this cape forementioned lie certain Indian towns, from whence, as we passed by, came many of the people in certain bawses made of seal's skins; of which two being joined together of a just length, and side by side, resemble in fashion or form a boat: they have in either of them a small gut, or some such thing blown full of wind, by reason whereof it floateth, and is rowed very swiftly, carrying in it no small burden. In these, upon sight of our ship, they brought store of fish of diverse sorts, to traffic with us for any trifles we would give them, as knives, glasses, and suchlike, whereof men of 60 and 70 years old were as glad as if they had received some exceeding rich commodity, being a most simple and plain dealing people. Their resort unto us was such, as considering the shortness of the time, was wonderful to us to behold.

Not far from this, viz., in 22 deg. 30 min., lay Mormorena, another great town of the same people, over whom 2 Spaniards held the government; with these our General thought meet to deal, or at least to try their courtesy, whether they would, in way of traffic, give us such things as we needed or no, and therefore, January 26, we cast anchor here. We found them (more for fear than for love) somewhat tractable, and received from them by exchange many good things, very necessary for our uses.

Amongst other things which we had of them, the sheep of the country (viz., such as we mentioned before, bearing the leathern bags) were most memorable. Their height and length was equal to a pretty cow, and their strength fully answerable, if not by much exceeding their size or stature. Upon one of their backs did sit at one time three well grown and tall men, and one boy, no man's foot touching the ground by a large foot in length, the beast nothing at all complaining of his burden in the mean time. These sheep have necks like camels, their heads bearing

78 The *Ark Royal* from a woodcut of 1587. The *Ark Royal* was the flagship of Lord Howard, who commanded the English fleet against the Spanish Armada in 1588.

79 Celestial planisphere – northern hemisphere. Detail from a woodcut by A. Dürer (1471 – 1528).

a reasonable resemblance of another sheep. The Spaniards use them to great profit. Their wool is exceeding fine, their flesh good meat, their increase ordinary, and besides they supply the room of horses for burden or travel: yea they serve to carry over the mountains marvellous loads, for 300 leagues together, where no other carriage can be made but by them only. Hereabout, as also all along, and up into the country throughout the Province of Cusko, the common ground, wheresoever it be taken up, in every hundred pound weight of earth, yieldeth 25 shillings of pure silver, after the rate of a crown an ounce.

The next place likely to afford us any news of our ships (for in all this way from the height where we builded our pinnace, there was no bay or harbour at all for shipping), was the port of the town of Arica, standing in 20 deg., whither we arrived February 7. This town seemed to us to stand in the most fruitful soil that we saw all along these coasts, both for that it is situate in the mouth of a most pleasant and fertile valley, abounding with

all good things, as also in that it hath continual trade of shipping, as well from Lima as from all other parts of Peru. It is inhabited by the Spaniards. In two barks here we found some forty and odd bars of silver (of the bigness and fashion of a brickbat, and in weight each of them about 20 pounds), of which we took the burden on ourselves to ease them and so departed towards Chowley, with which we fell the second day following, viz., February 9; and in our way to Lima, we met with another bark at Ariquipa, which had begun to load some silver and gold, but having had (as it seemed, from Arica by land) some notice of our coming, had unloaden the same again before our arrival. Yet in this passage we met another bark loaden with linen, some of which we thought might stand us in some stead, and therefore took it with us.

At Lima we arrived February 15, and notwithstanding the Spaniards' forces, though they had thirty ships at that present in harbour there, whereof 17 (most of them the especial ships in all the South Sea) were fully ready, we entered and anchored all night in the midst of them, in the *Calao*, and might have made more spoil amongst them in few hours, if we had been affected to revenge, than the Spaniard could have recovered again in many years. But we had more care to get up that company which we we had so long missed, than to recompense their cruel and hard dealing by an even requital, which now we might have took. This Lima stands in 12 deg. 30 min. South latitude.

from *The World Encompassed* by Sir Francis Drake the Younger, London 1628.

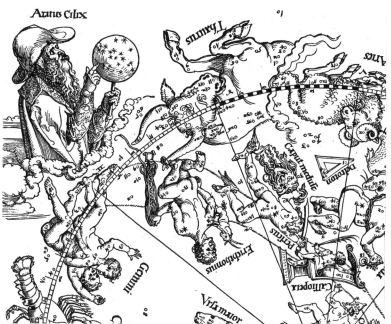

Sir Richard versus Don Beltran

By 1594 improvements in the design and armament of Spanish ships made things less easy for the privateers.

Richard Hawkins was the son of John Hawkins, one of the early privateers, and followed in his steps at sea. He served under Drake in the West Indies in 1585 and commanded the *Swallow* against the Armada in 1588. In 1593 he set out in the *Dainty* for a raid in the Drake manner into the Pacific. He got as far as Valparaiso where he was set upon and overpowered by numbers. He surrendered on the express understanding that the remainder of his men should be spared and set free.

In spite of the honourable protests of his captor Don Beltran de Castro, Richard was kept a prisoner for eight years in Lima and in Spain. In 1595 his father led an unsuccessful expedition to rescue him. Richard was knighted by James I and wrote a spirited account of his voyage. The following is the story of Richard Hawkins and his predecessors from the Spanish point of view. Francis Drake is 'Francisco Draque', Queen Elizabeth is 'Isabel', Cavendish is 'Candi' and Hawkins is 'Aquines'.

Several ships, commanded by English pirates, entered the South Sea in the time of former Viceroys, whose audacity was rewarded with success in the shape of prizes and notable plunder. The first who, entering by the Strait of Magellan, coasted along the land from south to north, was Francisco Draque. His Queen, Isabel, sent him three ships well armed and provisioned. Each ship had a crew of two hundred men, besides ten young gentlemen, who wished to perform the voyage with the object of seeing the world, and of showing their valour on such occasions as might offer themselves. He left the port of Plemua [Plymouth] to pass into the South Sea, and seek the above strait.

Having reached the strait after various events which have already been related by others, he passed it alone in the *Capitana* [the Admiral's ship]. While he was ranging over those seas and before he arrived at Callao, the port for which he was making, he fell in with a ship of Arica, the port of Potosi. She was coming from Callao, unarmed, and not expecting the appearance of pirates, laden with bars of iron and some gold. Draque boarded her, and giving good treatment to all, he asked the master, named San Juan de Anton, for the invoice of the cargo; who delivered up what he had got, item by item, without omitting anything, for which he received from Draque a receipt in full as his discharge. Observing that the others were sad, he consoled them by saying that they should cast off all care, seeing that they lived in so good and rich a land. With this he left them in their vessel, and went

80 A Spanish three-decker lying at Naples, oil painting by Abraham Willaerts (1613–69). This was the type of ship with which the Spaniards defended their South American colonies.

to Callao, where he came to amongst the other ships. Being there unknown, the people rose in arms, in consequence of which he made sail and proceeded to the coast of Nicaragua. On an island called Del Caño, on the coast of Costa Rica, there is abundance of wood and water. Here he careened the ship, and, without hurrying himself, he then shaped a course towards the west.

Draque continued his voyage, and arrived at the Malucos. He anchored at Ternate, where he had trade in cloves, and made a treaty of perpetual friendship with the king and queen. He then sailed for the coast of Guinea and Cape Verde, and continuing his course to his native land, he arrived there in triumph, with two ships laden with silver, gold, spices, and other riches. He delivered all to the Queen, without being richer by his robberies nor more esteemed by reason of his acts.

After this, in the time of Don Fernando de Torres, Conde de Villar and Viceroy of Peru, the Englishman, Tomas Candi,

entered by the same strait. He anchored in the port of Valparaiso (which is the principal port of the kingdom of Chile), and was attacked by a troop of Spaniards. They caught the English off their guard, and, killing fourteen, obliged Tomas to continue his voyage with much despite. He seized some vessels at anchor, on whose crews he avenged himself for the recent attack. The Viceroy was presently informed of his arrival, and he armed three good ships, which were sent in chase. Other precautions were taken for the pursuit of the pirates, and for giving notice by land and sea. The Audiencia of Quito sent soldiers to Guayaquil, where, finding the enemies on shore, six more were killed. This ship departed full of alarm at this second misfortune, and the ships of Lima, after a fruitless search, arrived at Panama. The Englishman sailed along the coast of Nicaragua, and went thence to the Cape of San Lucas of California, in a height of $22\frac{1}{2}$ deg. N. There he waited for the ship *Santa Ana*, that was coming from the Filipinas with a rich

81 An animated sixteenth-century engraving of a ship preparing for sea.

65

cargo. He found her (that sea being pacific) without a sword, and quite secure from such a mishap. Candi went on board, seized on everything, and landed all the crew except a priest whom he hanged. He then examined all the cargo, item by item. He found a large sum in gold, and, selecting the most valuable part of the cargo, he threw the rest into the sea. Lastly, he set fire to the ship, and sailed on towards the Filipinas, where he seized an Indian who showed him a passage by which he passed between the two islands of Taprobane and Java Major, a strait called Fundia [Sunda]. Finally, he arrived at London with his sails made of green damask, and all his sailors dressed in silk, to the general delight of that city.

Such were the results of the two first entries of these pirates whom (envious of their good luck) Ricardo Aquines, also an Englishman, desired to imitate. This man, with a famous ship called the Linda [the *Dainty*], entered by the strait, in the narrows of which he lost two other vessels which came with him, in the year 1594. He arrived at Valparaiso in need of provisions and other necessaries. Here he found five vessels off their guard, laden with provisions, cordage, and other stores. They surrendered without offering any resistance. He enjoyed himself for some days in this port, and at the end of them, wishing to depart, he came to an agreement with the people regarding the ransom of their vessels; without considering that he was setting those at liberty who could give notice of his arrival. Such was the opinion he had of his ship (as being so well armed and manned), and so cheap did he hold the maritime resources of all Peru. The Viceroy, Don Garcia, received news of this with all despatch, and although the tidings found him in bed, suffering from an attack of illness, he rose up at once, his first care being to send orders to collect the guards of lances and arquebuses at the port of Callao, to the end that it might be secure. He also gave commissions, as captains, to three soldiers who were experienced in martial affairs. Their names were Pulgar, Manrique, and Plaza. They had orders to raise a hundred soldiers each, and to man the ships which were being fitted out with all despatch. The Marquis, not altogether relying upon the diligence of the officers whom he had sent, went himself with a few attendants, on the following day, to see after everything, in spite of a fit of gout which he was suffering from at the time.

The Viceroy nominated Don Beltran de Castro y de la Cueva, as commander of the expedition, a son of the Count of Lemos, and his own brother-in-law. Don Beltran was an officer of distinguished talent and capacity equal to the greatest undertakings; as was proved by his former services. He was at Milan in the days when that province was governed, with so much ability,

by his uncle, Don Gabriel de la Cueva, Duke of Albuquerque. Knowing his talent, the Duke appointed him, when only twenty-two years of age, to the command of an army which was sent by order of His Majesty to take Final. The selection of Don Beltran, by the Viceroy, as General of the expedition, was approved by all, and he was not long before his deeds justified the appointment. He was scarcely appointed before he set out for the port, and devoted himself to the preparation of the fleet, without ever leaving the sea shore, morning or evening.

At last the three galleons were ready and well provided with soldiers, priests, arms, stores, and provisions, and they only waited for favourable weather to make sail. In the meanwhile the Marquis wished to honour the expedition with his presence. He, therefore, went to Callao and, getting into his boat, pulled towards the ships. On his approach the ships fired off all their pieces, and very high mountains of smoke ascended, while cheers resounded on all sides. The Viceroy visited them all, inciting the men and cheering them with his speeches. Finally, he returned to the shore, and, according to custom, the last gun was fired, and the ships sailed shortly afterwards, the three keeping company until they were out of sight.

Don Beltran had scarcely disappeared when the Viceroy received the news that Ricardo had appeared off Arica, with three ships. A fisherman brought this intelligence, from whom the pirate had taken a supply of fish, and then given him his liberty. It was supposed that the two other vessels might be the *Almiranta*, and another that was reported to have been lost in the straits. It, therefore, seemed good to the Viceroy to take some further precautions. He, therefore, prepared a *galizabra*,[1] built by his orders at Callao, together with another galleon and a brigantine. These were supplied with all necessaries, and their duty was to protect the thirty ships and packet boats that were in that port, so entirely without defence that one small vessel might almost have taken them all. The new vessels would also be in a position to reinforce the first fleet, and to fill up vacancies caused by any accidents. The coast was garrisoned, and all watched with such diligence that the pirate had scarcely been seen before the news had been announced to each port, being sent from one to the other by means of flaming beacons.

This constant vigilance was the reason why Aquines did not venture on shore, being fearful of destruction, as he saw the beaches crowded with cavalry, which was what caused most

[1] The Dictionary of the Spanish Academy describes a 'zabra' as a kind of small frigate used in the Bay of Biscay. The compound word, 'galizabra' is not given.

dismay to the enemy. Thus he had to continue his voyage without being able to do any harm, until he arrived off Chincha, which is a place at a distance of thirty leagues from Lima. Thence a runner set out to the Viceroy with the news, which was at once forwarded to his brother-in-law. During the twelve days that he had been at sea Don Beltran had not been able to obtain any news of Ricardo: so that, when the intelligence reached him, he altered his course with great joy, and steered towards the land. It was at dawn, one day, that he discovered the pirate under the land; but the enemy had got the first sight of our fleet, and strove to escape with all speed, by hauling his wind. Don Beltran wished to get the wind, but it was impossible, because a storm arose almost at the same time. Nevertheless he did his best to follow in spite of a heavy sea, until the gale increased and, losing sight of the chase, it was as much as he could do to save his own ships. This storm was considered to have been the greatest that had ever been encountered in those parts. It obliged the fleet, which was to follow Ricardo, to return to the port whence they had sailed, where they arrived in a very damaged condition. Nor did the tempest spare the fugitive, for those on board were obliged to throw part of the cargo overboard in order to save her.

At the first favourable wind the fleet sailed again, approaching the shore whenever there was a chance, to see whether Aquines was cruising under the land, or was at anchor in any bay or creek. A point had scarcely been doubled on a certain day, being the vespers of Santa Isabel, at about four in the afternoon,

when the enemy was discovered in the bay of San Mateo, which is on the coast of Esmeraldas.

Aquines saw the two ships and, supposing that they were not men-of-war, but suited for plunder, he prepared to capture them. He only had one ship and a launch, for considering that the two other ships, with which he appeared at Arica, would be a hindrance to his voyage, he had brought them no further. The pirate without leaving his position, sent his captain to reconnoitre the vessels that had come in sight. He did so, and approached within a little less than a cannon shot. Don Beltran, at the same time, had ordered his Admiral Lorenzo de Heredia to advance with the *Galizabra* to meet the enemy. He also gave instructions that, as his vessel was small, he should take up a position inshore, while, at the same time, Don Beltran selected a station to seaward of the enemy. The *Almiranta* fired off three pieces which, without doing any harm to the reconnoitering vessel, merely served to warn him that the strangers were enemies. The English captain returned, with sails and oars, to where Ricardo was waiting for him; and delivered a brief report of what had happened. Instantly weighing his anchors, and sounding a loud trumpet, Ricardo then came forth to do battle with the strangers. As he approached, the *Capitana* discharged the guns on the port side, and then going about fired two guns, from the poop, the shot from which hit the English ship. Presently the *Galizabra* came up, and discharging six guns at one time, the mizen was cut away and fell into the sea. The pirate sheered off, and again opening fire, two negroes and two sailors on board the *Capitana*, who were on the poop hauling aft the sheet, were cut in two near the bitts. This discharge was followed up so quickly by another that the ship of Don Beltran de Castro was hardly pressed. At this time the *Galizabra*, which had been chasing the launch, came up with the intention of running into the enemy, but the attempt turned out badly; for Ricardo defended his ship with renewed valour, shooting away the main mast of his assailant and killing fourteen men.

The ships then sheered off from each other somewhat and, the night coming on, those of the King followed Aquines, keeping a good look-out, and firing off their guns from time to time. At dusk they began the work of attending to the wounded, and of throwing the dead into the sea. The *Galizabra* rigged a jury main mast, and in the morning (being the day of the Visitation), she opened fire on the enemy, with all her guns and muskets. Presently Don Beltran came up, also firing off his pieces, but the enemy replied with so terrible a discharge that one ball shot away the figurehead and another entered the dead wood, passing out on the other side without doing any harm. Having exchanged these shots, the vessels came alongside each other and were so close that the gallant Hawkins himself seized the royal standard by means of a bowline knot which he threw over it. But the attempt failed, as Diego de Avila, Juan Manrique, Pedro de Reinalte, Juan Velazquez, and others came to the rescue, and defended it valorously. The Englishman paid for his audacity by two wounds, one in the neck and the other in the arm, both received from gun shots. At this moment the *Galizabra* attempted to run alongside, but the enemy hurled two harpoons into her sails, and four inboard, killing the *Condestable* and two sailors. The men in the *Galizabra* were not, however, dismayed; but, persevering in their attempt, they grappled the enemy and boarded her. The first to reach her deck were Juan Bantista Montañes and Juan de Torres Portugal, both valiant soldiers. The captain of the ship opposed the entry of Torres with a shield and sword, but, after some blows and wounds dealt on both sides, the Englishman fell on his back, giving place to the Spaniard to pass onwards. Meanwhile, Juan Bantista had killed two and driven others backwards until they were forced into the cabin under the poop, where they continued their resistance with signal courage. Finally they received quarter, the *Capitana* having also boarded, and sent her men into the enemy's ship.

from *Hechos de Don Garcia Hurtado de Mendoza*, Madrid 1614 (translated by Clements R. Markham).

North to China

After describing the two known routes to China—via the Cape of Good Hope and via the Straits of Magellan—William Bourne outlines three ways 'supposed'. The search for the North-west and North-east Passages was a constant magnet for explorers and geographers, who dreamed of circumventing the monopolies of the Spanish and Portuguese on the southern routes to China, and of finding a shorter sea route to the East (see p. 20). The ice conditions defeated all attempts until the age of steam. Amundsen's sailing ship *Gjöa* in which he navigated the North-west Passage in 1903 had an auxiliary engine. An interesting belief which lasted until well into the eighteenth century was the open polar sea, the reasons for which belief Bourne gives here.

A hydrographical discourse to show the passage unto Cathay five manner of ways, two of them known and the other three supposed

. . . And now furthermore, for to discourse the third way, that is not known, but supposed that it may be passageable, that is by the north-west, as now of late Captain Frobisher hath begun and hath discovered as far as a place now called *Meta Incognita*, which he himself did call *Frobisher's Straits*, but yet notwithstanding it is doubtful, whether that be a straits to give passage to come into the east ocean sea, or south sea, for anything that is known yet, it may be as well a bay as otherwise, but notwithstanding whether that be a strait or not, it is possible that there may be passage there about, between the northern part of America, as between Labrador and Greenland, and such lands as lie unto the North Polewards.

Wherefore now for to depart from England to go unto Cathay by the north-west, first this for to make their direction from the west of England, unto the place called *Meta Incognita*, the course is west norwest about 650 leagues, and the latitude thereof 63 degrees, and on the starboard is first Ireland and Iceland, and Freeseland, and on the larboard side, is the Ocean Sea. And now being at *Meta Incognita*, they must discover thereabouts, where that they may find sea for to give them passage, and yet if they do find sea, they must hold on their course west until that they have passed 1,000 or 1,100 leagues. For if that they should hold on any southerly course, then they should imbay themselves in the mainland of America, for the extension of the back side, or north side of America, is not much less than 1,000 leagues, before that they shall open the way into the East Ocean Sea, and in this west course on the starboard side is the North Pole, and such lands as lie that way if there be any, and on the larboard side, is the main of America.

And after that they have sailed west 1,000 leagues on the north part of America, they may then direct a more southerly course,

83 A Dutch ship from Zeeland at Anchor, oil painting by Abraham Willaerts (1613–69). The topsail yards are lowered on the cap (i.e. down to the truck of the lower mast). In this type of ship Dutch explorers sailed out to seek northern and southern routes to the East.

84 A school of navigation, depicted
in the frontispiece of a seventeenth-
century book of charts, showing
navigational aids of the period.

for that then they may be open of the East Ocean Sea, for that the most part of the best cosmographers lay the opening of that sea opposite unto us in our meridian, and then holding on a southerly course, then they may have unto the great bay of Quinsay about 400 or 500 leagues. And the latitude of the north part of the Bay of Quinsay in Cathay is about 46 degrees, and on the starboard side is the coast of Asia, as Mangie and Cathay, and on the larboard side America.

And now in like manner as touching the fourth way to go unto Cathay, not known but supposed, and that is by the north-east part or north part of Russia, about by that way that Master Barents began the discovery, about by a land that is called Nova Zembla, which is a country or point of a land that extendeth to the northwards, it is not known how far, and yet it may be possible that it is navigable that way if it were attempted.

And now for to pass that way unto Cathay, I will a little use my discourse. The way and distance unto the North Cape in Norway is not unknown unto a number of seamen, the latitude thereof is 71 deg. 20 min., therefore I do think it best to begin the direction and setting out the course east until that they do come with the land of Nova Zembla, and then falling with that place to make their discovery as the land will give them leave, and so in this direction it may be possible that they may find a sea to give them passage as it may be possible, that when they may meet with land, that they shall be constrained to go north-east or north noreast, until that the North Pole be raised 80 or 85 degrees, yet they may hold on their course until such time that they shall be encumbered with ice, for it may be so, that in the latitude of 80 degrees, there shall be no ice, for no man can tell until such time as it hath been put in experience, and now in this passage unto the eastwards from the North Cape until that they shall have the sea open to come into the southwards in the sea of Cathay, it may be about 1,000 or 1,200 leagues, and then in this passage on the starboard side is first Norway and Lapia, and the Bay of Saint Nicholas, and the great river of Ob and Nova Zembla, and the east part of Asia, and on the larboard side the North Pole, and those lands that lie that way if there be any, and now in the following of the coast of the land which may be south-east or south south-east or south, it may be 500 or 600 leagues unto the Bay of Quinsay in Cathay, and on the starboard side is Asia and the coast of Mangie and Cathay, and on the larboard side the mainland of America, &c.

And furthermore, it' may be possible for to find passage for to go to Cathay, between Nova Zembla, and the country of Samwetes, through the sea of Vagates, and this passage may be somewhat shorter, than for to go unto the norwards of Nova Zembla, and then you shall have in this passage upon the starboard side, first the country of Samwetes, as Pichora, and the river of Ob and Tartaria, &c. And on the larboard side, Nova Zembla, &c.

And furthermore as touching the fifth way to go unto Cathay, it is possible that in my discourse it is mere foolishness and a thing unpossible for it to be done, and yet notwithstanding no man can tell, before that it is put in experience, and yet it is the nearest way if that it be navigable, and my meaning is this, for to go directly unto the Pole, if so be that there is no land to let the passage. Now it is possible that some will say that it is the frozen zone, but notwithstanding if that there is not land that way,

69

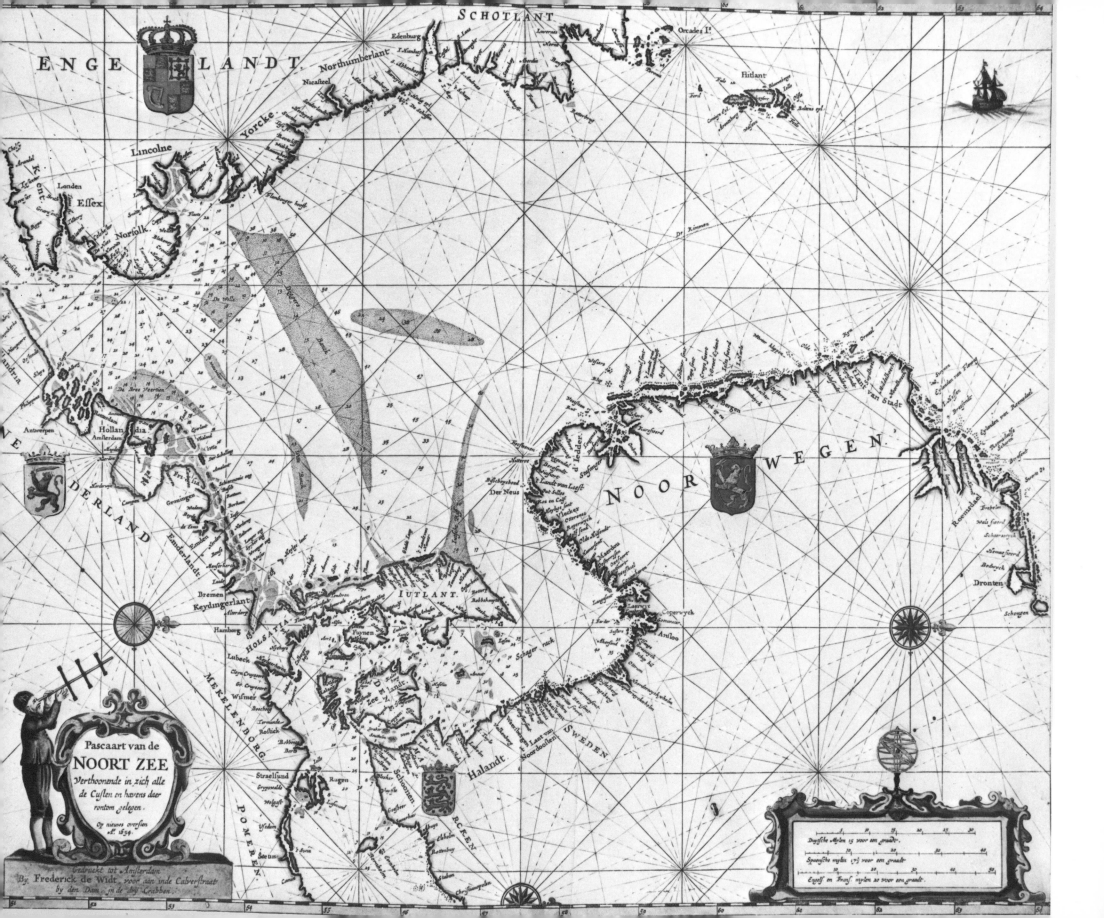

85 *opposite* A Dutch chart of the North Sea with a picture of a man using a cross-staff in the corner, 1654. North is not at the top but to the right in this map.

86 *below* Longitude 1: this print shows the early belief that longitude could be found by magnetic variation.

87 *right* Longitude 2: chronometer by Ferdinand Berthoud, 1788. In England John Harrison designed after several failures the first reliable marine chronometer and received in 1772 at the age of 80 the £20,000 reward offered by the Admiralty Board of Longitude. In France Berthoud made his first chronometer in 1763. This one is dated 1788 and is considered, rather than Harrison's instrument, the technical ancestor of our modern chronometers. Instead of being driven by a spring this clock is moved by a weight which descends in the brass cylinder and is hoisted again by winding the clockwork.

88 *bottom right* A drawing illustrating the use of the back-staff or Davis quadrant.

then it is not frozen, for the great salt sea never freezeth, and for that you do see the great quantity of ice on the coast of Labrador and Baculayas, it is a token that thereabouts is much land towards the North Polewards, and so is frozen in sounds and rivers, and so in the breaking up of the year, that then it doth come driving out to sea: for in respect they do seldom see any ice at the North Cape, nor 100 leagues north off from thence, which is a great token that there is no land towards the Polewards, and before that it hath been put in proof it cannot be known. But all the doubts for going unto the Polewards, is for fear of too much cold, and yet notwithstanding it may be reasonable warm right under the Pole for anything that is known unto the contrary, by the long continuance of the sun in summer, for that in the time of 9 weeks, that the sun is never less than 20 degrees above the horizon going round about them, so that the continuance of the sun must enforce the air to be reasonable warm, and especially if that there is no ice driving in the sea, for it is not so cold at *Meta Incognita,* if that they be not amongst the ice, for if that they be at sea and not amongst ice, then it is very warm, and also if that they be ashore, then it is warm in like manner, so that the cold is by no other means but the cold breath of air that cometh from the ice. And now for to proceed to go unto Cathay, and to go directly north till that they be right under the Pole, and then to go south to the opposite part beyond the Pole, which is to be done if that they be not let by any land that lieth in the way, then it may be possible for it to be done, and then the whole distance in this course from the river of Thames unto the Bay of Quinsay, is but 1680 leagues, which is a very short way in respect of the other.

from *A Regiment for the Sea,* by William Bourne, 1580 edition.

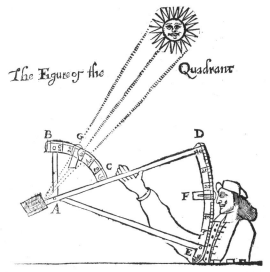

Barents' last voyage

The Dutchman, Willem Barents, made three voyages in search of the North-east Passage and was the discoverer of Spitzbergen and Bear Island, and explorer of the Barents Sea. His house on Novaya Zemlya was rediscovered in 1871, the clock and other relics being presented to the Dutch government. More even than the modern astronaut, the early explorer journeyed into a world of unknown wonders and terrors, for unlike the astronaut, he was completely isolated from his home base. Gerrit de Veer's journal, from which these extracts are taken, is an unconscious revelation, as the piece by Joseph Conrad on page 225 is a conscious one, of the direct, personal confrontation with the universe which was at the heart of the sailing ship experience.

89 'We saw a strange sight in the element'.

Plate 11 Dutch ships in a Gale with a Whale, oil painting by Adam Willaerts (1577–1664). A scene of melodrama typical of this artist's imagination, painted with obvious enjoyment.

The third voyage northward to the kingdoms of Cathaia and China, in Anno 1596

. . . in the beginning of this year, there was two ships rigged and set forth by the town of Amsterdam, to sail that voyage. In the one, Jacob Heemskerke Hendrickson was master and factor for the wares and merchandise, and William Barents chief pilot. In the other, John Cornelison Rijp was both master and factor for the goods that the merchants had laden in her . . .

June 1 we had no night, and June 2 we had the wind contrary; but upon June 4 we had a good wind out of the west north-west, and sailed north-east.

And when the sun was about south south-east [9.30 A.M.], we saw a strange sight in the element: for on each side of the sun there was another sun, and two rainbows that passed clean through the three suns, and then two rainbows more, the one compassing round about the suns, and the other cross through the great circle; the great circle standing with the uttermost point elevated above the horizon 28 degrees.

June 5 we saw the first ice, which we wondered at, at the first thinking that it had been white swans, for one of our men walking in the foredeck, on a sudden began to cry out with a loud voice, and said that he saw white swans: which we that were under hatches hearing, presently came up, and perceived that it was ice that came driving from the great heap, showing like swans, it being then about evening: at midnight we sailed through it, and the sun was about a degree elevated above the horizon in the north.

June 7 we took the height of the sun, and found the Pole to be 74 degrees: there we found so great a store of ice, that it was admirable: and we sailed along through it, as if we had passed between two lands, the water being as green as grass; and we supposed that we were not far from Greenland, and the longer we sailed the more and thicker ice we found . . .

July 1 . . . John Cornelison and his officers came aboard of our ship, to speak with us about altering of our course; but we being of a contrary opinion, it was agreed that we should follow on our course and he his: which was, that he (according to his desire) should sail unto 80 degrees again; for he was of opinion that there he should find a passage through, on the east side of the land that lay under 80 degrees.[1] And upon that agreement we left each other, they sailing northward, and we southward because of the ice, the wind being east south-east.

July 17 we took the height of the sun, and it was elevated above the horizon 37 deg. 55 min.; and when the sun was in the south [11 A.M.], we saw the land of Nova Zembla. I was the first that espied it. Then we altered our course, and sailed north-east and by north, and hoisted up all our sails except the fore-sail and the bezaan.

July 19 we came to the Cross Island[2], and could then get no further by reason of the ice, for there the ice lay still close upon

[1] In June they had discovered Bear Island and Spitzbergen.

[2] An island Barents had visited on an earlier voyage.

the land, at which time the wind was west and blew right upon the land, and it lay under 76 deg 20 min. There stood 2 crosses upon the land, whereof it had the name.

August 5 we set sail again towards Ice Point[1] with an east wind, and sailed south south-east, and then north north-east.

August 10, being Saturday, the ice began mightily to break, and then we first perceived that the great piece of ice whereunto we had made our ship fast, lay on the ground; for the rest of the ice drove along by it, wherewith we were in great fear that we should be compassed about with the ice, and therefore we used all the diligence and means that we could to get from thence, for we were in great doubt: and got to another piece of ice, whereunto we made our ship fast again with our sheet anchor, which we made fast upon it, and there we lay till evening. And when we had supped, in the first quarter the said piece of ice began on a sudden to burst and rend in pieces, so fearfully that it was admirable; for with one great crack it burst into four hundred pieces at the least: we lying fast to it, weighed our cable and got off from it. Under the water it was ten fathom deep and lay upon the ground, and two fathom above the water: and it made a fearful noise both under and above the water when it burst, and spread itself abroad on all sides.

And being with great fear gotten from that piece of ice, we came to another piece, that was six fathom deep under the water, to the which we made a rope fast on both sides.

August 16 ten of our men entering into one boat, rowed to the firm land at Nova Zembla, and drew the boat up upon the ice; which done, we went up a high hill to see the situation of the land, and found that it reached south-east and south south-east, and then again south, which we disliked, for that it lay so much southward: but when we saw open water south-east and east south-east, we were much comforted again, thinking that we had won our voyage, and knew not how we should get soon enough on board to certify William Barents thereof.

August 19 it was indifferent good weather, the wind blowing south-west, the ice still driving, and we set sail with an indifferent gale of wind, and passed by the Point of Desire, whereby we were once again in good hope. And when we had gotten above the point, we sailed south-east into the seaward 16 miles, but then again we entered into more ice, whereby we were constrained to turn back again, and sailed north-west until we came to the land again.

August 21 we sailed a great way into the Ice Haven, and that night anchored therein: next day, the stream going extreme hard

eastward, we hailed out again from thence, and sailed again to the Island Point; but for that it was misty weather, coming to a piece of ice, we made the ship fast thereunto, because the wind began to blow hard south-west and south south-west. There we went up upon the ice, and wondered much thereat, it was such manner of ice: for on the top it was full of earth, and there we found above 40 eggs, and it was not like other ice, for it was of a perfect azure colour, like to the skies, whereby there grew great contention in words amongst our men, some saying that it was ice, others that it was frozen land; for it lay unreasonable high above the water, it was at least 18 fathom under the water close to the ground, and 10 fathom above the water: there we stayed all that storm, the wind being south-west and by west.

August 23 we sailed again from the ice south-eastward into the sea, but entered presently into it again, and wound about to the Ice Haven. The next day it blew hard north north-west, and the ice came mightily driving in, whereby we were in a manner compassed about therewith, and withal the wind began more and more to rise, and the ice still drove harder and harder, so that the pin of the rudder and the rudder were shorn in pieces, and our boat was shorn in pieces between the ship and the ice, we expecting nothing else but that the ship also would be pressed and crushed in pieces with the ice.

August 25 the weather began to be better, and we took great pains and bestowed much labour to get the ice, wherewith we were so enclosed, to go from us, but what means soever we used it was all in vain. But when the sun was south-west [2.30 P.M.] the ice began to drive out again with the stream, and we thought to sail southward about Nova Zembla, and so westwards to the Straits of Vaygatz. For that seeing we could there find no passage, we having passed Nova Zembla, we were of opinion that our labour was all in vain and that we could not get through, and so agreed to go that way home again; but coming to the Stream Bay, we were forced to go back again, because of the ice which lay so fast thereabouts; and the same night also it froze, that we could hardly get through there with the little wind that we had, the wind then being north.

August 26 there blew a reasonable gale of wind, at which time we determined to sail back to the Point of Desire, and so home again, seeing that we could not get through by the way towards the Vaygatz, although we used all the means and industry we could to get forward; but when we had passed by the Ice Haven the ice began to drive with such force, that we were enclosed round about therewith, and yet we sought all the means we could to get out, but it was all in vain.

The same day in the evening we got to the west side of the

Plate 12 A Dutch attack on a Spanish fort, oil painting by Adam Willaerts (1577–1664). Two Spanish galleys and a galleon are going out to defend a fort against the attacking Dutch ships.

[1] The northernmost point of Novaya Zemlya.

Ice Haven, where we were forced, in great cold, poverty, misery, and grief, to stay all that winter; the wind then being east north-east.

August 27 the ice drove round about the ship, and yet it was good weather; at which time we went on land, and being there it began to blow south-east with a reasonable gale, and then the ice came with great force before the bow, and drove the ship up four foot high before, and behind it seemed as if the keel lay on the ground, so that it seemed that the ship would be overthrown in the place.

August 28 we got some of the ice from it, and the ship began to sit upright again; but before it was fully upright, as William Barents and the other pilot went forward to the bow, to see how the ship lay and how much it was risen, and while they were busy upon their knees and elbows to measure how much it was, the ship burst out of the ice with such a noise and so great a crack, that they thought verily that they were all cast away, knowing not how to save themselves.

September 1, being Sunday, while we were at prayer, the ice began to gather together again, so that the ship was lifted up two foot at the least, but the ice brake not. The same evening the ice continued in that sort still driving and gathering together, so that we made preparation to draw our scute and the boat over the ice upon the land, the wind then blowing south-east.

September 11 it was calm weather, and 8 of us went on land, every man armed, to see if that were true as our other three companions had said, that there lay wood about the river; for that seeing we had so long wound and turned about sometime in the ice, and then again got out, and thereby were compelled to alter our course, and at last saw that we could not get out of the ice but rather became faster, as also that it began to be winter, we took counsel together what we were best to do according to the time, that we might winter there and attend such adventure as God would send us: and after we had debated upon the matter, to keep and defend ourselves both from the cold and the wild beasts, we determined to build a house upon the land, to keep us therein as well as we could, and so to commit ourselves unto the tuition of God. And to that end we went further into the land, to find out the convenient place in our opinions to raise our house upon, and yet we had not much stuff to make it withal, in regard that there grew no trees, nor any other thing in that country convenient to build it withal. But we leaving no occasion unsought, as our men went abroad to view the country, and to see what good fortune might happen unto us, at last we found an unexpected comfort in our need, which was that we found certain trees roots and all (as our three companions had said before), which had been driven upon the shore, either from Tartaria, Muscovia, or elsewhere, for there was none growing upon that land; wherewith (as if God had purposely sent them unto us) we were much comforted, being in good hope that God would show us some further favour; for that wood served us not only to build our house, but also to burn and serve us all the winter long; otherwise without all doubt we had died there miserably with extreme cold.

September 13 it was calm but very misty weather, so that we could do nothing, because it was dangerous for us to go into the land, in regard that we could not see the wild bears; and yet they could smell us, for they smell better than they see.

September 19 it was calm sunshine weather, and we drew two sleds full of wood six thousand paces, and that we did twice a day.

September 23 we fetched more wood to build our house, which we did twice a day, but it grew to be misty and still weather again, the wind blowing east and east north-east. That day our carpenter died as we came aboard about evening.

September 24 we buried him in the cleft of a hill, hard by the water, for we could not dig up the earth by reason of the great frost and cold; and that day we went twice with our sleds to fetch wood.

September 26 we had a west wind and an open sea, but our ship lay fast, wherewith we were not a little grieved; but it was

90 'We fetched more wood to build our house, which we did twice a day . . .'

76

God's will, which we most patiently bore, and we began to make up our house: part of our men fetched wood to burn, the rest played the carpenters and were busy about the house. As then we were sixteen men in all, for our carpenter was dead, and of our sixteen men there was still one or other sick.

September 27 it blew hard north-east, and it froze so hard that as we put a nail into our mouths (as when men work carpenter's work they use to do), there would ice hang thereon when we took it out again, and made the blood follow. The same day there came an old bear and a young one towards us as we were going to our house, being all together (for we durst not go alone), which we thought to shoot at, but she ran away. At which time the ice came forcibly driving in, and it was fair sunshine weather, but so extreme cold that we could hardly work, but extremity forced us thereunto.

October 5 it blew hard north-west, and the sea was very open and without ice as far as we could discern; but we lay still frozen as we did before, and our ship lay two or three foot deep in the ice. The same day we broke up the lower deck of the fore-part of our ship, and with those deals we covered our house, and made it slope overhead that the water might run off; at which time it was very cold.

October 12 it blew north and at times somewhat westerly, and then half of our men went and slept in the house, and that was the first time that we lay in it; but we endured great cold because our cabins were not made, and besides that we had not clothes enough, and we could keep no fire because our chimney was not made, whereby it smoked exceedingly.

October 13 the wind was north and north-west, and it began again to blow hard, and then three of us went aboard the ship and loaded a sled with beer; but when we had laden it, thinking to go to our house with it, suddenly there rose such a wind and so great a storm and cold, that we were forced to go into the ship again, because we were not able to stay without; and we could not get the beer into the ship again, but were forced to let it stand without upon the sled. Being in the ship, we endured extreme cold because we had but a few clothes in it.

October 14, as we came out of the ship, we found the barrel of beer standing upon the sled, but it was fast frozen at the heads, yet by reason of the great cold the beer that purged out froze as hard upon the side of the barrel as if it had been glued thereon, and in that sort we drew it to our house and set the barrel on end, and drank it first up; but we were forced to melt the beer, for there was scant any unfrozen beer in the barrel, but in that thick yeast that was unfrozen lay the strength of the beer, so that it was too strong to drink alone, and that which was frozen tasted like

water; and being melted we mixed one with the other, and so drank it, but it had neither strength nor taste.

October 19 the wind blew north-east, and then there was but two men and a boy in the ship, at which time there came a bear that sought forcibly to get into the ship, although the two men shot at her with pieces of wood, and yet she ventured upon them, whereby they were in an extreme fear; and each of them seeking to save themselves, the two men leaped into the balast, and the boy climbed into the fore-mast top to save their lives; meantime some of our men shot at her with a musket, and then she ran away.

October 20 it was calm sunshine weather, and then again we saw the sea open, at which time we went on board to fetch the rest of our beer out of the ship, where we found some of the barrels frozen in pieces, and the iron hoops that were upon the barrels were also frozen in pieces.

October 24 the rest of our men, being 8 persons, came to the house, and drew the sick man upon a sled, and then with great labour and pain we drew our boat home to our house, and turned the bottom thereof upwards, that when time served us (if God saved our lives in the winter time) we might use it.

Things standing at this point with us, as the sun (when we might see it best and highest) began to be very low, we used all the speed we could to fetch all things with sleds out of our ship into our house, not only meat and drink but all other necessaries; at which time the wind was north.

October 26 we fetched all things that were necessary for the furnishing of our scute and our boat: and when we had laden the last sled, and stood ready to draw it to the house, our master looked about him and saw three bears behind the ship that were coming towards us, whereupon he cried out aloud to fear them away, and we presently leaped forth to defend ourselves as well as we could. And as good fortune was, there lay two halberds upon the sled, whereof the master took one and I the other, and made resistance against them as well as we could; but the rest of our men ran to save themselves in the ship, and as they ran one of them fell into a cleft of ice, which grieved us much, for we thought verily that the bears would have ran unto him to devour him; but God defended him, for the bears still made towards the ship after the men that ran thither to save themselves. Meantime we and the man that fell into the cleft of ice took our advantage, and got into the ship on the other side; which the bears perceiving, they came fiercely towards us, that had no other arms to defend us withal but only the two halberds, which we doubting would not be sufficient, we still gave them work to do by throwing billets of fire-wood and other things at them, and every time we threw they ran after them, as a dog useth to do at a stone that is cast at him. Meantime we sent a man down under hatches to strike fire, and another to fetch pikes; but we could get no fire, and so we had no means to shoot.[1] At the last, as the bears came fiercely upon us, we struck one of them with a halberd upon the snout, wherewith she gave back when she felt herself hurt, and went away, which the other two that were not so great as she perceiving, ran away; and we thanked God that we were so well delivered from them, and so drew our sled quietly to our house, and there showed our men what had happened unto us.

November 2 . . . we saw the sun rise south south-east, and it went down about south-west, but it was not full above the earth, but passed in the horizon along by the earth. And the same day one of our men killed a fox with a hatchet, which was flayed, roasted, and eaten.

November 3 the wind blew north-west with calm weather, and the sun rose south and by east and somewhat more southerly, and went down south and by west and somewhat more southerly; and then we could see nothing but the upper part of the sun above the horizon, and yet the land where we were was as high as the mast of our ship.

November 4 it was calm weather, but then we saw the sun no more, for it was no longer above the horizon. Then our surgeon prescribed and made a bath, to bathe us in, of a wine pipe, wherein we entered one after the other, and it did us much good and was a great means of our health. The same day we took a white fox, that often times came abroad, not as they used at other times; for that when the bears left us at the setting of the sun, and came not again before it rose, the foxes to the contrary came abroad when they were gone.

November 7 it was dark weather and very still, the wind west; at which time we could hardly discern the day from the night, specially because at that time our clock stood still, and by that means we knew not when it was day although it was day: and our men rose not out of their cabins all that day but only to make water, and therefore they knew not whether the light they saw was the light of the day or of the moon, whereupon they were of several opinions, some saying it was the light of the day, the others of the night; but as we took good regard thereunto, we found it to be the light of the day, about twelve of the clock at noon.

November 8 it was still weather, the wind blowing south and south-west. The same day we shared our bread amongst us, each man having four pound and ten ounces for his allowance in eight days; so that then we were eight days eating a barrel of bread, whereas before we ate it up in five or six days. As yet we had

91 'The bears still made towards the ship . . .'

92 'We presently leaped forth to defend ourselves as well as we could . . .'

[1] Their firearms had matchlocks.

no need to share our flesh and fish, for we had more store thereof; but our drink failed us, and therefore we were forced to share that also: but our best beer was for the most part wholly without any strength, so that it had no savour at all, and besides all this there was a great deal of it spilt.

November 9 the wind blew north-east and somewhat more northerly, and then we had not much daylight, but it was altogether dark.

November 12 the wind blew east, with a little light. That day we began to share our wine, every man had two glasses a day, but commonly our drink was water which we melted out of snow which we gathered without the house.

November 13 it was foul weather, with great snow, the wind east.

November 19 it was foul weather, with an east wind; and then the chest with linen was opened and divided amongst the men for shift, for they had need of them, for then our only care was to find all the means we could to defend our body from the cold.

November 20 it was fair still weather, the wind easterly. Then we washed our sheets, but it was so cold that when we had washed and wrung them, they presently froze so stiff out of the warm water, that although we laid them by a great fire, the side that lay next the fire thawed, but the other side was hard frozen; so that we should sooner have torn them in sunder than have opened them, whereby we were forced to put them into the seething water again to thaw them, it was so exceeding cold.

November 25 it was fair clear weather, the wind west; and that day we took two foxes with a springe that we had purposely set up.

December 1 it was foul weather, with a south-west wind and great store of snow, whereby we were once again stopped up in the house, and by that means there was so great a smoke in the house that we could hardly make fire, and so were forced to lie all day in our cabins, but the cook was forced to make fire to dress our meat.

December 3 we had the like weather, at which times as we lay in our cabins we might hear the ice crack in the sea, and yet it was at the least two miles from us, which made a huge noise, and we were of opinion that as then the great hills of ice which we had seen in the sea in summer time broke one from the other. And for that during those two or three days, because of the extreme smoke, we made not so much fire as we commonly used to do, it froze so sore within the house that the walls and the roof thereof were frozen two fingers thick with ice, and also in our cabins where we lay. All those three days, while we could not go out by reason of the foul weather, we set up the sand-glass of 12 hours, and when it was run out we set it up again, still watching it lest we should miss our time. For the cold was so great that our clock was frozen, and might not go although we hung more weight on it than before.

December 16 it was fair clear weather, the wind north-east.

93 'That day we took two foxes in a springe that we had purposely set up . . .'

94 'In our house . . .'

At that time we had no more wood in the house, but had burnt it all; but round about our house there lay some covered over with snow, which with great pain and labour we were forced to dig out and so shovel away the snow, and so brought it into the house, which we did by turns, two and two together, wherein we were forced to use great speed, for we could not long endure without the house, because of the extreme cold, although we wore the foxes' skins about our heads and double apparel upon our backs.

December 19 it was fair weather, the wind being south. Then we put each other in good comfort that the sun was then almost half over and ready to come to us again, which we sore longed for, it being a weary time for us to be without the sun, and to want the greatest comfort that God sendeth unto man here upon the earth, and that which rejoiceth every living thing.

January 5 it was somewhat still and calm weather. Then we digged our door open again, that we might go out and carry out all the filth that had been made during the time of our being shut in the house, and made everything handsome, and fetched in wood, which we cleft; and it was all our day's work to further ourselves as much as we could, fearing lest we should be shut up again. And as there were three doors in our portal, and for that our house lay covered over in snow, we took the middle door thereof away, and digged a great hole in the snow that lay without the house, like to a side of a vault, wherein we might go to ease ourselves and cast other filth into it. And when we had taken pains all day, we remembered ourselves that it was Twelfth Even, and then we prayed our master that in the midst of all our troubles we might be merry that night, and said that we were content to spend some of the wine that night which we had spared and which was our share every second day, and whereof for certain days we had not drunk; and so that night we made merry and drunk to the three kings. And therewith we had two pound of meal which we had taken to make paste for the cartridges, whereof we now made pancakes with oil, and we laid to every man a white biscuit which we sopped in the wine. And so supposing that we were in our own country and amongst our friends, it comforted us as well as if we had made a great banquet in our own house. And we also made tickets, and our gunner was king of Nova Zembla, which is at least eight hundred miles long and lies between two seas.

January 10 it was fair weather, with a north wind. Then seven of us went to our ship, well armed, which we found in the same state we left it in, and in it we saw many footsteps of bears, both great and small, whereby it seemed that there had been more than one or two bears therein. And as we went under hatches, we struck fire and lighted a candle, and found that the water was risen a foot higher in the ship.

January 19 it was fair weather, with a north wind. And then our bread began to diminish, for that some of our barrels were not full weight, and so the division was less, and we were forced to make our allowance bigger with that which we had spared before. And then some of us went aboard the ship, wherein there was half a barrel of bread, which we thought to spare till the last, and there quite secretly each of them took a biscuit or two out of it.

January 21 it was fair clear weather, with a west wind. At that time taking of foxes began to fail us, which was a sign that the bears would soon come again, as not long after we found it to be true; for as long as the bears stayed away the foxes came abroad, and not much before the bears came abroad the foxes were but little seen.

January 24 it was fair clear weather, with a west wind. Then I and Jacob Heemskerke, and another with us, went to the seaside on the south side of Nova Zembla, where, contrary to our expectation, I the first of all saw the edge of the sun; wherewith we went speedily home again, to tell William Barents and the rest of our companions that joyful news. But William Barents, being a wise and well experienced pilot, would not believe it, esteeming it to be about fourteen days too soon for the sun to shine in that part of the world; but we earnestly affirmed the contrary and said we had seen the sun whereupon divers wagers were laid.

January 25 and 26 it was misty and close weather, so that we could not see anything. Then they that laid the contrary wager with us, thought that they had won; but upon the twenty-seventh day it was clear and bright weather, and then we all saw the sun in his full roundness above the horizon, whereby it manifestly appeared that we had seen it upon the twenty-four day of January. And as we were of divers opinions touching the same, and that we said it was clean contrary to the opinions of all old and new writers, yea and contrary to the nature and roundness both of heaven and earth; some of us said, that seeing in long time there had been no day, that it might be that we had overslept ourselves, whereof we were better assured: but concerning the thing in itself, seeing God is wonderful in all his works, we will refer that to his almighty power, and leave it unto others to dispute of.

April 9 it was fair clear weather, but towards evening it was foul weather, the wind south-west, so that still the water became opener, whereat we much rejoiced, and gave God thanks that he had saved us from the aforesaid cold, troublesome, hard, bitter, and unsupportable winter, hoping that time would give us a happy issue.

April 14 it was fair clear weather with a west wind; then we saw greater hills of ice round about the ship then ever we had seen before, which was a fearful thing to behold, and much to be wondered at that the ship was not smitten in pieces.

April 15 it was fair calm weather with a north wind; then seven of us went aboard the ship, to see in what case it was, and found it to be all in one sort; and as we came back again there came a great bear towards us, against whom we began to make defence, but she perceiving that, made away from us, and we went to the place from whence she came to see her den, where we found a great hole made in the ice, about a man's length in depth, the entry thereof being very narrow, and within wide; then we thrust in our pikes to feel if there was anything within it, but perceiving it was empty, one of our men crept into it, but not too far, for it was fearful to behold. After that we went along by the seaside, and there we saw that in the end of March and the beginning of April the ice was in such wonderful manner risen and piled up one upon the other that it was wonderful, in such manner as if there had been whole towns made of ice, with towers and bulwarks round about them.

May 9 it was fair clear weather with an indifferent wind out of the north-east; at which time the desire that our men had to be gone from thence still more and more increased, and then they agreed to speak to William Barents to move the master to go from thence, but he held them off with fair words; and yet it was not done to delay them, but to take the best counsel with reason and good advice, for he heard all what they could say.

May 15 it was fair weather with a west wind, and it was agreed that all our men should go out to exercise their bodies with running, and other exercises, thereby to stir their joints and make them nimble. Meantime William Barents spake unto the master and showed him what the company had said, who made him answer that they should stay no longer than to the end of that month, and that if then the ship could not be loosed, that preparation should be made to go away with the scute and the boat.

May 27 it was foul weather with a great north-east wind, which drove the ice mightily in again, whereupon the master, at the motion of the company, willed us to make preparation to be gone.

May 29 in the morning it was reasonable fair weather with a west wind; then ten of us went unto the scute to bring it to the house to dress it and make it ready to sail, but we found it deep hidden under the snow, and were fain with great pain and labour to dig out, but when we had gotten it out of the snow, and thought to draw it to the house, we could not do it, because we were too weak, wherewith we became wholly out of heart, doubting that we should not be able to go forward with our

95 '. . . and shot three pieces at her, two from our doors and one out of the chimney . . .'

96 'But her death did us more hurt than her life, for after we ripped her belly we dressed her liver and ate it . . .'

labour; but the master encouraging us bade us strive to do more than we were able, saying that both our lives and our welfare consisted therein, and that if we could not get the scute from thence and make it ready, then he said we must dwell there as burghers of Nova Zembla, and make our graves in that place. But there wanted no good will in us, but only strength, which made us for that time to leave off work and let the scute lie still, which was no small grief unto us and trouble to think what were best for us to do. But after noon, being thus comfortless come home, we took hearts again, and determined to turn the boat that lay by the house with her keel upwards, and we began to amend it and to heighten the gunwales, so that it might be the fitter to carry us over the sea, for we made full account that we had a long troublesome voyage in hand, wherein we might have many crosses, and wherein we should not be sufficiently provided for all things necessary, although we took never so much care; and while we were busy about our work, there came a great bear unto us, wherewith we went into our house and stood to watch her in our three doors with arquebuses, and one stood in the chimney with a musket. This bear came boldlier unto us than ever any had done before, for she came to the nether step that went to one of our doors, and the man that stood in the door saw her not because he looked towards the other door, but they that stood within saw her and in great fear called to him, wherewith he turned about, and although he was in a maze he shot at her, and the bullet passed clean through her body, whereupon she ran away. Yet it was a fearful thing to see, for the bear was almost upon him before he saw her, so that if the piece had failed to give fire (as oftentimes they do) it had cost him his life, and it may be that the bear would have gotten into the house.

May 31 it was fair weather, but somewhat colder than before, the wind being south-west, whereby the ice drove away, and we wrought hard about our boat; but when we were in the chiefest part of work, there came another bear, as if they had smelt that we would be gone, and that therefore they desired to taste a piece of some of us, for that was the third day, one after the other, that they set so fiercely upon us; so that we were forced to leave our work and go into the house, and she followed us, but we stood with our pieces to watch her, and shot three pieces at her, two from our doors and one out of the chimney, which all three hit her, whereby she fared as the dog did with the pudding; but her death did us more hurt than her life, for after we ripped her belly we dressed her liver and ate it, which in the taste liked us well, but it made us all sick, specially three that were exceeding sick, and we verily thought that we should have lost them, for all their skins came off from the foot to the head, but yet they recovered

again, for the which we gave God hearty thanks, for if as then we had lost these three men, it was a hundred to one that we should never have gotten from thence, because we should have had too few men to draw and lift at our need.

June 13 it was fair weather; then the master and the carpenters went to the ship, and there made the scute and the boat ready, so that there rested nothing as then but only to bring it down to the waterside. The master and those that were with him, seeing that it was open water and a good west wind, came back to the house again, and there he spake unto William Barents (that had been long sick), and showed him that he thought it good (seeing it was a fit time) to go from thence, and so willed the company to drive the boat and the scute down to the waterside, and in the name of God to begin our voyage to sail from Nova Zembla . . . And so, having finished all things as we determined, we drew the boat to the waterside and left a man in it, and went and fetched the scute, and after that eleven sleds with goods, as victuals and some wine that yet remained, and the merchants' goods which we preserved as well as we could, viz., 6 packs with the finest woollen cloth, a chest with linen, two packets with velvet, two small chests with money, two trunks with the men's clothes, and other things, 13 barrels of bread, a barrel of cheese, a flitch of bacon, two runlets of oil, 6 small runlets of wine, two runlets of vinegar, with other packs belonging to the sailors and many other things; so that when they lay altogether upon a heap, a man would have judged that they would not have gone into the scutes. Which being all put into them, we went to the house, and first drew William Barents upon a sled to the place where our scutes lay, and after that we fetched Claes Adrianson, both of them having been long sick. And so we entered into the scutes and divided ourselves into each of them alike, and put into either of them a sick man.

June 14 in the morning, the sun easterly [4.30 A.M.], we by God's mercy put off from the land of Nova Zembla and the fast ice there unto adjoining, with our boat and our scute, having a west wind, and sailed east north-east all that day to the Island Point, which was twenty miles; but our first beginning was not very good, for we entered fast into the ice again, which there lay very hard and fast, which put us into no small fear and trouble; being there, four of us went on land, to know the situation thereof, and there we took many birds, which we killed with stones upon the cliffs . . . We put to the sea again with a south-east wind and drowsy mizzling weather, whereby we were all dankish and wet, for we had no shelter in our open scutes, and sailed west and west and by south to opposite the Ice Point. And being there, both our scutes lying hard by each other, the master called to William Barents to know how he did, and William Barents made answer

and said, 'Well, God be thanked, and I hope before we get to Warehouse to be able to go.' Then he spake to me and said, 'Gerrit, are we about the Ice Point? If we be, then I pray you lift me up, for I must view it once again'; at which time we made our scutes fast to a great piece of ice and there ate somwhat; but the weather was still fouler and fouler, so that we were once again enclosed with ice and forced to stay there.

June 17 in the morning, when we had broken our fasts, the ice came so fast upon us that it made our hairs stand upright upon our heads, it was so fearful to behold; by which means we could not make fast our scutes, so that we thought verily that it was a foreshowing of our last end; for we drove away so hard with the ice, and were so sore pressed between a flake of ice, that we thought verily the scutes would burst in a hundred pieces, which made us look pitifully one upon the other, for no counsel nor advise was to be found, but every minute of an hour we saw death before our eyes. At last, being in this discomfort and extreme necessity, the master said if we could take hold with a rope upon the fast ice, we might therewith draw the scute up, and so get it out of the great drift of ice. But as this counsel was good, yet it was so full of danger, that it was the hazard of his life that should take upon him to do it; and without doing it, was it most certain that it would cost us all our lives. This counsel (as I said) was good, but no man (like to the tale of the mice) durst hang the bell about the cat's neck, fearing to be drowned; yet necessity required to have it done, and the most danger made us choose the least. So that being in that perplexity and as a drowned calf may safely be risked, I being the lightest of all our company took on me to fasten a rope upon the fast ice; and so creeping from one piece of driving ice to another, by God's help got to the fast ice, where I made a rope fast to a high hummock, and they that were in the scute drew it thereby unto the said fast ice, and then one man alone could draw more than all of them could have done before. And when we had gotten thither, in all haste we took our sick men out and laid them upon the ice, laying clothes and other things under them, and then took all our goods out of the scutes, and so drew them upon the ice, whereby for that time we were delivered from that great danger, making account that we had escaped out of death's claws, as it was most true.

June 20 it was indifferent weather, the wind west, and when the sun was south-east [7.30 A.M.] Claes Adrianson began to be extreme sick, whereby we perceived that he would not live long, and the boatswain came into our scute and told us in what case he was, and that he could not long continue alive; whereupon William Barents spake and said, 'I think I shall not live long after him'; and yet we did not judge William Barents to be so sick,

Plate 14 Naples, detail from an oil painting by Gaspar van Vitelli (1674–1731) showing an un-rigged frigate careened for hull repairs.

97 'So that there rested nothing as then but only to bring it down to the waterside.'

98 'We by God's mercy put off from the land of Nova Zembla . . .'

for we sat talking one with the other, and spake of many things, and William Barents read in my chart which I had made touching our voyage; at last he laid away the chart and spake unto me, saying, 'Gerrit, give me some drink'; and he had no sooner drunk but he was taken with so sudden a qualm, that he turned his eyes in his head and died presently, and we had no time to call the master out of the scute to speak unto him; and so he died before Claes Adrianson who died shortly after him. The death of William Barents put us in no small discomfort, as being the chief guide and only pilot on whom we reposed ourselves next under God; but we could not strive against God, and therefore we must of force be content.

June 22, in the morning, it blew a good gale out of the south-east, and then the sea was reasonable open, but we were forced to draw our scutes over the ice to get unto it, which was great pain and labour unto us, for first we were forced to draw our scutes over a piece of ice of 50 paces long, and there put them into the water, and then again to draw them up upon other ice, and after draw them at the least 300 paces more over the ice, before we could bring them to a good place, where we might easily get out. And being gotten unto the open water, we committed ourselves to God and set sail, the sun being about east north-east, with an indifferent gale of wind out of the south and south south-east, and sailed west and west and by south . . .

June 28, when the sun was in the east, we laid all our goods upon the ice, and then drew the scutes upon the ice also, because we were so hardly pressed on all sides with the ice, and the wind came out of the sea upon the land, and therefore we were in fear to be wholly enclosed with the ice, and should not be able to get out thereof again. And being upon the ice, we laid sails over our scutes, and lay down to rest, appointing one of our men to keep watch; and when the sun was north there came three bears towards our scutes, wherewith he that kept the watch cried, 'Three bears, three bears'; at which noise we leaped out of our boats with our muskets, that were laden with hailshot to shoot at birds, and had no time to discharge them, and therefore shot at them therewith; and although that kind of shot could not hurt them much yet they ran away, and in the meantime they gave us leisure to load our muskets with bullets, and by that means we shot one of the three dead, which the other two perceiving ran away, but within two hours after they came again, but when they were almost at us and heard us make a noise, they ran away; at which time the wind was west and west and by north, which made the ice drive with great force into the east.

July 1 it was indifferent fair weather, with a west north-west wind; and in the morning, the sun being east, there came a bear

from the driving ice and swam over the water to the fast ice whereon we lay; but when she heard us she came no nearer, but ran away. And when the sun was south-east, the ice came so fast in towards us, that all the ice whereon we lay with our scutes and our goods broke and ran one piece upon another, whereby we were in no small fear, for at that time most of our goods fell into the water. But we with great diligence drew our scutes further upon the ice towards the land, where we thought to be better defended from the driving of the ice, and as we went to fetch our goods we fell into the greatest trouble that ever we had before, for that we endured so great danger in the saving thereof, that as we laid hold upon one piece thereof the rest sunk down with the ice, and many times the ice broke under our own feet; whereby we were wholly discomforted and in a manner clean out of all hope, expecting no issue thereof, in such sort that our trouble at that time surmounted all our former cares and impeachments. And when we thought to draw up our boats upon the ice, the ice broke under us, and we were carried away with the scute and all by the driving ice; and when we thought to save the goods the ice broke under our feet, and with that the scute broke in many places, especially that which we had mended; as the mast, the mast plank, and almost all the scute, wherein one of our men that was sick and a chest of money lay, which we with great danger of our lives got out from it; for as we were doing it, the ice that was under our feet drove from us and slid upon other ice, whereby we were in danger to burst both our arms and our legs. At which time, thinking that we had been clean quit of our scute, we beheld each other in pitiful manner, knowing not what we should do, our lives depending thereon; but God made so good provision for us that the pieces of ice drove from each other, wherewith we ran in great haste unto the scute and drew it to us again in such case as it was, and laid it upon the fast ice by the boat, where it was in more security, which put us unto an exceeding and great and dangerous labour from the time that the sun was south-east until it was west south-west, and in all that time we rested not, which made us extreme weary and wholly out of comfort, for that it troubled us sore, and it was much more fearful unto us than at that time when William Barents died; for there we were almost drowned, and that day we lost (which was sunk in the sea) two barrels of bread, a chest with linen cloth, a trunk with the sailors' best clothes, our astronomical ring, a pack of scarlet cloth, a runlet of oil, and some cheeses, and a runlet of wine, which bonged with the ice, so that there was not anything thereof saved.

July 3 in the morning, the sun being east, two of our men went to the water, and there they found two of our oars, our helm stick the pack of scarlet cloth, the chest with linen cloth, and a hat that fell out of the trunk, whereby we guessed that it was broken in pieces; which they perceiving, took as much with them as they could carry, and came unto us, showing us that they had left more goods behind them, whereupon the master with 5 more of us went thither, and drew all the goods upon the firm ice, that when we went away we might take it with us; but they could not carry the chest nor the pack of cloth (that were full of water) because of their weight, but were forced to let them stand till we went away, that the water might drop out of them and we might afterwards fetch them, and so they did.

July 4 it was so fair clear weather, that from the time we were first in Nova Zembla we had not the like. Then we washed the velvets, that had been wet with the salt water, in fresh water drawn out of snow, and then dried them and packed them up again; at which time the wind was west and west south-west.

July 5 it was fair weather, the wind west south-west. The same day died John Franson of Harlem (Claes Adrianson's nephew, that died the same day when William Barents died) the sun being then about north north-west; at which time the ice came mightily driving in upon us, and then six of our men went into the land, and there fetched some firewood to dress our meat.

July 20, having still a good gale, about the south-east sun we past along by the Black Point, which is forty-eight miles distant from the Cross Island, and sailed west south-west; and about the evening with the west sun we saw the Admirable Island, and about the north sun past along by it, which is distant from the Black Point thirty-two miles. And passing along by it, we saw about two hundred sea horses lying upon a flake of ice, and we sailed close by them and drove them from thence, which had almost cost us dear; for they, being mighty strong fishes and of great force, swam towards us (as if they would be revenged on us for the despite that we had done them) round about our scutes with a great noise, as if they would have devoured us; but we escaped from them by reason that we had a good gale of wind, yet it was not wisely done of us to wake sleeping wolves.

July 28 it was fair weather, with a north-east wind; then we sailed along by the land, and with the south-west sun got before St Laurence Bay, or Sconce Point, and sailed south south-east twenty-four miles; and being there, we found two Russian ships beyond the point, wherewith we were not a little comforted to think that we were come to the place where we found men, but were in some doubt of them because they were so many, for at that time we saw at least 30 men, and knew not what sort of persons they were. There with much pain and labour we got to the land, which they perceiving, left off their work and came towards us, but without any arms; and we also went on shore, as many as

were well, for divers of us were very ill at ease and weak by reason of the scurvy. And when we met together we saluted each other in friendly wise, they after theirs, and we after our manner. And when we were met, both they and we looked each other steadfastly in the face, for that some of them knew us, and we them to be the same men which the year before, when we passed through the Vaygatz, had been in our ship; at which time we perceived that they were abashed and wondered at us, to remember that at that time we were so well furnished with a splendid great ship, that was exceedingly provided of all things necessary, and then to see us so lean and bare, and with so small, open scutes into that country. And amongst them there were two that in friendly manner clapped the master and me upon the shoulder, as knowing us since the former voyage: for there was none of all our men that was as then in that voyage but we two only; and they asked us for our crable, meaning our ship, and we showed them by signs as well as we could (for we had no interpreter) that we had lost our ship in the ice; wherewith they said *Crable pro pal*, which we understood to be, 'Have you lost your ship?' And we made answer, *Crable pro pal*, which was as much as to say, that we had lost our ship. And many more words we could not use, because we understood not each other. Then they made

show to be sorry for our loss and to be grieved that we the year before had been there with so many ships, and then to see us in so simple manner, and made us signs that then they had drunk wine in our ship, and asked us what drink we had now; wherewith one of our men went into the scute and drew some water, and let them taste thereof; but they shaked their heads, and said *No dobbre,* that is, it is not good. Then our master went nearer unto them and showed them his mouth, to give them to understand that we were troubled with the scurvy, and to know if they could give us counsel to help it; but they thought we made show that we had great hunger, wherewith one of them went unto their boats and fetched a round rye loaf weighing about 8 pounds, with some smoked fowl, which we accepted thankfully, and gave them in exchange half a dozen of biscuit ... And we were much comforted to see the Russians, for that in thirteen months since that we departed from John Cornelison we had not seen any man, but only monstrous and cruel wild bears; and therewith we said unto each other, now we hope that it will fall out better with us, seeing we have found men again, thanking God with all our hearts, that he had been so gracious and merciful unto us, to give us life until that time.

July 29 it was reasonable fair weather, and that morning the Russians began to make preparation to be gone and to set sail; and we not knowing whither they would go, saw them sail towards the Vaygatz: at which time also we set sail and followed after them. But they sailing before us, and we following them along by the land, the weather being close and misty, we lost the sight of them, and knew not whether they put into any creek or sailed forward; but we held on our course south south-east, with a north-west wind, and then south-east.

August 16 in the morning, sailing forward north-west, we perceived that we were in a creek, and so made towards a Russian ship which we had seen on our starboard, which at last with great labour and much pain we got unto and coming to them about the south-east sun, with a hard wind, we asked them how far we were from Sembla de Cool[1] or Kilduin; but they shook their heads, and showed us that we were on the east side of Zembla de Candinaes [Cape Kanin], but we would not believe them. And then we asked them for some victuals, wherewith they gave us certain plaice, for the which the master gave them a piece of money, and we sailed from them again, to get out of that hole where we were, as it reached into the sea; but they perceiving that we took a wrong course and that the flood was almost past, sent two men unto us, in a small boat, with a great loaf of bread, which they gave us, and made signs unto us to come aboard of their ship again, for that they intended to have further speech with us and to help us, which we seemed not to refuse and desiring not to be unthankful, gave them a piece of money and a piece of linen cloth, but they stayed still by us, and they that were in the great ship held up bacon and butter unto us, to move us to come aboard of them again, and so we did. And being with them, we fetched our chart and let them see it, by the which they showed us that we were still on the east side of the White Sea and of Candinaes; which we understanding, were in some doubt with ourselves because we had so great a voyage to make over the White Sea.

August 18, in the morning we saw a point of land reaching into the sea, and on it certain signs of crosses, which as we went nearer unto we saw perfectly; and when the sun was west, we perceived that the land reached west and south-west, so that thereby we knew it certainly to be the point of Candinaes, lying at the mouth of the White Sea, which we were to cross, and had long desired to see it. This point is easily to be known, having five crosses standing upon it, which are perfectly to be discerned, one the east side in the south-east, and one the other side in the south-west. And when we thought to sail from thence to the west side of the White Sea towards the coast of Norway, we found that one of our runlets of fresh water was almost leaked out; and for

100 'And we were much comforted to see the Russians . . .'

[1] Kola in Lapland.

that we had about 160 miles to sail over the sea before we should get any fresh water, we sought means first to row on land to get some, but because the waves went so high we durst not do it; and so having a good north-east wind (which was not for us to slack) we set forward in the name of God, and when the sun was north-west we passed the point, and all that night and the next day sailed with a good wind, and in all that time rowed but while three glasses were run out; and the next night after ensuing having still a good wind, in the morning about the east north-east sun we saw land on the west side of the White Sea, which we found by the rushing of the sea upon the land before we saw it. And perceiving it to be full of cliffs, and not low sandy ground with some hills as it is on the east side of the White Sea, we assured ourselves that we were on the west side of the White Sea, upon the coast of Lapland, for the which we thanked God that he had helped us to sail over the White Sea in thirty hours, it being 160 miles at the least, our course being west with a north-east wind.

August 24 the wind blew east, and then, the sun being east, we got to the Seven Islands, where we found many fishermen, of whom we enquired after Cool and Kilduin, and they made signs that they lay east from us (which we likewise guessed to be so). And withal they showed us great friendship, and cast a cod into our scute, but for that we had a good gale of wind we could not stay to pay them for it but gave them great thanks, much wondering at their great courtesy. And so, with a good gale of wind, we arrived before the Seven Islands when the sun was south-west, and passed between them and the land, and there found certain fishermen, that rowed to us, and asked us where our crable (meaning our ship) was, whereunto we made answer with as much Russian language as we had learned, and said, *Crable pro pal* (that is, our ship is lost), which they understanding said unto us, *Cool Brabouse crable*, whereby we understood that at Cool there was certain Netherland ships, but we made no great account thereof, because our intent was to sail to Warehouse, fearing lest the Russians or great prince of the country would stay us there.

August 25, sailing along by the land with a south-east wind, about the south sun we had a sight of Kilduin, at which time we held our course west north-west . . . But as we were under sail, the wind blew so stiff that we durst not keep the sea in the night time, for that the waves of the sea went so hollow, that we were still in doubt that they would smite the scutes to the ground, and so took our course behind two cliffs towards our land. And when we came there, we found a small house upon the shore, wherein there was three men and a great dog, which received us very friendly, asking us of our affairs and how we got thither . . .

Then we asked them if they would go with one of our men by land to Coola, to look for a ship wherewith we might get into Holland, and said we would reward them well for their pains; but they excused themselves, and said that they could not go from thence, but they said that they would bring us over the hill, where we should find certain Laplanders whom they thought would go with us, as they did; for the master and one of our men going with them over the hill, found certain Laplanders there, whereof they got one to go with our man, promising him two royals of eight for his pains. And so the Laplander going with him, took a piece on his neck, and our man a boat hook, and about evening they set forward, the wind as then being east and east north-west.

August 29 it was indifferent weather, and we were still in good hope to hear some good news from Coola, and always looked up towards the hill to see if our man and the Laplander came; but seeing they came not we went to the Russians again, and there dressed our meat at their fire, and then meant to go to our scutes to lodge in them all night. In the meantime we spied the Laplander upon the hill coming alone without our man, whereat we wondered and were somewhat in doubt; but when he came unto us, he showed us a letter that was written unto our master, which he opened before us, the contents thereof being that he that had written the letter wondered much at our arrival in that place, and that long since he verily thought that we had been all cast away, being exceeding glad of our happy fortune, and how that he would presently come unto us with victuals and all other necessaries to succour us withal. We being in no small admiration who it might be that showed us so great favour and friendship, could not imagine what he was, for it appeared by the letter that he knew us well. And although the letter was subscribed 'by me John Cornelison Rijp,' yet we could not be persuaded that it was the same John Cornelison, who the year before had been set out in the other ship at the same time with us . . .

August 30 it was indifferent fair weather, we still wondering who that John Cornelison might be that had written unto us; and while we sat musing thereon, some of us were of opinion that it might be the same John Cornelison that had sailed out of Holland in company with us, which we could not be persuaded to believe because we were in as little hope of his life as he of ours, supposing that he had sped worse then we, and long before that had perished or been cast away. At last the master said, I will look amongst my letters, for there I have his name written, and that will put us out of doubt. And so, looking amongst them, we found that it was the same John Cornelison, wherewith we were as glad of his safety and welfare as he was of ours. And while we were speaking thereof, and that some of us would not believe that it was the same John Cornelison, we saw a Russian yawl come rowing, with John Cornelison and our companion that we had sent to Coola; who being landed, we received and welcomed each other with great joy and exceeding gladness, as if either of us on both sides had seen each other rise from death to life again; for we esteemed him, and he us, to be dead long since. He brought us a barrel of Roswick beer, wine, aqua vita, bread, flesh, bacon, salmon, sugar, and other things, which comforted and relieved us much. And we rejoiced together for our so unexpected meeting, and that time giving God great thanks for his mercy showed unto us.

September 2 in the morning we rowed up the river, and as we passed along we saw some trees on the riverside, which comforted us and made us as glad as if we had then come into a new world, for in all the time that we had been out we had not seen any trees; and when we were by the salt kettles, which is about twelve miles from Coola, we stayed there awhile and made merry, and then went forward again, and with the west north-west sun got to John Cornelison's ship, wherein we entered and drunk. There we began to make merry again with the sailors that were therein and that had been in the voyage with John Cornelison the year before and bade each other welcome. Then we rowed forward, and late in the evening got to Coola, where some of us went on land, and some stayed in the scutes to look to the goods, to whom we sent milk and other things to comfort and refresh them; and we were all exceeding glad that God of his mercy had delivered us out of so many dangers and troubles, and had brought us thither in safety: for as then we esteemed ourselves to be safe, although the place in times past, lying so far from us, was as much unknown unto us as if it had been out of the world, and at that time, being there, we thought that we were almost at home.

101 'We had sailed in those open scutes almost 1,600 miles, through and along by the sea coasts to the town of Coola . . .'

September 11, by leave and consent of the bayart, governor for the Great Prince of Muscovia, we brought our scute and our boats into the merchants' house, and there let them stand for a remembrance of our long, far, and never before sailed way, and that we had sailed in those open scutes almost 1,600 miles, through and along by the sea coasts to the town of Coola, whereat the inhabitants thereof could not sufficiently wonder.

September 17 in the evening John Cornelison and our master being come aboard, the next day about the east sun we set sail out of the river of Coola, and with God's grace put to sea to sail homewards; and being out of the river we sailed along by the land north-west and by north, the wind being south.

September 19, about the south sun, we got to Warehouse, and there anchored and went on land, because John Cornelison was there to take in more goods, and stayed there till October 6, in the which time we had a hard wind out of the north and north-west. And while we stayed there we refreshed ourselves somewhat better, to recover from our sickness and weakness again, that we might grow stronger, which asked some time, for we were much spent and exceeding weak.

October 6, about evening, the sun being south-west, we set sail, and with God's grace, from Warehouse for Holland; but for that it is a common and well known way, I will speak nothing thereof, only that upon October 29 we arrived in the Maas with an east north-east wind, and upon November 1 about noon got to Amsterdam, in the same clothes that we wore in Nova Zembla, with our caps furred with white fox's skins, and went to the house of Peter Hasselaer, that was one of the merchants that set out the two ships, which were conducted by John Cornelison and our master. And being there, where many men wondered to see us, as having esteemed us long before that to have been dead and rotten, the news thereof being spread abroad in the town, it was also carried to the Prince's Court in the Hague, at which time the Lord Chancellor of Denmark, ambassador for the king, was then at dinner with Prince Maurice. For the which cause we were presently fetched thither by the scout and two of the burghers of the town, and there in the presence of those ambassadors and the burgher masters we made rehearsal of our journey both forwards and backwards. And after that, every man that dwelt thereabouts went home, but such as dwelt not near to that place were placed in good lodging for certain days, until we had received our pay, and then every one of us departed and went to the place of his abode.

from *The Three Voyages of William Barents to the Arctic Regions,* by Gerrit de Veer (translated by William Phillip, London 1609).

A wonderful voyage

The early years of the seventeenth century saw Dutch enterprise at its height (see p. 34f). In 1615 Willem Cornelison Schouten set sail with the merchant Jacob Le Maire to look for a new southern route to the East via the Pacific, the Dutch government having given the Dutch East India Company a monopoly on the use of the Straits of Magellan and the Cape of Good Hope route. Passing through the strait which today bears Le Maire's name, they named its eastern side Staten Land (today Staten Island) in the belief that it was part of a southern land mass. They also rounded and named Cape Horn, thus discovering what was to become the most famous of the sailing ship routes. Though they completed their circumnavigation, their voyage was not an unalloyed success, as the following passages from *The Relation of a Wonderfull Voiage made by William Cornelison Schouten of Horne* show . . .

Upon the 14 of June 1615 we sailed out of the Texell, and the 16 of the same month, being in sight of Dunkerk, passed between Dover and Callis.

The 21 and 22, having a great storm we put into the Isle of Wight, where our Master would glady have hired a carpenter but could not.

The 25 we set sail from Wight and upon the 27 entered at Plymouth, where the Master hired a carpenter of Maydenblicke.

The 28 we left Plymouth and sailed with a north north-east wind and fair weather, and the 29 the Master and Merchant of the *Horne* came aboard the *Unity* to agree together about order to be taken upon the 4 of July, for sharing of our victuals, according to the manner and custom used in ships that sail long voyages, where they deliver the sailors their meat and drink by weight, and measure, to every man alike and according to his quality.

The 4 of July, according to the aforesaid resolution, it was ordered that every man should have a can of beer a day, 4 pound of biscuit, and half a pound of butter (besides sweet suet) a week, and five cheeses for the whole voyage.

The 8, being under 39 degrees and 25 minutes our carpenter's mate died . . .

The first of November we passed the sun, whereby at noon time, it was north from us . . .

The 17 [December] we laid our ship within the King's Island on the wall, with a high water, to make it clean, where it was dry that we might go round about it dry foot.

The 18 the *Horne* was also laid on shore about 2 musket shot from our ship, to make it clean.

The 19 as we were busy about both the ships to make them clean, and burned reeds under the *Horne*, the flame of the fire suddenly got into the ship, and presently took such hold thereof that in the twinkling of an eye, it was so great that we could by no means

high hills, that were all covered over with ice. We sailed along by that land, and about noon passed it and saw other land east from it, which also was very high and ragged.

These lands as we guessed lay about 8 leagues one from the other, and seemed as if there were a good passage between them, which we were the better persuaded unto, for that there ran a hard stream southward between both those lands.

Then about noon we were under 54 degrees and 46 minutes. There we saw an innumerable number of penguins and thousands of whales, so that we were forced to look well about us, and to wind and turn to shun the whales, lest we should sail upon them.

The 25, in the morning we were close by the east land, which was very high and craggy, which on the north side reacheth east south-east, as far as we could see, that land we called States Land, but the land that lay west from us, we named Maurice Land. We perceived that on both sides thereof, there were good roads, and sandy bays, for on either side it had sandy strands and very fair sandy ground. There are great store of fish, penguins and porpoises, as also birds and water enough, but we could see no trees . . . In the evening the wind was south-west, and that night we went south with great waves or billows out of the south-west, and very blue water, whereby we judged, and held for certain that we had great deep water to windward from us, nothing doubting but that it was the great south sea, whereat we were exceeding glad, to think that we had discovered a way, which

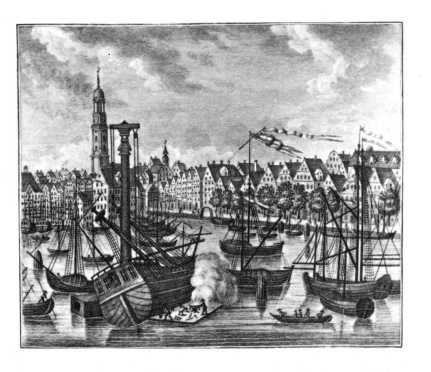

102 *above* A scene at Amsterdam in oil by Ludolf Bakhuysen (1631 – 1708), showing the lateen mizen which was in the seventeenth century to be replaced by a gaff spanker.

103 *right* Ship careened for caulking in a German port. After J. M. David, 1790.

quench it, by reason it lay 50 foot dry from the waterside, and by that means we were constrained to stand still, and see it burn before our eyes, not able to do anything to save it.

The 20 at a high water we launched the *Unity,* into the water again, and went to the *Horne* and quenched the fire, but the ship was burnt clean down to the water. The next day when we had cast the water out of that part of it that was left, we saved all the wood, ironwork, anchors, ordinance, and what else that was to be gotten and put it into our ship.

The 12 [January 1616] our Pinnace rowed to the Penguins Island, to fetch penguins, but the weather was so foul, that they could not get aboard again that day, and next morning came to us laden with penguins, but by reason of the great number of them, they were spoilt, and we cast them overboard.

The 20 we were under 53 degrees, and guessed we were about 20 leagues southward from the Straits of Magellan.

The 24 in the morning, we saw land on starboard not above a great league distant from us, there we had ground at 40 fathom, and a west wind, the land stretched east and south, with very

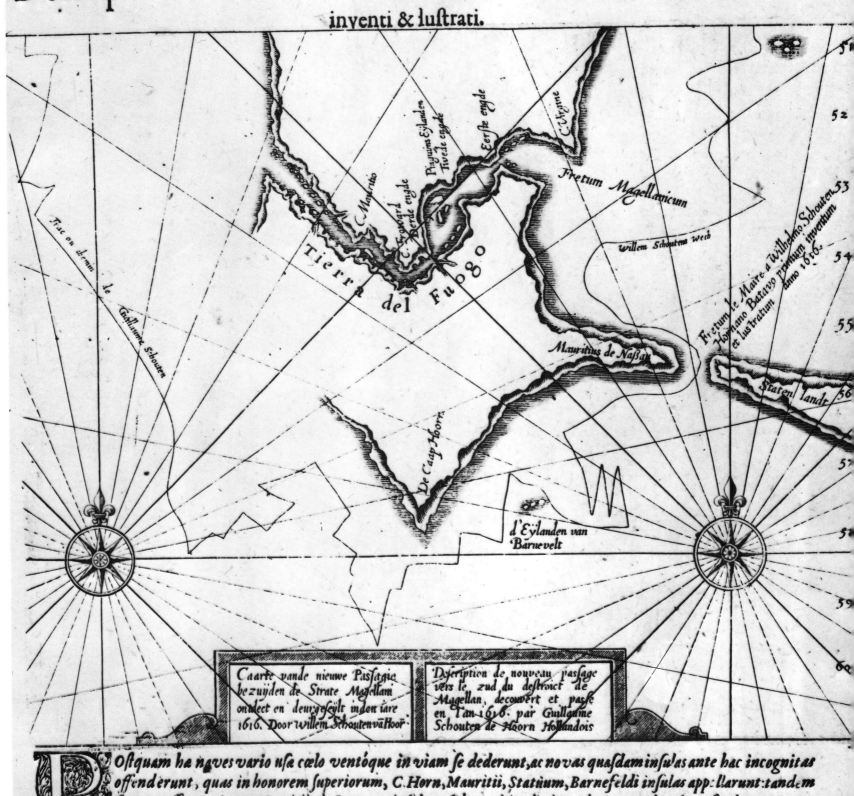

Descriptio freti Le Maire à Guilhelmo Schouten Hornano inventi & lustrati.

104 A page from the original edition showing Schouten's route round Cape Horn.

Postquam hæ naves vario usa cælo ventóque in viam se dederunt, ac novas quasdam insulas ante hac incognitas offenderunt, quas in honorem superiorum, C. Horn, Mauritii, Statuum, Barnefeldi insulas app: llarunt: tandem scopum assecutæ, inter Mauritii & Statuum insulam, sub 57. altitudinis gradu commodum in australem oceanum transitum reperērut, quem, urgente sic Jacobo Mairio commissario, Fretum Le Maire appellarunt, quamvis me-

until that time, was unknown to men, as afterwards we found it
to be true.

There we saw extreme great sea mews, bigger of body than
swans, their wings being spread abroad, were each of them above
a fathom long. These birds being unaccustomed to see men, came
to our ship, and sat thereon, and let our men take and kill them.

The 29, we had a north-east wind, and held our course south-
west and saw two islands before us, lying west south-west from us,
about noon we got to them but could not sail above them, so
that we held our course north, about them they had dry grey cliffs,
and some low cliffs about them, they lay under 57 degrees,
southward of the equinoctial line. We named them Barnevells
Islands, from them we sailed west north-west. About evening we
saw land again, lying north-west and north north-west from us,
which was the land that lay south from the Straits of Magellan
which reacheth southward, all high hilly land covered over with
snow, ending with a sharp point, which we called Cape Horne,
it lieth under 57 degrees and 48 minutes.

Then we had fair weather, and a north wind, with great
billows out of the west, we held on course west, and found a
strong stream that ran westward.

The 12 [February] our men had each of them three cups of wine
in sign of joy for our good luck, for then the Straits of Magellan
lay east from us: the same day by advice of all our counsel, at
the request of our chief Merchant, the new passage (by us discovered between Mauritius Land and the States Land), was
named the Straits of le Maire, although by good right it should
rather have been called William Schouten's Strait, after our

Master's name, by whose wise conduction and skill in sailing,
the same was found.

The 9 [May] we were under 15 degrees 20 minutes, and at that
time as we thought were 1,510 leagues distant from the coast of
Peru and Chile. About noon we saw a sail, which as we guessed
was a bark, coming out of the south, and went northward towards
us. We presently made towards it, and as it came near to us, we
shot at it with one of our pieces right over her, to make them strike,
but they would not. Then we shot again, but yet they would not
strike. With that we put out our shallop with 10 musketeers in it;
to take her, which calling to them we shot another piece, yet without any intent to reach or to hurt them, but they would not strike,
but sought as well as they could to get away from us, and got
to windward of us, but our shallop being too crafty for them
rowed to them, and being about half a musket shot from them
shot four muskets one after another, as they drew near to her,
and before they could reach her some of her men in great fear
leaped overboard, whereof one of them had a little child, and
another was hurt, and had three holes in his back, but not very
deep, for it was hail-shot, those we fetched out of the water again.
They also threw much of their goods overboard, and amongst
the rest three hens. Our men leaped into their ship, and carried
them into our ship, they not once resisting, for in truth they had
no arms. When they were in our ship we fetched two men more
that were left in theirs, which presently fell down before us, and
kissed our feet and hands. One of them was a very old man, the
other a young man. We could not understand them, but used
them kindly, and presently the shallop rowed to fetch those that
leaped overboard, to save their lives, but they got but two of them,
that drove upon one of their oars, and pointed to our men with
their hands to the ground, as much to say, that the rest were
drowned: one of those two that was hurt, whom we dressed had
long yellow hair. In that ship there was at least eight women,
three young sucking children, and some of nine or ten years old,
so that we made account they were three and twenty in all,
clean naked people, both men and women, only something
hanging before their privy members. About evening we set the
men on board their ship again, that were welcome to their wives,
which clasped them about the necks and kissed them. We gave
them beads (which they hung about their necks) and some knives,
and showed them all the friendship we could, and they the like
to us, giving us two fine matiens, and two coconuts, for they had
not many. That was all they had to eat and drink, and they had
drunk out all the water out of the nuts, so that they had no more
drink. We saw them drink salt water out of the sea, and gave it
also to their young children to drink, which we thought to be

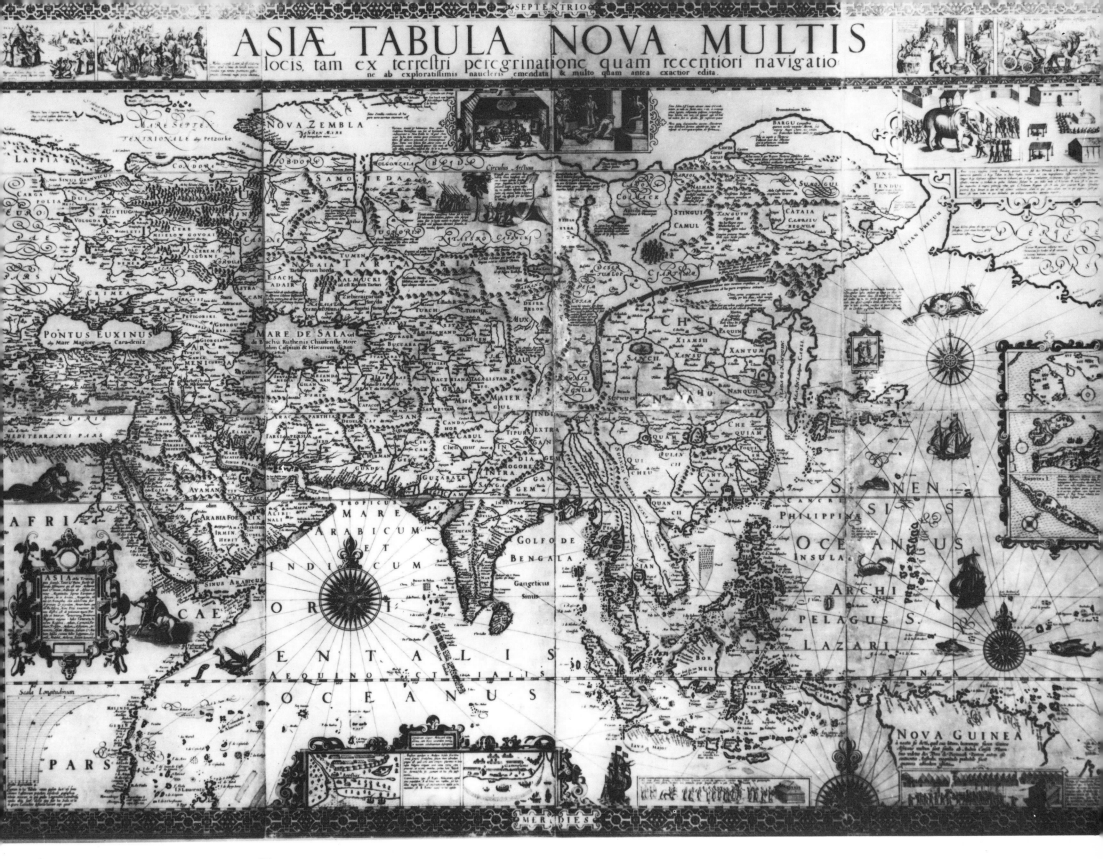

against Nature. They had certain cloths, which they wore before their privy members, and therewith covered themselves against the heat of the sun, of a yellowish colour. They were reddish people, that annointed themselves with oil: the women had short hair, like our men in Holland: men's hair was long, curled, and very black: their ship was of a strange fashion. It was made of 2 long fair canoes with a good space between them, in each canoe about the middle thereof, there lay two whole broad planks of fair red wood, to keep out the water, and divers planks laid cross over, from the one canoe to the other, which were made fast together, and hung a good way over on both ends, without the canoes, very close above to keep out the water, before at the end of one of the canoes, on starboard, there stood a mast, at the end thereof having a fork, whereon the yard lay. The sail was made of mats, and as the wind blew they sailed, without compass, or any instruments for the sea, but hooks to fish withal, whereof the upper part was stone, the other black bone, or tortoise's shells, and some of them were mother of pearl. Their ropes were very fair, and almost as thick as a cable. When they sailed from us, they held their course south-east.

The 14 in the morning, we saw another island right before us, about seven leagues distant from us . . . and made towards it . . . Then ten or twelve canoes came to our ship, but we would not let them come aboard, but showed them friendly countenance, and bartered with them for four flying fishes, for the which we gave them some beads, which we let down by a rope at the stern of the ship, and they taking them tied the fishes to the rope, and we pulled them up. In the meantime our shallop sounded along by the land, which they in the canoes seeing, presently made towards it, and being close by it, at first spake unto the men, but withal compassed them about with fourteen canoes, and therewith some of them leaped overboard, thinking to fall upon the shallop, or to draw it away with them, which our men perceiving, shot with their muskets among them (there being six muskets, and other arms, cutlasses and pikes in the shallop), and therewith killed two of the indians as they sat in their canoes, whereof one presently fell dead overboard, the other sat still with his hand wiping off the blood upon his breast, but at last fell likewise overboard: the rest in the canoes, were thereat in so great fear, that in all haste they made away, at which time we saw many men standing upon the shore, that cried and made a great noise. But for that we there could find no fit anchoring ground, we took our shallop in again, and went forward on our voyage, holding our course south-west, the better to get to the south, hoping there to find firm land.

The 15, after noon we came to 2 low inhabited islands, about half a league from the mainland, which stood full of coco trees . . . The Master rowed with the boat and the shallop well armed, to the land, thinking to get some coco-nuts, which there were upon the land in great abundance: but going on shore, the indians lay in a bush right against the place where we came to land, and watching for us, shot so fiercely at us with their bows, that they hurt at least 16 of our men, some in the arm, others in the leg, neck and hands, and other places. And we shot at them with muskets and slings, but at last by reason that the indians shot so thick we were forced to retire, there we were under 2 degrees and 54 minutes.

The 16 in the morning we sailed in with our ship between both the islands, and anchored at 9 fathom, where we had good lying. After noon our boat and shallop rowed to the lesser island, to fetch some coco-nuts, and burned 2 or 3 of the indian's houses, whereupon they that dwelt in the other island began mightily to cry and make a noise, but durst not come to us, for with our ordinance we shot along the shore, and into the wood, that the bullets entered into it with thundering noise, whereat the indians fled, and durst not once look out. About evening our men came aboard again, and brought so many coco-nuts, that everyone of us had three nuts for his part. That night there came one of the indians aboard our ship to make peace with us, with him bringing one of our men's caps which before fell off his head in the skirmish. Those people are clean naked, their privy members and all.

The 14 [October] in the morning, we saw Java, and that day sailed by Tuban.

The 23 we set sail, and the 28 went by Jakarta, where we anchored without the island, there we found three ships of Holland. The *Horne,* the *Eagle,* and the *Trou,* and 3 English ships. The next night, one of our men died, which was the first man that died that voyage in the *Unity,* besides 2 more that died in the *Horne,* the one John Cornelison Schouten, our Master's brother, in the south sea, and one about the coast of Portingale. So that until then, there died but 3 men in both the ships, and then we had left 84 men living, all indifferently well.

The 1 of November, the President John Peterson Koeven, sent for William Cornelison Schouten our master, and the merchants to come on land, where being come (in the presence of his counsel there assembled) he told them in name of the East India Company, that they must leave their ship and goods there and deliver it up into his hands: and although our Master showed him many reasons to persuade the contrary, saying that they did them great wrong, they were forced to do as the President appointed them, who told them, that if they thought they did them wrong, that they should right themselves in Holland:

and so our ship and goods was stayed, and attached there. To receive the ship and all her furniture, the President appointed two masters of ships, and two merchants, which was delivered by inventory unto them, by our Master and the merchant.

Our ship being in this manner taken from us, some of our men put themselves into service with the East India Company. The rest were put into two ships (that were to go home into Holland) called the *Amsterdam* and the *Zeland*. The master William Cornelison Schouten, and Jacob le Maire, ten of our men, went in the *Amsterdam*.

The 32 our merchant Jacob le Maire died.

The 1 of January 1617 we lost the sight of the *Zeland*.

The 6 of March, as we guessed, we passed the Cape, but saw it not.

The 31 we were under the Island of Saint Helena, where we found the *Zeland*, which arrived there certain days before us.

The 24 [April] in the morning, we were under the equinoctial line, and the 28 we saw the north star, which we had not seen in 20 months before.

The 1 of July we came with the *Amsterdam* into Zeland, where the day before, the *Zeland* likewise was arrived. And so performed our voyage in two years and eighteen days.

from *The Relation of a Wonderfull Voiage made by William Cornelison Schouten of Horne*, London 1619.

107, 108 and 109. The list of ingredients of a surgeon's chest and the two engravings of surgical instruments shown on this page are taken from *The Surgeon's Mate* by John Woodall, Surgeon General to the English East India Company. First published in 1617, the book went through several editions and was in use throughout the seventeenth century. Oddly enough, it mentions lemon juice as a cure for scurvy, but also recommends oil of vitriol.

Surgery at sea

A note of particular ingredients for a Surgeons Chest, and of other necessary Appendixes serving for Chirurgicall uses, whereof these next recited may be placed on the lidd of the Chest to open view, to manifest he hath them, if the Surgeon will have it so, or he that is to pay for them desire to see them in view.

INcision knives.
Dismembring knives.
Catlings.
Rasours.
Trapans.
Trafine.
Lavatories.
Head sawes.
Dismembring sawes.
Dismembring Nippers.
Mallet and chizel.
Speculum Oris.
Speculum Oris with a screw.
Speculum Lingua.
Speculum Ani.
Cauterizing irons.
Storks bills.
Ravens bills.
Crowes bils.
Terebellum.
Incision sheers.
Probes or flamules.
Spatulaes great and small
Spatulum Mondani.

For teeth. { Paces.
Pullicans.
Forcers or punches.
Crowes bills.
Flegmes.

Gravers,
Small files.
One bundle of small German instruments.
Glister strings.
Small strings.
Catheter.
Wax Lights.
These for the lidd of the Surgeons Chest, till the Surgeon see cause to remove them.

The rest that follow are no lesse necessary then the former for their particular uses: namely.

The salvatory furnished with such Vnguents as hereafter in their places are named.
The Plaster box furnished with the due instruments and medicines thereunto belonging.
The instruments for the Plaster box are as followeth ordinarily.
Scissers.
Forceps.
Spatula.

A

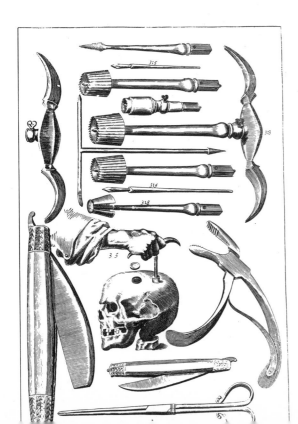

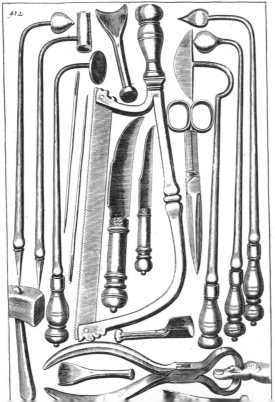

The *Sovereign of the Seas*

110 The *Resolution* in a gale by
W. van de Velde the Younger
(1633–1707). This oil painting shows
the luxuriant decoration on the hull
of a seventeenth-century warship.

What was a seventeenth-century ship like and how did people see it? The 'ginger-bread' or gilded carving on the hull was a dominant preoccupation, as witnessed by this quaint description (original spelling preserved), which gives little space to any other feature of the ship's design. As well as showing the current fondness for allegory it gives a good picture of the loving craftsmanship inspired by the sailing ship as an object of creation. The ships' crews did not receive such lavish

attention. The propaganda for King Charles I is ironical in view of the subsequent events mentioned at the beginning of our next piece. The *Sovereign of the Seas* (see p. 24) was an advanced design at the tail end of the period of British supremacy in shipbuilding. She was widely criticized.

Before I come to give you a true and exact dimension of her Bulke, burden, &c. it is necessary that I make some satisfaction to the world concerning those Decorements which beautifie and adorne her, and to render a faire account of mine owne invention and fancy concerning the carving worke, the figures, and Mottoes upon them, which some perhaps have too liberally taxed: Thus therefore to any who have formerly either doubted of their property, or are at this present desirous to understand their imagined obscurity, I thus freely deliver my selfe.

Upon the Beak-head sitteth royall King Edgar on horse-backe, trampling upon seven Kings. . . . This Edgar was the first that could truely write himselfe an absolute Monarch of this Island; for there were divers Reguli in those times, who were small Kings, and had absolute Dominion over divers Provinces.

His Navy Royall consisted of three thousand and six hundred Ships . . . to secure Navigators, from Enemies and Sea-Rovers . . . And those Islands, of which he was sole Prince and Monarch, being at his only charge, both quieted and secured, he did (as justly he might) write himselfe Lord of the Foure Seas.

My purpose is not to enter into a large discourse of his noble Acts and Atcheivements; what I have done, is onely to give the World a true and authentick expression, that whatsoever his sacred Maiesty challengeth concerning his absolute dominion over the foure Seas, hee justly, and with an unquestionable Title claimeth from this King Edgar, being his true and lawfull hereditary Successor.

I began at the Beak-head, where I desire you to take notice, that upon the stemme-head there is Cupid, or a Child resembling him, bestriding, and bridling a Lyon, which importeth, that sufferance may curbe Insolence, and Innocence restraine violence; which alludeth to the great mercy of the King, whose Type is a proper Embleme of that great Majesty, whose Mercy is above all his Workes.

On the Bulk-head right forward, stand six severall Statues in sundry postures, their Figures representing *Consilium*, that is, Counsell: *Cura*, that is, Care: *Conamen*, that is, Industry, and unanimous indeavour in one compartment: Counsell holding in her hand a closed or folded Scrole; Care a Sea-compasse; *Conamen*, or Industry, a Lint-stock fired. Upon the other, to correspond with the former, *Vis*, which implyeth force or strength; handing a Sword. *Virtus*, or Vertue, a sphearicall Globe: and

Jason, being figured with his Oare in his hand, as being the prime Argonaut, and say *Nava*. Shee pointeth to Hercules on the sinister side, with his club in his hand, with this Mottto, *Clava*; as if she should say, O Hercules, be thou as valiant with thy Club upon the Land, as Jason is industrious with his Oare upon the Water. Hercules againe pointing to Æolus, the god of Windes, saith *Flato*; who answereth him againe, *Flo*: Jason pointing to Neptune, the god of the Seas, (riding upon a Sea-horse) saith *Faveto*; to whom Neptune answereth, *No*: These words *Flo*, and *No*, were also much excepted at, as if there had beene no such Latine words, till some better examining their Grammar Rules found out *Flo*, *flas*, *flavi*, proper to Æolus, and *No*, *nas*, *navi*, to Neptune, &c.

In the lower Counter of the Sterne, on either side of the Helme is this Inscription,

> He who Seas, Windes, and Navies doth protect,
> Great Charles, thy great Ship in her course direct.

There are other things in the Vessell worthy remarke, at least, if not admiration; namely, that one Tree, or Oake made foure of the principall beames of this great Ship, which was Forty foure foote of strong and serviceable Timber in length, three foote Diameter at the top, and Ten foot Diameter at the stubbe or bottome.

Another, (as worthy of especiall Observation is) that one peece of Timber which made the Keelson, was so great, and weighty, that 28 Oxen, and 4 Horses with much difficulty drew it from the place where it grew, and from whence it was cut downe, unto the water-side.

There is one thing above all these, for the World to take especiall notice of, that shee is, besides her Tunnage, just so many Tuns in burden, as their have beene Yeeres since our Blessed Saviours Incarnation, namely, 1637 and not one under, or over: A most happy Omen, which though it was not at the first projected, or intended, is now by true computation found so to happen.

It would be too tedious to insist upon every Ornament belonging to this incomparable Vessel, yet thus much concerning Her outward appearance, She hath two Galleries of a side, and all of most curious carved Worke, and all the sides of the ship are carved also with Trophies of Artillery and Types of honour, as well belonging to Land as Sea, with Symboles, Emblemes, and Impresses appertaining to the Art of Navigation: as also their two sacred Majesties Badges of Honour, Armes, Escutchions, &c. with severall Angels holding their Letters in Compartements: all which workes are gilded quite over, and no other colour but gold and black to bee seene about her, and thus much in a succinct way I have delivered unto you concerning her inward and out-

Victoria, or Victory, a wreath of Lawrell. The Morall is, that in all high Enterprizes there ought to be first Counsell, to undertake; then Care to manage; and Industry, to performe: and in the next place, where there is ability and strength to oppose, and Vertue to direct, Victory consequently is alwayes at hand ready to crowne the undertaking.

Upon the Hances of the waste are foure Figures with their severall properties: Jupiter riding upon his Eagle, with his Trisulk (from which hee darteth Thunder) in his hand: Mars with his Sword and Target, a Foxe being his Embleme: Neptune with his Sea-horse, Dolphin, and Trident: and lastly Æolus upon a Camelion, (a beast that liveth onely by the Ayre) with the foure Windes, his Ministers or Agents, the East, call'd Eurus, Subsolanus, and Apeliotes: the North-winde, Septemtrio, Aquilo, or Boreas: the West, Zephyrus, Favonius, Lybs, and Africus: the South, Auster, or Notus.

I come now to the Stearne, where you may perceive upon the upright of the upper Counter, standeth Victory . . . Her wings are equally display'd; on one Arme she weareth a Crowne, on the other a Laurell, which imply Riches and Honour: in her two hands she holdeth two Mottoes; her right hand, which pointeth to *Jason*, beares this Inscription, *Nava* . . . I intreate thee Reader, but to examine Riders last Edition of his Dictionary, corrected, and greatly augmented by Mr. Francis Holy-oke, and he shall there read *Navo*, *navas*, (and therefore consequently *nava* in the Imperative Mood) *ex navus*, that is, to imploy with all ones power, to act, to ayde, to helpe, to indeavour with all diligence and industry; and therefore not unproperly may Victory point to

111 The return of Prince Charles from Spain, 1623 by H. C. Vroom (1566–1640) (oil). Note the long beakhead, persisting into the seventeenth century.

Cannon throughout, (being able to beare them). Her middle Tyre hath also thirty ports for Demi-Culverin, and whole Culverin: Her third Tyre hath Twentie six Ports for other Ordnance, her fore-Castle hath twelve ports, and her halfe Decke hath fourteene ports; She hath thirteene or foureteene ports more within Board for murdering pieces, besides a great many Loope holes out of the Cabins for Musket shot. She carrieth moreover ten pieces of chase Ordnance in her, right forward; and ten right aft, that is according to Land-service in the front and the reare. She carrieth eleven Anchors, one of them weighing foure thousand foure hundred, &c. and according to these are her Cables, Mastes, Sayles, Cordage; which considered together, seeing his Majesty is at this infinite charge, both for the honour of this Nation, and the security of his Kingdome, it should be a great spur and incouragement to all his faithful and loving Subjects to be liberall and willing Contributaries towards the Ship-money.

I come now to give you a particular Denomination of the prime Worke-men imployed in this inimitable Fabricke; as first Captayne Phines Pett, Over-seer of the Worke, and one of the principal Officers of his Majesties Navy; whose Ancestors, as Father, Grand-father, and Great-Grand-father, for the space of two hundred years and upwards, have continued in the same Name, Officers and Architectures in the Royall Navy; of whose knowledge, experience, and judgement, I can not render a merited Character.

The Master Builder is young Mr. Peter Pett, the most ingenious son of so much improoved a Father, who before he was full five and twenty yeares of age, made the Model, and since hath perfected the worke, which hath won not only the approbation but admiration of all men, of whom I may truely say, as Horace did of Argus, that famous Ship-Master, (Who built the great *Argo* in which the Grecian Princesse Rowed through the Hellespont to fetch the golden Fleece from Colchos), that Pallas herselfe flew into his bosome, and not only injoyn'd him to the undertaking, but inspired him in the managing of so exquisite and absolute an Architecture.

from *A True Description of His Majesties Royall Ship built this yeare 1637 at Woolwich in Kent to the great glory of our English nation and not paralelled in the whole Christian world*, by Thomas Heywood, London 1637.

112 The *Sovereign of the Seas* with Peter Pett, portrait attributed to P. Lely.

Plate 15 The *Sovereign of the Seas*, built 1637, showing the lavish gilding on the sides of the hull, engraving by J. Payne.

ward Decorements. I come now to Discribe her in her exact Dimension.

Her Length by the Keele, is 128 foot or there about, within some few inches. Her mayne breadth or widenesse from side to side 48 foote. Her utmost length from the fore-end of the Beake-head, unto the after end of the Sterne 232 foote, she is in height from the bottome of her Keele to the top of her Lanthorne seventy sixe foote, she beareth five Lanthornes, the biggest of which will hold ten persons to stand upright, and without shouldering or pressing one the other.

She hath three flush Deckes, and a Fore-Castle, an halfe Decke, a quarter Decke, and a round-house. Her lower Tyre hath thirty ports, which are to be furnished with Demy Cannon and whole

An ordinary voyage

After the Civil War between the English Crown and Parliament, resulting in the deposition and execution of King Charles I in 1649, many Royalists went to seek their fortunes abroad. A typical example was Norwood, of whom nothing is known but the account he left of his voyage to the colony of Virginia, which reveals the uncertainty of trans-Atlantic immigrant crossings as little less than that of voyages of exploration. Stranded on a desolate coast, Norwood and his friends survived and finally reached their destination thanks to the hospitality of the Red Indians. Here the actual sea voyage from Madeira to the American coast is described.

The month of August, *Anno* 1649 being the time I engaged to meet my two comrades, Major Francis Morrison, and Major Richard Fox, in order to a full accomplishment of our purpose to seek our fortunes in Virginia, all parties very punctually appeared at the time and place assigned, and were all still in the same mind, fully bent to put in practice what we had so solemnly agreed upon, our inclinations that way being nothing abated, but were rather quickened, by the new changes that we saw in the state of things, and that very much for the worse. For if our spirits were somewhat depressed in contemplation of a barbarous restraint upon the person of our king in the Isle of Wight; to what horrors and despairs must our minds be reduced at the bloody and bitter stroke of his assassination, at his palace of Whitehall? . . .

It was about the 22d of October that we look leave of Fyal. We had store of black pigs for fresh meat, and I carried peaches without number. We parted with an easterly wind, a topsail gale, which soon brought us into a trade wind that favoured us at fifty or sixty leagues in twenty-four hours, till we came to the height of Bermudas. In that latitude it is the general observation of seamen, that the seas are rough, and the weather stormy. It was my fortune to have a curiosity to look out, when the officer on the watch shewed me a more than ordinary agitation of the sea in one particular place above the rest; which was the effect of what they call a spout, a raging in the bowels of the sea (like a violent birth) striving to break out, and at last springs up like a mine at land, with weight and force enough to have hoisted our ship out of her proper element, into the air (had the helm been for it) and to have made her do the supersalt; but God's providence secured us from that danger.

The sight of the island was welcome to all: the mariners learned thereby our true distance from Cape Hatteras; and the passengers were relieved with hopes to be soon at shore from a hungry pestered ship and company.

The gale continued fair till November 8: then we observed the

water changed; and having the lead, we had thirty-five fathom of water, which was joyful news; our want of all things necessary for human life, made it so.

Towards the break of day, weary of my lodging, I visited mate Putts on the watch, and would have treated him with brandy, but he refused that offer, unless I could also give him tobacco, which I had not. He said, it was near break of day, and he would look out to see what change there was in the water. No sooner were his feet upon the deck, but with stamps and noise he calls up the seamen, crying out, *All hands aloft! Breaches, breaches on both sides! All hands aloft!*

The seamen were soon on deck with this dismal alarm, and saw the cause thereof; but instead of applying their hands for their preservation (through a general despondency) they fell on their knees, commending their souls as at the last gasp. The captain

Plate 16 The *Royal Prince* As She Appeared In 1679, by Jan van Beecq (oil). A typical warship of the period still carrying a lateen sail on the mizen and heavily decorated with gingerbread. This period was the high peak of gilt decoration.

113 Shipbuilding at Porto San Stefano by Renier Nooms, called Zeeman (1623–c 1663) (oil).

NAVE REALE
D'INGHILTERRA,
NOMINATA
IL GRAN
CARLO

Descritta
Nel suo Atlante Veneto
Dal P. Cosmografo Coronelli
e Dedicata

came out at the noise to rectify what was amiss; but seeing how the case stood, his courage failed. Mate Putts (a stout seaman) took heart again, and cried out, 'Is there no good fellow that will stand to the helm, and loose a sail?' But of all the ship's crew there were but two foremast men that would be persuaded to obey commands, namely, Thomas Reasin and John Smith, men of innate courage, who, for their good resolution on that and divers other occasions in the various traverses of this voyage, deserve to have their names kept in lasting remembrance.

One of them got up and loosed the fore topsail, to put the ship (if possible) in steerage way, and under command; the other stood to the helm, and he shifted it in a nick of time; for the ship was at the point of dashing on the starboard breach: and although, in the rest of the voyage she was wont to be blamed for the ill quality of not feeling the helm, she did, in this important instance, redeem her credit, and fell round off for our rescue from that danger. But the sense of this escape lasted but a moment; for no sooner was she fallen from that breach, but another on the larboard bow was ready to receive her. The ships' crew, by this time (reproached by the courage of Reasin and Smith) were all at work; and the helm shifting opportunely, she fell off again as before. The light of the day (which now broke forth) did discover our condition to be altogether as perilous as possible; for we now saw ourselves surrounded with breaches; scarce any water like a channel appeared for a way to shun them. In this sad condition the ship struck ground, and raised such a war of water and sand together, which fell on the main chains, that now all hopes of safety were laid aside; but the ship being still afloat, and the seamen all of them now under command, nothing was omitted for our preservation that was in their power.

Tom Reasin, seeing the ship go ahead in the likeliest water for a channel, and ordering the helm accordingly, heaved the lead; and after a little further advance into that new channel, wholly against his hopes, he had a good deal of water more than the ship drew, which soon mended upon us, the next cast of the lead affording eighteen or twenty foot. We stood to this channel, and the light of the morning enabling the quartermasters to con the ship, we were by this miraculous mercy of God, soon clear of the breaches at Cape Hatteras, and got out to sea.

No sooner was the ship freed of this danger, and gotten a little into the offing, but the seamen (like so many spirits) surveyed each other, as if they doubted the reality of the thing, and shook hands like strangers, or men risen from the other world, and did scarce believe they were, what they seemed to be, men of flesh and blood. As they recovered force, they made what sail they could to stand to seaward.

The gale came fresh at north-west, and this fresh gale did soon grow up to a violent storm, which increased to so great a rigour, separating us from the land at the rate of eight leagues a watch, merely with our fore-courses, insomuch that the master thought it necessary to stop that career; and, in order thereunto, he did advise with his officers to bring the ship about, to furl all sails, and to try with the mizen.

The mountainous towering north-west seas that this storm made, were so unruly, that the seamen knew not how to work the ship about. We were already at a great distance from land, and something must be done to hinder our running off at that excessive rate. The first thing they did, was to lower the main-yard, to give some ease to that mast, by laying it on the ship's waist. Our great difficulty was, how to deal so with the fore-sails, that the ship might work about with safety, or at least with as little hazard as possible. All hands were too little to hale the sheet close, in order to bring the ship about. Many great seas were shipped as she came to work through the trough of the sea: amongst the rest one chanced to break upon the poop (where we were quartered) and that with so sad a weight, that we guessed a ton of water (at the least) did enter the tarpaulin, and set us all on float who were in the round-house. The noise it made by discharging itself in that manner, was like the report of a great gun, and did put us all into a horrible fright, which we could not soon shake off. This shock being past, the ship about, and our fore-sail handled, we now lay trying with our mizen.

I cannot forget the prodigious number of porpoises that did that evening appear about the ship, to the astonishment of the oldest seamen in her. They seemed to cover the surface of the sea as far as our eyes could discern; insomuch that a musket bullet, shot at random, could hardly fail to do execution on some of them. This the seamen would look upon as of bad portent, predicting ill weather; but in our case, who were in present possession of a storm, they appeared too late to gain the credit of foretelling what should come upon us in that kind.

The seas thus enraged, and all in foam, the gale still increasing upon us, the officers on the watch made frequent visits to the round-house, to prepare the captain for some evil encounter which this mighty tempest must bring forth: and their fears proved reasonable; for, about the hours of ten or eleven, our new disasters did begin with a crash from aloft. All hands were summoned up with loud cries, that the fore-topmast was come by the board, not alone, but in conjunction with the foremast head broken short off, just under the cap.

This was a sore business, and put all to their wits end to recover to any competent condition; what could be done was done to

114 The *Gran Carlo*, an imaginary ship, based on the *Sovereign of the Seas*. The intricacy and the beautifully combined balance of the full-rigged ship are admirably shown in this engraving.

prevent further mischiefs; but the whole trim and rigging of a ship depending much upon stays and tackle fixed to that mast, we had reason to expect greater ruins to follow, than what had already befallen us. Mate Putts was then on the watch, and did not want his apprehension of what did soon ensue, which in all likelihood was to end in our utter perdition; for about the hours of twelve or one at night, we heard and felt a mighty sea break on our fore-ship, which made such an inundation on the deck where the mate was walking, that he retired back with all diligence up to his knees in water, with short ejaculations of prayers in his mouth, supposing the ship was foundering, and at the last gasp. This looked like a stroke of death in every seaman's opinion: the ship stood stock still, with her head under water, seeming to bore her way into the sea. My two comrades and myself lay on our platform, sharing liberally in the general consternation. We took a short leave of each other, men, women, and children. All assaulted with the fresh terror of death, made a most dolorous outcry throughout the ship, whilst mate Putts perceiving the deck almost freed of water, called out aloud for hands to pump. This we thought a lightning before death, but gave me occasion (as having the best sea legs) to look out and learn the subject of this astonishing alarm, which proved to arise from no less cause than the loss of our forecastle, with six guns, and our anchors (all but one that was fastened to a cable) together with our two cooks, whereof one was recovered by a strange providence.

This great gap, made by want of our forecastle, did open a passage into the hold for other seas that should break there before a remedy was found out to carry them off, and this made our danger almost insuperable; but it fell out propitiously, that there were divers land-carpenter passengers, who were very helpful in this distress; and, in a little time, a slight platform of deal was tacked to the timbers, to carry off any ordinary sea in the present strait we were in; every moment of this growing tempest cutting out new work to employ all hands to labour.

The bowsprit, too top-heavy in itself, having lost all stays and rigging that should keep it steady, swayed to and fro with such bangs on the bows, that at no less rate than the cutting it close off, could the ship subsist.

All things were in miserable disorder, and it was evident our danger increased upon us: the stays of all the masts were gone, the shrouds that remained were loose and useless, and it was easy to foretell, our main-topmast would soon come by the board. Tom Reasin (who was always ready to expose himself) with an axe in his hand, ran up with speed to prevent that evil, hoping thereby to ease the main-mast, and preserve it; but the danger of his person in the enterprise, was so manifest, that he was called

down again; and no sooner was his foot upon the deck, but what was feared came to pass with a witness, both main and top-mast all came down together, and, in one shock, fell all to the windward clear into the sea, without hurt to any man's person.

Our main-mast thus fallen to the broadside, was like to incommode us more in the sea, than in her proper station; for the shrouds and rigging not losing the hold they had of the ship, every surge did so check the mast (whose butt-end lay charged to fall perpendicular on the ship's side) that it became a ram to batter and force the plank, and was doing the last execution upon us, if not prevented in time by edge-tools, which freed the ship from that unexpected assault and battery.

Abandoned in this manner to the fury of the raging sea, tossed up and down without any rigging to keep the ship steady, our seamen frequently fell overboard, without anyone regarding the loss of another, every man expecting the same fate, though in a different manner. The ceilings of this hulk (for it was no better) were for the same cause so uneasy, that, in many tumbles, the deck would touch the sea, and there stand still as if she would never make another. Our mizen mast only remained, by which we hoped to bring the ship about in proper season, which now lay stemming to the east.

In this posture did we pass the tenth and eleventh days of November; the twelfth in the morning we saw an English merchant, who showed his ensign, but would not speak with us, though the storm was abated, and the season more fit for communication. We imagined the reason was, because he would not be compelled to be civil to us: he thought our condition desperate, and we had more guns than he could resist, which might enable us to take what he would not sell or give. He shot a gun to leeward, stood his course, and turned his poop upon us.

Before we attempted to bring the ship about, it was necessary to refresh the seamen, who were almost worn out with toil and want of rest, having had no leisure of eating set meals for many days. The passengers, overcharged with excessive fears, had no appetite to eat; and (which was worst of all) both seamen and passengers were in a deplorable state as to the remaining victuals, all like to fall under extreme want; for the storm, by taking away the forecastle, having thrown much water into the hold, our stock of bread (the staff of life) was greatly damnified; and there remained no way to dress our meat, now that the cook-room was gone: the incessant tumbling of the ship (as has been observed) made all such cookery wholly impracticable. The only expedient to make fire betwixt decks, was, by sawing a cask in the middle, and filling it with ballast, which made a hearth to parch pease, and broil salt beef; nor could this be done but with great attendance,

115 Jonah and the Whale by
Pieter Mulier the Younger (1637–
1701) (oil), an evocative storm scene.
Although this rather splendid picture
has more drama than accuracy, the
long curved yard of the lateen
foresail is clearly illustrated

which was many times frustrated by being thrown topsy-turvy in spite of all circumspection, to the great defeat of empty stomachs.

The seas were much appeased the seventeeth day, and divers English ships saw, and were seen by us, but would not speak with us; only one, who kept the pump always going, for having tasted too liberally of the storm, he was so kind as to accost us. He lay by till our wherry (the only surviving boat that was left us) made him a visit. The master showed our men his leaks, and proposed that ours would spare him hands to pump in lieu of any thing he could spare for our relief. He promised however to keep us company, and give us a tow to help to weather the cape, if occasion offered; but that was only a copy of his countenance; for in the night we lost each other, and we never heard more of him, though he was bound to our port.

The weather now invited us to get the ship about with our mizen; and having done so, the next consideration was, how to make sail. The foremast, all this while (as much as was of it)

stood its ground: and as it was without dispute, that a yard must in the first place be fixed to it, so was it a matter of no small difficulty how to advance to the top of that greasy, slippery stump, since he that would attempt it, could take no hold himself, nor receive any help for his rise, by other hands. This was a case that put all the ship's crew to a nonplus; but Tom Reasin (a constant friend at need, that would not be baffled by any difficulty) showed by his countenance, he had a mind to try his skill to bring us out of this unhappy crisis. To encourage him the more, all passengers did promise and subscribe to reward his service, in Virginia, by tobacco, when God should enable us so to do. The proportions being set down, many were the more generous, because they never thought to see the place of payment, but expected to anticipate that by the payment of a greater debt to nature, which was like to be exacted every hour by an arrest of the merciless sea, which made small show of taking bail for our appearance in Virginia.

The manner of Tom Reasin's ascent to this important work, was thus. Among the scattered parcels of the ship's stores he had the luck to find about half a dozen iron spikes fit for his purpose. His first onset was to drive one of them into the mast, almost to the head, as high as he could reach; which being done, he took a rope of about ten foot long, and having threaded the same in a block or pulley, so as to divide it in the middle, he made both ends meet in a knot upon the spike, on both sides of the mast; so that the block falling on the contrary side, became a stirrup to mount upon for driving another spike in the same manner: and thus from step to step, observing the best advantage of striking with his hammer in the smoothest sea, he got aloft, drove cleats for shrouds, to rest upon, and was soon in a posture of receiving help from his comrades, who got a yard and sails (with other accommodation) such as could be had, and thus we were enabled, in few hours' time, to make some sail for our port.

The main-yard, that in the storm had been lowered to the waist to lie out of harm's way, was now preferred to the place of a main mast, and was accordingly fitted and accoutred, and grafted into the stump of what was left in the storm, some eight or ten foot from the deck. It was a hard matter to find out rigging answerable to that new-fashioned mast and yard; top-gallant sails and yards were most agreeable to this equipage, and was the best part of our remaining stores. The seas grew every moment smoother, and the weather more comfortable; so that for a while we began to shake off the visage of utter despair, as hoping ere long to see ourselves in some capacity to fetch the cape. We discovered another ship bound to Virginia, who as frankly promised to stand by us, the wind at N. N. W. We did what could be done by

a ship so mangled, to get the weather-gauge of the Cape Henry, conceiving ourselves to the southward of Cape Hatteras: but by taking an observation on a sunshine day, we found ourselves carried by a current we knew not of, to the windward, much beyond all our dead reckonings and allowances for sailing, insomuch that when we thought we had been to the southward of the cape, we found ourselves considerably shot to the north of Achomat, and that in the opinion of mate Putts, who was as our north star.

We passed this night with greater alacrity than we had done any other since we had left Fyal; for mate Putts, our trusty pilot, did confidently affirm, that, if the gale stood, there would be no question of our dining the next day within the capes. This was reasonable news, our water being long since spent, our meat spoiled (or useless) no kind of victuals remaining to sustain life, but a biscuit cake a day for a man; at which allowance there was not a quantity to hold out many days. In the dark time of the night, in tacking about, we lost our new comrade, and with much impatience we expected the approaching day; the wind N. W.

The morning appeared foggy, as the wind veered to the east, and that did cover and conceal the land from our clearer sight; howbeit we concluded by mate Putts' computation, we were well to the northward of the capes. Many times he would mount the mizen top for discovery, as the weather seemed to clear up, and would espy and point at certain hummocks of trees that used to be his several landmarks in most of the twenty-two voyages he had made to that plantation. Under this confidence he made more sail, the daylight confirming him in what he thought was right.

All the forenoon we lost the sight of land and marks by trees, by reason of the dark fogs and mists that were not yet dispelled; but as soon as the sun, with a north-west gale, had cleared all the coast (which was about the hours of two or three o'clock) mate Putts perceived his error from the deck, and was convinced, that the hummocks of trees he had seen and relied on for sure landmarks, had counter points to the south cape, which had misguided him; and that it was the opening of the bay which made the land at distance out of sight.

This fatal disappointment (which was now past human help) might have met an easy remedy, had our sails and rigging been in any tolerable condition to keep the windward gauge (for we had both the capes in our sight) but under our circumstances it was vain to endeavour such a thing; all our equipage, from stem to stern, being no better than that of a western barge, and we could not lie within eleven or twelve points of the wind.

Defeated thus of lively hopes we had the night before entertained

to sleep in warm beds with our friends in Virginia, it was a heavy spectacle to see ourselves running at a round rate from it, notwithstanding all that could be done to the contrary. Nothing was now to be heard but sighs and groans through all that wretched family, which must be soon reduced to so short allowance, as would just keep life and soul together. Half a biscuit cake a day to each (of which five whole ones made a pound) was all we had to trust to. Of liquors there remained none to quench thirst: Malaga sack was given plentifully to everyone, which served rather to inflame and increase thirst, than to extinguish it.

The gale blew fresh (as it used to do) towards night, and made a western sea that carried us off at a great rate. Mate Putts, extremely abashed to see his confidence so miserably deluded, grew sad and contemplative, even to the moving compassion in those whom his unhappy mistake had reduced to this misery. We cherished him the best we could, and would not have him so profoundly sad, for what was rather his misfortune than his fault.

The wind continued many days and nights to send us out into the ocean, insomuch that until we thought ourselves at least an hundred leagues from the capes, the north-west gale gave us no truce to consider what was best to do. All little helps were used by top-gallant sails, and masts placed where they could be fixed, to keep the windward gauge; but, for lack of bowlines and other tackle to keep them stiff to draw, every great head-sea would check them in the wind, and rend and tear them in pieces; so that it was an ordinary exercise with us to lie tumbling in the sea a watch or two together, driving to leeward, whilst the broken sails were in hand to be repaired.

It would be too great a trial of the reader's patience to be entertained with every circumstance of our sufferings in the remaining part of this voyage, which continued in great extremity for at least forty days from the time we left the land, our miseries increasing every hour: I shall therefore omit the greatest number of our ill encounters, which were frequently repeated on us, and remember only what has in my thoughts been most remarkable, and have made the deepest impression in my memory.

To give us a little breathing, about the nineteenth day the wind shifted to the east, but so little to our avail (the gale so gentle, and the seas made against us like a strong current) that, with the sail we were able to make, we could hardly reckon the ship shortened the way, but that she rather lost ground. In less than two watches the gale faced about; and if we saved our own by the change, it was all we could pretend unto.

Our mortal enemy, the north-west gale, began afresh to send us out to sea, and to raise our terrors to a higher pitch. One of

116 A 1657 chart of the southern part of Virginia. Unexplored inland areas are decorated with trees, representing forest, and with fanciful beasts.

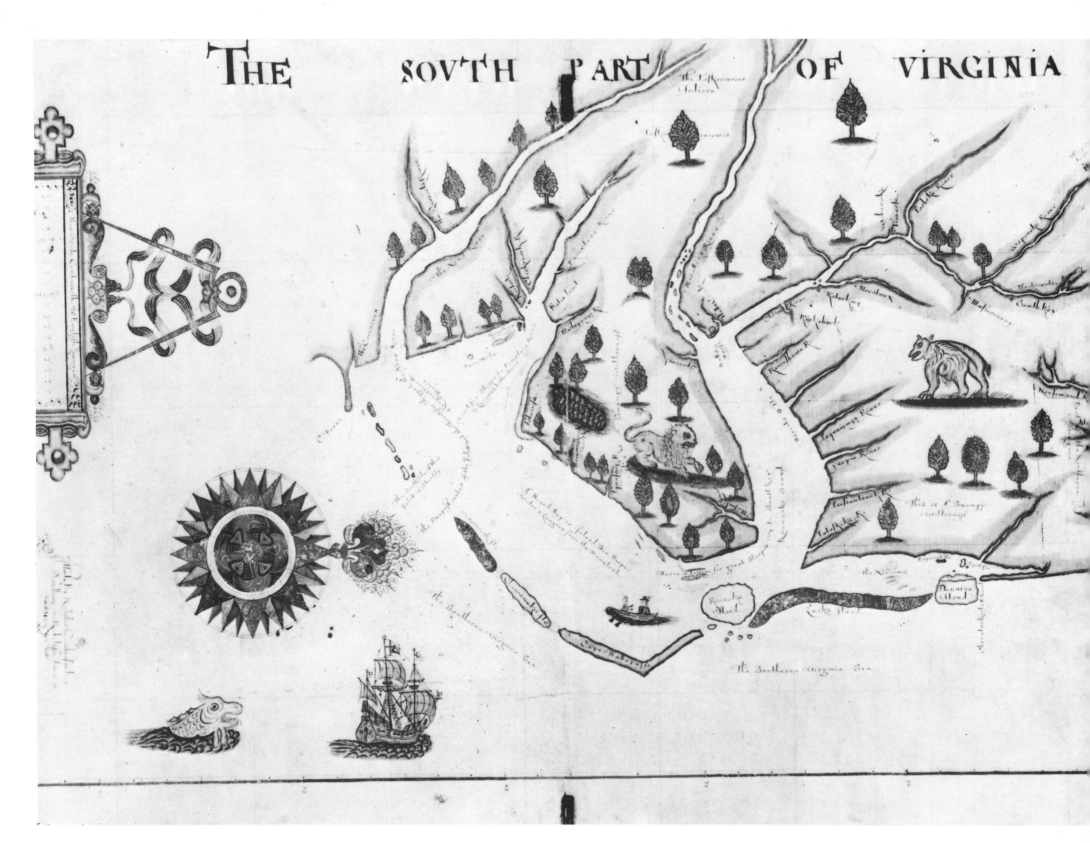

our pumps grew so unfixed, that it could not be repaired; the other was kept in perpetual motion; no man was excused to take his turn that had strength to perform it. Amongst the manifold perils that threatened every hour to be our last, we were in mortal apprehension, that the guns which were all aloft, would show us a slippery trick, and some of them break loose, the tackle that held them being grown very rotten: and it was another providence they held so long, considering how immoderately the ship rolled, especially when the sails were mending that should keep them steady, which was very near a third part of our time, whilst we plied to the windward with a contrary gale.

To prevent this danger which must befall when any one gun should get loose, mate Putts found an expedient by a more than ordinary smooth water; and by placing timber on the hatchway, to supply the place of shrouds, he got them safe in hold; which tended much to our good, not only in removing the present danger, but by making the ship (as seamen say) more wholesome, by having so great weight removed from her upper works into her centre, where ballast was much wanted.

But the intolerable want of all provisions, both of meat and drink, jostled the sense of this happiness soon out of our minds. And to aggravate our misery yet the more, it was now our interest to pray, that the contrary gale might stand; for whilst the westerly wind held, we had rain water to drink, whereas at east the wind blew dry.

In this miserable posture of ship and provision, we reckoned ourselves driven to the east, in less than week's time, at least two hundred leagues, which we despaired ever to recover without a miracle of divine mercy. The storm continued so fresh against us, that it confounded the most knowing of our ship's company in advising what course to take. Some reckoned the ship had made her way most southerly, and therefore counselled we should put ourselves in quest of the Bermudas islands, as to the nearest land we could hope to make: but that motion had great opposition in regard of the winter season, which would daily produce insuperable difficulties, and give greater puzzle in the discovery of it, than our circumstances would admit. Others would say, The furthest way about, in our case, would prove the nearest way home; and judged it best to take advantage of the westerly winds, and impetuous seas made to our hands, to attempt returning back to the western islands, as a thing more likely to succeed (though at a great distance) than thus to strive against the stream without any hopeful prospect of gaining the capes. But that motion met with a more general aversion, because the run was so long, that, though the gale had been in our own power to continue it, we could not have subsisted. Backwards we could not go, nor

forwards we could not go in the course we desired: it followed then of consequence, that we must take the middle way; and it was resolved, that, without further persisting in endeavouring to gain our port by a close haul, we should raise our tackle, and sail tardy for the first American land we could fetch, though we ran to the leeward as far as the coast of New England.

Whilst this determination was agreed and put in practice, the famine grew sharp upon us. Women and children made dismal cries and grievous complaints. The infinite number of rats that all the voyage had been our plague, we now were glad to make our prey to feed on; and as they were ensnared and taken, a well grown rat was sold for sixteen shillings as a market rate. Nay, before the voyage did end (as I was credibly informed) a woman great with child offered twenty shillings for a rat, which the proprietor refusing, the woman died.

Many sorrowful days and nights we spun out in this manner, till the blessed feast of Christmas came upon us, which we began with a very melancholy solemnity; and yet, to make some distinction of times, the scrapings of the meal-tubs were all amassed together to compose a pudding. Malaga sack, sea water, with fruit and spice, all well fried in oil, were the ingredients of this regale, which raised some envy in the spectators; but allowing some privilege to the captain's mess, we met no obstruction, but did peaceably enjoy our Christmas pudding.

My greatest impatience was of thirst, and my dreams were all of cellars, and taps running down my throat, which made my waking much the worse by that tantalizing fancy. Some relief I found very real by the captain's favour in allowing me a share of some butts of small claret he had concealed in a private cellar . . . It wanted a mixture of water for qualifying it to quench thirst; however, it was a present remedy, and a great refreshment to me.

I cannot forget another instance of the captain's kindness to me, of a like obligation. He singled me out one day to go with him into the hold to seek fresh water in the bottoms of the empty casks. With much ado we got a quantity to satisfy our longing, though for the thickness thereof it was not palatable. We were now each of us astride on a butt of Malaga, which gave the captain occasion to taste of their contents. We tasted and tasted it again; and though the total we drank was not considerable, yet it had an effect on our heads that made us suspend (though we could not forget) our wants of water. The operation this little debauch had upon the captain, was very different from what it wrought on me, who felt myself refreshed as with a cordial; but the poor captain fell to contemplate (as it better became him) our sad condition; and being troubled in mind for having brought so many wretched souls into misery, by a false confidence he gave

Plate 17 The Battle of the Texel, 1673, by W. van de Velde the Younger, showing Cornelis Tromp's flagship, the *Gouden Leeuw* (Golden Lion) in the foreground, engaged with the *Royal Prince*. This was the last battle of the third Anglo-Dutch war, when De Ruyter drove off the allied English and French fleet from the Dutch coast.

them of his having a good ship, which he now thought would prove their ruin; and being conscious, that their loss would lie all at his door, it was no easy matter to appease his troubled thoughts. He made me a particular compliment for having engaged me and my friends in the same bottom, and upon that burst into tears. I comforted him the best I could, and told him, We must all submit to the hand of God, and rely on his goodness, hoping, that the same providence which had hitherto so miraculously preserved us, would still be continued in our favour till we were in safety. We retired obscurely to our friends, who had been wondering at our absence.

The westerly wind continued to shorten our way to the shore, though very distant from our port; but this did not at all incline us to change our resolution of sailing large for the first land; it did rather animate and support us in our present disasters of hunger and thirst, toil and fatigue. The hopes of touching land was food and raiment to us.

In this wearisome expectation we passed our time for eight or nine days and nights, and then we saw the water change colour, and had soundings. We approached the shore the night of January 3d with little sail; and, as the morning of the fourth day gave us light, we saw the land; but in what latitude we could not tell, for that the officers, whose duty it was to keep the reckoning of the ship, had for many days past totally omitted that part; nor had we seen the sun a great while, to take observations, which (though a lame excuse) was all they had to say for that omission. But in truth it was evident, that the desperate state of the ship, and hourly jeopardy of life did make them careless of keeping either log or journal; the thoughts of another account they feared to be at hand, did make them neglect that of the ship as inconsiderable.

About the hours of three or four in the afternoon of the twelfth eve, we were shot in fair to the shore. The evening was clear and calm, the water smooth; the land we saw nearest was some six or seven English miles distant from us, our soundings twenty-five fathoms in good ground for anchor-hold.

These invitations were all attractive to encourage the generality (especially the passengers) to execute what we had resolved on for the shore: but one old officer who was husband for the ship's stores whilst there were any, would not consent on any terms to trust the only anchor that was left us for preservation, out of his sight at sea. His arguments to back his opinion were plausible; as, first, the hazard of losing that only anchor by any sudden storm, bringing with it a necessity to cut or slip, on which every life depended. Secondly, the shortness of the cable, very unfit for anchorage in the ocean: And thirdly, the weakness of the ship's crew, many dead and fallen overboard, and the passengers weakened by hunger, dying every day on the decks, or at the pump, which with great difficulty was kept going, but must not rest.

Against the old man's reasonings was urged the very small remains of biscuit, at our short allowance, which would hardly hold a week; the assurance of our loss by famine if we should be forced to sea again by a north-west storm, and the great possibility of finding a harbour to save our ship, with our lives and goods, in some creek on the coast. These last reasons prevailed upon the majority against all negatives: and when the anchor was let loose, mate Putts was ordered to make the first discovery of what we might expect from the nearest land. He took with him twelve sickly passengers, who fancied the shore would cure them; and he carried Major Morrison on shore with him in pursuit of such adventures as are next in course to be related; for according to the intelligence that could be got from land, we were to take our measures at sea, either to proceed on in our voyage in that sad condition that has been in some proportion set forth, or to land ourselves, and unload the ship, and try our fortunes amongst the Indians.

In four or five hours time we could discover the boat returning with mate Putts alone for a setter, which we looked upon as a signal of happy success. When he came on board his mouth was full of good tidings, as namely, that he discovered a creek that would harbour our ship, and that there was a depth of water on the bar, sufficient for her draught when she was light. That there was excellent fresh water, (a taste whereof Major Morrison had sent me in a bottle.) That the shore swarmed with fowl, and that Major Morrison stayed behind in expectation of the whole ship's company to follow.

I opened mine ears wide to the motion, and promoted the design of our landing there with all the rhetoric and interest I had. The captain was no less forward for it, hoping thereby to save the lives of the passengers that remained: and that he might not wholly rely on mate Putts's judgement in a matter wherein he was most concerned, he embarked with me in the wherry, with a kinsman of his, and some others; and the seamen were glad of my help to put the boat to shore, my hands having been very well seasoned at the pump, by taking my turn for many weeks at the rate of three hours in twenty four. My passionate desires to be on shore at the fountain head to drink without stint, did not a little quicken me, insomuch that the six or seven miles I rowed on this occasion, were no more than the breadth of the Thames at London, at another time, would have been toilsome to me.

As soon as I had set my foot on land, and had rendered thanks to almighty God for opening this door of deliverance to us,

Plate 18 The Hamburg whaler *Die Sonne*, 1680 by F. Stuhr. This appears to have been built in the style of a Dutch fluyt ship. A stage is hung over the side for the men who are cutting up the whale.

117 The Dutch ship *Kampveere* by
W. van de Velde the Elder, *c.* 1664.

after so many rescues even from the jaws of death at sea, Major Morrison was pleased to oblige me beyond all requital, in conducting me to the running stream of water, where, without any limitation of short allowance, I might drink my fill. I was glad of so great liberty, and made use of it accordingly, by prostrating myself on my belly, and setting my mouth against the stream, that it might run into my thirsty stomach without stop. The rest of the company were at liberty to use their own methods to quench their thirst; but this I thought the greatest pleasure I ever enjoyed on earth.

After this sweet refreshment, the captain, myself, and his kinsman crossed the creek in our wherry, invited thither by the cackling of wild-fowl. The captain had a gun charged, and the moon shining bright in his favour, he killed one duck of the flock that flew over us, which was roasted on a stick out of hand by the seamen, whilst we walked on the shore of the creek for further discovery.

In passing a small gullet we trod on an oyster bank that did happily furnish us with a good addition to our duck. When the cooks had done their parts, we were not long about ours, but fell on without using the ceremony of calling the rest of our company, which would have been no entertainment to so many, the proverb telling us, *The fewer the better cheer*. The bones, head, legs, and inwards were agreed to be the cook's fees; so we gave God thanks, and returned to our friends, without making boast of our good fortunes.

Fortified with this repast, we informed ourselves of the depth of water at the bar of the creek, in which the captain seemed satisfied, and made shows in all his deportment, of his resolution to discharge the ship there in order to our safety. Towards break of day he asked me in my ear, If I would go back with him on board the ship? I told him, No, because it would be labour lost, in case he would persist in his resolution to do what he pretended, which he ratified again by protestations, and so went off with his kinsman, who had a large coarse cloth gown I borrowed of him to shelter me from the sharpest cold I ever felt.

No sooner had the captain cleared himself of the shore but the daybreak made me see my error in not closing with his motion in my ear. The first object we saw at sea was the ship under sail, standing for the capes with what canvas could be made to serve the turn. It was a very heavy prospect to us who remained (we knew not where) on shore, to see ourselves thus abandoned by the ship, and more, to be forsaken by the boat, so contrary to our mutual agreement. Many hours of hard labour and toil were spent before the boat could fetch the ship: and the seamen (whose act it was to set sail without the captain's order, as we were told

after) cared not for the boat while the wind was large to carry them to the capes. But mate Putts, who was more sober and better natured, discovering the boat from the mizen-top, lay by till she came with the captain on board.

from *A Collection of Voyages*, ed. A. and J. Churchill, 1732.

Worms of several sorts

The external beauty of a sailing ship is apt to banish from the mind thoughts of the revolting conditions in which her people often lived. Even the very real perils of the sea in those days before seas were well charted or the chronometer had come to the aid of navigation, seem to fade . . .

Gemelli was an Italian priest who sailed round the world as a passenger out of curiosity and wrote an account dated 1697. Here he is experiencing the eastward Pacific crossing, from the Philippines to Mexico.

The poor people stowed in the cabins of the galleon bound towards the Land of Promise of New Spain, endure no less hardships than the children of Israel did, when they went from Egypt towards Palestine. There is hunger, thirst, sickness, cold, continual watching, and other sufferings; besides the terrible shocks from side to side, caused by the furious beating of the waves. I may further say they endure all the plagues God sent upon Pharaoh to soften his hard heart; for if he was infected with leprosy, the galleon is never clear of a universal raging itch, as an addition to all other miseries. If the air then was filled with gnats; the ship swarms with little vermin, the Spaniards call *Gorgojos*, bred in the biscuit; so swift that they in a short time not only run over cabins, beds, and the very dishes the men eat on, but insensibly fasten upon the body. Instead of the locusts, there are several other sorts of vermin of sundry colours, that suck the blood. Abundance of flies fall into the dishes of broth, in which there also swim worms of several sorts . . . I had a good share in these misfortunes; for the boatswain, with whom I had agreed for my diet, as he had fowls at his table the first days, so when we were out at sea he made me fast after the Armenian manner, having banished from his table all wine, oil and vinegar; dressing his fish with fair water and salt. Upon flesh days he gave me *Tassajos Fritos*, that is, steaks of beef or buffalo, dried in the sun or wind, which are so hard that it is impossible to eat them, without they are first well beaten like stockfish; nor is there any digesting them without the help of a purge. At dinner another piece of that same sticky flesh was boiled without any other sauce but its own hardness, and fair water. At last he deprived me of the satisfaction of gnawing a good biscuit, because he would spend no more of his own, but laid the king's allowance on the table; in every mouthful whereof there went down abundance of maggots and *Gorgojos* chewed and bruised. On fish days the common diet was old rank fish boiled in fair water and salt; at noon we had *Mongos*, something like kidney beans, in which there were so many maggots, that they swam at top of the broth, and the quantity was so great, that besides the loathing they caused, I doubted whether the dinner was fish or flesh. This bitter fare was sweetened after dinner with a little water and sugar; yet the allowance was but a small cocoa shell full, which rather increased than quenched drought . . . Abundance of poor sailors fell sick, being exposed to the continual rains, cold, and other hardships of the season; yet they were not allowed to taste of the good biscuit, rice, fowls, Spanish bread and sweetmeats, put into the custody of the master by the king's order, to be distributed among the sick; for the honest master spent all at his own table. Notwithstanding the dreadful sufferings

in this prodigious voyage, yet the desire of gain prevails with many to venture through it, four, six, and some ten times. The very sailors, though they forswear the voyage when out at sea; yet when they come to Acapulco, for the lucre of two hundred seventy-five pieces of eight, the king allows them for the return, never remember past sufferings; like women after their labour. The whole pay is three hundred and fifty pieces of eight; but they have only seventy-five paid them at Cavite, when they are bound for America; for if they had half, very few would return to the Philippine Islands for the rest. The merchants, there is no doubt, get by this voyage, an hundred and fifty, or two hundred per cent and factors have nine in the hundred, which in two or three hundred thousand pieces of eight amounts to money. And indeed it is a great satisfaction to return home in less than a year with seventeen or eighteen thousand pieces of eight clear gains, besides a man's own venture; a sum that may make a man easy as long as he lives.

Captain Emanuel Arguelles told me, that he without having any employment, should clear to himself that voyage by commissions twenty-five or thirty thousand pieces of eight. It was reckoned the pilot would make twenty thousand pieces of eight; his mates nine thousand each. The captain of the galleon forty thousand. The master, his mate, and boatswain, who may put aboard several bales of goods, may make themselves rich in one voyage. He that borrows money at fifty per cent may get as much more, without standing to the hazard of losses. The extraordinary gains induce many to expose themselves to so many dangers and miseries. For my own part, these or greater hopes shall not prevail with me to undertake that voyage again, which is enough to destroy a man, or make him unfit for anything as long as he lives. I have made this digression, to show the reader through what thorns men must venture to come at the so much coveted roses of riches. The Spaniards and other geographers, have given this the name of the Pacific Sea, as may be seen in the maps; but it does not suit with its tempestuous and dreadful motion, for which it ought rather to be called the Restless. But the truth is, the Spaniards gave it this fine name in sailing from Acapulco to the Philippine Islands, which is performed very easily in three months, without any boisterous motion in the sea, and always before the wind, as was said before.

from *A Collection of Voyages*, ed. A. and J. Churchill, 1732.

Caress and humour them

Even the hardships endured by sailors, officers and passengers in the seventeenth and eighteenth centuries were insignificant compared with the sufferings of the slaves, shipped from Africa and packed as tightly as the owners could cram them in the stinking holds for the long voyages to the markets of the West Indies and America. Many writers have commented on the musty, miasmic stench that trailed behind these slave ships. It took forty-eight years of campaigning, from 1759 to 1807, to make the slave trade illegal in British law. Here is the voice of one Barbot, from the early eighteenth century, which some may find an interesting self-exposure of a certain type of 'liberal' mentality.

As to the management of our slaves aboard, we lodge the two sexes apart, by means of a strong partition at the main mast; the forepart is for men, the other behind the mast for the women. If it be in large ships carrying five or six hundred slaves, the deck in such ships ought to be at least five and a half or six foot high, which is very requisite for driving a continual trade of slaves: for the greater height it has, the more airy and convenient it is for such a considerable number of human creatures; and consequently far the more healthy for them, and fitter to look after them. We build a sort of half-decks along the sides with deals and spars provided for that purpose in Europe, that half-deck extending no farther than the sides of our scuttles, and so the slaves lie in two rows, one above the other, and as close together as they can be crowded.

The Dutch company's ships exceed all other Europeans in such accommodations, being commonly built designedly for those voyages, and consequently contrived very wide, lofty, and airy, betwixt decks, with gratings and scuttles, which can be covered with tarpaulins in wet weather; and in fair uncovered, to let in the more air. Some also have made small ports, or lights along the sides at proper distances, well secured with thick iron bars, which they open from time to time for the air; and that very much contributes to the preservation of those poor wretches, who are so thick crowded together.

The Portuguese of Angola, a people in many respects not to be compared to the English, Dutch or French, in point of neatness aboard their ships, though indeed some French and English ships in those voyages for slaves are slovenly, foul, and stinking, according to the temper and the want of skill of the commanders; the Portuguese, I say, are commendable in that they bring along with them to the coast, a sufficient quantity of coarse thick mats, to serve as bedding under the slaves aboard, and shift them every fortnight or three weeks with such fresh mats: which, besides that it is softer for the poor wretches to lie upon than the bare deals or

decks, must also be much healthier for them, because the planks, or deals, contract some dampness more or less, either from the deck being so often washed to keep it clean and sweet, or from the rain that gets in now and then through the scuttles or other openings, and even from the very sweat of the slaves; which being so crowded in a low place, is perpetual, and occasions many distempers, or at best great inconveniencies dangerous to their health: whereas, lying on mats, and shifting them from time to time, must be much more convenient; and it would be prudent to imitate the Portuguese in this point, the charge of such mats being inconsiderable.

We are very nice in keeping the places where the slaves lie clean and neat, appointing some of the ship's crew to do that office constantly, and several of the slaves themselves to be assistant to them in that employment; and thrice a week we perfume betwixt decks with a quantity of good vinegar in pails, and red-hot iron bullets in them, to expel the bad air, after the place has been well washed and scrubbed with brooms: after which, the deck is cleaned with cold vinegar, and in the daytime, in good weather, we leave all the scuttles open, and shut them again at night.

It has been observed before, that some slaves fancy they are carried to be eaten, which makes them desperate; and others are so on account of their captivity: so that if care be not taken, they will mutiny and destroy the ship's crew in hopes to get away.

To prevent such misfortunes, we use to visit them daily, narrowly searching every corner between decks, to see whether they have not found means, to gather any pieces of iron, or wood, or knives, about the ship, notwithstanding the great care we take not to leave any tools or nails, or other things in the way: which, however, cannot be always so exactly observed, where so many people are in the narrow compass of a ship.

We cause as many of our men as is convenient to lie in the quarter-deck and gunroom, and our principal officers in the great cabin, where we keep all our small arms in a readiness, with sentinels constantly at the door and avenues to it; being thus ready to disappoint any attempts our slaves might make on a sudden.

These precautions contribute very much to keep them in awe; and if all those who carry slaves duly observed them, we should not hear of so many revolts as have happened. Where I was concerned, we always kept our slaves in such order, that we did not perceive the least inclination in any of them to revolt, or mutiny, and lost very few of our number in the voyage.

It is true, we allowed them much more liberty, and used them with more tenderness than most other Europeans would think prudent to do; as, to have them all upon deck every day in good

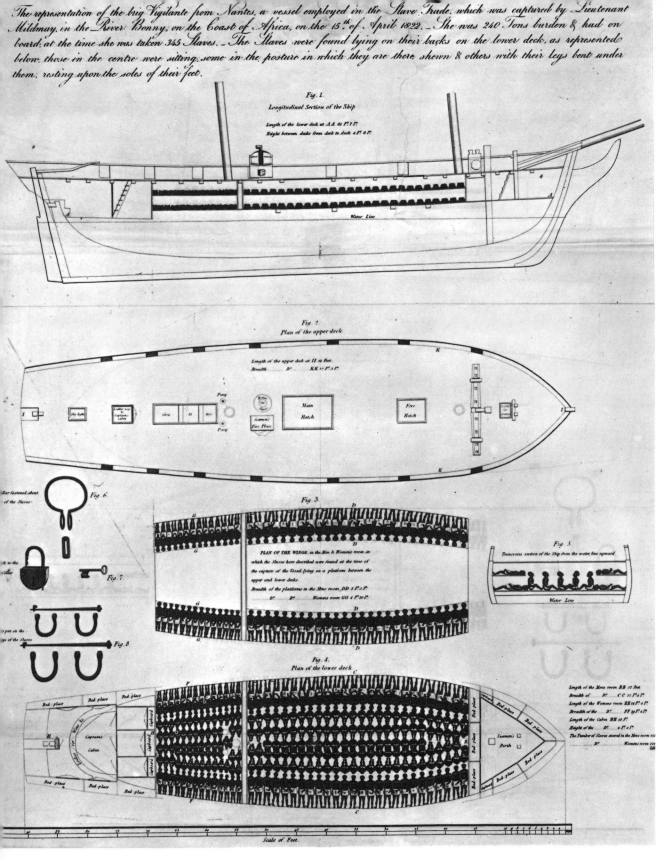

The representation of the brig Vigilante from Nantes, a vessel employed in the Slave Trade, which was captured by Lieutenant Mildmay, in the River Bonny, on the Coast of Africa, on the 15th of April 1822. — She was 240 Tons burden & had on board, at the time she was taken 345 Slaves. — The Slaves were found lying on their backs on the lower deck, as represented below; those in the centre were sitting; some in the posture in which they are there shewn & others with their legs bent under them, resting upon the soles of their feet.

weather; to take their meals twice a day, at fixed hours, that is, at ten in the morning, and at five at night; which being ended, we made the men go down again between decks: for the women were almost entirely at their own discretion, to be upon deck as long as they pleased, nay even many of the males had the same liberty by turns, successively; few or none being fettered or kept in shackles, and that only on account of some disturbances, or injuries offered to their fellow-captives, as will unavoidably happen among a numerous crowd of such savage people. Besides, we allowed each of them betwixt their meals a handful of Indian wheat and mandioca, and now and then short pipes and tobacco to smoke upon deck by turns, and some coco-nuts; and to the women a piece of coarse cloth to cover them, and the same to many of the men, which we took care they did wash from time to time, to prevent vermin, which they are very subject to; and because it looked sweeter and more agreeable. Towards the evening they diverted themselves on the deck, as they thought fit, some conversing together, others dancing, singing, and sporting after their manner, which pleased them highly, and often made us pastime; especially the female sex, who being apart from the males, on the quarter-deck, and many of them young sprightly maidens, full of jollity and good humour, afforded us abundance of recreation; as did several little fine boys, which we mostly kept to attend on us about the ship.

We messed the slaves twice a day, as I have observed; the first meal was of our large beans boiled, with a certain quantity of Muscovy lard, which we have from Holland, well packed up in casks. The beans we have in great plenty at Rochel. The other meal was of peas, or of Indian wheat, and sometimes meal of mandioca; this provided in Prince's Island, the Indian wheat at the Gold Coast; boiled with either lard, or suet, or grease, by turns: and sometimes with palm-oil and malaguette or Guinea pepper. I found they had much better stomachs for beans, and it is proper fattening food for captives; in my opinion far better to maintain them well, than Indian wheat, mandioca or yams; though the Calabar slaves value this root above any other food, as being used to it in their own country: but it is not at certain times of the year to be had in so great a quantity as is requisite to subsist such a number of people for several months; besides that they are apt to decay, and even to putrify as they grow old. Horse-beans are also very proper for slaves in lieu of large beans: there is good plenty of them in Great Britain, which, as well as the other beans, will keep, if well put up in dry vats or casks.

We distributed them by ten in a mess, about a small flat tub, made for that use by our coopers, in which their victuals were served; each slave having a little wooden spoon to feed himself handsomely, and more cleanly than with their fingers, and they were well pleased with it.

At each meal we allowed every slave a full coco-nut shell of water, and from time to time a dram of brandy, to strengthen their stomachs.

The Dutch commonly feed their slaves three times a day, with indifferent good victuals, and much better than they eat in their own country. The Portuguese feed them most with mandioca.

As for the sick and wounded, or those out of order, our surgeons, in their daily visits betwixt decks, finding any indisposed, caused them to be carried to the Lazaretto, under the forecastle, a room reserved for a sort of hospital, where they were carefully looked after. Being out of the crowd, the surgeons had more conveniency and time to administer proper remedies; which they cannot do leisurely between decks, because of the great heat that is there continually, which is sometimes so excessive, that the surgeons would faint away, and the candles would not burn; besides, that in such a crowd of brutish people, there are always some very apt to annoy and hurt others, and all in general so greedy, that they will snatch from the sick slaves the fresh meat or liquor that is given them. It is no way advisable to put the sick slaves into the long-boat upon deck, as was very imprudently done in the *Albion* frigate, spoken of in the description of New Calabar; for they being thus exposed in the open air, and coming out of the excessive hot hold, and lying there in the cool of the nights, for some time just under the fall of the wind from the sails, were soon taken so ill of violent cholics and blood fluxes, that in a few days they died, and the owners lost above three hundred slaves in the passage from St Tome to Barbados; and the two hundred and fifty that survived, were like skeletons, one half of them not yielding above four pounds a head there: an oversight, by which fifty per cent of the stock or outset was lost.

Much more might be said relating to the preservation and maintenance of slaves in such voyages, which I leave to the prudence of the officers that govern aboard, if they value their own reputation and their owner's advantage; and shall only add these few particulars, that though we ought to be circumspect in watching the slaves narrowly, to prevent or disappoint their ill designs for our own conservation, yet must we not be too severe and haughty with them, but on the contrary, caress and humour them in every reasonable thing. Some commanders, of a morose peevish temper are perpetually beating and curbing them, even without the least offence, and will not suffer any upon deck but when unavoidable necessity to ease themselves does require; under pretence it hinders the work of the ship and sailors, and that they are troublesome by their nasty nauseous stench, or their noise: which makes those poor wretches desperate, and besides their falling into distempers through melancholy, often is the occasion of their destroying themselves.

from *A Collection of Voyages*, ed. A. and J. Churchill, 1732.

A naval hero

Jean-Bart (*c.* 1650–1702) came of a family of merchant captains in Dunquerque. Serving against the Dutch and English from an early age, he distinguished himself as a privateer and blockade runner, bringing a vital grain fleet safely into Dunquerque. Noticed by Louis XIV, he was given command of a squadron and became one of France's greatest naval heroes. One of his many daring exploits was an escape from prison in Plymouth, at which time he rowed across the English Channel. Here is another . . .

While Jean-Bart was at Bergen an Englishman in command of two ships landed there, and going to a public place where foreigners were wont to resort for refreshment, perceived a man whose proud and resolute mien, whose tall and robust stature impressed him. Hearing him speak English without the least difficulty, he was curious to know who the man was, and asking, was told that he was Jean-Bart. 'That is the name of a man I seek,' said he. 'This is no other than he,' he was told.

The Englishman began a conversation with Jean-Bart and after a brief exchange, said that he was seeking him, that he longed to engage him in battle. 'That is simple enough,' replied Jean-Bart. 'I am in need of munitions and shall sail as soon as I have received them.'

'I shall be waiting for you,' replied the Englishman. Learning that a ship which had sailed from Brest to bring him supplies had been captured, Jean-Bart sold one of his prizes to buy munitions.

Having made all preparations for his departure, he informed the English captain that he would set sail the following day. The Englishman replied that they would fight when they were in the open sea, but being in a neutral port they ought to treat each other with friendship; he therefore invited him to take refreshment the next day aboard his ship before leaving. 'When two enemies like you and me meet,' replied Jean-Bart, 'our refreshment should be of cannon shots and blows of the sword!'

The English captain insisted. Jean-Bart was brave, therefore incapable of base guile. Judging the captain's heart by his own,

119 The slave trade persisted well into the nineteenth century, long after the principal governments of the world had declared it illegal.
The brig *Vigilante* from Nantes was captured in 1822 off the coast of Africa. On board were found 345 slaves—225 men and 120 women—appallingly crowded into the lower deck and on platforms between the upper and lower decks, as shown in the diagram opposite, on which the iron collars fastened round the necks of the slaves and the fetters put on their arms and legs may also be seen.

he accepted his invitation and came aboard his ship. Having taken a glass of spirits and smoked a pipe, he said to the English captain: 'It is time to leave.' 'You are my prisoner,' replied the Englishman. 'I have made a promise that I shall capture you and take you back to England.'

Jean-Bart turned upon him a look which spoke his indignation and contempt. Lighting his slow-match, with a shout of 'To me!' he knocked down a number of English who were on the deck and cried: 'No! I shall never be your prisoner! The ship shall blow up first!' Holding the lighted slow-match, he hurled himself towards a barrel of gunpowder which by chance had been brought out of the powder room. Seeing themselves near the point of death, all the English crew were seized with terror. The Frenchmen in Jean-Bart's ships had heard his call. Quickly taking to their boats, they climbed aboard the ship where he was, hacked some of the English to pieces, took the remainder prisoner and captured the ship. In vain did the English captain protest. that he was in a neutral port; Jean-Bart carried him away to Dunquerque, leaving in the port of Bergen the other English ship which was not a party to the captain's treachery.

from *Vies des Plus Célèbres Marins, Tome VIII: Jean-Bart*, by A. Richer, Paris 1789.

120 Jean-Bart at Bergen. 'I shall never be your prisoner!'

Blackbeard the pirate

From wartime privateer to peacetime pirate was often a small step, the same qualities being adulated in the one and condemned in the other. Of all the pirates who haunted the coast of America, even until the mid-nineteenth century, Captain Teach or Thatch was the most notorious, at a time (the early eighteenth century) when piracy was at its worst. The account of him here, written under the pseudonym of Captain Charles Johnson, may possibly be by Daniel Defoe.

Edward Thatch (commonly called Blackbeard) was born in Jamaica, and was from a boy bred up to the sea; in the late war he sailed for the most part in privateers, yet, though he had often distinguished himself for his uncommon boldness, and personal courage, he was never raised to any command. The first of his going upon the pirating account, was with Major Bonnet, a gentleman of Barbados, worth £500 a year real estate, who being, as 'tis supposed a little distracted, fitted out a sloop from that island, to become a pirate, as has been taken notice of in his Life. With him Thatch shipped himself as a fore-mast man; the pirates soon found Major Bonnet to be a person unfit for this condition of life; and though the sloop was his own, yet they deposed him from the command, and by common consent, placed this Thatch in his room.

We have already given an account of the piracies of Thatch, to the time of his parting with Major Bonnet, which was, when he lost his ship in Topsail Inlet, in North Carolina, where some of his men were drowned, and others dispersed about the country; after which, he, and twenty or thirty more of the crew, went up to Bath-Town, and surrendered to His Majesty's mercy, as offered by proclamation, and they all received certificates from His Excellency Charles Eden, Esq; governor of that province. It did not appear that their submitting to this proclamation, was from any reformation of manners, but only to wait a more favourable opportunity to play the same game over again; which he soon after effected, with greater security to himself, and with much better prospect of success, having in this time cultivated a very good understanding with the governor above mentioned.

The first piece of service this kind governor did to Blackbeard, was, to give him a right to the vessel which he had taken, when he was a-pirating in the great ship, called the *Queen Ann's Revenge*, for which purpose, a Court of Vice-Admiralty was held at Bath-Town; and, though Thatch had never any Commission in his life, and the sloop belonging to the English merchants, and taken in time of peace; yet was she condemned as a prize taken from the

121 Blackbeard the Pirate.

Spaniards, by the said Thatch. These proceedings show that governors are but men.

Before he sailed upon his adventures, he married a young creature, of about sixteen years of age, the governor performing the ceremony. As it is a custom to marry here by a priest, so it is there by a magistrate; and this, as I have been informed, made Thatch's fourteenth wife, whereof, about a dozen might be still living. His behaviour in this state, was something extraordinary; for, while his sloop lay in Okerecock Inlet; and he ashore at a plantation, where his wife lived, with whom, after he had lain all night, it was his custom to invite five or six of his brutal companions to come ashore, and he would force her to prostitute herself to them all, one after another, before his face.

In June 1718, he went to sea, upon his second expedition, and steered his course towards Bermuda; he met with two or three English vessels in his way, but robbed them only of provisions, stores, and other necessaries, for his present expense; but, near the island aforementioned, he fell in with two French ships, one of them was loaden with sugar, and cocoa, and the other light, both bound to Martinico; the ship that had no lading, he let go, and putting all the men of the loaded ship aboard her, Thatch brought home the other with her cargo, to North Carolina, where the governor and the pirates shared the plunder.

When Thatch and his prize arrived, he and four of his crew, went to His Excellency, and made affidavit, that they found the French ship at sea, without a soul on board her; and then a court was called, and the ship condemned. The governor had sixty hogsheads of sugar for his dividend, and one Mr Knight, who was his secretary, and collector of the province, twenty, and the rest was shared among the other pirates.

The business was not yet done, the ship remained, and it was possible, one or other might come into the river, that might be acquainted with her, and so discover the roguery; but Thatch, thought of a contrivance to prevent this, for, upon a pretence that she was leaky, and that she might sink, and so stop up the mouth of the inlet, or cove, where she lay, he obtained an order from the governor, to bring her out into the river, and set her on fire, which was accordingly executed, and she was burnt down to the water's edge, and her bottom sunk, and with it, their fears of her ever rising in judgment against them.

Captain Thatch, alias Blackbeard, passed three or four months in the river, sometimes lying at anchor in the coves, at other times, sailing from one inlet to another, trading with such sloops as he met, for all things he wanted, whether provisions, or stores, and giving them something else in exchange, that is, when he happened to be in a giving humour; at other times he made bold with them,

and took what he liked, without saying, by your leave, knowing well, they dare not send him in a bill for the payment. He often diverted himself with going ashore among the planters, where he revelled night and day: by these he was well received, but whether out of love or fear, I cannot say; sometimes he used them courteously enough, and made them presents of rum, and sugar, in recompense of what he took from them; but, as for liberties (which 'tis said) he and his companions often took with the wives and daughters of the planters, I cannot take upon me to say, whether he paid them *ad Valorem*, or no. At other times he carried it in a lordly manner towards them, and would lay some of them under contribution; nay, he often proceeded to bully the governor, not, that I can discover the least cause of quarrel betwixt them, but it seemed only to be done, to show he dare do it.

The sloops trading up and down this river, being so frequently pillaged by Blackbeard, consulted with the traders, and some of the best of the planters, what course to take; they saw plainly it would be in vain to make any application to the governor of North Carolina, to whom it properly belonged, to find some redress; so that if they could not be relieved from some other quarter, Blackbeard would be like to reign with impunity; therefore, with as much secrecy as possible, they sent a deputation to Virginia, to lay the affair before the governor of that colony, and to solicit an armed force, from the men-of-war lying there, to take this pirate.

This governor consulted with the captains of the two men-of-war, *viz* the *Pearl*, and *Lime*, who had lain in St James's River, about ten months. It was agreed that the governor should hire a couple of small sloops, and the men-of-war should man them; this was accordingly done, and the command of them given to Mr Robert Maynard, First Lieutenant of the *Pearl*, an experienced officer, and a gentleman of great bravery and resolution, as will appear by his gallant behaviour in this expedition. The sloops were well manned, and furnished with ammunition and small arms, but had no guns mounted.

The 17th of November, 1718, the Lieutenant sailed from Kicquetan, in James River in Virginia, and the 21st in the evening, came to the mouth of Okerecock Inlet, where he got sight of the pirate. This expedition was made with all imaginable secrecy, and the officer managed with all the prudence that was necessary, stopping all boats and vessels he met with, in the river, from going up, and thereby preventing any intelligence from reaching Blackbeard, and receiving at the same an account from them all, of the place where the pirate was lurking; but notwithstanding this caution, Blackbeard had information of the design, from His Excellency of the province; and his secretary, Mr Knight, wrote him a letter, particularly concerning it, intimating, that he had sent him four of his men, which were all he could meet with, in or about town, and so bid him be upon his guard. These men belonged to Blackbeard, and were sent from Bath-Town, to Okerecock, where the sloop lay, which is about 20 leagues.

Blackbeard had heard several reports, which happened not to be true, and so gave the less credit to this, nor was he convinced till he saw the sloops: thereupon he put his vessel in a posture of defence; he had no more than twenty-five men on board, though he gave out to all the vessels he spoke with, that he had forty. When he had prepared for battle, he set down and spent the night in drinking with the master of a trading sloop, who, 'twas thought, had more business with Thatch, than he should have had.

Lieutenant Maynard came to an anchor, for the place being shoal, and the channel intricate, so that there was no getting in, where Thatch lay, that night; but in the morning he weighed, and sent his boat ahead of the sloops, to sound, and coming within gunshot of the pirate, received his fire; whereupon Maynard hoisted the king's colours, and stood directly towards him, with the best way that his sails and oars could make. Blackbeard cut his cable, and endeavoured to make a running fight, keeping a continual fire at his enemies, with his guns, Mr Maynard not having any, kept a constant fire with small arms, while some of his men laboured at their oars; Blackbeard's sloop ran aground, and Mr Maynard's drawing more water than that of the Pirate, he could not come near him, so he anchored within half gunshot of the enemy; and, in order to lighten his vessel, that he might run him aboard; the Lieutenant ordered all his ballast to be thrown overboard, and all the water to be staved, and then weighed and stood for him; upon which Blackbeard, hailed him in this rude manner: 'Damn you for villains, who are you? And, from whence came you?' The Lieutenant made him answer, 'You may see by our colours, we are no pirates.' Blackbeard bid him send his boat on board, that he might see who he was; but Mr Maynard replied thus: 'I cannot spare my boat, but I will come aboard of you, as soon as I can, with my sloop.' Upon this, Blackbeard took a glass of liquor, and drank to him with these words: 'Damnation seize my soul if I give you quarters, or take any from you.' In answer to which, Mr Maynard told him, that he expected no quarters from him, nor should he give him any.

By this time Blackbeard's sloop fleeted, as Mr Maynard's sloops were rowing towards him, which being not above a foot high in the waist, and consequently the men all exposed, as they came near together (there being hitherto, little or no execution done, on either side), the pirate fired a broadside, charged with all manner of small shot. A fatal stroke to them! The sloop the Lieutenant was in, having twenty men killed and wounded, and the other sloop nine: this could not be helped, for there being no wind, they were obliged to keep to their oars, otherwise the pirate would have got away from him, which it seems, the Lieutenant was resolute to prevent.

After this unlucky blow, Blackbeard's sloop fell broadside to the shore; Mr Maynard's other sloop, which was called the *Ranger*, fell astern, being for the present disabled, so the Lieutenant finding his own sloop had way, and would soon be on board of Thatch, he ordered all his men down, for fear of another broadside, which must have been their destruction, and the loss of their expedition. Mr Maynard was the only person that kept the deck, except the man at the helm, whom he directed to lie down snug, and the men in the hold were ordered to get their pistols and their swords ready for close fighting, and to come up at his command; in order to which, two ladders were placed in the hatchway for the more expedition. When the Lieutenant's sloop boarded the other, Captain Thatch's men threw in several new fashioned sort of grenades, *viz* case-bottles filled with powder, and small shot, slugs, and pieces of lead or iron, with a quick-match in the mouth of it, which being lighted withoutside, presently runs into the

124

bottle to the powder, and as it is instantly thrown on board, generally does great execution, besides putting all the crew into a confusion; but by good providence, they had not that effect here; the men being in the hold, and Blackbeard seeing few or no hands aboard, told his men, that 'They were all knocked on the head, except three or four, and therefore,' says he, 'let's jump on board and cut them to pieces.'

Whereupon, under the smoke of one of the bottles just mentioned, Blackbeard enters with fourteen men, over the bows of Maynard's sloop, and were not seen by him, till the air cleared; however, he just then gave a signal to his men, who all rose in an instant, and attacked the pirates with as much bravery as ever was done upon such an occasion: Blackbeard and the Lieutenant fired the first pistol at each other, by which the pirate received a wound, and then engaged with swords, till the Lieutenent's unluckily broke, and stepping back to cock a pistol, Blackbeard, with his cutlass, was striking at that instant, that one of Maynard's men gave him a terrible wound in the neck and throat, by which the Lieutenant came off with a small cut over his fingers.

They were now closely and warmly engaged, the Lieutenant and twelve men, against Blackbeard and fourteen, till the blood run out of the scuppers in streams; Blackbeard received a shot into his body, from the pistol that Lieutenant Maynard cocked, yet still stood his ground and fought with great fury, till he received sixteen wounds, and five of them by shot. At length, as he was cocking another pistol, having fired several before, he fell down dead by which time, eight more out of the fourteen dropped, and all the rest much wounded, jumped overboard, and called out for quarters; which was granted, though it was only prolonging their lives for a few days. The sloop *Ranger* came up, and attacked the men that remained in Blackbeard's sloop with equal bravery, till they likewise cried for quarters.

Here was an end of that courageous brute, who might have passed in the world for a hero, had he been employed in a good cause; his destruction which was of such consequence to the plantations, was entirely owing to the conduct and bravery of Lieutenant Maynard, and his men, who might have destroyed him with much less loss, had they had a vessel with great guns; but they were obliged to use small vessels, because the holes and places he lurked in, would not admit of others, of greater draught; for it was no small difficulty for this gentleman to get to him, having grounded his vessel at least a hundred times in getting up the river, besides other discouragements, enough to have turned back any gentleman without dishonour, who was less resolute and bold than this Lieutenant. The broadside that did so much mischief before they boarded, in all probability, saved

The Boats of the victorious going to Board the American Privateer Diomede; which escaped by a breeze springing up

the rest from destruction; for before that, Thatch had little or no hopes of escaping, and therefore had posted a resolute fellow a Negro, whom he had bred up, with a lighted match, in the powder room, with commands to blow up, when he should give him orders, which was as soon as the Lieutenant and his men should have entered, that so he might have destroyed his conquerors: and when the Negro found how it went with Blackbeard, he could hardly be persuaded from that rash action, by two prisoners that were then in the hold of the sloop.

What seems a little odd, is, that some of these men, who behaved so bravely against Blackbeard, went afterwards a-pirating themselves, and one of them was taken along with Roberts; but I do not find that any of them were provided for, except one that was hanged; but this is a digression.

The Lieutenant caused Blackbeard's head, to be severed from his body, and hung up at the boltsprit end, and sailed to Bath-Town, to get relief for his wounded men.

It must be observed, that in rummaging the pirate's sloop, they found several letters and written papers, which discovered the correspondence betwixt Governor Eden, the secretary and collector, and also some traders at New York, and Blackbeard. It is likely he had regard enough for his friends, to have destroyed

123 *opposite* British Sailors Boarding an Algerine Pirate. An early nineteenth-century print.

124 *right* The American privateer *Diomede* of Salem, built 1809, an early nineteenth-century hermaphrodite brig, showing the vast amount of sail she carried including studding sails. Here she is shown escaping from the boats of the British warship *Victorious,* sent to seize her when becalmed, but foiled by a breeze springing up.

these papers before the action, in order to hinder them from falling into such hands, where the discovery would be of no use, either to the interest or reputation of these fine gentlemen, if it had not been his fixed resolution, to have blown up altogether, when he found no possibility of escaping.

When the Lieutenant came to Bath-Town, he made bold to seize in the governor's store-house, the sixty hogsheads of sugar, and from honest Mr Knight, twenty; which it seems was their dividend of the plunder taken in the French ship; the latter did not long survive this shameful discovery, for being apprehensive that he should be called to an account for these trifles, fell sick with the fright and died in a few days.

After the wounded men were pretty well recovered, the Lieutenant sailed back to the men-of-war, in James River, in Virginia, with Blackbeard's head still hanging at the boltsprit end, and fifteen prisoners, thirteen of whom were hanged. It appearing upon trial, that one of them, *viz* Samuel Odell, was taken out of the trading sloop, but the night before the engagement. This poor fellow was a little unlucky at his first entering upon his new trade, there appearing no less than 70 wounds upon him after the action, notwithstanding which, he lived, and was cured of them all. The other person that escaped the gallows, was one Israel Hands, the master of Blackbeard's sloop, and formerly captain of the same, before the *Queen Ann's Revenge* was lost in Topsail Inlet.

The aforesaid Hands happened not to be in the fight, but was taken afterwards ashore at Bath-Town, having been sometime before disabled by Blackbeard, in one of his savage humours, after the following manner. One night drinking in his cabin with Hands, the pilot, and another man; Blackbeard without any provocation privately draws out a small pair of pistols, and cocks them under the table, which being perceived by the man, he withdrew, and went upon deck, leaving Hands, the pilot, and the captain together. When the pistols were ready, he blew out the candle, and crossing his hands, discharged them at his company; Hands, the master, was shot through the knee, and lamed for life; the other pistol did no execution. Being asked the meaning of this, he only answered by damning them, that if he did not now and then kill one of them, they would forget who he was.

Hands being taken, was tried and condemned, but just as he was about to be executed, a ship arrives at Virginia with a proclamation for prolonging the time of His Majesty's pardon, to such of the pirates as should surrender by a limited time therein expressed: notwithstanding the sentence, Hands pleaded the pardon, and was allowed the benefit of it, and is alive at this time in London, begging his bread.

Now that we have given some account of Thatch's life and actions, it will not be amiss, that we speak of his beard, since it did not a little contribute towards making his name so terrible in those parts.

Plutarch, and other grave historians, have taken notice, that several great men amongst the Romans, took their surnames from certain odd marks in their countenances; as Cicero, from a mark or vetch on his nose; so our hero, Captain Thatch, assumed the cognomen of Blackbeard, from that large quantity of hair, which like a frightful meteor, covered his whole face, and frightened America, more than any comet that has appeared there a long time.

This beard was black, which he suffered to grow of an extravagant length; as to breadth, it came up to his eyes; he was accustomed to twist it with ribbons, in small tails, after the manner of our Ramellies wigs, and turn them about his ears: in time of action, he wore a sling over his shoulders, with three brace of pistols, hanging in holsters like bandoliers; he wore a fur cap, and stuck a lighted match on each side, under it, which appearing on each side his face, his eyes naturally looking fierce and wild, made him altogether such a figure, that imagination cannot form an idea of a fury, from Hell, to look more frightful.

If he had the look of a fury, his humours and passions, were suitable to it; we shall relate two or three more of his extravagances, which we omitted in the body of his history, by which it will appear, to what a pitch of wickedness, human nature may arrive, if its passions are not checked.

In the commonwealth of pirates, he who goes the greatest length of wickedness, is looked upon with a kind of envy amongst them, as a person of a more extraordinary gallantry, and is thereby entitled to be distinguished by some post, and if such a one has but courage, he must certainly be a great man. The hero of whom we are writing was thoroughly accomplished this way, and some of his frolics of wickedness, were so extravagant, as if he aimed at making his men believe he was a devil incarnate; for being one day at sea, and a little flushed with drink: 'Come,' says he, 'let us make a Hell of our own, and try how long we can bear it.' Accordingly he, with two or three others went down into the hold, and closing up all the hatches, filled several pots full of brimstone, and other combustible matter, and set it on fire, and so continued till they were almost suffocated, when some of the men cried out for air; at length he opened the hatches, not a little pleased that he held out the longest.

The night before he was killed, he sat up and drank the whole night, with some of his own men, and the master of a merchantman, and having had intelligence of the two sloops coming to attack

125 and 126 *opposite* French sailor of the seventeenth century by Goichon and French sailor about 1795 by Maleuvre. Regular uniform for the lower deck was not introduced until about 1830. Before then common sailors wore their own clothes until they wore out and then bought clothes from the ship's slop chest, a shop run by the petty officers. This did make for some homogeneity in sailors' dress.

him, as has been before observed; one of his men asked him, in case anything should happen to him in the engagement, with the sloops, whether his wife knew where he had buried his money? He answered, that nobody but himself, and the devil, knew where it was, and the longest liver should take all.

Those of his crew who were taken alive, told a story which may appear a little incredible; however, we think it will not be fair to omit it, since we had it from their own mouths. That once upon a cruise, they found out, that they had a man on board more than their crew; such a one was seen several days amongst them, sometimes below, and sometimes upon deck, yet no man in the ship could give an account who he was, or from whence he came; but that he disappeared a little before they were cast away in their great ship, as has been related in the history of Bonnet; but, it seems, they all verily believed it was the Devil.

One would think, these things should induce them to reform their lives, but so many reprobates together, encouraged and spirited one another up in their wickedness, to which a continual course of drinking did not a little contribute; for in Blackbeard's journal, which was taken, there were several memorandums of the following nature, found writ with his own hand.

'Such a day, rum all out: our company somewhat sober: a damned confusion amongst us! Rogues a-plotting; talk of separation. So I looked sharp for a prize; such a day, took one, with a great deal of liquor on board, so kept the company hot, damned hot, then all things went well again.'

Thus it was these wretches passed their lives, with very little pleasure or satisfaction, in the possession of what they violently take away from others, and sure to pay for it at last, by an ignominious death.

from *A General History of the Robberies and Murders of the Most Notorious Pirates*, by Captain Charles Johnson, London 1724.

The scurvy

Commodore George Anson was sent on a voyage of circumnavigation in order to attack Spanish trade. Departing in September 1740 with a squadron of five men-of-war, the *Centurion*, the *Gloucester*, the *Severn*, the *Pearl*, and the *Wager*, a sloop and two victualling ships (see p. 38), he returned in the *Centurion* alone in June 1744. He later became First Lord of the Admiralty and reformed the British navy.

The scurvy which he described was perhaps the greatest hazard of any on long sea voyages until lemon juice was discovered to be an easily stored supply of the vitamins missing from the seaman's diet.

Soon after our passing Straits Le Maire, the scurvy began to make its appearance amongst us; and our long continuance at sea, the fatigue we underwent, and the various disappointments we met with, had occasioned its spreading to such a degree, that at the latter end of April there were but few on board, who were not in some degree afflicted with it, and in that month no less than forty-three died of it on board the *Centurion*. But though we thought that the distemper had then risen to an extraordinary height, and were willing to hope, that as we advanced to the northward its malignity would abate, yet we found, on the contrary, that in the month of May we lost near double that number. And as we did not get to land till the middle of June, the mortality went on increasing, and the disease extended itself so prodigiously, that after the loss of above two hundred men, we could not at last muster more than six fore-mast men in a watch capable of duty.

This disease so frequently attending all long voyages, and so particularly destructive to us, is surely the most singular and unaccountable of any that affects the human body. For its symptoms are inconstant and innumerable, and its progress and effects extremely irregular; for scarcely any two persons have the same complaints, and where there hath been found some conformity in the symptoms, the order of their appearance has been totally different. However, though it frequently puts on the form of many other diseases, and is therefore not to be described by any exclusive and infallible criterions; yet there are some symptoms which are more general than the rest, and therefore, occurring the oftenest, deserve a more particular enumeration. These common appearances are large discoloured spots dispersed over the whole surface of the body, swelled legs, putrid gums, and above all, an extraordinary lassitude of the whole body, especially after any exercise, however inconsiderable; and this lassitude at last degenerates into a proneness to swoon on the least exertion of strength, or even on the least motion.

This disease is likewise usually attended with a strange dejection of the spirits, and with shiverings, tremblings, and a disposition to be seized with the most dreadful terrors on the slightest accident. Indeed it was most remarkable, in all our reiterated experience of this malady, that whatever discouraged our people, or at any time damped their hopes, never failed to add new vigour to the distemper; for it usually killed those who were in the last stages of it, and confined those to their hammocks, who were before capable of some kind of duty, so that it seemed as if alacrity of mind, and sanguine thoughts, were no contemptible preservatives from its fatal malignity.

But it is not easy to complete the long roll of the various concomitants of this disease; for it often produced putrid fevers, pleurisies, the jaundice, and violent rheumatic pains, and sometimes it occasioned an obstinate costiveness, which was generally attended with a difficulty of breathing; and this was esteemed the most deadly of all the scorbutic symptoms. At other times the

whole body, but more especially the legs, were subject to ulcers of the worst kind, attended with rotten bones, and such a luxuriancy of funguous flesh, as yielded to no remedy. But a most extraordinary circumstance, and what would be scarcely credible upon any single evidence, is, that the scars of wounds which had been for many years healed, were forced open again by this virulent distemper. Of this, there was a remarkable instance in one of the invalids on board the *Centurion,* who had been wounded above fifty years before at the battle of the Boyne; for though he was cured soon after, and had continued well for a great number of years past, yet on his being attacked by the scurvy, his wounds, in the progress of his disease, broke out afresh, and appeared as if they had never been healed. Nay, what is still more astonishing, the callous of a broken bone, which had been completely formed for a long time, was found to be hereby dissolved, and the fracture seemed as if it had never been consolidated. Indeed, the effects of this disease were in almost every instance wonderful; for many of our people, though confined to their hammocks, appeared to have no inconsiderable share of health, for they ate and drank heartily, were cheerful, and talked with much seeming vigour, and with a loud strong tone of voice; and yet on their being the least moved, though it was only from one part of the ship to the other, and that in their hammocks, they have immediately expired; and others, who have confided in their seeming strength, and have resolved to get out of their hammocks, have died before they could well reach the deck; and it was no uncommon thing for those who were able to walk the deck, and to do some kind of duty, to drop down dead in an instant, on any endeavours to act with their utmost vigour, many of our people having perished in this manner during the course of this voyage.

from *A Voyage Round the World in the Years MDCCXL, I, II, III, IV,* by George Anson, Esq. . . . Compiled from Papers and other Materials of the Right Honourable George Lord Anson, and published under his Direction by Richard Walter, M.A., Chaplain of his Majesty's Ship the *Centurion* in that Expedition, London 1748.

127 George, Lord Anson, 1697 – 1762, from whose journal this passage is taken, (oil, artist unknown). After his circumnavigation, Anson became First Lord of the Admiralty and reformed the British navy. His modest and retiring manner prompted the saying that he 'had been round the world but was never in it'.

Plate 19 View of a Port at Sunset by Claude Gellée, called Le Lorrain, (1600 – 82). The visual excitement of a sea port in the age of sail could appeal to even the most classical of artists.

Wednesday, 22 [April 1741]. The first part moderate and fair, the latter fresh gales and squally weather. The *Gloucester*'s people informed us that so great a number of rats were seen between decks, as would appear incredible to any but an eye-witness; that they were infested with them to that prodigious degree, that they could scarce keep them from running over their victuals, during the time they were at dinner, and that they had never seen so great a number before this day.

Friday, 24. The first part little winds and calm, the latter part
hard gales and squally, with a large sea, that carried away the
Gloucester's fore-topsail yard in the slings, and split her foresail,
which obliged them to bring to under their mizen; they likewise
found the oakham, washed out of the whale between wind and
water; on which they nailed a piece of lead over the place that
was leaky. The ship's company being still in a sick and miserable
condition, at 8 a.m. they brought to, and stowed her foresail,
which was split by the buntlines breaking, and also the clewlines.

Friday, 15 [May]. Fresh gales and squally with much rain.
The crew of the *Gloucester* are extremely sickly, they having very
few capable of working the ship; and what still adds to their
unfortunate condition is, the prodigious increase of rats, which
plague them to that degree, that they can get no sleep; for they
are no sooner laid down in their hammocks, but immediately a
swarm of these vermin come running over them, and frequently
give them sad bites; nay, some of those who kept their hammocks,
and, through the force of their distemper, were almost insensible
of pain, have had part of their toes eaten off as they lay there;
the destruction and deformity which these vermin make on the
dead bodies, that lie about the deck (they having at this time, ten
or a dozen dying in a day) makes the most shocking spectacle
that ever man beheld, one having his eyes eat out, another his
cheeks eaten off, and others part of their arms, legs, &c.

from *An Authentic Journal of the Late Expedition Under the Command of Commodore
Anson*, by John Philips, Midshipman of the *Centurion*, London 1744.

130 *left* The *Royal George* off Deptford by J. Cleveley the Elder (*d.* 1777). These are ships of the classical age of the sailing ship of war. In the background is a three-decker under construction and another actually being launched, with cheering figures on board. The *Royal George* went down with great loss of life on the morning of 29 August 1782, when being heeled over for repairs at Spithead. The guns had been run out to one side and at the same time a large quantity of rum was being loaded; the combined weight allowed water to enter through the open gun ports. The Lieutenant of the watch ignored the warnings of the ship's carpenter and, to assert his authority, delayed giving the order to right ship for a fatal two minutes.

131 Greenwich hospital by Antonio Canaletto (1677–1768) (oil). This hospital for seamen was founded in 1694 and the chief architect was Sir Christopher Wren, who also designed St Paul's Cathedral.

The loss of the *Wager*

The principal peril to the square-rigged sailing ship of the eighteenth century was that of being caught on a lee shore. With its limited ability to beat against the wind, it was often difficult for a ship to avoid being swept inshore. The most dramatic illustration of this is the loss of the *Wager* on an island off the inhospitable south-western coast of South America, during Anson's voyage in 1741, a story which reveals the brutality of the seagoing life of that time.

Captain Cheap and a few officers eventually reached Santiago de Chile in an open boat after many hardships, while a small remnant of the mutinous crew reached Rio Grande in Brazil after an arduous journey through the Straits of Magellan.

What may be said to have chiefly contributed to the fatal catastrophe of the *Wager,* after her separation from us, on Sunday, April 19, 1741, was the captain's too scrupulously adhering to the letter of his instructions. The first rendezvous agreed upon, was to be at Nostra Signora di Socora, in Lat. 44; and that being upon a lee shore, little agreed with the distressed condition of a ship with her shrouds and main chain-plates broke, her mizen-mast gone, with her standing rigging fore and aft, and all her people down, as was her case. The captain, however, it must be owned, did not propose coming nearer shore than seven leagues, and only to sail off and on for 24 hours, to see if he could meet with the commodore; designing, in case he did not meet him in that time, to go for Juan Fernandez. Accordingly, they laid the ship to for the first four nights after their separation from us, the wind at S. and S.S.W. steering N.W. by N. and

al Caroline Yacht.

when, at half an hour past 4 in the morning of this fatal day, the ship struck abaft on a sunken rock, and the miserable people found themselves surrounded on every side with rocks. She struck a second time, which broke the head of the tiller; and in a short time after, she struck, bilged, and grounded, between two small islands (about five leagues distant from the main) and not above a musket shot from the shore. They immediately launched the barge, cutter, and yawl over the gunnel; cut the main and fore masts by the board, and the sheet anchor from the gunnel. The captain sent the barge ashore to see if the place was inhabited, but the people not returning on board, as directed, the lieutenant was sent in the yawl, with orders to bring off the barge. This he sent off, but stayed ashore himself. As soon as the barge came on board, the captain was persuaded, being very ill, to go ashore, which he accordingly did, accompanied with the land officers, mate, and midshipmen. The officers remaining on board were the master, boatswain, gunner, and carpenter. Upon the principal officers leaving the ship, several of the crew fell into the most violent outrage and disorder. And though it blowed very hard, with a tumbling sea, and it was expected every moment, that the ship would part, they were yet so insensible of their danger, that they began with broaching the wine in the lazaretto, then fell to breaking open cabins and chests, arming themselves with swords and pistols, threatening to murder any who should oppose them. Being now drunk, and mad with liquor, they plundered chests and cabins of money, and other things of value, and tricked themselves up in the richest apparel they could meet with. The next day, the ship being bilged in the midships, after securing some powder, ball, and bread, the gunner and carpenter, with several of those imaginary lords, went ashore. Upon their landing, the purser, and Lieutenant Hamilton, of the marines, presented their pistols to several of their breasts, upon which, those grandees suffered themselves very quietly to be disrobed of all their finery.

They found the island uninhabited, without beast, or bird, except some wild fowls, nor producing any other vegetable but celery, which grows here in abundance, and was of great use, as the crew in general had the scurvy. There was indeed a plenty of mussels, limpets, and other shell-fish. The captain took up his lodging in a little hut, supposed to have been built by the Indians. The marine officers pitched their tents. Others sheltered themselves from the inclemency of the weather under trees, making large fires, and others hauled up the cutter, and propped her up bottom upwards: these remained thus exposed several days, when they were at length distributed into tents.

On the 16th of May, the boatswain made a signal for a boat to come aboard, but finding no appearance of any, he brought a

132 *left* The *Royal Caroline* by John Cleveley the Elder (*d.* 1777). The royal yacht of the eighteenth century. The original yacht design was developed in Holland but by this time yachts had been elaborated into miniature ships.

133 Wreck of the *Dutton* in Plymouth Sound, oil by T. Luny (1759–1837). It was seldom that the crew of a ship had the good fortune to find rescuers on the lee shore where they were being wrecked.

N.N.W. and the 5th and every night after made sail, till the 13th of May, when they saw land from the forecastle: of which the captain being made acquainted, and coming forward, he unhappily received a fall, which dislocated his shoulder, so that he was obliged to be put into the surgeon's cabin. They had now a disabled captain; they were upon a lee shore, and under a necessity of crowding the ship off. In this sad condition they could only muster 12 men, officers included, in both watches (the rest of the ship's company being all sick below), and it blew so very hard, that it was impossible to set their main topsail; while the other topsails at the yards were so bad, that if they attempted to loose them for making sail, they were in danger of being split, and they had not a spare sail in the ship, that could be brought to the yard without being repaired. It rained violently besides, and withal was so very dark, that they could not see the length of the ship.

Such was their deplorable situation, till May the 14th, 1741

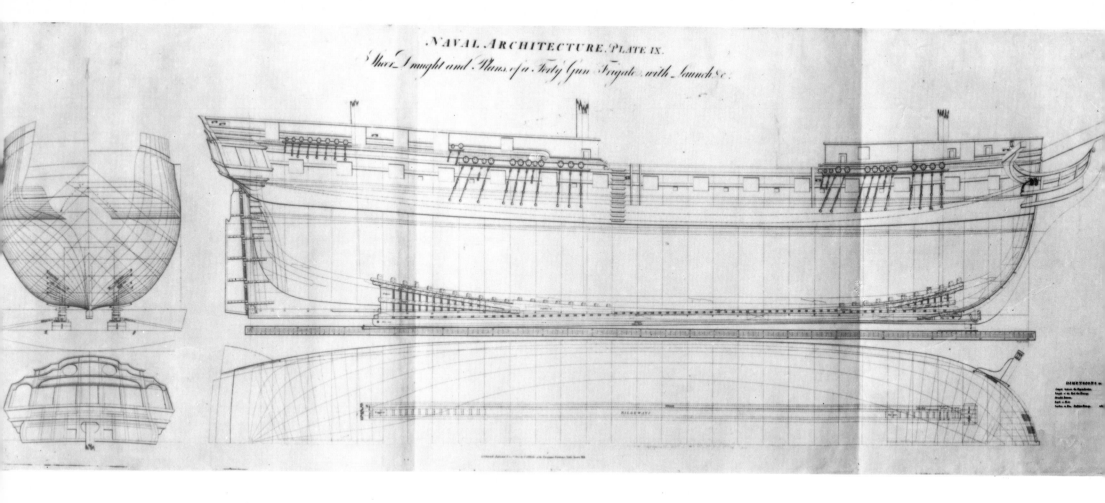

134 Sheer draught and plans of a forty-gun frigate, a drawing from a late eighteenth-century book on naval architecture.

quarter-deck gun to bear on the captain's hut and fired two shot, which grazed over it, without doing any other damage. As soon as he came ashore, the captain, for this, struck him a blow with his cane, that knocked him down, and he lay motionless, and to appearance dead, for some time. When he came to himself, and saw a pistol cocked in the captain's hand, he presented his naked breast to him; but the captain only told him he deserved to be shot, and said no more then.

In scuttling the decks they found several men dead, and some drowned in the ship, supposed to have drank till they were not able to get from the water, as it flowed into the vessel. As they were at work one day on the wreck, there came alongside a canoe with several Indians, bowing and crossing themselves, giving the *Wager's* folks to understand they were of the Romish religion. They are a most simple and inoffensive people, of a very low stature, scarce four feet high, flat-nosed, with little eyes sunk very deep in their heads, and not much bigger than a bean. They live continually in smoke, and are never without a fire,

even in their canoes; yet although the climate be excessive cold, they have nothing to cover their nakedness but a piece of an old blanket, which they throw over their shoulders. Captain Cheap gave them hats, and presented each of them with a soldier's coat.

The *Wager's* people bought dogs of them, which they killed and ate, esteeming the flesh little inferior to English mutton. The Indians soon left them, they never staying long in a place.

About this time, ten of the crew (having been detected in a design to blow up the captain, the surgeon, and Lieutenant Hamilton), deserted; among whom was the carpenter's mate, a very useful person in their distressed circumstances, which rendered his loss the more considerable. They had no way to get to the main, but by building themselves a punt out of the wreck of the ship, or by seizing a canoe; nor had they anything to live upon but seaweed and shell-fish. This seaweed is of a dark green colour, called by the seamen *slaugh*. Upon this accident, the captain ordered the oars to be secured, and the boats hauled up, to prevent the deserters or any others going away by night.

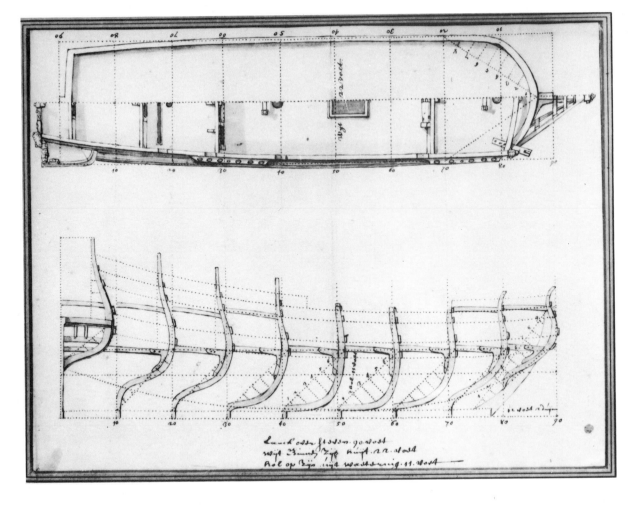

offenders being generally marines, were punished in the military way by whipping; but the punishment not appearing adequate to the heinousness of the crime, the crew were unanimous for making it capital; this was overruled, but at last they agreed in this punishment, namely, that any person whatever, who should be convicted for the future of so atrocious a depredation, should straight be set ashore on the next desolate island, and live upon

135 Mid seventeenth-century plans for a Dutch pinnace. The peculiar manner of showing the sections was in use until the first half of the eighteenth century.

136 *right* Design for the *Illustrious* by the famous shipbuilder Henry Adams who built many great ships at Buckler's Hard near Southampton Water in the south of England.

The several things that drove ashore were put into a tent, and a watch was set over them. Everyone was obliged to do duty, except the captain and carpenter which last was employed in fitting up the long-boat, that was cut in two, and lengthened eleven feet, ten inches and a half by the keel. They had above one hundred men to be victualled, and it behoved them to be very frugal, as well as vigilant; they were therefore put to an allowance, *viz* first, of half a pound of flour and one piece of pork for three men per day; then it came to a quarter of a pound of flour a man per day, and one pint of wine; and such as liked brandy had half a pint in lieu of wine; till at last their chief support was mussels, limpets, and clams, which they picked up about the rocks, and are a shell-fish not unlike our cockles. They used likewise to boil a large seaweed called *thromba,* and eat a broad green weed called *saragraza,* fried in tallow. The vigilance of the captain indeed did not answer the good purposes for which it was calculated. The store-tent was robbed several times, and the

what they could get, till the rest were ready for sailing. This expedient was not sufficient to create the intended terror. The store-tent was again robbed, and five of the suspected marines, dreading the punishment due to their crime, made off to the deserters; four others, who stayed to be tried, received sentence to be carried off to the main, and there shift for themselves.

These repeated depredations however caused great murmuring among the seamen, who insisted on having a pint of brandy per day, each man, and some of them went to the captain with a two-gallon keg, and asked it full of wine. He refused them at first, but apprehending they would make no ceremony of filling it without leave, he thought proper to order it to be given them.

Now it was that the captain began to perceive the ticklish situation he was in, and how difficult it was to support his authority, of which the following unlucky affair is a melancholy instance. Mr Henry Cozens, midshipman, was one day confined by order from the captain, on an accusation of drunkenness. It seems Mr

137

137, 138 and 139 Sailors of the second half of the eighteenth century, from a series of etchings by Dominic Serres, 1777.
Left to right: a seaman; a lieutenant; a master and commander.

In colour opposite: Four eighteenth-century shipping scenes.

Plate 22 *top left* The Thames at Deptford, oil painting by Samuel Scott (*c.* 1702–72). On the left is a two-decker fitting out. Now part of London, Deptford then presented a charming country scene. The dockyard was closed down at the end of the eighteenth century.

Plate 23 *top right* English Whalers in the Ice, oil painting by Charles Brooking (1723–59).

Plate 24 *bottom left* A merchant Ship and Royal Yacht Beating to Windward off Dover, oil painting by Charles Brooking (1723–59). The royal yacht flying the union jack and the red ensign and carrying a gaff sail and topsail on the mizen, is very close by the wind. The smaller vessels carry jibs, but the larger ship carries a fore staysail. An early example of the transition from the square spritsail can be seen furled in the merchant ship.

Plate 25 *bottom right* A Danish Timber Barque, by Samuel Scott (*c.* 1702–72). England was heavily dependent on the Baltic countries for her timber for ship-building. The unusually bluff bows were to enable her to carry long timbers.

Plate 26 *overleaf* Marseille, by Joseph Vernet (1714–89). One of Vernet's famous series of the ports of France. A lateen-sailed zebec and a ceremonial barge approach the jetty in front of a man-of-war at left centre. *Musée de la Marine, Paris.*

Cozens was rolling a cask of peas up a steep beach, but finding it too heavy for him he stopped for some time; the captain looking on, told him he was drunk; Mr Cozen's replied, 'With what should I get drunk, unless it be with water?' The captain then said, 'You scoundrel get more hands, and roll the cask up,' and afterwards struck him with his cane. 'Tis said that Cozens then talked to the captain about Captain Shelvocke, and the following night he was heard to use very unbecoming language again to the captain telling him, that he was come into those seas to pay Shelvocke's debts, and also insolently added, 'Though Shelvocke was a rogue, he was no fool, and by G—d you are both.' When he spoke this he was a prisoner in the store-tent, and asked the captain if he was to be kept there all night? On these provocations, the captain attempted to strike him again; but the sentinel said he should strike no prisoner of his; and Cozens endeavouring to stave a cask of brandy, was soon after released.

Two days after Mr Cozens had a dispute with the surgeon. The latter having words with him in the tent, on his going away, Mr Cozens followed him; they soon fell to blows, but the surgeon had so much the advantage of the midshipman, that he tied his hands behind him. The next day as they were serving the provisions, the boatswain's servant, a Portuguese boy talking bad English, and bringing in the allowance of wine, the boatswain, Mr Cozens, and the cook, his messmates, with some difficulty, understood by the boy's talk that one of the men had his allowance stopped. Mr Cozens went to know the reason. The purser and he having a dispute the day before, the purser told him, when he asked for his wine, that he was come to mutiny, and without further ceremony discharged a pistol at his head, and would have shot him, had he not been prevented by the cooper's canting the pistol with his elbow, at the instant of its going off. The captain, and lieutenant H——n, hearing the report of the pistol, the latter ran out with a firelock, and then called the captain out of his tent, telling him that Cozens was come to mutiny. The captain on this jumped out, asking where the villain was, then clapped a cocked pistol to Mr Cozens' cheek, and precipitately shot him, without asking any questions. Immediately on this the lieutenant went to one of the tents, where several of the officers were together, and called all hands to the captain. Accordingly they went unarmed. When they came before the captain, he told them what he had done, and that he was still their commander. One of the officers, observing that the captain, purser, surgeon,

140 The Loss of the *Magnificent*, by J. C. Schetky (1778 – 1874) (oil). Cutter, brig, and two frigates and ship's boats rendering assistance. Topmasts gone on main and mizen – perhaps cut away in effort to right ship by reducing top hamper. Windward guns run out in efforts to provide leverage to right the ship.

lieutenant H——n, E——rs, and F——ng of the marines, were all armed, said to the captain, 'Sir, you see we are unarmed.' On this the captain dropped his firelock to the ground, saying, 'I see you are, and have only sent for you, to let you all know that I am still your commander, so let every man go to his tent.' Accordingly everyone obeyed him.

It was thought that the captain and the gentlemen above-mentioned, had some suspicion of the gunner and carpenter, who had eighteen of the stoutest fellows that belonged to the ship in

their tent, believing they could sway most of the seamen on shore. But doubtless their behaviour on this occasion was a sufficient indication of the fairness of their intentions, and their detestation of mutiny, by their not appearing in arms on the report of Mr Cozens being shot. They walked up with the captain, to the place where Mr Cozens lay, with his elbow on the ground, resting his right cheek on the palm of his hand, alive, and to appearance sensible, but speechless. The captain ordered him to the sick-tent, the surgeon's mate dressed his left cheek where

he was shot, and felt a ball about three inches under his right eye; the surgeon refused dressing him. This was attributed to his late quarrel with Mr Cozens, which has been already mentioned. The shooting of Mr Cozens was a very unhappy affair; the person whose allowance was stopped, made no complaint to him; he was too officious in the business, and his preceding behaviour,. and notorious disrespectful words to the captain, might probably make the captain suspect his design was mutiny, though this may be said, that Mr Cozens neither on this, or any other occasion, appeared in arms since the loss of the ship. However, his fate laid foundation of a great deal of mischief which afterwards followed.

On the 11th of June, Dr O——y, of the land forces, was desired to assist the surgeon's mate, to take the ball out of Mr Cozens' cheek, which he then was inclinable to do; but in the afternoon, finding it not agreeable to the captain, he refused to go. The ball however was taken out, and for some time supposed to be lost, but was afterwards found.

On the 12th, the carpenter saw the surgeon at the medicine chest, who asked him how that unfortunate creature did, meaning Mr Cozens; the carpenter told him he had not seen him today. The surgeon then said he would have visited him, but the captain would not give him leave. This was looked on as an act of inhumanity in the captain, and contributed very much to his losing the affections of the people; whose opinion was, that as Mr Cozens was very strong and healthy, with proper assistance he might recover, they did not scruple to say that the captain would act a more honourable part to discharge another pistol at him, and dispatch him at once, than to deny him relief, and suffer him to languish in a cold wet place in pain and misery.

On the 13th, Mr Cozens being, to all outward appearance, likely to recover, desired he might be removed to the gunner and carpenter's tent, which was his place of residence before this unhappy accident. But these officers being unwilling to disoblige the captain, waited on him, before they would admit the patient into their tent, and told him, they were come to ask a favour, hoping that he would have so much mercy and compassion on the unhappy man who was in the sick tent, as to permit them to remove him to his former lodging. The captain answered, 'No; I am so far from it, that if he lives, I will carry him a prisoner to the commodore, and hang him.'

On the 17th, the surgeon's mate took out of Mr Cozen's cheek a ball much flatted, and a piece of bone, supposed to be part of the upper jaw, which was desired by Mr Cozens to be delivered to Mr Bulkeley, who received it, together with the first ball mentioned to have been lost.

On the 18th, the carpenter cut the longboat in two, and

lengthened her eleven feet ten inches and half by the keel.

On the 21st, part of the crew went aboard the ship; but it being dangerous going about anything, by reason of her working much, and a great sea tumbling in, the boats were employed in going about the rocks in search of subsistence.

On the 24th, departed this life Mr Henry Cozens, midshipman, after languishing fourteen days with the wound he had received in his cheek. He was buried in as decent a manner as time, place, and circumstances would allow. There died sundry ways (since the ship first struck, to this time) forty-five men, and seven deserted.

from *An Authentic Journal of the Late Expedition Under the Command of Commodôre Anson*, by John Philips, Midshipman of the *Centurion*, London 1744.

Landing on Tahiti

Louis Antoine de Bougainville (see p. 39) was not a seaman by profession. After studying law he had been a soldier, reaching high rank and serving under Montcalm in Canada during the Seven Years War. His career as an explorer followed his leadership of an enterprise to colonize the Falkland Isles. In 1767, when he handed over the French interest to the Spaniards, he sailed in a frigate, the *Boudeuse*, accompanied by a store-ship the *Etoile* into the Pacific.

The principal discovery of his voyage was that of Tahiti, though in this he had, in fact, been preceded by Wallis a year earlier. His extravagant eulogy of what he called the 'New Cythera' and its people encouraged the contemporary cult of 'the noble savage'.

The second of April, at ten in the morning, we perceived to the N.N.E. a high and very steep mountain, seemingly surrounded by the sea. I called it the *Boudoir*, or the *Peak of the Boudeuse*. We stood to the northward, in order to make it plain, when we saw another land, bearing W. by N. the coast of which was not so high, but afforded an indeterminate extent to our eyes. We had a very urgent necessity for touching at some place where we might get refreshments and wood, and we flattered ourselves to find them on this land.

During the night, between the third and fourth, we turned to windward, in order to get more to the northward. With joy we saw fires burning on every part of the coast, and from thence concluded that it was inhabited.

The 4th, at daybreak, we discovered that the two lands, which before appeared separate, were united together by a low land,

which was bent like a bow, and formed a bay open to the N.E. We ran with all sails set towards the land, standing to windward of this bay, when we perceived a piragua coming from the offing, and standing for the land, and making use of her sail and paddles. She passed athwart us, and joined a number of others, which sailed ahead of us, from all parts of the island. One of them went before all the rest; it was manned by twelve naked men, who presented us with branches of bananas; and their demonstrations signified that this was their olive branch. We answered them with all the signs of friendship we could imagine; they then came alongside of our ship; and one of them, remarkable for his prodigious growth of hair, which stood like bristles divergent on his head, offered us, together with his branch of peace, a little pig, and a cluster of bananas. We accepted his present, which he fastened to a rope that was thrown over to him; we gave him caps and handkerchiefs; and these first presents were the pledges of our alliance with these people.

The two ships were soon surrounded with more than a hundred piraguas of different sizes, all which had outriggers. They were laden with coco-nuts, bananas, and other fruits of the country. The exchange of these fruits, which were delicious to us, was made very honestly for all sorts of trifles; but without any of the islanders venturing to come aboard. We were obliged either to come into their piraguas, or show them at a distance what we offered in exchange; when both parties were agreed, a basket or a net was let down by a rope; they put their goods in it, and so we did ours; giving before they had received, or receiving before they gave indifferently, with a kind of confidence, which made us conceive a good opinion of their character. We further saw no kind of arms in their piraguas, in which there were no women at this first interview. The piraguas kept alongside of the ships, till the approach of night obliged us to stand offshore, when they all retired.

We endeavoured, during night, to go to the northward, never standing further than three leagues from the land. All the shore was, till near midnight, covered as the night before, with little fires at a short distance from each other: it seemed as if it was an illumination made on purpose, and we accompanied it with several sky-rockets from both our ships.

The 5th we spent in plying, in order to work to windward of the island, and in letting the boats sound for an anchoring place. The aspect of this coast, elevated like an amphitheatre, offered us the most enchanting prospect. Notwithstanding the great height of the mountains, none of the rocks has the appearance of barrenness; every part is covered with woods.

As we ran along the coast, our eyes were struck with the sight

Opposite Two eighteenth-century caricatures – or are they drawings of photographic accuracy?

141 The Liberty of the Subject, 1779, by James Gillray, shows the British navy's method of solving its difficulty in manning its ships in the eighteenth century – the use of press gangs. These gangs of brutal seamen seized without pity any able bodied men they could find, who had not purchased an indemnity from the Admiralty.

142 'An Irish Leap or a *Pat* Reply to a Plain Question'.

Another isle now came within sight: but seeing several breakers that seemed to obstruct the passage between the two isles, I determined to return in search of anchorage in the first bay, which we saw on the day of our landfall. Our boats which sounded ahead of us towards shore, found the north side of the bay everywhere surrounded, at a quarter of a league's distance, by a reef which appears at low water. However, about a league from the north point, they discovered a gap in the reef, of the width of twice a cable's length at most, where there was 30 and 35 fathom of water, and within it a pretty extensive road, where the bottom varied from nine to thirty fathom. This road was bounded to the south by a reef, which, proceeding from the land, joined that which surrounded the shore. Our boats had constantly found a sandy bottom, and discovered several little rivers fit for watering at. Upon the reef, on the north side, there are three little islands.

As we came nearer the shore, the number of islanders surrounding our ships increased. The piraguas were so numerous all about the ships, that we had much to do to warp in amidst the crowd of boats and the noise. All these people came crying out *tayo*, which means friend, and gave a thousand signs of friendship; they all asked nails and ear-rings of us. The piraguas were full of females; who, for agreeable features, are not inferior to most European women; and who in point of beauty of the body might, with much reason, vie with them all. Most of these fair females were naked; for the men and the old women that accompanied them, had stripped them of the garments which they generally dress themselves in. The glances which they gave us from their piraguas, seemed to discover some degree of uneasiness, notwithstanding the innocent manner in which they were given; perhaps, because nature has everywhere embellished their sex with a natural timidity; or because even in those countries, where the ease of the golden age is still in use, women seem least to desire what they most wish for. The men, who were more plain, or rather more free, soon explained their meaning very clearly. They pressed us to choose a woman, and to come on shore with her; and their gestures, which were nothing less than equivocal, denoted in what manner we should form an acquaintance with her. It was very difficult, admidst such a sight, to keep at their work four hundred young French sailors, who had seen no women for six months. In spite of all our precautions, a young girl came on board, and placed herself upon the quarter-deck, near one of the hatchways, which was open, in order to give air to those who were heaving at the capstan below it. The girl carelessly dropped a cloth, which covered her, and appeared to the eyes of all beholders, such as Venus showed herself to the Phrygian shepherds, having, indeed, the celestial form of that goddess. Both sailors

of a beautiful cascade, which came from the tops of the mountains, and poured its foaming waters into the sea. A village was situated at the foot of this cascade, and there appeared to be no breakers in this part of the coast. We all wished to be able to anchor within reach of this beautiful spot; we were constantly sounding aboard the ships, and our boats took soundings close under the shore; but we found a bottom of nothing but rocks in this port, and were forced to go in search of another anchorage.

The piraguas returned to the ship at sun-rising, and continued to make exchanges all the day. We likewise opened new branches of commerce; for, besides the fruits, which they brought the day before, and other refreshments, such as fowls and pigeons, the islands brought with them several instruments for fishing; stone chisels, strange kinds of cloth, shells, &c. They wanted iron and ear-rings in exchange. This bartering trade was carried on very honestly, as the day before: this time some pretty and almost naked women came in the piraguas. One of the islanders went on board the *Etoile*, and stayed there all night, without being in the least uneasy.

This night was likewise spent in plying; and on the 6th in the morning we were got to the most northerly extremity of the island.

VÜE DU VAISSEAU DU ROY   LE DUC DE BOURGOGNE,

Lancé a la Mer dans le Port   *de Rochefort le 20 Octobre 1751.*

Dedié a Monseigneur Le Duc de Bourgogne, Par son très humble et de l'Academie   *et très obéissant Serviteur Ozanne, Dessinateur de la Marine a Brest.*

144 French shipyard scene: the launching of the royal ship *Duc de Bourgogne* at Rochefort, 20th October 1751. Engraving after N. Ozanne.

and soldiers endeavoured to come to the hatchway; and the capstan was never hove with more alacrity than on this occasion.

At last our cares succeeded in keeping these bewitched fellows in order, though it was no less difficult to keep the command of ourselves. One single Frenchman, who was my cook, having found means to escape against my orders, soon returned more dead than alive. He had hardly set his feet on shore, with the fair whom he had chosen, when he was immediately surrounded by a crowd of Indians, who undressed him from head to feet. He thought he was utterly lost, not knowing where the exclamations of those people would end, who were tumultuously examining every part of his body. After having considered him well, they returned him his clothes, put into his pockets whatever they had taken out of them, and brought the girl to him, desiring him to content those desires which had brought him on shore with her. All their persuasive arguments had no effect; they were obliged to bring the poor cook on board, who told me, that I might reprimand him as much as I pleased, but that I could never frighten him so much, as he had just now been frightened on shore.

from *A Voyage Round the World in 1766, 1767, 1768 and 1769,* by Louis de Bougainville.

Scenes from Cook's voyages

The three voyages of James Cook (1768–71, 1772–5 and 1776–9) were the world's first scientific expeditions (see p. 39*f*). As well as astronomers and naturalists, artists were taken to record the events of the voyages and to bring back accurate natural history drawings. In contrast to Anson's voyage some thirty years earlier, the problem of scurvy hardly arose, thanks to the numerous experimental foods showered on Cook by the Admiralty (including sauerkraut and blocks of 'portable soup' made from the concentrated juices of lemons and other fruit), and thanks also to Cook's forceful way of administering them to his sailors and his insistence that on every visit ashore sailors should bring back some green food to the ship.

145 *below* Matavai Bay and Point Venus, Tahiti, oil painting by W. Hodges (1744–97).

'SATURDAY 3rd [June 1769]. This day prov'd as favourable to our purpose as we could wish, not a Clowd was to be seen the whole day and the Air was perfectly clear, so that we had every advantage we could desire in Observing the whole of the passage of the Planet Venus over the Suns disk: we very distinctly saw an Atmosphere or dusky shade round the body of the Planet which very much disturbed the times of the Contacts particularly the two internal ones. Dr Solander observed as well as Mr Green and my self, and we differ'd from one another in observeing the times of the Contacts much more than could be expected. Mr Greens Telescope and mine were of the same Magnifying power but that of the D^r was greater than ours. It was nearly calm the whole day and the Thermometer expose'd to the Sun about the middle of the Day rose to a degree of heat (119) we have not before met with.'

from the journal of Captain Cook on his first voyage.

146 *below* Waterspout off Cape Stephens, New Zealand by W. Hodges.
'TUESDAY 18*th* [May 1773]. At 4 o'Clock in the PM the sky became suddenly obscured and seemed to indicate much Wind which occasioned us to clew up all our sails, presently after Six Water Spouts were seen, four rose and spent themselves between us and the land, the fifth was at some distance without us and the Sixth pass'd under our Stern at about fifty yards from us, the diameter of the base of this spout I judged to be about fifty or sixty feet, during the time these Spouts lasted which was near a hour we had light puffs of wind from all points of the Compass. Water Spouts are caused by whirl winds which carries the Water in a stream upwards, the Sea below them is much agitated and all in a foam from which a tube or round boddy is formed by which the water is conveyed up to the Clowds, some of our people said they saw a bird in the one near us which was whirled round in the same manner as the fly of a Jack while it was carried upwards; we had thick hazey weather for some hours after with variable Winds, but by middnight the

Weather was clear at which time we pass'd Stephen's Isle at the distance of one mile.'
from the journal of Captain Cook on his second voyage.

147 *below* A bearded penguin by G. Forster.
'WEDNESDAY 15*th* [December 1773]. *Therm.r. Noon 31. Winds WBN, NNW, & West. Course S 60° 15' E. Dist. Sailed 116 Miles. Lat. in South 65° 52'. Longde. in West Reck.g. 159° 20'. Long. made from C. Pallisser 25° 19'.*
Fresh gales and thick Foggy weather with snow, except in the PM when we had some intervals of clear Weather in one of which we found the Variation to be 14° 12' E. At 6 o'Clock double reefed the Top-sails and handed the Main sail and Mizen Top-sail. The Ice begins to increase fast, from Noon till 8 o'Clock in the evening we saw but two islands, but from 8 to 4 AM we passed fifteen, besides a quantity of loose Ice which we sailed through, this last increased so fast upon us that at 6 o'Clock we were obliged to alter the Course

more to the East, having to the South an extensive feild of loose ice; there were several partitions in the feild and clear water behind it, but as the wind blew strong the Weather foggy, the going in among this Ice might have been attended with bad concequences, especially as the wind would not permit us to return. We therefore hauled to the NE on which course we had stretched but a little way before we found our selves quite imbayed by the ice and were obliged to Tack and stretch back to the SW having the loose field ice to the South and many large islands to the North. After standing two hours on this tack the wind very luckily veered to the westward with which we tacked and stretched to the Northward (being at this time in Lat 66°0′s) and soon got clear of all the loose ice but had yet many huge islands to incounter, which were so numerous that we had to luff for one and bear up for a nother, one of these mases was very near proving fatal to us, we had not weather[ed] it more than once or twice our length, had we not succeeded this circumstance could never have been related. According to the old proverb a miss is as good as a mile, but our situation requires more misses than we can expect, this together with the improbability of meeting with land to the South and the impossibility of exploreing it for the ice if we did find any, determined me to haul to the north. This feild or loose ice is not such as is usually formed in Bays or Rivers, but like such as is broke off from large Islands, round ill-shaped pieces from the size of a small Ship's Hull downwards, whilst we were amongst it we frequently, notwithstanding all our care, ran against some of the large pieces, the shoks which the Ship received thereby was very considerable, such as no Ship could bear long unless properly prepared for the purpose. Saw a great number of Penguins on an ice island and some Antartick Petrels flying about.'
from the journal of Captain Cook on his second voyage.

148 *left* Poedoua by John Webber (1750–93) (oil). Poedoua was a princess of Raiatea, one of the Society Islands.

'We were no sooner in safty then Numbers of the Natives flock'd on board of us from all parts amongst which were many of our old Friends, they seem'd very happy to see us. Amongst the rest that came off was the King named *Oreo,* this man was pecularly fond of Captain Cook; and Insisted on his going on shore that evening to see a Play or Heva, the Principal Parts of which was to be perform'd by his Daughter a young Lady about 15 years of age – and in consequence we all went, and were conducted up to his house amidst a vast concourse of People where we were entertain'd with Cocoa Nuts &ca and Introduced to the young Princess; she was of the middleing stature rather Slender, and Delicate, with good teeth and Eyes and a regular set of features, Black Hair and her complexion so fair that I have seen many Ladies in England much more of a Brunett.

After we had been in this House a little while Miss *Poedoua* for that was her name desired me to go and see her dress; we went to an ajacent House, the front of which was open and opposite it at the distance of about Ten yards between these two Houses was a space neatly cover'd with Matts, on these Matts they acted; in the first house sat the audience and in the second the Musick, one end being inclosed for the actress to dress in, which was inclosed; into this Place she carried me, where undressing an old woman came in to dress her, her dress consisted of large Pieces of Painted cloths made up in folds and girded tort round her to an amazing thickness, and her head dressed in the Manner of a Turband with fine Platted black hair orniemented with flowers. All the actors being ready they began with a Dance, the Musick consisting of 4 Drums and some Boys to sing, this ending the Men came out and acted their Parts which consisted in rediculeing the Chief People about

them so that the whole together made up a kind of a Burletta, indeed the men seem'd to go thro' their Parts exceedingly well but their Danceing consisted of the most ludicrous gestures I ever beheld.'
from the journal of Lieutenant Richard Pickersgill on Cook's second voyage.

149 *above* Boats of the Friendly Isles, by W. Hodges (1744-97). Cook visited the Tonga Group or Friendly Isles on both his second and third voyages.

150 *facing page* Anchorage at Nuku'alofa, aquatint by J. Cleveley (1747–86).
'Soon after we had anchored which was about noon several of the Inhabitants came off in their canoes to the Ships. These as also our two Pilots assured us we should find deep water farther in and a bottom free from rocks, and so it proved for about 4 PM the boats made the signal for having found good anchorage – upon which we weighed and stood in till dark, then anchored in 9 fathom a fine clear sandy bottom. During the night had some showers of rain, but towards the morning the wind shifted to the South & SE and brought on fair weather. At day break weighed and worked in for the shore, meeting with no obstruction but what was vissible and easily avoided. While we were plying up to the harbour the Natives directed us to, the King kept sailing round us in his Canoe, there were at the same time a great many small Canoes about the Ships; two who could not get out of his way he run quite over with as little concern as if they had been bits of wood. Amongst many others who came on board the Ship was Otaga who was so usefull to me when I was here last voyage, and one Toobough who at the same time was the Friend of Captain Furneaux. They brought each of them a hog and some yams as a testimony of their friendship and I was not wanting on my part in making them a suitable return.

At length about 2 PM we arrived at our intended Station, being a very snug place formed by the shore of Tongatabu on the SE and two small islands on the East and NE: here we anchored in 10 fathom Water over a bottom of owsey sand, distant from the shore one third of a mile. Soon after we had Anchored, I landed accompanied by Omai and some of the Officers, we found the King waiting for us on the beach, ready to conduct us to a small neat house, situated a little within the skirts of the woods with a fine large area

before it; this house the Cheif told me was at my service during my stay and a better situation we could not wish for.'
From the journal of Captain Cook on his third voyage, 10 June 1777.

151 *overleaf* The Refit at Nootka Sound, by J. Webber (1750–93). In late March 1778, on his third voyage, on the way from Hawaii to search for a western entrance to the North-west Passage, Cook put into Nootka Sound on Vancouver Island (which he thought was part of the American mainland) for

repairs to the *Resolution,* necessitated by faulty work in Deptford Dockyard. 'MONDAY APRIL 6TH. The Indians trading about the Ship as usual. We found the Head of our foremast so much damaged that it became necessary to get it on shore to be repaired, this Business & caulking the ship's Sides employed the Carpenters of both Ships. Hitherto we had seen none of their young Women tho' we had often given the men to understand how agreeable their Company would be to us & how profitable to themselves, in consequence of which they about this time brought two or three Girls to the Ships; tho' some of them had no bad faces yet as they were exceedingly dirty their Persons at first sight were not very inviting, however our young Gentlemen were not to be discouraged by such an obstacle as this which they found was to be removed with Soap & warm water, this they called the Ceremony of Purification and were themselves the Officiators at it, & it must be mentioned to their praise that they performed it with much piety & Devotion, taking as much pleasure in cleansing a naked young Woman from all Impurities in a Tub of Warm Water, as a young Confessor would to absolve a beutiful Virgin who was about to sacrifice that Name to himself. This Ceremony appeared very strange to the Girls, who in order to render themselves agreeable to us had taken particular pains to daub their Hair and faces well with red oaker which to their great astonishment we took much pains to wash off. Such are the different Ideas formed by different nations of Beauty & cleanliness; they were prevailed upon to sleep on board the Ships, or rather forced to it by their Fathers or other Relations who brought them on board. In their behaviour they were very modest and timid, in which they differed very much from the South Sea Island Girls who in general are impudent & loud.

Their Fathers who generally accompanied them made the Bargain & received the price of the Prostitution of their Daughters, which was commonly a Pewter plate well scoured for one Night. When they found that this was a profitable Trade they brought more young women to the Ships, who in compliance with our preposterous Humour spared themselves the trouble of laying on their Paint & us of washing it off again by making themselves tolerable clean before they came to us, by which they found they were more welcome Visitors and thus by falling in with our ridiculous Notions (for such no doubt they deemed them) they found means at last to disburthen our young Gentry of their Kitchen furniture, many of us after leaving this Harbour not being able to muster a plate to eat our Salt beef from.'
from the journal of David Samwell, Surgeon of the Discovery.

152 *opposite.* A walrus, 1778, by William Ellis.
'WEDNESDAY 19*th* [August 1778]. The 19th at 8 AM the Wind veering back to West I tacked to the Northward and at Noon the Latitude was 70°06′ N, Longitude 196°42′ E. In this situation we had a good deal of drift ice about us and the main ice was about two leagues to the North.

At ½ past 1 PM we got close in with the edge of the main ice, it was not so compact as that which we had seen more to the Northward, but it was too close and in too large pieces to force the ships through it.

On the ice lay a prodigious number of Sea horses and as we were in want of fresh provisions the boats from each ship were sent to get some. By 7 oclock in the evening we had got on board the Resolution Nine of these Animals which till now we had supposed to be Sea Cows, so that we were not a little disappointed, especially some of the Seamen who for the Novelty of the thing, had been feasting their eyes for some days past, nor would they have been disappointed now, or known the difference, if we had not happened to have one or two on board who had been in Greenland and declared what animals

150

these were, and that no one ever eat of them. But not withstanding this we lived upon them so long as they lasted and there were few on board who did not prefer it to salt meat. They lay in herds of many hundred upon the ice, huddling one over the other like swine, and roar or bray very loud, so that in the night or foggy weather they gave us notice of the ice long before we could see it. We never found the Whole herd a sleep, some were always upon the watch, these, on the approach of the boat, would wake those next to them and these the others, so that the whole herd would be awake presently. But they were seldom in a hurry to get away till after they had been once fire[d] at, then they would tumble one over the other into the sea in the utmost confusion, and if we did not at first discharge kill those we fired at out right we generally lost them tho' mortally wounded. They did not appear to us to be that dangerous animal some Authors have discribed, not even when attacked, they are rather more so to appearance than reality; Vast numbers of them would follow and come close up to the boats, but the flash of a Musket in the pan, or even pointing one at them would send them down in an instant. The feemale will defend the young one to the very last and at the expence of her life whether in the Water or on the ice; nor will the young quit the dam though she be dead so that if you kill one you are sure of the other. The Dam when in the Water holds the young one between her fore fins.'
from the journal of Captain Cook on his third voyage.

153 *overleaf* The Death of Captain Cook at Hawaii, 14 February 1779, aquatint by J. Cleveley (1747–86).
'Capt Cook landed at the Town situate within the NW point with his Pinnace & Launch, leaving the small Cutter off the Point to prevent the escape of any Canoes that might be dispos'd to get off, at his Landing he order'd 9 Marines which we had in the Boats and myself onshore to attend him and immediately march'd into the Town where he enquir'd for Terre'oboo and the 2 Boys (his sons who had liv'd principally with Capt Cook

onboard the Resolution since Terre'oboo's first arrival among us). Messengers were immediately dispatch'd and the 2 Boys soon came and conducted us to their Fathers house. After waiting some time on the outside Capt Cook doubted the old Gentlemans being there and sent me in that I might inform Him. I found our old acquaintance just awoke from Sleep when upon my acquainting him that Capt Cook was at the door, he very readily went with me to Him. Capt Cook after some little conversation observ'd that Terre'oboo was quite innocent of what had happen'd [the theft of the expedition's large cutter] and proposed to the old Gentleman to go onboard with him, which he readily agree'd to, and we accordingly proceeded towards the Boats, but having advanc'd near to the Water side an elderly Woman whose name was Kar'na'cub'ra one of his Wives came to him and with many tears and intreaties beg'd he would not go onboard, at the same time 2 Chiefs laid hold of him and insisting that he should not, made him sit down; the old Man now appear'd dejected and frighten'd. It was at this period we first began to suspect that they were not very well dispos'd towards us, and the Marines being huddled together in the midst of an immense Mob compos'd of at least 2 or 3 thousand People, I propos'd to Capt Cook that they might be arrang'd in order along the Rocks by the Water side which he approving of, the Croud readily made way for them and they were drawn up accordingly: we now clearly saw they were collecting their Spears &c, but an Artful Rascal of a Priest was singing & making a ceremonious offering of a Coco Nut to the Capt and Terre'oboo to divert their attention from the Manœuvres of the surrounding multitude. Capt Cook now gave up all thoughts of taking Terre'oboo onboard with the following observation to me, "We can never think of compelling him to go onboard without killing a number of these People," and I believe was just going to give orders to embark, when he was interrupted by a fellow arm'd with a long Iron Spike (which they call a Pah'hoo'ah) and a Stone; this Man made a flourish with his Pah'hoo'ah, and threaten'd to throw his stone upon which Capt Cook discharg'd a load of small shot at him but he having his Mat on the small shot did not penetrate it, and had no other effect than farther to provoke and encourage them, I could not observe the least fright it occasion'd; immediately upon this an Aree [a warrior] arm'd with a Pah'hoo'ah attempted to stab me but I foil'd his attempt by giving him a severe blow with the Butt End of my Musket, just at this time they began to throw stones, and one of the Marines was knock'd down, the Capt then fir'd a ball and kill'd a Man. They now made a general attack and the Capt gave orders to the Marines to fire and afterwards called out "Take to the Boats".'
from the report of Lieutenant Phillips of the Marines who accompanied Cook.

'Captain Cook was advanced a few paces before the Marines when they fired, the Stones flew as thick as hail which knocked the Lieut. down & as he was rising a fellow struck him in the back with a Spear, however he recovered himself shot the Indian dead and escaped into the Water. Captain Cook was now the only Man on the Rock, he was seen walking down towards the Pinnace, holding his left hand against the Back of his head to guard it from the Stones & carrying his Musket under the other Arm. An Indian came running behind him, stopping once or twice as he advanced, as if he was afraid that he should turn round, then taking him unaware he sprung to him, knocked him on the back of his head with a large Club taken out of a fence, & instantly fled with the greatest precipitation; the blow made Captain Cook stagger two or three paces, he then fell on his hand & one knee & dropped his Musket, as he was rising another Indian came running to him & before he could recover himself from the Fall drew out an iron Dagger he concealed

under his feathered Cloak & stuck it with all his force into the back of his Neck, which made Capt. Cook tumble into the Water in a kind of a bite by the side of the rock where the water is about knee deep; here he was followed by a crowd of people who endeavoured to keep him under water, but struggling very strongly with them he got his head up & looking towards the Pinnace which was not above a boat hook's Length from him waved his hands to them for Assistance, which it seems it was not in their Power to give. The Indians got him under water again but he disengaged himself & got his head up once more & not being able to swim he endeavoured to scramble on the Rock, when a fellow gave him a blow on the head with a large Club and he was seen alive no more.'
from the journal of David Samwell, Surgeon of the Discovery.

Naval tactics

To load a gun, it had first to be hauled inboard by means of tackles secured to ring-bolts in the deck amidships and to the carriage. After the first shot this was done by the recoil. Before reloading it was first necessary to clean the bore of the smouldering material left by the previous cartridge. This was done with a cork-screw-like object on the end of a pole, known as a 'worm', and followed up with a wet sponge. A cartridge made of specially treated paper and containing black powder was then fed into the barrel by a ladle, followed by the wad and the shot and the whole rammed home.

The gun's crew then manned the two tackles rigged for hauling the carriage into its firing position with the gun muzzle protruding beyond the square gun-ports in the ship's side. The gun-captain would clear out the touch-hole or vent with a priming iron, which would also prick a hole in the cartridge, and fill the touch-hole with powder from his powder flask. At the order to fire he would apply the glowing end of the slow-match fixed to the end of his linstock.

Wooden ships were remarkably hard to sink, and boarding was often the only way to bring an action to a decisive conclusion. An added incentive was that the capture rather than the destruction of a ship brought prize money to the victors. Some captains returned from the wars as very rich men.

154 Battle of Negapatam, 6 July 1782, oil by Dominic Serres (1722–93), fought by British and French fleets off India. This is a rather idealized picture which illustrates the rigid lines adopted for fleet actions. The line of men-of-war moved towards their opponents, while the frigates etc. kept to the outside. The only manoeuvre was to seize the weather gauge, which the possessor could use to force a closer fight or break off the action at will.

Epitome of a general engagement

The whole economy of a naval engagement may be arranged under the following heads, *viz* the PREPARATION; the ACTION; and the REPAIR, or refitting for the purposes of navigation.

The PREPARATION is begun by issuing an order to clear the ship for action, which is repeated by the boatswain and his mates at all the hatchways, or staircases, leading to the different batteries. As the cannon cannot be worked while the hammocks are suspended in their usual situations, it becomes necessary to remove them as quick as possible. By this circumstance a double advantage is obtained: the batteries of cannon are immediately cleared of an encumbrance, and the hammocks are converted into a sort of parapet, to prevent the execution of small shot on the quarter-deck, tops, and forecastle. At the summons of the boatswain, *Up all hammocks!* every sailor repairs to his own; and, having stowed his bedding properly, he cords it firmly with a lashing, or line, provided for that purpose. He then carries it to the quarter-deck, poop, or forecastle, or wherever it may be necessary. As each side of the quarter-deck and poop is furnished with a double network, supported by iron cranes fixed immediately above the gunwale, or top of the ship's side, the hammocks thus corded are firmly stowed by the quarter-master between the two parts of the netting, so as to form an excellent barrier. The tops, waist, and forecastle, are then fenced in the same manner.

Whilst these offices are performed below, the boatswain and his mates are employed in securing the sail-yards, to prevent them from tumbling down when the ship is cannonaded, as she might thereby be disabled, and rendered incapable of attack, retreat, or pursuit. The yards are now likewise secured by strong chains, or ropes, additional to those by which they are usually suspended. The boatswain also provides the necessary materials to repair the rigging, wherever it may be damaged by the shot of the enemy; and to supply whatever parts of it may be entirely destroyed. The carpenter and his crew in the meanwhile prepare his shot plugs and mauls, to close up any dangerous breaches that may be made near the surface of the water; and provide the iron-work necessary to refit the chain-pumps, in case their machinery should be wounded in the engagement. The gunner, with his mates and quarter-gunners, is busied in examining the cannon of the different batteries, to see that their charges are thoroughly dry and fit for execution: to have everything ready for furnishing the great guns and small arms with powder, as soon as the action begins: and to keep a sufficient number of cartridges continually filled, to supply the place of those expended in battle. The master and his mates are attentive to have the sails properly trimmed, according to the situation of the ship; and to reduce or multiply

them, as occasion requires, with all possible expedition. The lieutenants visit the different decks, to see that they are effectually cleared of all encumbrance, so that nothing may retard the execution of the artillery; and to enjoin the other officers to diligence and alertness, in making the necessary dispositions for the expected engagement, so that everything may be in readiness at a moment's warning.

When the hostile ships have approached each other to a competent distance, the drums beat to arms. The boatswain and his mates pipe, *all hands to quarters!* at every hatchway. All the persons appointed to manage the great guns immediately repair to their respective stations. The crows, handspecs, rammers, sponges, powder-horns, matches and train-tackles, are placed in order by the side of every cannon. The hatches are immediately laid, to prevent anyone from deserting his post by escaping into the lower apartments. The marines are drawn up in rank and file, on the quarter-deck, poop and forecastle. The lashings of the great guns are cast loose, and the tompions withdrawn. The whole artillery, above and below, is run out at the ports, and levelled to the point-blank range ready for firing.

The necessary preparations being completed, and the officers and crew ready at their respective stations, to obey the order, the commencement of the action is determined by the mutual distance and situation of the adverse ships, or by the signal from the commander in chief of the fleet or squadron. The cannon being levelled in parallel rows, projecting from the ship's side, the most natural order of battle is evidently to range the ships abreast of each other, especially if the engagement is general. The most convenient distance is properly within the point-blank range of a musket, so that all the artillery may do effectual execution.

The ACTION usually begins by a vigorous cannonade, accompanied with the whole efforts of the swivel guns and the small-arms. The method of firing in platoons, or volleys of cannon at once, appears inconvenient in the sea-service, and perhaps should never be attempted, unless in the battering of a fortification. The sides and decks of the ship, although sufficiently strong for all the purposes of war, would be too much shaken by so violent an explosion and recoil. The general rule observed on this occasion throughout the ship, is to load, fire, and sponge the guns with all possible expedition, yet without confusion or precipitation. The captain of each gun is particularly enjoined to fire when the piece is properly directed to its object, that the shot may not be fruitlessly expended. The lieutenants, who command the different batteries, traverse the deck to see that the battle is prosecuted with vivacity; and to exhort and animate the men to their duty. The midshipmen second these injunctions, and give the necessary assistance, wherever it may be required, at the guns

155 The Capture of the *Glorioso* 9 October 1747, oil by C. Brooking (1723–59). Note the burnt-out ship in the background. Fire in battle was particularly dreaded, for wooden ships soon blazed down to the waterline or blew up. It was often caused in close range fighting by the flaming wads from the opponent's guns being hurled amongst the splintered timbers.

156 The French victory on 27 June 1693, at the Bay of Lagos on the south coast of Portugal, the scene of more than one naval battle in the age of sail. Tourville, the French admiral, was an original strategist and naval thinker. After Gudin.

157 The Battle of Malaga, 24 August 1704, after Ozanne. Like most naval battles of the period, it was indecisive.

158 HMS *Agamemnon*, 64 guns, getting in lower masts at Portsmouth in 1781. Pen drawing by Harold Wyllie. The *Agamemnon* was built by the famous Henry Adams at Buckler's Hard near Southampton Water. She was the favourite ship of Horatio Nelson, who admired her sailing qualities, and she took part in the Battle of Trafalgar in 1805.

committed to their charge. The gunner should be particularly attentive that all the artillery is sufficiently supplied with powder, and that the cartridges are carefully conveyed along the decks in covered boxes. The havoc produced by a continuation of this mutual assault may be readily conjectured by the reader's imagination. The defeated ship having acknowledged the victor, by striking her colours, is immediately taken possession of by the conqueror, who secures her officers and crew as prisoners in his own ship and invests his principal officer with the command of the prize until a captain is appointed by the commander in chief.

The engagement being concluded, they begin the REPAIR: the cannon are secured by their breechings and tackles, with all convenient expedition. Whatever sails have been rendered unserviceable are unbent; and the wounded masts and yards struck upon the deck, and fished or replaced by others. The standing rigging is knotted, and the running rigging spliced wherever necessary. Proper sails are bent in the room of those which have been displaced as useless. The carpenter and his crew are employed in repairing the breaches made in the ship's hull, by shot-plugs, pieces of plank, and sheet lead. The gunner and his assistants are busied in replenishing the allotted number of

charged cartridges, to supply the place of those which have been expended, and in refitting whatever furniture of the cannon may have been damaged by the late action.

Such are the usual process and consequences of an engagement between two ships of war, which may be considered as descriptive of a general battle between fleets or squadrons. The latter, however, involves a greater variety of incidents, and necessarily requires more comprehensive skill and judgment in the commanding officer.

Of boarding

Boarding is the art of approaching the ship of an enemy so near, that you can easily, and in spite of him, throw on board the grapplings, which are fixed on the lower yard-arms, at the forecastle, gangways, &c. for the purpose of being thrown into the enemy's ship, as soon as alongside, in order to confine the vessels together, and give the people an opportunity of getting on board, to carry the adverse ship sword in hand.

To board to windward, or to avoid being boarded

If it be desired to board a ship which keeps her wind under

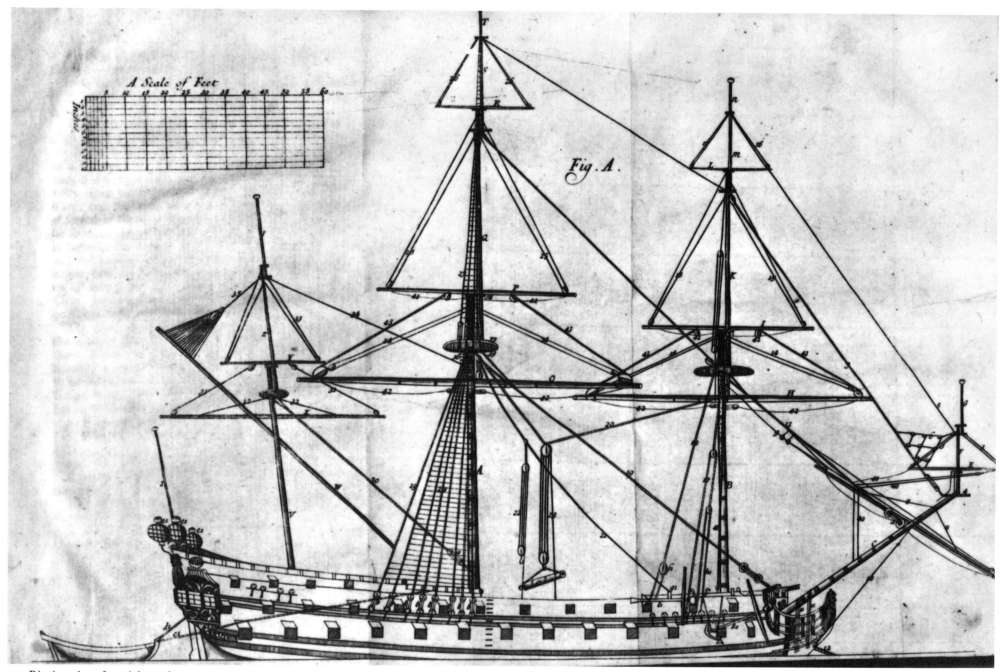

A Scale of Feet

Fig. A.

159 Rigging plan of an eighteenth-century frigate showing method of hoisting in and out guns and other heavy stores.

Plate 27 Rogers Capturing the *Jeune Richard,* by Samuel Drummond (1765–1844). A typical boarding action of the mid eighteenth century.

an easy sail; or that does not shorten sail, but over which the boarding vessel has the advantage of sailing; she must get on the weather quarter of the ship she means to board, within half a pistol shot. She should then begin the action, and continue it with vivacity, to cover her manoeuvre by the smoke of the cannon and musketry of both ships; then, under the cover of this cloud, let her make more sail if she has not way enough, in order to augment the velocity of the ship and the rapidity of her movements, that she may more readily lay on board her enemy, on the weather side, either exactly abreast or a little abaft. This is very easily executed, by edging down suddenly upon her; so, however, as not to be raked by the enemy's fire. The ship boarded by this manoeuvre can hardly suspect the design but at the moment when, or very little before, the grapnels will be on board of her. In this situation

the boarded vessel has but one doubtful expedient to try, and which even will be of no service if the boarder observes her well. For, the moment she braces sharp aback her head sails, to cause the ship's falling off, and squares those aft to give her sternway, the boarder has only to perform briskly the same manoeuvre, and they will then be both as near for boarding as before, provided the boarding ship feels quickly the impulse of her sails and helm, which ought to be put a-weather and kept so till the ship's head-way ceases, when it is to be put a-lee, to assist her in falling off, in manoeuvering as is box-hauling, in order to board the enemy to leeward; for, the boarder ought to be on the quarter of the other, since at the moment the two ships were right before the wind, she who was directly to windward, and wished to board, had only to continue her movements of rotation, and render her velocity equal to that of her adversary, by shortening sail in order not to pass her. If therefore, the circular motion is kept up by the boarder, which at first caused him to fall off, and now brings him to the wind on the other tack, he will join the enemy to leeward; for, it is evident that, if this motion of turning be more rapid than that of the ship which wishes to avoid boarding, the boarder will close her before she can range to the wind on the other tack, since the boarder comes round with greater celerity. However, if the ship which fears boarding was pressed thus closely, she could make no other attempt than to throw once more all her sails to the mast, by bracing them only perpendicular to the keel to give her sternway, and putting the helm a-weather, to keep her to the wind, as soon as her headway ceases; observing that, she being to windward, this manoeuvre may cause her to drive on the boarder, as he is then watching for her under her lee. As there is no other resource, necessity obliges her to this expedient; because, if the ship which is attacked could go astern with sufficient velocity, she might let the boarder pass ahead, veer under his stern, and rake him, if he is not as quick as the other to foresee this manoeuvre, and as nimble in manoeuvering in the same manner as the enemy's ship: because, the great velocity with which he comes to the wind and goes ahead (his sails being still full), puts him in this bad situation, which may prevent his persisting in the inclination of boarding. It is however very clear that the boarder will attain his purpose, if he takes care to throw all his sails aback at the same time as the ship to windward; because, the attacked ship dropping to leeward, and having sternway first, approaches a little the boarder, who has still preserved his position on the quarter, and longer kept his luff, by having gone astern somewhat later than the weather ship. It must be farther observed, that when the two ships are right before the wind, if the vessel which fears boarding moves quicker to the wind than the one which attacks, she will

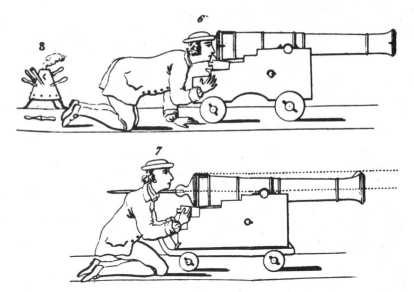

avoid it, as the retreating ship will be close to the wind before the other, and able to get ahead of her by making all sail to keep her wind, or to heave in stays and get upon the other tack. But, it must be considered that this last movement is dis-advantageous; as, by so doing, it will present the stern to a ship, which no doubt will take advantage of that situation, and rake her; which might be more destructive than a well-opposed attack by boarding.

There is, however, no doubt that if the ship inclined to board sails better than the other, it will always be in her power to execute that design, if she is manoeuvered as the ship which flies.

To board to leeward, when close to the wind, or to avoid being boarded
In order to execute this manoeuvre, the boarder is to come within pistol shot, close in the wake, or, at most, to the weather quarter of the ship he means to attack; taking care to continue steering, so as not to be raked by any of the guns which belong to the quarter he stands on. Then, to come up with his adversary, he must edge away a little, and range round aft, so close upon the enemy's lee quarter, that his cat-head may almost touch her quarter gallery. Now, when you have shot sufficiently ahead, your ship being parallel to your adversary's so as to bring your forecastle abreast of your enemy's mainmast, the mizen and mizen staysail sheets are to be hauled well aft, the helm put hard a-lee, and the head sheets let fly; then, your ship, coming rapidly to the wind, shivers her sails, and closes the opposing vessel side to side. This manoeuvre is infallible when you have the advantage of sailing, provided very great attention is paid to it. But great

NAVAL CUTLASS EXERCISE.

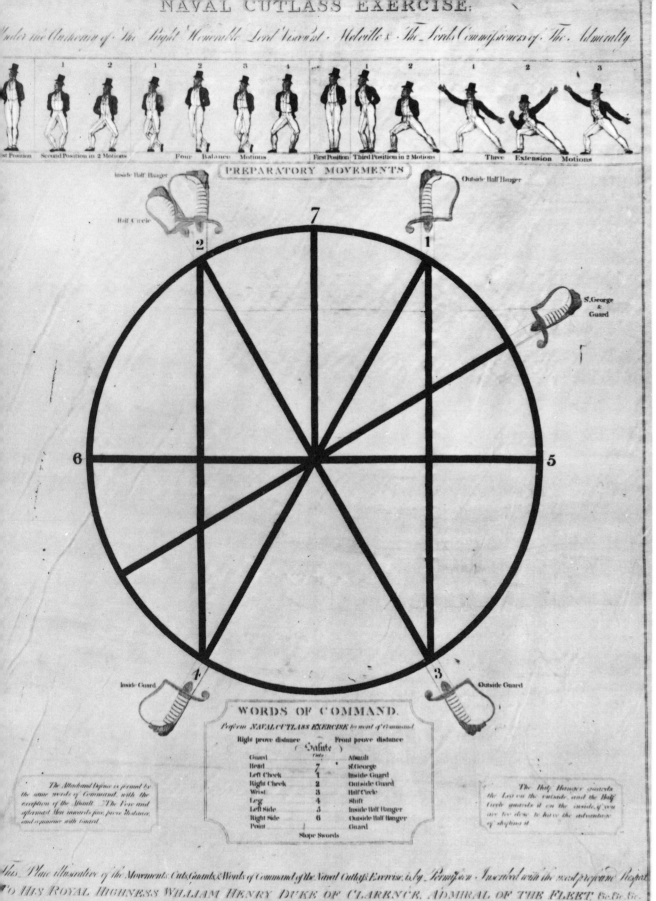

Under the Authority of The Right Honorable Lord Viscount Melville & The Lords Commissioners of The Admiralty.

PREPARATORY MOVEMENTS

First Position · Second Position in 2 Motions · Four Balance Motions · First Position · Third Position in 2 Motions · Three Extension Motions

Inside Half Hanger · Half Circle · Outside Half Hanger · S. George & Guard · Inside Guard · Outside Guard

WORDS OF COMMAND.

Perform NAVAL CUTLASS EXERCISE by word of Command.

Right prove distance · Front prove distance

Salute

	Cuts	
Guard		Assault
Head	7	St George
Left Cheek	1	Inside Guard
Right Cheek	2	Outside Guard
Wrist	3	Half Circle
Leg	4	Shift
Left Side	5	Inside Half Hanger
Right Side	6	Outside Half Hanger
Point		Guard

Slope Swords

The Attack and Defence is formed by the same words of Command, with the exception of the Assault. The Fire and aftermost Men inwards face, prove distance, and commence with Guard.

The Half Hanger guards the Leg on the outside, and the Half Circle guards it on the inside, if you are too close to have the advantage of stopping it.

This Plate illustrative of the Movements, Cuts, Guards, & Words of Command of the Naval Cutlass Exercise, is by Permission Inscribed with the most profound Respect to HIS ROYAL HIGHNESS WILLIAM HENRY DUKE OF CLARENCE, ADMIRAL OF THE FLEET, &c &c &c.

by HENRY ANGELO Jun.r

161 *facing, left* Diagrams illustrating naval cutlass exercise in the late eighteenth century.

162 *facing, right* French naval officers' uniforms 1678–1845. *Top row (left to right):* 1678 (Louis XIV) Officier de Marine; 1758 (Louis XV) Gentilhomme garde du pavillon amiral; 1793 (République) Officier de Marine. *Bottom row (left to right):* 1810 (Empire) Capitaine de Vaisseau; 1819 (Restauration) Officier de Marine; 1845 (Louis-Philippe I) Capitaine de Vaisseau.

163 The French corvette *Bayonnaise*, 20 guns, and the English frigate *Ambuscade*, 42 guns. In this engagement on the 14 December 1798 the French crew boarded the English ship which struck its colours. The *Bayonnaise*, being totally dismasted was towed into La Rochelle by the captured frigate. Painting by Crépin.

attention is necessary; because, if at this moment the weather ship, which wishes to avoid the boarding, either sets her courses, or lays all those flat aback which she had set, she may perchance break the grapnels if you have neglected to trim your sails in the same manner as hers: for, by making more sail, if the wind be a little fresh, she will shoot ahead through the water, and drag the boarder with such force as to break the chains or hawsers by which the two ships are confined together. By laying all flat to the mast, the boarded vessel is still more likely to succeed, since the sails of one ship will be full, while those of the other are aback.

This mode of boarding may, as shown before, be anticipated and avoided, if the boarder does not pay the strictest attention to his own as well as to his adversary's manoeuvres: but it may be still more readily avoided; if the last mentioned vessel braces her head sails sharp aback, setting only, if necessary, the foresail, at the same instant laying to the mast or shivering (according to the necessity for more or less sternway) all those which are abaft, and putting the helm hard a-lee. All this is to be executed when the boarder is still about a ship's length (more or less) astern of the other vessel. The quickness of this evolution, and the rapid veering of the weather ship, may bring the boarding vessel, which is a little to leeward or astern of the other, into the most dangerous situation, if she does not manoeuvre in the same manner and with equal celerity; as the boarder's sails, being full, keep up his velocity, and may, before he can veer, engage his bowsprit in the main shrouds of the enemy, who pays short round on her head.

This terrible and dangerous situation is infinitely to be dreaded; and it is of the highest importance to pay the strictest attention to your own manoeuvres, and to those of your opponent, which you are to endeavour to foresee and avoid as much as possible.

from *Rigging and Seamanship*, vol. 2, 1794.

164 Horatio Nelson (1758–1805), oil painting by L. F. Abbott (1760–1805).

Documents of Trafalgar

The novel features of Nelson's famous Trafalgar Memorandum were his decision *a*) not to form the single line-ahead for battle, hitherto sacrosanct and strictly enjoined by the Fighting Instructions, but to attack in the order of sailing (normally two or three columns) in such a way as to overwhelm the rear half of the enemy's line; *b*) to delegate the direction of one line to the Second in Command; *c*) to release captains of ships from too rigid a conformity with standing instructions by his statement that 'No Captain can do very wrong if he places his ship alongside that of an enemy'.

Prior to Nelson, two fleets meeting and fighting in a formal line of battle rarely achieved a decisive result. Nelson aimed to cause a mêlée in which the experience of the British sailors, who spent all their time at sea, would be decisive.

Lord Nelson's Plan of Attack, given out on board His Majesty's Ship Victory, dated off Cadiz, October 10, 1805

MEM.

Thinking it almost impossible to bring a fleet of forty sail of the line into a line of battle; invariable winds, thick weather, and other circumstances which must occur; without such a loss of time, that the opportunity would probably be lost of bringing the enemy to battle, in such a manner as to make the business decisive;—I have therefore made up my mind to keep the fleet in that position of sailing (with the exception of the first and second in command), that the order of sailing is to be the order of battle; placing the fleet in two lines of sixteen ships each, with an advanced squadron of eight of the fastest sailing two-decked ships; which will always make, if wanted, a line of twenty-four sail, on whichever line the Commander in Chief may direct. The second in command will, after my intentions are made known to him, have the entire direction of his line to make the attack upon the enemy, and to follow up the blow until they are captured, or destroyed.—If the enemy's fleet should be seen to windward in line of battle, and that the two lines and advanced squadron could fetch them; they will probably be so extended, that their van could not succour their rear.—I should therefore probably make the second in command's signal, to lead through about their twelfth ship from their rear (or wherever he could fetch, if not able to get so far advanced): my line would lead through about their centre, and the advanced squadron two, three, or four ships ahead of their centre, so as to ensure getting at their Commander in Chief; on whom every effort must be made to capture. The whole impression of the British fleet must be to overpower from two or three ships ahead of their Commander in Chief (supposed to be in the centre) to the rear of their fleet.—

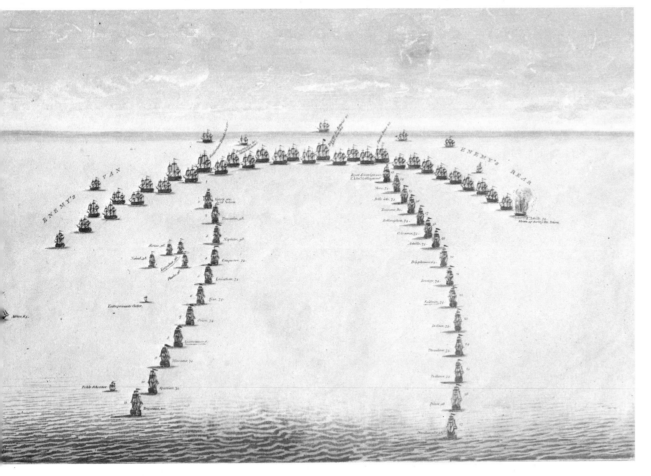

movements of his line, by keeping them as compact as the nature of the circumstances will admit. Captains are to look to their particular line, as their rallying point; but in case signals cannot be seen, or clearly understood, no Captain can do very wrong, if he places his ship alongside that of an enemy. The divisions of the British fleet will be brought nearly within gun-shot of the enemy's centre. The signals will most probably then be made for the lee line to bear up together, to set all sails, even their steering sails, in order to get as quickly as possible to the enemy's line, and to cut through, beginning at the twelfth ship from the enemy's rear: some ships may not get through their exact place, but they will always be at hand to assist friends. If any are thrown in the rear of the enemy, they will effectually complete the business of twelve of the enemy.

Should the enemy wear together, or bear up and sail large, still the twelve ships composing, in the first position, the enemy's rear, are to be the object of attack of the lee line; unless otherwise directed by the Commander in Chief, which is scarcely to be expected, as the entire management of the lee line, after the intentions of the Commander in Chief are signified, is intended to be left to the Admiral commanding that line. The remainder of the enemy's fleet, thirty-four sail, are to be left to the management of the Commander in Chief, who will endeavour to take care that the movements of the second in command are as little interrupted as possible.

By Command of the Vice-Admiral
NELSON AND BRONTE

165 The fleet dispositions at Trafalgar, showing the highly original tactics described on these pages.

I will suppose twenty sail of the enemy to be untouched, it must be some time before they could perform a manoeuvre to bring their force compact, to attack any part of the British fleet, or to succour their own ships; which indeed would be impossible without mixing with the ships engaged.—The enemy's fleet is supposed to consist of forty-six sail of the line; British forty; if either is less, only a proportional number of the enemy's ships are to be cut off. Something must be left to chance, nothing is sure in a sea fight beyond all others; shot will carry away masts and yards of friends, as well as foes: but I look with confidence to a victory before the van of the enemy could succour their retreat; and then, that the British fleet would be ready to receive their twenty sail of the line, or to pursue them should they endeavour to make off. If the van of the enemy tacks, the captured ships must run to leeward of the British fleet; if the enemy wears, the British must place themselves between the enemy and the captured and disabled British ships; and should the enemy close, I have no fear as to the result. The second in command will in all possible things direct the

Gazette Extraordinary
November 6
Dispatches, of which the following are copies, were received at the Admiralty this day, at one o'clock a.m., from Vice-Admiral Collingwood, Commander in Chief of His Majesty's Ships and Vessels off Cadiz.

SIR, *Euryalus, off Cape Trafalgar, October 22, 1805*
The ever to be lamented death of Vice-Admiral Lord Viscount Nelson, who, in the late conflict with the enemy, fell in the hour of victory, leaves to me the duty of informing my Lords Commissioners of the Admiralty, that on the 19th instant it was communicated to the Commander in Chief from the ships watching the motions of the enemy in Cadiz, that the combined fleets had put to sea; as they sailed with light winds westerly, his Lordship concluded their destination was the Mediterranean,

166 HMS *Victory,* by R. Dodd (1748–1815) (oil). An early rig of the ship which was later to be Nelson's flagship, showing the spritsail and spritsail topsail yards which were later discarded. The *Victory* is now preserved in dry dock at Portsmouth and is open to the public.

and immediately made all sail for the Strait's entrance, with the British squadron, consisting of twenty-seven ships, three of them sixty-fours, where his Lordship was informed by Capt. Blackwood (whose vigilance in watching, and giving notice of the enemy's movements, has been highly meritorious), that they had not yet passed the Straits.

On Monday the 21st instant, at daylight, when Cape Trafalgar bore E. by S. about seven leagues, the enemy was discovered six or seven miles to the eastward, the wind about west, and very light; the Commander in Chief immediately made the signal for the fleet to bear up in two columns, as they are formed in order of sailing; a mode of attack his Lordship had previously directed, to avoid the inconvenience and delay in forming a line of battle in the usual manner. The enemy's line consisted of thirty-three ships (of which eighteen were French and fifteen Spanish), commanded in chief by Admiral Villeneuve; the Spaniards, under the direction of Gravina, wore, with their heads to the northward, and formed their line of battle with great closeness and correctness; but as the mode of attack was unusual, so the structure of their line was new;—it formed a crescent convexing to leeward—so that, in leading down to their centre, I had both their van and rear abaft the beam: before the fire opened, every alternate ship was about

167 Battle of Trafalgar, oil by
J. M. W. Turner (1775–1851).
The *Victory* laying alongside, with
Nelson's famous signal ('England
expects that every man will do his
duty') still hoisted at the main.
Gives a fine impression of the
confusion of battle. Note hammocks
along the *Victory's* bulwarks, meant to
give some protection against flying
splinters, a great danger in wooden
ships, and shot.

a cable's length to windward of her second ahead and astern, forming a kind of double line, and appeared, when on their beam, to leave a very little interval between them; and this without crowding their ships. Admiral Villeneuve was in the *Bucentaure* in the centre, and the *Prince of Asturias* bore Gravina's flag in the rear; but the French and Spanish ships were mixed without any apparent regard to order of national squadron.

As the mode of our attack had been previously determined on, and communicated to the flag-officers and captains, few signals were necessary, and none were made, except to direct close order as the lines bore down.

The Commander in Chief in the *Victory* led the weather column; and the *Royal Sovereign,* which bore my flag, the lee.

The action began at twelve o'clock, by the leading ships of the columns breaking through the enemy's line, the Commander in Chief about the tenth ship from the van, the second in command about the twelfth from the rear, leaving the van of the enemy unoccupied; the succeeding ships breaking through in all parts, astern of their leaders, and engaging the enemy at the muzzles of their guns, the conflict was severe; the enemy's ships were fought with a gallantry highly honorable to their officers, but the attack on them was irresistible; and it pleased the Almighty Disposer of all events to grant His Majesty's arms a complete and glorious victory. About three p.m. many of the enemy's ships having struck their colours, their line gave way; Admiral Gravina, with ten ships, joining their frigates to leeward, stood towards Cadiz. The five headmost ships in their van tacked, and standing to the southward, to windward of the British line, were engaged, and the sternmost of them taken; the others went off, leaving to His Majesty's squadron nineteen ships of the line (of which two are first-rates, the *Santissima Trinidada* and the *Santa Anna*), with three flag officers; *viz.* Admiral Villeneuve, the Commander in Chief; Don Ignatio Maria d'Aliva, Vice-Admiral; and the Spanish Rear-Admiral, Don Baltazar Hidalgo Cisneros.

After such a victory it may appear unnecessary to enter into encomiums on the particular parts taken by the several commanders; the conclusion says more on the subject than I have language to express; the spirit which animated all was the same: when all exert themselves zealously in their country's service, all deserve that their high merits should stand recorded; and never was high merit more conspicuous than in the battle I have described.

The *Achille* (a French 74), after having surrendered, by some mismanagement of the Frenchmen, took fire and blew up: two hundred of her men were saved by the tenders.

A circumstance occurred during the action, which so strongly marks the invincible spirit of British seamen, when engaging the enemies of their country, that I cannot resist the pleasure I have in making it known to their Lordships. The *Temeraire* was boarded by accident, or design, by a French ship on one side, and a Spaniard on the other; the contest was vigorous; but in the end, the combined ensigns were torn from the poop, and the British hoisted in their places.

Such a battle could not be fought without sustaining a great loss of men. I have not only to lament, in common with the British Navy, and the British Nation, in the fall of the Commander in Chief, the loss of a hero, whose name will be immortal, and his memory ever dear to his country; but my heart is rent with the most poignant grief for the death of a friend, to whom, by many years' intimacy, and a perfect knowledge of the virtues of his mind, which inspired ideas superior to the common race of men, I was

shifted my flag to her, that I might more easily communicate my orders to, and collect the ships, and towed the *Royal Sovereign* out to seaward. The whole fleet were now in a very perilous situation; many dismasted; all shattered; in thirteen fathoms water, off the shoals of Trafalgar; and when I made the signal to prepare to anchor, few of the ships had an anchor to let go, their cables being shot; but the same good Providence which aided us through such a day preserved us in the night, by the wind shifting a few points, and drifting the ships off the land, except four of the captured dismasted ships, which are now at anchor off Trafalgar, and I hope will ride safe until those gales are over.

Having thus detailed the proceedings of the fleet on this occasion, I beg to congratulate their Lordships on a victory which, I hope, will add a ray to the glory of His Majesty's crown, and be attended with public benefit to our country.
William Marsden Esq.   I am, &c. C. COLLINGWOOD

General Order   *Euryalus, October 22, 1805*
The ever-to-be-lamented death of Lord Visc. Nelson, Duke of Bronte, the Commander in Chief, who fell in the action of the 21st, in the arms of victory, covered with glory, whose memory will be ever dear to the British Navy, and the British nation; whose zeal for the honour of his king, and for the interests of his country, will be ever held up as a shining example for a British Seaman,—leaves to me a duty to return my thanks to the Right Hon. Rear-Admiral, the captains, officers, seamen, and detachments of Royal Marines serving on board His Majesty's squadron now under my command, for their conduct on that day; but where can I find language to express my sentiments of the valour and skill which were displayed by the officers, the seamen, and marines in the battle with the enemy, where every individual appeared an hero, on whom the glory of his country depended; the attack was irresistible, and the issue of it adds to the page of naval annals a brilliant instance of what Britons can do, when their king and their country need their service.

To the Right Honourable Rear-Admiral the Earl of Northesk, to the captains, officers, and seamen, and to the officers, non-commissioned officers, and privates of the Royal Marines, I beg to give my sincere and hearty thanks for their highly meritorious conduct, both in the action, and in their zeal and activity in bringing the captured ships out from the perilous situation in which they were, after their surrender, among the shoals of Trafalgar, in boisterous weather.

And I desire that the respective captains will be pleased to communicate to the officers, seamen, and Royal Marines, this

bound by the strongest ties of affection; a grief to which even the glorious occasion in which he fell, does not bring the consolation which perhaps it ought: his Lordship received a musket ball in his left breast, about the middle of the action, and sent an officer to me immediately with his last farewell; and soon after expired.

I have also to lament the loss of those excellent officers, Captains Duff of the *Mars,* and Cooke of the *Bellerophon*; I have yet heard of none others.

I fear the numbers that have fallen will be found very great when the returns come to me; but it having blown a gale of wind ever since the action, I have not yet had it in my power to collect any reports from the ships.

The *Royal Sovereign* having lost her masts, except the tottering foremast, I called the *Euryalus* to me, while the action continued, which ship lying within hail, made my signals, a service Captain Blackwood performed with great attention. After the action I

168 Nelson falls at the Battle of Trafalgar, 21 October 1805, by D. Dighton (1792–1827) (oil).

public testimony of my high approbation of their conduct, and my thanks for it.

To the Rt. Hon. Rear-Admiral, the Earl of   C. COLLINGWOOD
Northesk, and the respective Captains and Commanders

SIR,   *Euryalus, off Cadiz, October 24, 1805*
In my letter of the 22d, I detailed to you, for the information of my Lords Commissioners of the Admiralty, the proceedings of His Majesty's squadron on the day of the action, and that preceding it, since which I have had a continued series of misfortunes, but they are of a kind that human prudence could not possibly provide against, or my skill prevent.

On the 22d, in the morning, a strong southerly wind blew, with squally weather, which however did not prevent the activity of the officers and seamen of such ships as were manageable from getting hold of many of the prizes (thirteen or fourteen), and towing them off to the westward, where I ordered them to rendezvous round the *Royal Sovereign*, in tow by the *Neptune*: but on the 23d the gale increased, and the sea ran so high, that many of them broke the tow rope, and drifted far to leeward before they were got hold of again; and some of them taking advantage of the dark and boisterous night, got before the wind, and have perhaps drifted upon the shore and sunk; on the afternoon of that day the remnant of the combined fleet, ten sail of ships, who had not been much engaged, stood up to leeward of my shattered and straggled charge, as if meaning to attack them, which obliged me to collect a force out of the least injured ships, and form to leeward for their defence; all this retarded the progress of the hulks, and the bad weather continuing, determined me to destroy all the leewardmost that could be cleared of the men, considering that keeping posession of the ships was a matter of little consequence compared with the chance of their falling again into the hands of the enemy: but even this was an arduous task in the high sea which was running. I hope, however, it has been accomplished to a considerable extent; I entrusted it to skilful officers, who would spare no pains to execute what was possible. The captains of the *Prince* and *Neptune* cleared the *Trinidada* and sunk her. Captains Hope, Bayntun, and Malcolm, who joined the fleet this moment from Gibraltar, had the charge of destroying five others. The *Redoubtable* sunk astern of the *Swiftsure* while in tow. The *Santa Anna*, I have no doubt, is sunk, as her side was almost entirely beat in; and such is the shattered condition of the whole of them, that unless the weather moderates, I doubt whether I shall be able to carry a ship of them into port. I hope their Lordships will approve of what I (having only in consideration the destruction of the enemy's

fleet) have thought a measure of absolute necessity.

I have taken Admiral Villeneuve into this ship; Vice-Admiral don Aliva is dead. Whenever the temper of the weather will permit, and I can spare a frigate (for there were only four in the action with the fleet, *Euryalus*, *Sirius*, *Phoebe*, and *Naiad*; the *Melpomene* joined the 22d, and the *Eurydice* and *Scout* the 23d), I shall collect the other flag officers, and send them to England with their flags (if they do not go to the bottom), to be laid at His Majesty's feet.

There were four thousand troops embarked, under the command of General Contamin, who was taken with Admiral Villeneuve in the *Bucentaure*.

I am, Sir, &c. C. COLLINGWOOD

Gazette Extraordinary
November 27

Copy of a Letter received last Night by the Honourable Captain Blackwood, from Vice-Admiral Lord Collingwood, Commander in Chief of His Majesty's Ships and Vessels in the Mediterranean, to William Marsden, Esq.; dated on board His Majesty's Ship the Queen, off Cape Trafalgar, November 4, 1805.

SIR,
On the 28th ultimo I informed you of the proceedings of the squadron to that time. The weather continuing very bad, the wind blowing from the S.W., the squadron not in a situation of safety, and seeing little prospect of getting the captured ships off the land, and great risk of some of them getting into port, I determined no longer to delay the destroying them, and to get the squadron out of the deep bay.

The extraordinary exertion of Captain Capel, however, saved the French *Swiftsure*; and his ship the *Phoebe* together with the *Donegal*, Captain Malcolm, afterwards brought out the *Bahama*. Indeed, nothing can exceed the perseverance of all the officers employed in this service. Captain Hope rigged and succeeded in bringing out the *Ildefonso*; all of which will, I hope, have arrived safe at Gibraltar. For the rest, Sir, I enclose you a list of all the enemy's fleet, which were in the action, and how they are disposed of, which, I believe, is perfectly correct.

I informed you, in my letter of the 28th, that the remnant of the enemy's fleet came out a second time to endeavour, in the bad weather, to cut off some of the hulks, when the *Rayo* was dismasted, and fell into our hands; she afterwards parted her cable, went on shore, and was wrecked. The *Indomptable*, one of the same squadron, was also driven on shore, wrecked, and her crew perished.

Overleaf and facing Disaster at sea held fascination for many painters. Here it is seen by two great artists of contrasting styles.

Plate 29 *overleaf* Le Radeau de la Méduse, by Théodore Géricault (1791–1824). The *Méduse*, a 44 gun French frigate, carrying a new governor to Senegal, struck a reef 60 miles from the African coast. The captain, the governor and the latter's entourage made off in well-provisioned boats, leaving 200 people, mostly soldiers, with four boats and a hastily constructed raft. The boats were supposed to tow the raft, but abandoned it 50 miles from land with 147 people on board, including one woman. There was room only to stand on the raft and the sea washed knee deep over it at times, causing the loose timbers to crush the feet of the occupants. With provisions for one day, the raft drifted for twelve nights before being found on 17 July 1816 by the brig *Argus*, by which time only fifteen survivors remained to tell a tale of madness, murder and cannibalism.

Plate 30 Fire at Sea by J. M. W. Turner (1775–1851). Fire was one of the most terrifying hazards of the wooden ship. The combination of the most violent of the elements is portrayed in several of Turner's paintings.

The *Santa Anna* and *Algeziras* being driven near the shore of Cadiz, got such assistance as has enabled them to get in; but the ruin of their fleet is as complete as could be expected, under the circumstances of fighting them close to their own shore. Had the battle been in the ocean, still fewer would have escaped. Twenty sail of the line are taken or destroyed; and of those which got in, not more than three are in a repairable state for a length of time.

Rear-Admiral Louis in the *Canopus,* who had been detached with the *Queen, Spencer,* and *Tigre,* to complete the water, &c. of these ships, and to see the convoy in safety a certain distance up the Mediterranean, joined me on the 30th.

In clearing the captured ships of prisoners, I found so many wounded men, that to alleviate human misery as much as was in my power, I sent to the Marquis de Solana, Governor-General of Andalusia, to offer him the wounded to the care of their country, on receipts being given: a proposal which was received with the greatest thankfulness; not only by the Governor, but the whole country resounds with expressions of gratitude. Two French frigates were sent out to receive them, with a proper officer to give receipts, bringing with them all the English who had been wrecked in several of the ships, and an offer from the Marquis de Solana of the use of their hospitals for our wounded, pledging the honour of Spain for their being carefully attended.

I have ordered most of the Spanish prisoners to be released; the officers on parole; the men for receipts given, and a condition that they do not serve in war, by sea or land, until exchanged.

By my correspondence with the Marquis, I found that Vice-Admiral d'Aliva was not dead, but dangerously wounded; and I wrote to him a letter, claiming him as a prisoner of war: a copy of which I enclose, together with a state of the Flag Officers of the combined fleet.

I am, Sir, &c. C. COLLINGWOOD

169 Heaving the Lead, 1807. The seaman is standing in the chains, using a short sea lead. This was marked by different materials being incorporated into the line at one fathom intervals – leather, calico and hemp, for instance, were used in an arbitrary order so that the seaman could tell by feel in the dark the depths reached.

170 'Equity or a Sailor's Prayer before Battle. Anecdote of the Battle of Trafalgar'. Cartoons such as this anonymous one, published by Thomas Tegg, were a wry dissenting voice in an age when war was glorified. Prize money was an important source of income to officers. An admiral posted to the West Indies in wartime could expect to return a millionaire, while occasionally the prizes were so great that even the common sailors came home rich men. One crew fried gold watches on the beach on returning from an unusually successful campaign.

The *Constitution* versus the *Guerrière*

1812 saw the climax of the short sea war between Britain and the USA in which the bigger, better designed, more powerfully armed and better trained American frigates gained a number of victories over their British opponents who had grown carelessly over-confident (after years of easy ascendancy over the French) and had neglected gun-drill and fighting practice in favour of 'spit and polish' and showy seamanship. The trend was reversed largely owing to the influence of Captain Broke of the *Shannon*, who gained a spectacular victory over USS *Chesapeake*, and became an inspiration for a rebirth of British naval gunnery skill.

United States' Frigate Constitution, *off Boston Light*
August 30, 1812

SIR,

I have the honour to inform you that on the 19th instant, at 2 P.M. being in latitude 41 deg. 41 min. and longitude 55 deg. 48 min. with the *Constitution* under my command, a sail was discovered from the mast-head, bearing E. by S. or E.S.E. but at such a distance we could not tell what she was. All sail was instantly made in chase, and soon found we came up with her. At 3 P.M. could plainly see that she was a ship on the starboard tack under easy sail, close on a wind—at half past 3 P.M. made her out to be a frigate— continued the chase until we were within about three miles, when

171 The *Constitution* and the *Guerrière*. The *Constitution*, a 44 gun frigate of 1,576 tons was launched in 1797 and took part in the bombardments of Tripoli in 1804. Her nickname 'Old Ironsides' was earned in her fight with the *Guerrière* on 19 August 1812, because her hull received so little injury from the English shot. In her fight with HMS *Java* on 29 December 1812 her wheel was shot away, but her crew's superior gunnery carried the day for her. In 1830 a tear-jerking poem (*Old Ironsides*) by Oliver Wendell Holmes happily saved her from the breaker's yard. After further service as a training ship and a barrack ship she was restored by public subscription and is now preserved at Boston.

AMERICAN NAVAL VICTORIES.

GLORIOUS & BRILLIANT FLEET ON LAKE VICTORY OBTAINED BY COMMODORE O.H.PERRY OVER THE BRITISH ERIE COMMANDED

BY CAPT. BARCLAY.

U.S. FRIGATE CONSTITUTION CAPT. HULL capturing H.B.M.Frigate Guerrier Capt. DACRES August 19th 1812.

FRIGATE U. STATES COMMODORE DECATUR capturing H.B.M. Frigate Macedonian Capt. CARDEN October 25th 1812.

U.S. SLOOP OF WAR WASP CAPTAIN JONES taking H.B.M.Sloop of War Frolic Capt. WHINYATES October 18th 1812.

U.S. BRIG ENTERPRIZE LIEUT. COMt. BURROWS CAPTURING

CONSTITUTION SETTING FIRE TO THE GUERRIER August 19th 1812.

U.S. FRIGATE CONSTITUTION CAPT. BAINBRIDGE capturing H.B.M. Frigate Java Capt. LAMBERT December 29th 1812.

U.S. SLOOP OF WAR HORNET CAPT. LAWRENCE Capturing H.B.M. Sloop of War Peacock Capt. PEAK February 24th 1813.

H.B.M. BRIG BOXER CAPTAIN BLYTH ESQ. September 4th 1813.

Don't give up the Ship.

New York Published by J. Ticken, Nº 432 Waterst December 1813.
Printed by Riley & Adams 23 Chatham St.

I ordered the light sails taken in, the courses hauled up, and the ship cleared for action. At this time the chase had backed her main-topsail, waiting for us to come down. As soon as the *Constitution* was ready for action, I bore down with an intention to bring him to close action immediately: but on our coming within gunshot, she gave us a broadside, and filled away and wore, giving us a broadside on the other tack, but without effect, her shot falling short. She continued wearing and manoeuvring for about threequarters of an hour, to get a raking position—but finding she could not, she bore up and run under her top-sails and jib, with the wind on the quarter. I immediately made sail to bring the ship up with her, and at five minutes before 6 P.M. being alongside within half pistol shot, we commenced a heavy fire from all our guns, double-shotted with round and grape, and so well directed were they, and so warmly kept up, that in 16 minutes her mizen-mast went by the board, and his main-yard in the slings, and the hull, rigging, and sails, very much torn to pieces. The fire was kept up with equal warmth for 15 minutes longer, when his main-mast and fore-mast went, taking with them every spar, excepting the bowsprit; on seeing this we ceased firing; so that in thirty minutes after we got fairly alongside of the enemy, she surrendered, and had not a spar standing, and her hull below and above water so shattered, that a few more broadsides must have carried her down.

After informing that so fine a ship as the *Guerriere*, commanded by an able and experienced officer, had been totally dismasted and otherwise cut to pieces, so as to make her not worth towing into port, in the short space of 30 minutes, you can have no doubt of the gallantry and good conduct of the officers and ship's company I have the honour to command. It only remains, therefore, for me to assure you, that they all fought with great bravery; and it gives me great pleasure to say, that from the smallest boy in the ship, to the oldest seaman, not a look of fear was seen. They all went into action giving three cheers, and requesting to be laid close alongside the enemy.

Enclosed I have the honour to send you a list of the killed and wounded on board the *Constitution*, and a report of the damages she sustained—also a list of killed and wounded on board the enemy, with his quarter bill, &c. I have the honour to be, with very great respect, sir, your obedient servant,

ISAAC HULL
The Hon. Paul Hamilton, &c. &c.

Before the mast

Richard Dana was a Harvard law student who, suffering from weakness of the eyes, decided to go to sea in order to take two years away from his books. The result was *Two Years Before the Mast*, the most articulate account of life at sea ever written from the forecastle. He embarked in 1834 in the brig *Pilgrim* bound from Boston to California via Cape Horn. On his return in another ship he resumed his university career and became a lawyer specializing in the defence of the common seaman.

As we had now a long 'spell' of fine weather, without any incident to break the monotony of our lives, there can be no better place to describe the duties, regulations, and customs of an American merchantman, of which ours was a fair specimen.

The captain, in the first place, is lord paramount. He stands no watch, comes and goes when he pleases, and is accountable to no one, and must be obeyed in everything, without a question, even from his chief officer. He has the power to turn his officers off duty, and even to break them and make them do duty as sailors in the forecastle. Where there are no passengers and no super-cargo, as in our vessel, he has no companion but his own dignity; and no pleasures, unless he differs from most of his kind, but the consciousness of possessing supreme power, and, occasionally, the exercise of it.

The prime minister, the official organ, and the active and superintending officer, is the chief mate. He is first lieutenant,

boatswain, sailing-master, and quarter-master. The captain tells him what he wishes to have done, and leaves to him the care of overseeing, of allotting the work, and also the responsibility of its being well done. *The* mate (as he is always called, *par excellence*) also keeps the log-book, for which he is responsible to the owners and insurers, and has the charge of the stowage, safe keeping, and delivery of the cargo. He is also, ex-officio, the wit of the crew; for the captain does not condescend to joke with the men, and the second mate no one cares for; so that when 'the mate' thinks fit to entertain 'the people' with a coarse joke or a little practical wit, everyone feels bound to laugh.

The second mate's is proverbially a dog's berth. He is neither officer nor man. The men do not respect him as an officer, and he is obliged to go aloft to reef and furl the topsails, and to put his hands into the tar and slush with the rest. The crew call him the 'sailor's waiter', as he has to furnish them with spun-yarn, marline, and all other stuffs that they need in their work, and has charge of the boatswain's locker, which includes serving-boards, marline-

172 *opposite* A print celebrating the successes of the young American navy in the War of 1812.

173 *bottom left* 'Catch Me Who Can'. An American topsail schooner running the British blockade and boasting of its advantage over the ship in the background when sailing closehauled. It was from this type of vessel, which was noted for speed and fine lines, that the first *America* was developed, to challenge and found the America's Cup.

174 *top right* 'Captains', mid nineteenth century.

but, being employed all day, are allowed to 'sleep in' at night, unless all hands are called.

The crew are divided into two divisions, as equally as may be, called the watches. Of these the chief mate commands the larboard, and the second mate the starboard. They divide the time between them, being on and off duty, or, as it is called, on deck and below, every other four hours. If, for instance, the chief mate with the larboard watch have the first night-watch from eight to twelve; at the end of the four hours, the starboard watch is called, and the second mate takes the deck, while the larboard watch and the first mate go below until four in the morning, when they come on deck again and remain until eight; having what is called the morning watch. As they will have been on deck eight hours out of the twelve, while those who had the middle watch—from twelve to four, will only have been up four hours, they have what is called a 'forenoon watch below', that is, from eight A.M., till twelve M. In a man-of-war, and in some merchantmen, this alternation of watches is kept up throughout the twenty-four hours; but our ship, like most merchantmen, had 'all hands' from twelve o'clock till dark, except in bad weather, when we had 'watch and watch'.

An explanation of the 'dog watches' may, perhaps, be of use to one who has never been at sea. They are to shift the watches each night, so that the same watch need not be on deck at the same hours. In order to effect this, the watch from *four* to *eight* P.M., is divided into two half, or dog watches, one from four to six, and the other from six to eight. By this means they divide the twenty-four hours into *seven* watches instead of *six*, and thus shift the hours every night . . .

Before I end my explanations, it may be well to define a *day's work*, and to correct a mistake prevalent among landsmen about a sailor's life. Nothing is more common than to hear people say —'Are not sailors very idle at sea?—what can they find to do? This is a very natural mistake, and being very frequently made, it is one which every sailor feels interested in having corrected. In the first place, then, the discipline of the ship requires every man to be at work upon *something* when he is on deck, except at night and on Sundays. Except at these times, you will never see a man on board a well-ordered vessel standing idle on deck, sitting down, or leaning over the side. It is the officer's duty to keep everyone at work, even if there is nothing to be done but to scrape the rust from the chain cables. In no state prison are the convicts more regularly set to work, and more closely watched. No conversation is allowed among the crew at their duty, and though they frequently do talk when aloft, or when near one another, yet they always stop when an officer is nigh.

spikes, &c. &c. He is expected by the captain to maintain his dignity and to enforce obedience, and still is kept at a great distance from the mate, and obliged to work with the crew. He is one to whom little is given and of whom much is required. His wages are usually double those of a common sailor, and he eats and sleeps in the cabin; but he is obliged to be on deck nearly all his time, and eats at the second table, that is, makes a meal out of what the captain and chief mate leave.

The steward is the captain's servant, and has charge of the pantry, from which everyone, even the mate himself, is excluded. These distinctions usually find him an enemy in the mate, who does not like to have anyone on board who is not entirely under his control; the crew do not consider him as one of their number, so he is left to the mercy of the captain.

The cook is the patron of the crew, and those who are in his favour can get their wet mittens and stockings dried, or light their pipes at the galley in the night watch. These two worthies, together with the carpenter and sailmaker, if there be one, stand no watch,

175 The Mess Kid
'seeing what is thought a "smooth spell" to go forward from the Galley with the Mess when a heavy sea lifts the ship's stern out of water and dropping it down again scatters the whole precious mess of hot "scouse" rolling in the scuppers.'
from a series 'A Sailor's Life at Sea' No. 2.

174

176 *left* The *Topaz* of New York, Saml. Macoduck Master, 1832. An American snow. Watercolour by Edmund Camellate.

177 *right* The Brigantine *Experiment* of Newbury Port Captain Joseph Browon Going Out of Marseilles. An interesting feature is the studding sails of the square foresails and the two large staysails between the mast and foremasts. Water colour by Nicolas Cammillieri (*fl.* 1798-1820).

With regard to the work upon which the men are put, it is a matter which probably would not be understood by one who has not been at sea. When I first left port, and found that we were kept regularly employed for a week or two, I supposed that we were getting the vessel into sea trim, and that it would soon be over, and we should have nothing to do but to sail the ship; but I found that it continued so for two years, and at the end of the two years there was as much to be done as ever. As has often been said, a ship is like a lady's watch, always out of repair. When first leaving port, studding-sail gear is to be rove, all the running rigging to be examined, that which is unfit for use to be got down, and new rigging rove in its place: then the standing rigging is to be overhauled, replaced, and repaired, in a thousand different ways; and wherever any of the numberless ropes or the yards are chafing or wearing upon it, there 'chafing gear', as it is called, must be put on. This chafing gear consists of worming, parcelling, roundings, battens, and service of all kinds—both rope-yarns, spun-yarn, marline and seizing-stuffs. Taking off, putting on, and mending the chafing gear alone, upon a vessel, would find constant employ-ment for two or three men, during working hours, for a whole voyage.

The next point to be considered is, that all the 'small stuffs' which are used on board a ship—such as spun-yarn, marline, seizing stuff, &c. &c.—are made on board. The owners of a vessel buy up incredible quantities of 'old junk', which the sailors unlay, after drawing out the yarns, knot them together, and roll them up in balls. These 'rope-yarns' are constantly used for various purposes, but the greater part is manufactured into spun-yarn. For this purpose every vessel is furnished with a 'spun-yarn winch'; which is very simple, consisting of a wheel and spindle. This may be heard constantly going on deck in pleasant weather; and we had employment, during a great part of the time, for three hands in drawing and knotting yarns, and making spun-yarn.

Another method of employing the crew is, 'setting up' rigging. Whenever any of the standing rigging becomes slack (which is continually happening), the seizings and covering must be taken off, tackles got up, and, after the rigging is bowsed well taut, the seizings and coverings replaced; which is a very nice piece

in different parts of the ship, so that the sailors might not be idle in the *snatches* between the frequent squalls upon crossing the equator. Some officers have been so driven to find work for the crew in a ship ready for sea, that they have set them to pounding the anchors (often done) and scraping the chain cables. The 'Philadelphia catechism' is,

'Six days shalt thou labour and do all thou art able,
And on the seventh—holystone the decks and scrape the cable.'

This kind of work, of course, is not kept up off Cape Horn, Cape of Good Hope, and in extreme north and south latitudes; but I have seen the decks washed down and scrubbed, when the water would have frozen if it had been fresh; and all hands kept at work upon the rigging, when we had on our pea-jackets, and our hands so numb that we could hardly hold our marline-spikes . . .

Sunday Sept. 7th.—To enhance the value of the Sabbath to the crew, they are allowed on that day a pudding, or, as it is called, a 'duff'. This is nothing more than flour boiled with water, and eaten with molasses. It is very heavy, dark, and clammy, yet it is looked upon as a luxury, and really forms an agreeable variety with salt beef and pork. Many a rascally captain has made friends of his crew by allowing them duff twice a week on the passage home.

178 The packet ship *Massachusetts* in a squall, 10 November 1845. The topsails have been let fly and will quickly thrash themselves to pieces.

179 *right* 'Mates', mid nineteenth century.

180 *facing* Shore profiles of the Cape of Good Hope, Juan Fernandez Island and other coasts by Captain J. Hildreth *c.* 1850. Gives wind forces and directions, anchorages and shows the convict settlement and fort on Juan Fernandez Island.

of work. There is also such a connexion between different parts of a vessel, that one rope can seldom be touched without altering another. You cannot stay a mast aft by the back stays, without slacking up the head stays, &c. &c. If we add to this all the tarring, greasing, oiling, varnishing, painting, scraping, and scrubbing which is required in the course of a long voyage, and also remember this is all to be done in *addition to* watching at night, steering, reefing, furling, bracing, making and setting sail, and pulling, hauling and climbing in every direction, one will hardly ask, 'What can a sailor find to do at sea?'

If, after all this labour—after exposing the lives and limbs in storms, wet and cold . . . the merchants and captains think that they have not earned their twelve dollars a month (out of which they clothe themselves), and their salt beef and hard bread, they keep them picking oakum—*ad infinitum*. This is the usual resource upon a rainy day, for then it will not do to work upon rigging; and when it is pouring down in floods, instead of letting the sailors stand about in sheltered places, and talk, and keep themselves comfortable, they are separated to different parts of the ship and kept at work picking oakum. I have seen oakum stuff placed about

176

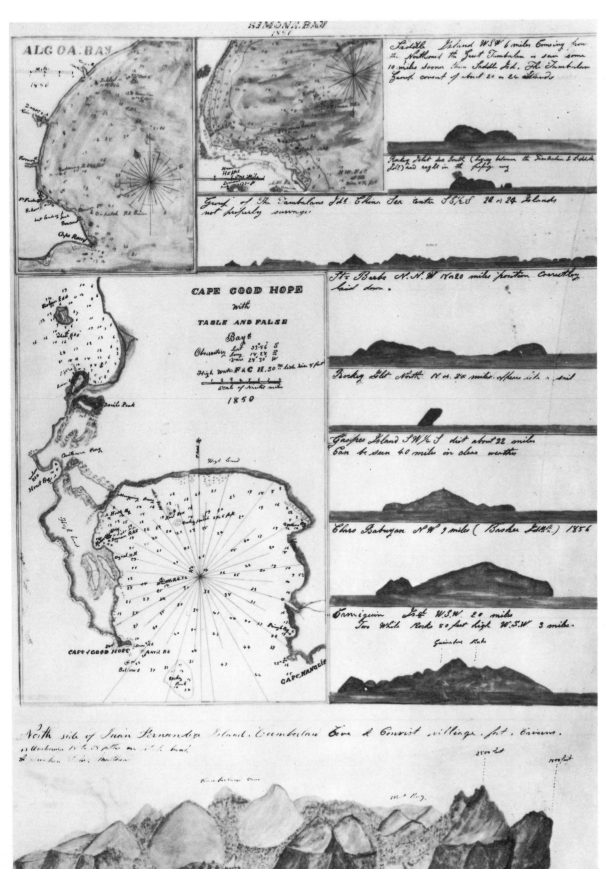

On board some vessels this is made a day of instruction and of religious exercises; but we had a crew of swearers, from the captain to the smallest boy; and a day of rest, and of something like quiet, social enjoyment, was all that we could expect . . .

Monday, Nov. 19th.—This was a black day in our calendar. At seven o'clock in the morning, it being our watch below, we were aroused from a sound sleep by the cry of 'All hands ahoy! a man overboard!' This unwonted cry sent a thrill through the heart of everyone, and hurrying on deck, we found the vessel hove flat aback, with all her studding-sails set; for the boy who was at the helm left it to throw something overboard, and the carpenter, who was an old sailor, knowing that the wind was light, put the helm down and hove her aback. The watch on deck were lowering away the quarter-boat, and I got on deck just in time to heave myself into her as she was leaving the side; but it was not until out upon the wide Pacific, in our little boat, that I knew whom we had lost. It was George Ballmer, a young English sailor, who was prized by the officers as an active and willing seaman, and by the crew as a lively, hearty fellow, and a good shipmate. He was going aloft to fit a strap round the main topmast-head, for ringtail halyards, and had the strap and block, a coil of halyards, and a marline-spike about his neck. He fell from the starboard futtock shrouds, and not knowing how to swim, and being heavily dressed, with all those things round his neck, he probably sank immediately. We pulled astern, in the direction in which he fell, and though we knew that there was no hope of saving him, yet no one wished to speak of returning, and we rowed about for nearly an hour, without the hope of doing anything, but unwilling to acknowledge to ourselves that we must give him up. At length we turned the boat's head and made towards the vessel . . .

We had hardly returned on board with our sad report, before an auction was held of the poor man's clothes. The captain had first, however, called all hands aft, and asked them if they were satisfied that everything had been done to save the man, and if they thought there was any use in remaining there longer. The crew all said that it was in vain, for the man did not know how to swim, and was very heavily dressed. So we then filled away, and kept her off to her course.

The laws regulating navigation make the captain answerable for the effects of a sailor who dies during the voyage; and it is either a law, or a universal custom established for convenience, that the captain should immediately hold an auction of his things, in which they are bid off by the sailors, and the sums which they give are deducted from their wages at the end of the voyage. In this way the trouble and risk of keeping his things through the voyage

In fact, we had been too long from port. We were getting tired of one another, and were in an irritable state, both forward and aft. Our fresh provisions were, of course, gone, and the captain had stopped our rice, so that we had nothing but salt beef and salt pork throughout the week, with the exception of a very small duff on Sunday. This added to the discontent; and a thousand little things, daily and almost hourly occurring, which no one who has not himself been on a long and tedious voyage can conceive of or properly appreciate—little wars and rumours of wars,—reports of things said in the cabin,—misunderstanding of words and looks,—apparent abuses,—brought us into a state in which everything seemed to go wrong. Every encroachment upon the time allowed for rest, appeared unnecessary. Every shifting of the studding-sails was only to 'haze'[1] the crew.

[1] *Haze* is a word of frequent use on board ship, and never, I believe, used elsewhere. It is very expressive to a sailor, and means to punish by hard work. Let an officer once say, 'I'll *haze* you,' and your fate is fixed. You will be 'worked up' if you are not a better man than he is.

181 Sailors on shore: an engagement with a storm. 'Determined to have more Grog, they board the Enemy's "Ship", enter BEN TACK's cabin, and commence the Engagement yard-arm and yard-arm. The YOUNKER, with the red-hot poker, is putting the Parlour-Customers to the rout; JACK is flung on his beam-ends, and threatened with a broadside; STEADY is endeavouring to hammer a little spirits into the philosophising CLOD, who, in his turn, is accommodating TOM with a tooth-pick; DICK HAULYARD is playing the Commander hard, who nearly runs down TIMBERTOE, one of his best customers, a Veteran of Battalion who however, appears to regard his ale more than his person.'

are avoided, and the clothes are usually sold for more than they would be worth on shore. Accordingly, we had no sooner got the ship before the wind, than his chest was brought up upon the forecastle, and the sale began. The jackets and trousers in which we had seen him dressed but a few days before, were exposed and bid off while the life was hardly out of his body, and his chest was taken aft and used as a store-chest, so that there was nothing left which could be called *his*. Sailors have an unwillingness to wear a dead man's clothes during the same voyage, and they seldom do so, unless they are in absolute want . . .

Thursday, Dec. 25th.—This day was Christmas, but it brought us no holiday. The only change was that we had a 'plum duff' for dinner, and the crew quarrelled with the steward because he did not give us our usual allowance of molasses to eat with it. He thought the plums would be a substitute for the molasses, but we were not to be cheated out of our rights in this way.

Such are the trifles which produce quarrels on shipboard

182 below, left 'Common sailor' mid nineteenth century. Uniforms for the lower deck were not introduced until well into the nineteenth century.

183 A Scene on the Main Deck.

EXPLANATION. - In the fore-ground are three *Seamen* playing at cards, one of whom, by the archness of his countenance, appears to have an advantage, and seems desirous of betting with his *Antagonist*, who, by his clenched fist, is evidently *losing*: the *third*, from his gravity, seems to be doubtful of the result. The *Group* to the right consists of two, apparently, *Messmates*, the one reading a letter with much satisfaction; while a *Female* is slily looking over the gun, listening to the contents, and seems, by her smiling, to enter into the full enjoyment of it. In the middle *Group* are represented two *Seamen* and their *Girls* dancing a reel; the *Fiddler*, supposed to be the *Ship's Cook* by his wooden leg, is evidently groggy, from his having one eye closed, while the other is significantly employed: the principal *Male Figure*, who sets to his *Partner*, has had more than his usual allowance of grog, being in the act of snapping his fingers, and literally reeling towards her: the *younger Female* and her *Partner* are not less interesting from their attitude. On the left is a *Sailor-Boy* with a can of grog in his hand; his attention being wholly taken up with the Group dancing, occasions him to spill the liquor, which a *Seaman* underneath is eagerly catching. Near these figures, to the right, is seen a fair *Damsel* descending the ladder, and is received into the arms of her *Admirer*. Next to them appears a *Sailor* handing down a box, supposed to contain the wares of an *Israelite*, brought on board for sale, who, from his attitude and countenance, appears most anxious for their safety. The two figures behind the *Jew* are seemingly a *Brother* and *Sister* joyously meeting. The *Group* near the quarter-deck-ladder represents an affray between two *Females,* who are jealous of each other, to the no small delight of the surrounding *Seamen.* On the quarter-deck-ladder is seen the flowing robe of a *Female* descending.

In the midst of this state of things, my messmate S—— and myself petitioned the captain for leave to shift our berths from the steerage, where we had previously lived, into the forecastle. This, to our delight, was granted, and we turned in to *bunk* and mess with the crew forward. We now began to feel like sailors, which we never fully did when we were in the steerage. While there, however useful and active you may be, you are but a mongrel,—and sort of afterguard and 'ship's cousin'. You are immediately under the eye of the officers, cannot dance, sing, play, smoke, make a noise, or *growl* (i.e. complain), or take any others sailor's pleasure; and you live with the steward, who is usually a go-between; and the crew never feel as though you were *one of them*. But if you live in the forecastle, you are 'as independent as a wood-sawyer's clerk' (nauticè), and are a *sailor*. You hear sailors' talk, learn their ways, their peculiarities of feeling as well as speaking and acting; and moreover pick up a great deal of curious and useful information in seamanship, ships' customs, foreign countries, &c., from their long yarns and equally long disputes. No man can be a sailor, or know what sailors are, unless he has lived in the forecastle with them—turned in and out with them, eaten of their dish, and drank of their cup. After I had been a week there, nothing would have tempted me to go back to my old berth; and never afterwards, even in the worst of weather, when in a close and leaking forecastle off Cape Horn, did I for a moment wish myself in the steerage. Another thing which you learn better in the forecastle than you can anywhere else, is, to make and mend clothes, and this is indispensable to sailors. A large part of their watches below they spend at this work, and here I learned that art which stood me in so good stead afterwards . . .

Jan. 14th, 1835, we came to anchor in the spacious bay of Santa Barbara, after a voyage of one hundred and fifty days from Boston . . .

For several days the captain seemed very much out of humour. Nothing went right or fast enough for him. He quarrelled with the cook, and threatened to flog him for throwing wood on deck; and had a dispute with the mate about reeving a Spanish burton; the mate saying that he was right, and had been taught how to do it by a man *who was a sailor!* This the captain took in dudgeon, and they were at sword's points at once. But his displeasure was chiefly turned against a large, heavy-moulded fellow from the Middle states, who was called Sam. This man hesitated in his speech, and was rather slow in his motions, but was a pretty good sailor, and always seemed to do his best; but the captain took a dislike to him, thought he was surly and lazy; and 'if you once give a dog a bad name'—as the sailor-phrase is—'he may as well jump overboard'. The captain found fault with everything this man did,

wrestling and heaving, as though the man was trying to turn him. 'You may as well keep still, for I have got you', said the captain. Then came the question, 'Will you ever give me any more of your jaw?'

'I never gave you any sir,' said Sam; for it was his voice that we heard, though low and half choked.

'That's not what I ask you. Will you ever be impudent to me again?'

'I never have been, sir,' said Sam.

'Answer my question, or I'll make a spread eagle of you! I'll flog you, by G—d.'

'I'm no Negro slave,' said Sam.

'Then I'll make you one,' said the captain; and he came to the hatchway, and sprang on deck, threw off his coat, and rolling up his sleeves, called out to the mate—'Seize that man up, Mr A——! Seize him up! Make a spread eagle of him! I'll teach you all who is master aboard!'

The crew and officers followed the captain up the hatchway, and after repeated orders the mate laid hold of Sam, who made no resistance, and carried him to the gangway.

'What are you going to flog that man for, sir?' said John, the Swede, to the captain.

Upon hearing this, the captain turned upon him, but knowing him to be quick and resolute, he ordered the steward to bring the irons, and calling upon Russell to help him, went up to John.

'Let me alone,' said John. 'I'm willing to be put in irons. You need not use any force'; and putting out his hands, the captain slipped the irons on, and sent him aft to the quarter deck. Sam by this time was *seized up*, as it is called, that is, placed against the shrouds, with his wrists made fast to the shrouds, his jacket off, and his back exposed. The captain stood on the break of the deck, a few feet from him, and a little raised, so as to have a good swing at him, and held in his hand the bight of a thick, strong rope. The officers stood round, and the crew grouped together in the waist. All these preparations made me feel sick, and almost faint, angry and excited as I was. A man—a human being, made in God's likeness—fastened up and flogged like a beast! A man, too, whom I had lived with and eaten with for months, and knew almost as well as a brother. The first and almost uncontrollable impulse was resistance. But what was to be done? The time for it had gone by. The two best men were fast, and there were only two beside myself, and a small boy of ten or twelve years of age. And then there were (beside the captain) three officers, steward, agent, and clerk. But beside the numbers, what is there for sailors to do? If they resist, it is mutiny; and if they succeed, and take the vessel, it is piracy. If they ever yield again, their punishment must

184 The ship *Alfred* of Salem leaving Marseille harbour under topsails and setting more sail. Sailing under topsails alone allowed maximum control for manoeuvre. Watercolour by Nicolas Cammillieri (*fl.* 1798–1820).

and hazed him for dropping a marline-spike from the main-yard, where he was at work. This, of course, was an accident, but it was set down against him. The captain was on board all day Friday, and everything went on hard and disagreeably. 'The more you drive a man, the less he will do', was as true with us as with any other people. We worked late Friday night, and were turned-to early Saturday morning. About ten o'clock the captain ordered our new officer, Russell, who by this time had become thoroughly disliked by all the crew, to get the gig ready to take him ashore. John, the Swede, was sitting in the boat alongside, and Russell and myself were standing by the main hatchway, waiting for the captain, who was down in the hold, where the crew were at work, when we heard his voice raised in violent dispute with somebody, whether it was with the mate, or one of the crew, I could not tell; and then came blows and scuffling. I ran to the side and beckoned to John, who came up, and we leaned down the hatchway; and though we could see no one, yet we knew that the captain had the advantage, for his voice was loud and clear—

'You see your condition! You see your condition! Will you ever give me any more of your *jaw*?' No answer; and then came

185 The Merry Ship's Crew, or the Nautical Philosophers.
'For all the happiness mankind can gain
Is not in pleasure but in rest from pain'
                                    – Dryden.
Flogging was just one aspect of the brutality of seagoing life.

186 The Burning of the Clipper Ship *Golden Light*, 23 February 1853 after being struck by lightning on the voyage from Boston to California.

come; and if they do not yield, they are pirates for life. If a sailor resist his commander, he resists the law, and piracy or submission are his only alternatives. Bad as it was, it must be borne. It is what a sailor ships for. Swinging the rope over his head, and bending his body so as to give it full force, the captain brought it down upon the poor fellow's back. Once, twice—six times. 'Will you ever give me any more of your jaw?' The man writhed with pain, but said not a word. Three times more. This was too much, and he muttered something which I could not hear; this brought as many more as the man could stand; when the captain ordered him to be cut down, and to go forward.

'Now for you,' said the captain, making up to John and taking his irons off. As soon as he was loose, he ran forward to the fore-castle. 'Bring that man aft', shouted the captain. The second mate, who had been a shipmate of John's, stood still in the waist, and the mate walked slowly forward; but our third officer, anxious to show his zeal, sprang forward over the windlass, and laid hold of John; but he soon threw him from him. At this moment I would have given worlds for the power to help the poor fellow; but it was all in vain. The captain stood on the quarter-deck, bare-headed, his eyes flashing with rage, and his face as red as blood, swinging the rope, and calling out to his officers, 'Drag him aft!— Lay hold of him! I'll *sweeten* him!' &c. &c. The mate now went forward and told John quietly to go aft; and he, seeing resistance in vain, threw the blackguard third mate from him; said he would go aft of himself; that they should not drag him; and went up to the gangway and held out his hands; but as soon as the captain began to make him fast, the indignity was too much, and he began to resist; but the mate and Russell holding him, he was soon seized up. When he was made fast, he turned to the captain, who stood turning up his sleeves and getting ready for the blow, and asked him what he was to be flogged for. 'Have I ever refused my duty, sir? Have you ever known me to hang back, or to be in-solent, or not to know my work?'

'No,' said the captain; 'it is not that that I flog you for; I flog you for your interference—for asking questions.'

'Can't a man ask a question here without being flogged?'

'No,' shouted the captain; 'nobody shall open his mouth aboard this vessel, but myself'; and began laying the blows upon his back, swinging half round between each blow, to give it full

and turning round, I found that the mate, at a signal from the captain, had cut him down. Almost doubled up with pain, the man walked slowly forward, and went down into the forecastle. Everyone else stood still at his post, while the captain, swelling with rage and with the importance of his achievement, walked the quarterdeck, and at each turn, as he came forward, calling out to us,—'You see your condition! You see where I've got you all, and you know what to expect!—You've been mistaken in me—you didn't know what I was! Now you know what I am!—I'll make you toe the mark, every soul of you, or I'll flog you all, fore and aft, from the boy, up!—You've got a driver over you! Yes a *slave-driver—a Negro-driver*! I'll see who'll tell me he isn't a Negro slave!' With this and the like matter, equally calculated to quiet us, and to allay any apprehensions of future trouble, he entertained us for about ten minutes, when he went below. Soon after John came aft, with his bare back covered with stripes and wales in every direction, and dreadfully swollen, and asked the steward to ask the captain to let him have some salve, or balsam, to put upon it. 'No,' said the captain, who heard him from below; 'tell him to put his shirt on; that's the best thing for him; and pull me ashore in the boat. Nobody is going to lay-up on board this vessel.' He then called to Mr Russell to take those two men and two others in the boat, and pull him ashore. I went for one. The two men could hardly bend their backs, and the captain called to them to 'give way, give way!' but finding they did their best, he let them alone. The agent was in the stern-sheets, but during the whole pull—a league or more—not a word was spoken. We landed; the captain, agent, and officer went up to the house, and left us with the boat. I, and the man with me, stayed near the boat, while John and Sam walked slowly away, and sat down on the rocks. They talked some time together, but at length separated, each sitting alone. I had some fears of John. He was a foreigner, and violently tempered, and under suffering; and he had his knife with him; and the captain was to come down alone to the boat. But nothing happened; and we went quietly on board. The captain was probably armed, and if either of them had lifted a hand against him, they would have had nothing before them but flight, and starvation in the woods of California, or capture by the soldiers and Indian blood-hounds, whom the offer of twenty dollars would have set upon them.

from *Two Years Before the Mast*, by Richard Dana, 1840.

effect. As he went on, his passion increased, and he danced about the deck, calling out as he swung the rope,—'If you want to know what I flog you for, I'll tell you. It's because I like to do it!—because I like to do it! It suits me! That's what I do it for!'

The man writhed under the pain, until he could endure it no longer, when he called out, with an exclamation more common among foreigners than with us—'Oh, Jesus Christ! Oh, Jesus Christ!'

'Don't call on Jesus Christ,' shouted the captain; '*he can't help you. Call on Captain T——. He's the man! He can help you! Jesus Christ can't help you now!'*

At these words, which I never shall forget, my blood ran cold. I could look no longer. Disgusted, sick, and horror-struck, I turned away and leaned over the rail, and looked down into the water. A few rapid thoughts of my own situation, and of the prospect of future revenge, crossed my mind; but the falling of the blows and the cries of the man called me back at once. At length they ceased,

187 The *Cherokee* of Boston at Smyrna in 1832. A fine example of a full-rigged brig. Watercolour, attributed to Raffael Corsini.

Homeward bound round the Horn

Richard Dana visits the scenery which we first met with Willem Cornelison Schouten in 1615.

Saturday, July 2d.—This day the sun rose fair, but it ran too low in the heavens to give any heat, or thaw out our sails and rigging; yet the sight of it was pleasant; and we had a steady 'reef-top-sail breeze' from the westward. The atmosphere, which had previously been clear and cold, for the last few hours grew damp, and had a disagreeable, wet chilliness in it; and the man who came from the wheel said he heard the captain tell 'the passenger' that the thermometer had fallen several degrees since morning, which he could not account for in any other way than by supposing that there must be ice near us; though such a thing had never been heard of in this latitude, at this season of the year. At twelve o'clock we went below, and had just got through dinner, when the

188 The USS *Vincennes* in the ice.

cook put his head down the scuttle, and told us to come on deck and see the finest sight that we had ever seen. 'Where away, cook?' asked the first man who was up. 'On the larboard bow.' And there lay, floating in the ocean, several miles off, an immense irregular mass, its top and points covered with snow, and its centre of a deep indigo colour. This was an iceberg, and of the largest size, as one of our men said who had been in the Northern ocean. As far as the eye could reach, the sea in every direction was of a deep blue colour, the waves running high and fresh, and sparkling in the light; and in the midst lay this immense mountain-island, its cavities and valleys thrown into deep shade, and its points and pinnacles glittering in the sun. All hands were soon on deck, looking at it, and admiring in various ways its beauty and grandeur. But no description can give any idea of the strangeness, splendour, and, really, the sublimity, of the sight. Its great size—for it must have been from two to three miles in circumference, and several hundred feet in height; its slow motion, as its base rose and sank in the water, and its high points nodded against the clouds; the dashing of the waves upon it, which, breaking high with foam, lined its base with a white crust; and the thundering sound of the cracking of the mass, and the breaking and tumbling down of huge pieces; together with its nearness and approach, which added a slight element of fear—all combined to give to it the character of true sublimity. The main body of the mass was, as I have said, of an indigo colour, its base crusted with frozen foam; and as it grew thin and transparent toward the edges and top, its colour shaded off from a deep blue to the whiteness of snow. It seemed to be drifting slowly toward the north, so that we kept away and avoided it. It was in sight all the afternoon; and when we got to leeward of it, the wind died away, so that we lay-to quite near it for a greater part of the night. Unfortunately, there was no moon; but it was a clear night, and we could plainly mark the long, regular heaving of the stupendous mass, as its edges moved slowly against the stars. Several times in our watch loud cracks were heard, which sounded as though they must have run through the whole length of the iceberg, and several pieces fell down with a thundering crash, plunging heavily into the sea. Toward morning, a strong breeze sprang up, and we filled away, and left it astern, and at daylight it was out of sight . . .

Having a fine wind, we were soon up with and passed the latitude of the Cape; and having stood far enough to the southward to give it a wide berth, we began to stand to the eastward, with a good prospect of being round, and steering to the northward on the other side, in a very few days. But ill luck seemed to have lighted upon us. Not four hours had we been standing on in this course before it fell dead calm; and in half-an-hour it clouded up; a but we had an abundance of what is worse to a sailor in cold weather—drenching rain. Snow is blinding, and very bad when coming upon a coast; but, for genuine discomfort, give me rain with freezing weather. A snow-storm is exciting, and it does not wet through the clothes (which is important to a sailor); but a constant rain there is no escaping from. It wets to the skin, and makes all protection vain. We had long ago run through all our dry clothes; and as sailors have no other way of drying them than by the sun, we had nothing to do but to put on those which were the least wet. At the end of each watch, when we came below, we took off our clothes and wrung them out; two taking hold of a pair of trousers—one at each end—and jackets in the same way. Stockings, mittens, and all, were wrung out also, and then hung up to drain and chafe dry against the bulk-heads. Then, feeling of all our clothes, we picked out those which were the least wet, and put them on, so as to be ready for a call, and turned-in, covered ourselves up with blankets, and slept until three knocks on the scuttle, and the dismal sound of 'All starbowlines ahoy! Eight bells, there below! Do you hear the news?' drawled out from on deck, and the sulky answer of 'Ay, ay!' from below, sent us up again . . .

After about eight days of constant easterly gales, the wind hauled occasionally a little to the southward, and blew hard, which, as we were well to the southward, allowed us to brace in a little and stand on, under all the sail we could carry. These turns lasted but a short while, and sooner or later it set in again from the old quarter; yet at each time we made something, and were gradually edging along to the eastward. One night, after one of these shifts of the wind, and when all hands had been up a great part of the time, our watch was left on deck, with the main-sail hanging in the buntlines, ready to be set, if necessary. It came on to blow worse and worse, with hail and snow beating like so many furies upon the ship, it being as dark and thick as night could make it. The main-sail was blowing and slatting with a noise like thunder, when the captain came on deck, and ordered it to be furled. The mate was about to call all hands, when the captain stopped him, and said that the men would be beaten out, if they were called up so often; that as our watch must stay on deck, it might as well be doing that as anything else. Accordingly we went upon the yard; and never shall I forget that piece of work. Our watch had been so reduced by sickness, and by some having been left in California, that, with one man at the wheel, we had only the third mate and three beside myself to go aloft; so that, at most, we could only attempt to furl one yard-arm at a time. We manned the weather yard-arm, and set to work to make a furl of it. Our lower masts being short, and our yards very square, the

189 Off the coast in a snowstorm. An American ship taking a pilot.

Plate 31 Sun Rising through Vapour, J. M. W. Turner (1775–1851). On the left are two spritsail fishing craft of a rig which has survived until the present day in the Thames barge. The men-of-war are seventeenth-century ships taken from the Dutch painters. *National Gallery, London.*

few straggling blasts, with spits of snow and sleet, came from the eastward; and in an hour more we lay hove-to under a close-reefed main top-sail, drifting bodily off to leeward before the fiercest storm that we had yet felt, blowing dead ahead from the eastward. It seemed as though the genius of the place had been roused at finding that we had nearly slipped through his fingers, and had come down upon us with tenfold fury. The sailors said that every blast, as it shook the shrouds, and whistled through the rigging, said to the old ship, 'No, you don't! no, you don't!'

For eight days we lay drifting about in this manner. Sometimes—generally towards noon—it fell calm; once or twice a round copper ball showed itself for a few moments in the place where the sun ought to have been; and a puff or two came from the westward, giving some hope that a fair wind had come at last. During the first two days we made sail for these puffs, shaking the reefs out of the top-sails, and boarding the tacks of the courses; but finding that it only made work for us when the gale set in again, it was soon given up, and we lay-to under our close-reefs. We had less snow and hail than when we were farther to the westward;

sail had a head of nearly fifty feet, and a short leach made still shorter by the deep reef which was in it, which brought the clew away out on the quarters of the yard, and made a bunt nearly as square as the mizen royal-yard. Beside this difficulty, the yard over which we lay was cased with ice, the gaskets and rope of the foot and leach of the sail as stiff and hard as a piece of suction-hose, and the sail itself about as pliable as though it had been made of sheets of sheathing-copper. It blew a perfect hurricane, with alternate blasts of snow, hail, and rain. We had to *fist* the sail with bare hands. No one could trust himself to mittens, for if he slipped he was a gone man. All the boats were hoisted in on deck, and there was nothing to be lowered for him. We had need of every finger God had given us. Several times we got the sail upon the yard, but it blew away again before we could secure it. It required men to lie over the yard to pass each turn of the gaskets; and when they were passed, it was almost impossible to knot them so that they would hold. Frequently we were obliged to leave off altogether, and take to beating our hands upon the sail, to keep them from freezing. After some time, which seemed for ever, we got the weather side stowed after a fashion, and went over to leeward for another trial. This was still worse, for the body of the sail had been blown over to leeward; and as the yard was a-cock-bill by the lying over of the vessel, we had to light it all up to windward. When the yard-arms were furled, the bunt was all adrift again, which made more work for us. We got all secure at last; but we had been nearly an hour-and-a-half upon the yard, and it seemed an age. It had just struck five bells when we went up, and eight were struck soon after we came down. This may seem slow work; but, considering the state of everything, and

that we had only five men to a sail with just half as many square yards of canvas in it as the main-sail of the *Independence*, sixty-gun-ship, which musters seven hundred men at her quarters, it is not wonderful that we were no quicker about it. We were glad enough to get on deck, and still more to go below. The oldest sailor in the watch said, as he went down, 'I shall never forget that main-yard; it beats all my going a-fishing. Fun is fun; but furling one yard-arm of a course, at a time, off Cape Horn, is no better than man-killing'.

During the greater part of the next two days the wind was pretty steady from the southward. We had evidently made great progress, and had good hope of being soon up with the Cape, if we were not there already. We could put but little confidence in our reckoning, as there had been no opportunies for an observation, and we had drifted too much to allow of our dead reckoning being anywhere near the mark. If it would clear off enough to give a chance for an observation, or if we could make land, we should know where we were; and upon these, and the chances of falling in with a sail from the eastward, we depended almost entirely.

Friday, July 22nd.—This day we had a steady gale from the southward, and stood on under close sail, with the yards eased a little by the weather braces, the clouds lifting a little, and showing signs of breaking away. In the afternoon, I was below with Mr H——, the third mate, and two others, filling the bread-locker in the steerage from the casks, when a bright gleam of sun-shine broke out and shone down the companion-way and through the skylight, lighting up everything below, and sending a warm glow through the heart of every one. It was a sight we had not seen for weeks—an omen, a God-send. Even the roughest and hardest face acknowledged its influence. Just at that moment we heard a loud shout from all parts of the deck, and the mate called out down the companion-way to the captain, who was sitting in the cabin. What he said we could not distinguish; but the captain kicked over his chair, and was on deck at one jump. We could not tell what it was; and, anxious as we were to know, the discipline of the ship would not allow of our leaving our places. Yet, as we were not called, we knew there was no danger. We hurried to get through with our job, when, seeing the steward's black face peering out of the pantry, Mr H—— hailed him, to know what was the matter. 'Lan' o, to be sure, sir! No you hear 'em sing out, "Lan' o?" De cap'em say 'im Cape Horn!' . . .

The land was the island of Staten Land, just to the eastward of Cape Horn; and a more desolate-looking spot I never wish to set eyes upon;—bare, broken, and girt with rocks and ice, with here and there, between the rocks and broken hillocks, a little stunted vegetation of shrubs. It was a place well suited to stand at the

Plate 32 Calais Pier – French Fishermen Preparing for Sea, the English Packet Arriving, by J. M. W. Turner (1775 – 1851) (detail). The English packet is built for speed rather than comfort and the picture gives a good idea of the misery of a Channel crossing in the early nineteenth century. *National Gallery. London.*

190 Reefing topsails, by W. Huggins 1832.

junction of the two oceans, beyond the reach of human cultivation, and encounter the blasts and snows of a perpetual winter. Yet, dismal as it was, it was a pleasant sight to us; not only as being the first land we had seen, but because it told us that we had passed the Cape, were in the Atlantic, and that, with twenty-four hours of this breeze, might bid defiance to the Southern Ocean. It told us, too, our latitude and longitude better than any observation; and the captain now knew where we were, as well as if we were off the end of Long Wharf . . .

We left the land gradually astern; and at sundown had the Atlantic Ocean clear before us.

It is usual in voyages round the Cape from the Pacific to keep to the eastward of the Falkland Islands; but as it had now set in a strong, steady, and clear south-wester, with every prospect of its lasting, and we had had enough of high latitudes, the captain determined to stand immediately to the northward, running inside the Falkland Islands. Accordingly, when the wheel was relieved at eight o'clock, the order was given to keep her due north, and all hands were turned up to square away the yards and make sail. In a moment the news ran through the ship that the captain was keeping her off, with her nose straight for Boston,

and Cape Horn over her taffrail. It was a moment of enthusiasm. Everyone was on the alert; and even the two sick men turned out to lend a hand at the halyards. The wind was now due south-west, and blowing a gale to which a vessel close-hauled could have shown no more than a single close-reefed sail; but as we were going before it, we could carry on. Accordingly, hands were sent aloft, and a reef shaken out of the top-sails, and the reefed fore-sail set. When we came to mast-head the top-sail yards, with all hands at the halyards, we struck up 'Cheerily, men', with a chorus which might have been heard halfway to Staten Land. Under her increased sail, the ship drove on through the water. Yet she could bear it well; and the captain sang out from the quarter-deck—'Another reef out of that fore top-sail, and give it to her!' Two hands sprang aloft; the frozen reef-points and earings were cast adrift, the halyards manned, and the sail gave out her increased canvas to the gale. All hands were kept on deck to watch the effect of the change. It was as much as she could well carry, and with a heavy sea astern, it took two men at the wheel to steer her. She flung the foam from her bows; the spray breaking aft as far as the gangway. She was going at a prodigious rate. Still everything held. Preventer braces were reeved and hauled taught; tackles got upon the back-stays; and each thing done to keep all snug and strong. The captain walked the deck at a rapid stride, looked aloft at the sails, and then to windward; the mate stood in the gangway rubbing his hands, and talking aloud to the ship— 'Hurrah, old bucket! the Boston girls have got hold of the tow-rope!' and the like; and we were on the forecastle, looking to see how the spars stood it, and guessing the rate at which she was going, when the captain called out—'Mr Brown, get up the top-mast studding-sail! what she can't carry she may drag!' The mate looked a moment; but he would let no one be before him in daring. He sprang forward—'Hurrah, men! rig out the top-mast studding-sail boom! lay aloft, and I'll send the rigging up to you!' We sprang aloft into the top; lowered a girt-line down, by which we hauled up the rigging; rove the tacks and halyards; ran out the boom and lashed it fast; and sent down the lower halyards as a preventer. It was a clear starlight night, cold and blowing; but everybody worked with a will. Some, indeed, looked as though they thought the 'old man' was mad, but no one said a word. We had had a new top-mast studding-sail made with a reef in it —a thing hardly ever heard of, and which the sailors had ridiculed a good deal, saying that when it was time to reef a studding-sail, it was time to take it in. But we found a use for it now; for there being a reef in the top-sail, the studding-sail could not be set without one in it also. To be sure, a studding-sail with reefed top-sails was rather a new thing; yet there was some reason in it,

for if we carried that away, we should lose only a sail and a boom; but a whole top-sail might have carried away the mast and all.

While we were aloft, the sail had been got out, bent to the yard, reefed, and ready for hoisting. Waiting for a good opportunity, the halyards were manned and the yard hoisted fairly up to the block; but when the mate came to shake the catspaw out of the downhaul, and we began to boom-end the sail, it shook the ship to her centre. The boom buckled up and bent like a whip-stick, and we looked every moment to see something go; but, being of the short, tough upland spruce, it bent like whalebone, and nothing could break it. The carpenter said it was the best stick he had ever seen. The strength of all hands soon brought the tack to the boom-end, and the sheet was trimmed down, and the preventer and the weather-brace hauled taught to take off the strain. Every rope-yarn seemed stretched to the utmost, and every thread of canvas; and with this sail added to her, the ship sprang through the water like a thing possessed. The sail being nearly all forward, it lifted her out of the water, and she seemed actually to jump from sea to sea. From the time her keel was laid, she had never been so driven; and had it been life or death with every one of us, she could not have borne another stitch of canvas.

Finding that she would bear the sail, the hands were sent below, and our watch remained on deck. Two men at the wheel had as much as they could do to keep her within three points of her course, for she steered as wild as a young colt. The mate walked the deck, looking at the sails, and then over the side to see the foam fly by her—slapping his hands upon his thighs and talking to the ship —'Hurrah, you jade, you've got the scent!—you know where you're going!' And when she leaped over the seas, and almost out of the water, and trembled to her very keel, the spars and masts snapping and creaking,—'There she goes!—There she goes—handsomely!—As long as she cracks she holds!'—while we stood with the rigging laid down fair for letting go, and ready to take in sail and clear away, if anything went. At four bells we hove the log, and she was going eleven knots fairly; and had it not been for the sea from aft which sent the log-ship home, and threw her continually off her course, the log would have shown her to have been going much faster. I went to the wheel with a young fellow from the Kennebec, who was a good helmsman; and for two hours we had our hands full. A few minutes showed us that our monkey-jackets must come off; and cold as it was, we stood in our shirt-sleeves, in a perspiration; and were glad enough to have it eight bells, and the wheel relieved. We turned-in and slept as well as we could, though the sea made a constant roar under her bows, and washed over the forecastle like a small cataract.

At four o'clock we were called again. The same sail was still

on the vessel, and the gale, if there was any change, had increased a little. No attempt was made to take the studding-sail in; and, indeed, it was too late now. If we had started anything towards taking it in, either tack or halyards, it would have blown to pieces, and carried something away with it. The only way now was to let everything stand, and if the gale went down, well and good; if not, something must go—the weakest stick or rope first—and then we could get it in. For more than an hour she was driven on at such a rate that she seemed actually to crowd the sea into a heap before her; and the water poured over the sprit-sail yard as it

192 – 8 An anonymous American artist's record of the different sail necessitated by the weather on the first few days of an Atlantic voyage, from a series of watercolours, probably by a person on board the ship.

192 Ship *Belisarius* leaving Baker's Island, January 1, 1802.

193 *Belisarius*, two days out scudding under reefed foresail and close-reefed main topsail.

off the swinging boom. No sooner was it set than the ship tore on again like one that was mad, and began to steer as wild as a hawk. The men at the wheel were puffing and blowing at their work, and the helm was going hard up and hard down, constantly. Add to this, the gale did not lessen as the day came on, but the sun rose in clouds. A sudden lurch threw the man from the weather wheel across the deck and against the side. The mate sprang to the wheel, and the man, regaining his feet, seized the spokes, and they hove the wheel up just in time to save her from broaching to, though nearly half the studding-sail went under water; and as she came to, the boom stood up at an angle of forty-five degrees. She had evidently more on her than she could bear; yet it was in vain to try to take it in—the clewline was not strong enough; and they were thinking of cutting away, when another wide yaw and a come-to snapped the guys, and the swinging boom came in with a crash against the lower rigging. The out-

194 *top Belisarius* four days out under reefed foresail and mizen staysail.

195 *centre Belisarius* five days out hove to under reefed mizen staysail.

196 *right Belisarius* six days from Salem with reefed topsails, foresail and staysail.

would over a dam. Toward daybreak the gale abated a little, and she was just beginning to go more easily along, relieved of the pressure, when Mr Brown determined to give her no respite, and depending upon the wind's subsiding as the sun rose, told us to get along the lower studding-sail. This was an immense sail, and held wind enough to last a Dutchman a week,—hove-to. It was soon ready, the boom topped up, preventer guys rove, and the idlers called up to man the halyards; yet such was still the force of the gale, that we were nearly an hour setting the sail; carried away the outhaul in doing it, and came very near snapping

haul block gave way, and the top-mast studding-sail boom bent in a manner which I never before supposed a stick could bend. I had my eye on it when the guys parted, and it made one spring and buckled up so as to form nearly a half circle, and sprang out again to its shape. The clewline gave way at the first pull; the cleat to which the halyards were belayed was wrenched off, and the sail blew round the sprit-sail yard and head guys, which gave us a bad job to get it in. A half-hour served to clear all away, and she was suffered to drive on with her top-mast studding-sail set, it being as much as she could stagger under . . .

Sail after sail was added, as we drew into fine weather; and in one week after leaving Cape Horn, the long top-gallant masts were got up, top-gallant and royal yards crossed, and the ship restored to her fair proportions . . .'

Sunday, July 31st.—At noon we were in Lat. 36 deg. 41 min. S., Long. 38 deg. 8 min. W.; having traversed the distance of two thousand miles, allowing for changes of course, in nine days. A thousand miles in four days and a half!—this is equal to steam . . .

Notwithstanding all that has been said about the beauty of a ship under full sail, there are very few who have ever seen a ship, literally, under all her sail. A ship coming in or going out of port, with her ordinary sails, and perhaps two or three studding-sails, is commonly said to be under full sail; but a ship never has all her sail upon her, except when she has a light, steady breeze, very nearly, but not quite, dead aft, and so regular that it can be trusted, and is likely to last for some time. Then, with all her sails, light and heavy, and studding-sails on each side, alow and aloft, she is the most glorious moving object in the world. Such a sight very few, even some who have been at sea a good deal, have ever beheld; for from the deck of your own vessel you cannot see her as you would a separate object.

One night, while we were in these tropics, I went out to the end of the flying-jib-boom, upon some duty, and having finished it, turned round, and lay over the boom for a long time, admiring the beauty of the sight before me. Being so far out from the deck, I could look at the ship, as at a separate vessel—and, there rose up from the water, supported only by the small black hull, a pyramid of canvas, spreading out far beyond the hull, and towering up almost, as it seemed in the indistinct night air, to the clouds. The sea was as still as an inland lake; the light trade-wind was gently and steadily breathing from astern; the dark blue sky was studded with the tropical stars; there was no sound but the rippling of the water under the stem; and the sails were spread out, wide and high;—the two lower studding-sails stretching, on each side, far beyond the deck; the top-mast studding-sails, like wings to the top-sails; the top-gallant studding-sails spreading fearlessly out above them; still higher, the two royal studding-sails, looking like two kites flying from the same string; and, highest of all, the little sky-sail, the apex of the pyramid, seeming actually to touch the stars, and to be out of reach of human hand. So quiet, too, was the sea, and so steady the breeze, that if these sails had been sculptured marble, they could not have been more motionless. Not a ripple upon the surface of the canvas; not even a quivering of the extreme edges of the sail—so perfectly were they distended by the breeze. I was so lost in the sight, that I forgot the presence of the man who came out with me, until he said (for he, too, rough old man-of-

war's-man as he was, had been gazing at the show), half to himself, still looking at the marble sails—'How quietly they do their work!'...

From the latitude of the West Indies, until we got inside the Bermudas, where we took the westerly and south-westerly winds, which blow steadily off the coast of the United States early in the autumn, we had every variety of weather, and two or three moderate gales, or, as sailors call them, double-reef-top-sail breezes, which came on in the usual manner, and of which one is a specimen of all.

197 *above Belisarius* seven days out under reefed foresail.

198 *below Belisarius* nine days out, under close-reefed main topsail, foresail and staysail.

elasticity, so that if it was pressed in, it would not return to its shape; and his gums swelled until he could not open his mouth. His breath, too, became very offensive; he lost all strength and spirit; could eat nothing; grew worse every day; and, in fact, unless something was done for him, would be a dead man in a week, at the rate at which he was sinking. The medicines were all, or nearly all gone; and if we had had a chest-full, they would have been of no use; for nothing but fresh provisions and terra firma has any effect upon the scurvy. This disease is not so common now as formerly; and is attributed generally to salt provisions, want of cleanliness, the free use of grease and fat (which is the reason of its prevalence among whalemen), and last of all to laziness. It never could have been from the latter cause on board our ship; nor from the second, for we were a very cleanly crew, kept our forecastle in neat order, and were more particular about washing and changing clothes than many better-dressed people on shore. It was probably from having none but salt provisions, and possibly from our having

199 The missionary packet *Morning Star*, 1866. A good view of a mid nineteenth-century hermaphrodite brig. Note the helmsman's clear view of the compass binnacle and the sails – the two most important things for him to watch. Two prominent deckhouses are a feature of this vessel. Lithograph by Endicott.

200 *right* A hermaphrodite brig, the *Kingston* of Boston, W. D. Phelps master leaving the Port of Smyrna, 1833. This popular rig for smaller trading ships required a smaller crew than a full-rigged brig. Watercolour attributed to Raffael Corsini.

Our captain had been married only a few weeks before he left Boston; and, after an absence of over two years, it may be supposed that he was not slow in carrying sail. The mate, too, was not to be beaten by anybody; and the second mate, though he was afraid to press sail, was afraid as death of the captain, and being between two fears, sometimes carried on longer than any of them. We snapped off three flying-jib booms in twenty-four hours, as fast as they could be fitted and rigged out; sprung the sprit-sail yard; and made nothing of studding-sail booms. Beside the natural desire to get home, we had another reason for urging the ship on. The scurvy had begun to show itself on board. One man had it so badly as to be disabled and off duty, and the English lad, Ben, was in a dreadful state, and was daily growing worse. His legs swelled and pained him so that he could not walk; his flesh lost its

run very rapidly into hot weather, after having been so long in the extremest cold.

Depending upon the westerly winds, which prevail off the coast in the autumn, the captain stood well to the westward, to run inside of the Bermudas, and in hope of falling in with some vessel bound to the West Indies or the Southern States. The scurvy had spread no farther among the crew, but there was danger it might; and these cases were bad ones.

Sunday, Sept. 11th.—Lat. 30 deg. 4 min. N., Long. 63 deg. 23 min. W.; the Bermudas bearing north-north-west, distant one hundred and fifty miles. The next morning, about ten o'clock, 'Sail ho!' was cried on deck, and all hands turned up to see the stranger. As she drew nearer, she proved to be an ordinary-looking hermaphrodite brig, standing south-south-east; and probably bound out from the Northern States to the West Indies; and was just the thing we wished to see. She hove-to for us, seeing that we wished to speak her; and we ran down to her; boom-ended our studding-sails; backed our main top-sail, and hailed her—'Brig, ahoy!'—'Hallo!'—'Where are you from, pray?' —'From New York, bound to Curacoa.'—'Have you any fresh provisions to spare?'—'Ay, ay! plenty of them!' We lowered away the quarter-boat instantly; and the captain and four hands sprang in, and were soon dancing over the water, and alongside the brig. In about half-an-hour they returned with half a boat-load of potatoes and onions, and each vessel filled away, and kept

on her course. She proved to be the brig *Solon*, of Plymouth, from the Connecticut river, and last from New York, bound to the Spanish Main, with a cargo of fresh provisions, mules, tin bake-pans, and other *notions*. The onions were genuine and fresh; and the mate of the brig told the men in the boat, as he passed the bunches over the side, that the girls had strung them on purpose for us the day he sailed. We had supposed on board, that a new president had been chosen the last winter; and, just as we filled away, the captain hailed and asked who was president of the United States. They answered, Andrew Jackson; but thinking that the General could not have been elected a third time, we hailed again, and they answered—Jack Downing; and left us to correct the mistake at our leisure.

It was just dinner-time when we filled away; and the steward, taking a few bunches of onions for the cabin, gave the rest to us, with a bottle of vinegar. We carried them forward, stowed them away in the forecastle, refusing to have them cooked, and ate them raw, with our beef and bread. And a glorious treat they were. The freshness and crispness of the raw onion, with the earthy taste, give it a great relish to one who has been a long time on salt provisions. We were perfectly ravenous after them. It was like a scent of blood to a hound. We ate them at every meal, by the dozen; and filled our pockets with them, to eat in our watch on deck; and the bunches, rising in the form of a cone from the largest at the bottom to the smallest, no larger than a strawberry at the top, soon disappeared. The chief use, however, of the fresh provisions was for the men with the scurvy. One of them was able to eat, and he soon brought himself to by gnawing upon raw potatoes; but the other, by this time, was hardly able to open his mouth; and the cook took the potatoes raw, pounded them in a mortar, and gave him the juice to drink. This he swallowed, by the tea-spoonful at a time, and rinsed it about his gums and throat. The strong earthy taste and smell of this extract of the raw potato at first produced a shuddering through his whole frame, and after drinking it, an acute pain, which ran through all parts of his body; but knowing by this that it was taking strong hold, he persevered, drinking a spoonful every hour or so, and holding it a long time in his mouth; until, by the effect of this drink, and of his own restored hope (for he had nearly given up in despair), he became so well as to be able to move about, and open his mouth enough to eat the raw potatoes and onions pounded into a soft pulp. This course soon restored his appetite and strength; and ten days after we spoke the *Solon*, so rapid was his recovery, that, from lying helpless and almost hopeless in his berth, he was at the mast-head, furling a royal.

With a fine south-west wind, we passed inside of the Bermudas;

and notwithstanding the old couplet, which was quoted again and again by those who thought we should have one more touch of a storm before our voyage was up,—

If the Bermudas let you pass,
You must beware of Hatteras—'

we were to the northward of Hatteras, with good weather, and beginning to count, not the days, but the hours, to the time when we should be at anchor in Boston harbour.

from *Two Years Before the Mast*, by Richard Dana, 1840.

202 *above* US surveying ship *Washington* near Cape Hatteras in the hurricane of 8 September 1846, lithograph by A. Hoffy. The sailors' doggerel about West Indian hurricanes went:

July – Stand by
August – Go you must
September – Remember
October – All over.

203 A view of Boston, 1779, from the *Atlantic Neptune*, a book of collected views.

Plate 33 Ship Aground, by J. M. W. Turner (1775–1851). The ship is a man-of-war. The yards being struck down and the men in the top working the yards can be clearly seen.

Whaling

Whaling changed very little between the sixteenth and nineteenth centuries. Captain Chippendale who went on several whaling voyages in the last years of the nineteenth century describes what must have been, with minor differences, the experiences of generations of whalers throwing their harpoons from open boats.

Sailing day on the *Falcon* was a great disappointment to me. The crew was a motley crowd, and as they stood about in little groups watching the narrow strip of headland fade from view, one or two furtively produced flasks from their hip pockets and passed them round. By the time we had passed the Sow and Pigs Lightship most of the gang were feeling their liquor and reeling over the deck. It was a wonder that they were able to keep their equilibrium when going aloft to unfurl the lighter sails.

The fo'c'sle floor below was wet and slippery and littered with rubbish. Often a bottle was dropped in the passing or an empty one smashed to the floor. The air was smoky and foul, and enormous cockroaches scurried about the walls and bulkheads. Oilskins swung to and fro like pendulums and gave off creaky noises, and limp articles of clothing hung on pegs all over the place. A whale-oil lamp spluttered in the draught from the scuttle and cast a gleam on the jumble of forms sitting on their sea-chests or lying half out of their bunks. It was squalid, congested, filthy, and no false glamour of adventure could compensate for the wretchedness.

The mate on deck was trying to bring order as the ship rolled through smooth seas and the wind hummed merrily through the tautened rigging.

The next morning all hands were mustered aft for watches to be told off and boats' crews picked. As I said before, they were a motley crowd: Kanakas, Portuguese, Irish, English, Dutch, and swamp Yankees—all with bloodshot eyes and swollen lips from their orgies of the night before.

In colour opposite: Nineteenth-century shipping from the Blackwaller to the late schooner.

Plate 34 *top left* The *Roxburghe Castle* rescuing people from a burning ship by J. Harris (*fl.* 1846–76). One of the famous Blackwall frigates.

Plate 35 *top right* ss *Europe* built in New York in 1833. A pioneer of the Black Ball line of America and a forerunner of the clipper ship, here seen sailing between New York and Liverpool. After S. Walters.

Plate 36 *bottom left* The clipper ship *William le Lacheur,* 1100 tons burden, on her first voyage from Punta Arenas (Straits of Magellan) to London in 97 days. Lithograph by T. G. Dutton, 1865.

Plate 37 *bottom right* The *Thomas W. Lawson.* The only seven-masted schooner ever built. Watercolour by John F. Leavitt (1905–   ).

204 The Dutch Whaling Fleet by Jacob F. de Vries (*d.* 1660) (oil).

Captain Handy was hard and tough, the bully type, and soon began to live up to his reputation. I never had any trouble with him, which might have been due to the fact that my father was U.S. Consul at St Helena, though I made it my business to keep out of his way. Even though I knew Mr Fuller and Mr Glass well, I stood on my own two feet and never cast an eye to either of them for any favours. So with that feeling of independence I went through the voyage without trouble.

Another reason for my sailing on the *Falcon* was that she was to cruise in the Indian Ocean. Barring my trip to Desolation Island on the barque *Swallow* and a short cruise off Herd's Island, all my voyages had been in the South Atlantic and off the West African coast. The rumour was that the *Falcon* was to make a straight run to the Indian Ocean, but we had no more cleared the coast when mastheads were the order of the day, and while we never shortened at night or did any cruising, the lookouts were ever on the watch for sperm whales. We raised one school in the North Atlantic, which gave us a catch of four cows and an oil take of more than a hundred barrels.

Shortly after we crossed the line we raised a lone bull and spent a hard day in the equatorial sun chasing the critter. Never once did we get near enough to him to cast an iron, and when the sun began to dip below the horizon we called it a day and went back to the ship. Captain Handy's rage was without bounds and the language he used was enough to melt the tar out of the deck seams.

We by-passed St Helena, rounding the Cape of Good Hope, and began our cruising south-east of Madagascar. We had been cruising about three weeks when the first episode occurred. It was typical Indian Ocean weather, so said those who had been there before. The sky was clear and the sun very bright, with the sea in little hills like furrows in ploughed land, and just enough wind to carry a sail, which spared us the back-breaking work of swinging an eighteen-foot white ash. Suddenly the welcome sound of 'Thar she blo-o-o-o-o-w-s!' came rolling down to the deck. About three miles away on the lee beam a big bull whale was breeching, coming down like a mountain and throwing a geyser of water into the air.

'Hard aport—braces!' shouted Mr Fuller, who had the deck. And then, as the heavy spars swung and the ship came round and gathered headway, 'Call all hands'. Soon we were running down to the monarch of the deep with all hands standing by and with all sails set, as we now had the wind well on the port quarter.

The boats had been made ready. We came up into the wind and were about to hop in and lower away when the big bull reared his enormous tail and down he went. We waited on board until he

205 *above* Dutch whalers in the ice, eighteenth century.

206 *opposite, top* Whaling, *c.* 1750.

207 *opposite bottom* Nineteenth-century American and British whalers off the Cape of Good Hope. Lithograph by Lebreton.

Captain Handy was pacing the afterdeck with a chip on his shoulder, and stopping before them he roared his disgust: 'You are a hard-looking crowd—where the agents picked you up I don't know and I don't care a damn, but I want you all to know that I am boss aboard this ship, and when I tell you to walk, I want you to run; and when I tell you to run, I want you to fly; and I'll spread-eagle in the mizzen riggin' the first man that I catch breaking the rules of this ship.' Then he continued his pacing, casting a sharp glance at us now and again while the mate took over.

The mates had already picked their boat-steerers: a whale-man named Scott steered Mr Fuller; a Portuguese named Viera from the island of Pico in the Azores steered Mr Glass; another whaleman named Bradford steered Mr Hartman; while a huge West Indian steered Mr Slocum. Then came the picking of the boats' crews. I chose to pull bow oar in the boat of Mr Glass.

broke water again, since many times when a lone bull whale sounds he is never seen again, especially if he is looking for his school of cows. Sometimes a lone bull will go flukes and sound when only a few cable-lengths away from the ship, and when he breaks water again he may be away off on the horizon and going strong, with nothing but his spout shining in the sun to indicate his whereabouts. Captain Handy was now aloft and in the rings, the regular station for the skipper when whales were sighted.

While waiting for the whale to come up again we gathered in small groups about the deck, with some of the men in the rigging scanning the sea, and then the captain's bellow was heard again: 'Thar she b-l-o-o-o-o-o-w-s! Thar she b-l-o-o-o-o-o-w-s!'

Every man belonging to the boats' crews made a break for the rails and the boats, and in no time at all the sheaves were creaking as the falls ran through them, the boats were in the water and the chase was on. Captain Handy had a unique way of letting the boats know when the whale had broken water. Besides the usual custom of hoisting the flag to the masthead, he had a pointer which consisted of a six-foot pole with a white canvas-covered hoop, about three feet in diameter, fastened to the end of it. When he pointed it in the direction of the whales it could be seen about a mile away, but at times when the boats were too far away he would raise the flag and head the ship in the direction of the whales. We could tell the ship's direction from the boat's compass, then bear away, always keeping a good lookout.

But this was an educated whale. He had been up against the enemy before, as was shown when we finally caught up with him by the number of irons belonging to other ships that he still had in him. He must either have parted the lines or else they were cut away on account of darkness. One of the irons was from the barque *Rousseau* and another from the barque *Sea Queen*. Both ships at that time were whaling on the other side of the world.

We had been chasing this huge bull whale for more than two hours and it seemed as if we would never get near enough to him to fasten. Every time we thought we had him cornered he would either settle or go flukes. We would then come up into the wind and wait for him to break water again, and in this way he led us a merry chase. Twice, before we caught up with him, Mr Fuller thought he had him cornered. As he flattened his sail and made the run to go on from behind, the whale threw his mighty flukes into the air and went down, leaving Mr Fuller some fifty feet away, much to his disappointment and chagrin.

Eventually we had to take him on the weather side. Now, no whaleman will go on a big bull whale on the weather side if he can help it, as it is a very dangerous undertaking. When a bull sperm whale is struck he rolls to windward and on top of the boat,

many times killing all or some of the boat's crew, and is always sure to roll the boat over. This last is just what happened to us.

The mammoth whale had been up and spouting for nearly an hour and all the boats had been chasing him but could not get close enough to him to fasten, when Mr Glass cut across him to take him head and head. As we got near he practically stopped moving and lay there as if listening. All the while our boat was getting nearer. Then he must have heard or seen us, for we were not more than twenty feet away when he was ready for the dip. Since we could not get to the lee side of him Mr Glass brought the boat to windward and shouted to Antone Viera, the harpooner, 'Let him have it before he goes'.

The Portuguese harpooner fastened him for'ard of the hump. Then over went the boat, bottom side up, with the six of us caught under it and trying desperately to extricate ourselves from the sail, oars, lances, and spare irons, while the line went whistling round the loggerhead at a terrific speed. It would have been destruction for any one of us if the line had caught us, but luckily we got from under the boat and climbed on the keel, while the line went whizzing through the cleat. When we thought the end of the line was in sight it got caught in some way round the loggerhead and held, and we were on our way at the end of a tow-line.

The other three boats had already started legging it for our upturned boat, but by this time the whale was off to windward at a mad rate. Antone Viera grabbed the boat's painter and passed the end of it along to the rest of us to hang on to while taking our wild ride, right up into the wind's eye. The wind had now freshened and as this educated whale went galloping to windward he gave us a fresh soaking every few minutes. As my station in the boat as bow oarsman placed me behind Viera, the harpooner, I gripped the painter that he had passed along, and as I sat astride the keel of the boat I pulled my legs up jockey fashion to keep from sliding off. Viera and I, who were nearest to the bow of the boat, took a continuous drenching, and acted as a sort of buffer for the rest of the men who were behind us.

Picture to yourself six men sitting astride an upturned boat, being towed to wind'ard by a 100-foot whale! It might have been funny at first until I heard Mr Glass shout, 'What we goin' to do when he sounds?'

Then it couldn't have been funny any more. There seemed no escape for us, no means by which we could cut away. Our hatchets, our sheath-knives, our oars were all lost when the boat overturned. Moreover, if we left the boat there was nothing that we could get hold of to keep ourselves afloat. The ship was now to lee'ard and the other three boats were legging it to windward as fast as they could. We might slide off the boat into the water, but where would we swim to?

As the bull's huge tail went into the air and slowly disappeared under the sea we turned and looked at each other silently. Everybody was thinking the same thing: This is the end, we'll meet at Fiddlers Green. Resignedly, we clung to the bottom of the boat and waited for the last pull that would take us down. But the last pull never came. Instead, the whale rose and again started off to windward at breakneck speed, spouting blood.

A whale spouting blood cannot live long under water as the blood coagulates and prevents underwater breathing, consequently he stays on the surface. But he can still tow a boat far away from any help, so all was not over yet. The tropical night might descend before the other boats could catch up with us.

Even though he was spouting blood, he was still strong, and it was some time before we noticed that he had begun to slacken speed, as the mast and sail had acted as a drag and apparently he had begun to tire. Just when it seemed a sure thing that we would soon be sitting at the board of Davy Jones, and listening to the old guy brag about the water being fresh when he was here, we saw the *Falcon* come up into the wind and back her main yards. We stopped looking scary-eyed. Help was on the way, for Captain Handy had dropped the bow boat and it was coming down to us.

Captain Handy himself was at the tiller, and as we carried no spare harpooners, the cooper, who was a six-footer, was in the bow of the boat. The ship had been left in charge of the steward, and since she was up in the wind with her main yards aback she was quite safe as she rose and fell with the swells. After a few loudly shouted exchanges between Mr Glass and Captain Handy, the latter grabbed a boathook and with great difficulty (because of the speed at which we were still travelling) fished a bight of our line out of the water. Pulling up on the line, he managed to get enough slack to take a few turns round his loggerhead and, bending the line to his, he cut our boat away. He lost no time in pulling up to the whale and, after lancing him a few times, shot a bomb into him. This effectively stopped his gallop to windward, and he began milling.

Captain Handy was now fighting the whale alone, and while Antone Viera's harpoon had found a vital spot, the tough old bull was still a long way from rolling over, fin out. During his milling he passed within a hundred feet of the ship and close to our upturned boat. His spout sounded like thunder, and sent a shiver up and down my spine. I certainly had some of the complacency and conceit taken out of me. The boats of the first, third and fourth mates had been following us from the time they saw us roll over. At that time they had been too far away to render any assistance, for when a whale sounds the boats usually spread out

208 *opposite* South Sea whale fishery after Louis Garneray (1755–1837). Whaling as in Melville's *Moby Dick*. In the background can be seen the flensing of a captured whale.

201

As for the old bull, it looked now as if his time was running out, as the mates had him in a bad way 'with his chimney afire', which means he was spouting thick blood. A dying whale is always dangerous until he rolls over, fin out, but by nightfall it was all over and we ran the ship down to fluke him.

Whales were always fluked on the starboard side of the ship, as the waist rail and the cutting-in stage were on that side. Where the ship was to lee'ard of the dead whale, the seizing was cut from the pole and the pole taken off, leaving the iron in the whale. Holes were then cut into his huge flukes and a line roved through them and fastened. Then the whale was towed tail first to the ship.

In the event the ship was to windward of the boats with the dead whale, she would run down and bring the whale alongside the ship tail for'ard and head astern. A bight of the line was then put round the small of the whale close to his flukes. A heavy chain with an eye ring, at the end of which a short line was attached, was passed over the rail and the line put over and under the small of the whale and run back through the eye ring. The chain was run through a hawsepipe in the shoulder of the ship and secured to a bitt, leaving enough play for the ship's rise and fall.

The whale once alongside and fluked, sails were shortened, the ship having been brought up into the wind with foreyards aback. All hands were ordered to turn in, ship-keepers excepted, as at sun-up the task of 'cuttin' in' would begin.

The cutting-in falls were sent aloft and rove through the blocks, which were already aloft and housed under the main top. The travelling blocks were also roved and the ends of the falls were taken for'ard to the windlass and passed under and over the drums. The cutting-in staging, which was carried lashed to the rail when not in use, was then lowered. It extended about ten feet beyond the side of the ship, giving working space to the cutters, the dead whale being directly beneath.

The mates, with spades in hand, then took up their positions on the staging and the work of cutting in would begin with the severing of the head from the body. This job was supervised by the skipper, who was usually in the bow of the starboard boat. A boat-steerer was stationed on the staging with a spade to keep the sharks away and prevent them from devouring the blubber before it could be stripped from the whale. Every time they rolled over to grab a hunk of the whale or a man's leg he would clip them on the snout.

It was necessary for a man with a monkey-rope round his waist to be lowered to the whale's back to cut holes in the blanket pieces for the hooks of the cutting-in falls and to cut holes in the head so that a steel needle could be passed through and a rope secured to the bitt aft of the main chains. Footholds were cut into the back

209 Whaling in the Davis Straits, watercolour by W. J. Huggins, 1829.

and wait for it to break water again. In that way one of them is pretty sure to be near enough to the whale to go on.

All this time we had been sitting on the bottom of our upturned boat, as it was too much of a job to roll it over. The mast and sail acted as a drag and kept the gunwales level with the water. We just had to be patient and wait for the whale to be killed. The sun was still above the horizon when Captain Handy was joined by the other three boats that had eventually come up to the whale. Passing the line over to the first mate while the third and fourth put their irons into him, he went back to the ship and ran her down to our boat. Casting us a line, he soon had us alongside and on the davits with nothing more than a cracked thwart, but with the loss of all the boat's gear. We then saw how the line had caught round the loggerhead and held, causing a near-tragedy.

But before the carcass was set adrift, spades were plunged into the bowels in search of ambergris. Then attention was given the head, which would be floating near the stern of the ship. As the head of a whale is about one-third its size, it was too heavy to be brought aboard intact, consequently it was cut in two parts, separating the junk (upper part) from the case (lower part).

of the whale, but at times when the sea was rough and with the ship rolling, the rope-tender had to be alert or the man might slip from the greasy back of the whale and be crushed to death between its ponderous body and the side of the ship. Sometimes, before the blanket piece was hooked on to the heaving-in falls, the whale would be washed away and lie at right angles to the ship. With the hundreds of sharks spearing at the whale, the man's position would then become very dangerous.

The cutting in of the body would begin by securing the hoisting tackle to what was called a blanket piece, beginning where the head was cut away. As the men at the windlass would heave away, the mates and the boat-steerers stripped the blubber from the carcass, rolling him the whole time. When one blanket piece was hove high enough to the main top and the stationary blocks, another fall was hooked on, and the piece was cut away, swung inboard and lowered to the deck. In the case of a big whale, the blanket pieces were sometimes lowered into the main hatchway to give more room for the rest of the blubber to be lowered to the main deck, where the slicing and mincing was done. This procedure continued until the whale was fully stripped, then the carcass was cast adrift to be devoured by sharks and gulls.

The case of the head included the jaw, and was full of liquid oil, which was dipped out with buckets, while the junk was brought aboard and cut up into strips and minced like the body blubber. The oil obtained from the junk and the case is the finest quality of sperm oil.

After the cutting-in was finished, then came the work of mincing and trying out. The blanket pieces were cut up into strips, minced with huge knives and tossed into the try pots with pikes. The oil was then dipped out and put into a copper cooler secured at the starboard side of the try pots, while the scrap was used as fuel. When cooled, the oil was run into the casks in the holds by means of a leather hose.

Next came the stripping of the ivory (taking out the whale's teeth). Some of the teeth were a foot long. A strap would be placed round a piece of the gum then hooked on to a watch tackle, and while two or three hands bent to the pull another hand with a spade would cut away the gum. The teeth were then cut into singles and left for the gum and meaty stuff to rot away before curing.

from Sails and Whales, by H. A. Chippendale, 1951.

210 *left* A bear hunt in the Arctic by Wigerius Vitringa (1657–1721) (oil).

211 *right* A whale sounding (oil) by Antoine Léon Morel Fatio (1810–71).

212 *below* The clipper *Blackadder* dismasted, 6 April 1881, watercolour by D'Esposito, 1895.

213 *opposite, top* Whampoa in China — two ships of war and Cantonese junks with their highly decorated sides and bulwarks. The lattice sails are a peculiarity of the Orient and made for great ease of handling and reefing. Aquatint after W. J. Huggins (1781 – 1845).

214 *opposite, bottom* The *Montezuma*, a packet clipper of the Black Ball line. Oil by Charles Robert Patterson (1875–1958).

China clippers

The clipper ships (see p. 42f) developed first by the Americans and perfected by the British, represent the apotheosis of the full-rigged sailing ship, achieving remarkable top speeds and fast passages.

The handling of a tea clipper was a ticklish business, and the captain who went into the tea races after being used to slower and less sensitive craft often found himself all at sea and made a bad mess of it at first.

A case in point was the dismasting of the *Titania*. In clipper ships it was bad practice to put your helm up in a squall, though the Board of Trade only recognised that manoeuvre when one was passing the examiners.

Experienced tea-ship captains invariably gave strict orders to an officer, who had just come out of a non-clipper, never to keep away in a squall, but to luff and shake the squall out of her, though the officer had, of course, to be careful not to get his ship aback, and there was also the danger of splitting sails.

The danger of putting the helm up in a sensitive and heavily-sparred clipper was this. As the wind freed the ship gathered more way, and, her yards being more fore and aft owing to her long lower masts than those of other ships, the sails got the full weight of the squall abeam. If the ship was the least bit tender, or it was an extra heavy puff, she would put her rail under so far that the helm lost its power over her. Then, probably, the halliards would be let fly, but, owing to the angle at which the ship was heeled, the yards would not come down, which meant that something had to go.

In *Titania's* case, she encountered a fierce squall just north of the Cape Verds. Her captain, Bobby Deas, who had come from a wagon called the *Reigate*, ordered the helm to be put up. Even so, if he had been in time to get the ship off the wind before the weight of the squall struck her, all would have been well; but he was too late. The squall caught her square on the beam. She went right over until her fairleads were in the water. The topsail yards stuck at the mastheads, and away went the foremast, jibboom, main topmast and mizen topgallant mast.

The *Titania, Ariel*, and *Sir Lancelot* were ships that required very careful handling and wanted knowing, but once a captain got the hang of them they would do anything for him but speak.

These three ships were very fine aft, with a counter like a yacht, which had a nasty habit in bad weather of dishing up the seas. The fineness aft also caused them to be troublesome boats to put about in a rough sea, as they fetched sternway so quickly, and, of course, then took heavy water aboard aft. Thus it was customary to wear them round when there was a nasty sea running.

No greater proof of the way these Steele clippers were cut away aft can be given than the story of how Captain England backed the *Titania* up the Shanghai River. In turning up the river he found that she stirred the mud up every time she came about and was very slow in stays. So on one board, instead of staying, he threw everything aback, brought her stern up to the wind, and sailed her across backwards; and this he continued, making one tack bow first and the other stern first.

The fact is that the Steele clippers were a wee bit too fine aft. On the other hand, the early Aberdeen clippers did not have

enough bearing forward, with the result that they were terribly wet in anything of a head sea.

Most of the tea clippers were inclined to be on the tender side. Some of them, indeed, were so overhatted as to be dangerously crank, but such ships were never in the first flight. But when cleverly handed no square-rigged ship that ever sailed the seas was as handy and willing as these beautiful little tea ships . . .

The captains

No man had more to do with the reputation of a ship than her captain. In the China trade daring, enterprise, and endurance were the *sine qua nons* of a successful skipper. And many a speedy ship, as we shall see, was never given a chance of doing herself justice, owing to her misfortune in the way of captains. First-class men were so scarce that I can barely scrape up a dozen worthy of remembrance.

There were many safe, steady goers, but these were not the passage makers. It required dash and steadiness, daring and prudence to make a crack racing skipper, and these are not attributes of character which are often found in conjunction. A born racing skipper has always been as rare as a born cavalry leader, and those in command of the tea-ships proved no exception to this rule. Most men were either too cautious or too reckless— added to which the China Coast was very wet (sailor's parlance) in those days, and a drunken captain was too often the explanation of a fine ship's non-success.

However, there were a few men, who held the necessary qualities of a tea-ship commander, whose endurance equalled their energy, whose daring was tempered by good judgment, whose business capabilities were on a par with their seamanship, and whose nerves were of cast iron. These men could easily be picked out of the ruck, for their ships were invariably in the front of the battle. Amongst the best known were Robinson of *Sir Lancelot*, Keay of *Ariel*, McKinnon of *Taeping*, Kemball of *Thermopylae*, Andrew Shewan of *Norman Court*, Burgoyne of *Titania*, John Smith of *Lahloo*, and Orchard of *Lothair*.

There are many ways of making a passage, and as many of sailing a ship. Some captains invariably made good tracks, others did not bother about mileage as long as they could keep their ships moving, others again prided themselves on their daring navigation in cutting corners and dashing through narrow channels at night.

The clippers, like thoroughbred horses, responded to the master touch like things of life; Robinson, for instance, was said to be worth an extra half-knot an hour on any ship; this could only be done by the most sleepless vigilance.

Thus the strain of a three months' race was naturally tremen-

dous. Some captains only went below to change their clothes or take a bath; others used the settee in the chart-room or even a deck-chair as a bed. This was the habit of old Captain Robertson, of the *Cairngorm*, who during the homeward run never turned in but dozed with one eye open in a deck-chair on the poop.

Captain Keay, of *Ariel*, writing of his passage down the China Coast, remarks: 'My habit during those weeks was never to undress except for my morning bath, and that often took the place of sleep. The naps I had were of the briefest and were mostly on deck.'

Many a man broke down after a few years of it, but the giants, such as Keay or Robinson, went on and on without a rest, and, still more wonderful, with hardly a serious accident.

Ruses used by the captains against one another
The excitement of the racing was, of course, doubled when the ships were in company. Some captains had a strong dislike to sailing in company, as it increased the tension; thus Captain Care of the *Lord Macaulay* invariably had a man stationed on his fore royal yard, whose timely warning enabled him to keep the horizon between himself and a rival.

Speaking of this habit of Captain Care's reminds me of a trick he once played on the *Elizabeth Nicholson*.

The *Lord Macaulay* was approaching a narrow passage between two islands in the Java Seas, and it was getting on for sundown when her rival, a new ship, the *Elizabeth Nicholson*, with a captain who was also new to the China Seas, was sighted astern bringing up a breeze.

Captain Care who knew the passage well, and, who had meant to go through it during the night, determined to take advantage of the other captain's inexperience in an effort to shake him off.

He began to shorten sail as if he meant to bring up for the night, and was at once gratified by seeing the guileless captain of the *Elizabeth Nicholson* prepare to follow suit. In order to give the other ship time, Captain Care pretended to miss stays, then as soon as the *Nicholson* was within hearing distance, he sang out loudly: 'Stand by and let go the anchor'. It was then just on dusk. Care waited until he heard the plunge of the *Nicholson's* anchor and the roar of the chain through the hawse-pipe, upon which he at once filled away again on the *Lord Macaulay*, and slipping through the channel during the night, was thus enabled to gain a lead of 70 miles.

He did not sight the *Nicholson* again until he was off the Scillies, when she was seen away to the norrard. Care managed to get into the Lizard, then the nor'-west wind coming away strong, he boomed up channel and arrived nearly a week ahead. He was

215 *opposite, top* The *Joseph Cunard*.
In the later clippers the topsails and
the topgallants were divided in two
to allow them to be worked by
smaller crews. Oil by S. Walters 1839.

216 *opposite, bottom* The clipper ship
Lord Warden. Note the clipper lines,
the raking bow. A lightship of the
period can be seen in the
background. Lithograph 1862 by
T. G. Dutton.

217 The peak period of beauty of the
sailing ship – The *Taeping* and the
Ariel racing home from China with
the season's tea crop in 1866.
Lithograph by T. G. Dutton.
(See p. 147.)

specially pleased at this victory, as the skipper of the *Elizabeth Nicholson* had treated the idea of the *Lord Macaulay* being able to beat his new ship with scorn, and was so strait-laced into the bargain that he refused even to bet the proverbial hat on the result.

It was in quite a different fashion that Captain Robinson of the *Sir Lancelot* fooled Captain Innes of the *Spindrift* in the 1869 race. The *Spindrift* had sailed from Foochow on the 4th of July, 13 days before *Sir Lancelot*; nevertheless Robinson managed to overhaul Innes off the Cape, and one fine clear morning the *Spindrift* sighted a ship on her starboard beam, which signalled the number of the *City of Dunedin*. On his arrival Captain Innes reported speaking the *City of Dunedin* on 31st August off the Cape, little knowing that the vessel was in reality his rival, the *Sir Lancelot*, which had already arrived in the Thames, five days ahead of him.

On another occasion Captain Keay in the *Ariel* got the better of *Spindrift*. This was in 1868. The two vessels had travelled nearly the whole length of the China Coast in company until one evening found them almost becalmed off the West Coast of Borneo. Both ships stood in to get the land breeze until at 8 p.m. they were so close on top of the land that *Spindrift* went about and stood out

to sea again. But Captain Keay, putting out all his lights, held on and with his lead going crept nearer and nearer the shore. At midnight he had 9 fathoms. Then came the first puff of the land breeze and he immediately hove round on the port tack. The next three casts of the lead gave 5, 4½, and 4 fathoms, so he was obliged to keep off a bit, but all the time the breeze was freshening, and as he stood away on his course he was rewarded for his daring by a last glimpse of *Spindrift's* port light as she lay becalmed in the offing.

from *The China Clippers*, by Basil Lubbock, 1916.

Smashed wheels, shifting ballast, weed and barnacles

With the cutting of the Suez Canal, the tea trade, which had brought the clipper ships to their beautiful perfection, transferred itself to the new steamers. Sailing ships were diverted to the transport of wool from Australia and, later, of fertilizer and iron ore from South America, for which greater size and less speed was called for. This led to the construction of the four and five (or more) masted ships, barques and schooners of the last days of the age of sail (see p. 48f).

The great jute clipper *Liverpool* . . . lost her whole second mate's watch overboard with the exception of the wheel and look-out; and it was not discovered until 8 bells. The little tea clipper *Undine* also lost her second mate and his watch overboard in 1882, whilst her captain was found dead under the spare spars on the following morning.

The wool clipper *Ben Voirlich* lost 9 men in a broach to when running heavy in 1878. Most of these were torn from the braces, but two of them were actually washed off the lee fore yard-arm, as it dragged in the water.

Such accidents were unknown in the days of wood and hemp. Nor had the high-sterned Elizabethans and Stuarts any fear of being badly pooped—a terror which never left the mind of a helmsman when steering a modern sailing ship before a gale of wind.

Instances of smashed wheels, broken helmsmen, gutted cabins and swept decks are so numerous that one can only wonder how many missing ships may not have been lost in this way . . .

In 1899, the iron barque *Gogoburn* was running for the Channel before a fierce S.W.ly gale. As she was filling her maindeck to the rail with every sea, Captain Climo prepared to heave her to. The main upper topsail had been made fast and all hands were busy clewing up the fore lower topsail when a gigantic sea broke over the poop and swept the ship from end to end.

The wheel was smashed to staves and the two helmsmen were found, when the water had run off, lying bleeding and insensible under the mizen fife-rail. Captain Climo and a seaman named Cleavan were tossed overboard and never seen again. The cabin was filled with water, the captain's wife and children being driven on deck by the flood; the boats were broken up, and the ship left in such a waterlogged condition that cargo had to be jettisoned in order to save her.

In January, 1889, the ship *Troop* was pooped in 45 deg. S., 12 deg. E. The sea washed the two men at the wheel down on to the maindeck, one of them being severely injured. The binnacle was laid flat and the compass magnets torn up from the deck.

In the autumn of 1910 a big sea broke over the stern of the barque *Glenshee* and buried her so deep that the watch had to take refuge in the rigging. The men at the wheel were lashed, and both they and the wheel survived on this occasion, but the poop-rail was laid flat, the bulwarks were torn up and the boats smashed . . .

In 1887, the famous Waverley clipper *Cedric the Saxon*, after beating for six weeks off the Horn in May and June when bound from Hull to 'Frisco, at last got a slant from S.E. which soon freshened to a full gale. At 7.30 a.m., after she had been shortened down to lower topsails, foresail and fore topmast staysail, a bad

218 *opposite* Beam view of the four-masted barque *Carradale,* an original photograph of one of the last of the windjammers.

219 and 220 The *Potosi,* a five masted barque of the famous P-Line, owned by Ferdinand Laeisz of Hamburg.

219 *above* under full sail in light airs and 220 *below* with sails unbent, being refitted in harbour.

221 *left* A clipper ship in a hurricane, *c.* 1860, loses her fore topmasts as she broaches to.

222 *right* The four-masted barque *Priwall* of the Laeisz line of Hamburg in ballast. As Basil Lubbock wrote, being in ballast showed up all the faults of a ship's lines, and while the clipper ships could still look beautiful in ballast, the last windjammers betrayed their functional design, intended for cargo capacity rather than speed.

sea was pooped, which carried away the wheel and both helmsmen, who were swept up against the rail at the break of the poop. The ship broached to, every shred of canvas was blown away, and she lay in the trough of the sea with the water waist high on the maindeck until preventer steering tackles could be rigged and some sail set on the mizen, when she was hove to and lay quietly. In the 18½ hours between noon of the previous day and the time of the pooping the *Cedric* had actually covered 322 miles.

And here is Captain R. H. Potter's account of the pooping of the barque *Meinwen*:

'It was in lat. 42 deg. 30 min. S., long. 76 deg. 30 min E., while we were scudding before a fresh westerly wind that the mishap occurred. I had just gone to breakfast at 8 a.m. when a great wave swept over the poop and the cabin was flooded. Rushing up on deck I found that a sea had swept the decks from aft to the mainmast. The barque broached to and the clatter aloft was deafening, but in a few minutes she shook herself clear, all hands being busily engaged in preventing further danger. Then I found that the

wheel had been smashed, the chief officer had his face cut and two teeth knocked out by the broken spokes; both of the hands who had been at the wheel were lying near the main hatch severely bruised and disabled, and four other hands had wounds and bruises which required dressing. The uninjured members of the crew were promptly got to work and we rigged tackles on the tiller. The first set carried away but the second held and the barque was soon on her course again.'

The most extraordinary case of a broach to that I have ever come across was that of the beautiful tea clipper *Oberon* (Shaw, Maxton & Co.), in 1883. Luckily the men at the wheel were lashed and the watch were aloft furling the foresail, but Captain John England was swept overboard and drowned. The ship must have come up almost head to sea on this occasion, for the water swept her from forward aft, and the boats on the skids were actually floated over the heads of the men at the wheel and so over the taffrail, whilst the ratlines of the mizen rigging were broken 9 feet above the poop by wreckage, which was washed aft.

In 1903, when bound from New York to Sydney, the four-mast barque *Torresdale* lay on her beam ends for two days with the sea making a clean breach over her; her sails were blown to ribbons, boats stove, topgallant rail and poop stanchions gone and cabin flooded.

A curious case was that of the ship *Leicester Castle* when bound from Monte Video to Melbourne in 1909. She was sailing along in a quiet sea, when a monster wave, which the captain estimated to be 100 feet high, suddenly heeled her over until the deck was up and down. This was a disastrous passage, for a week later she was badly dismanted.

The fate of the 'Dalgonar'

The *Dalgonar* left Callao for Taltal on September 24, 1913, ballasted with shingle.

In these latter days of big ships, stability is by far the most anxious and worrying problem which a commander has to solve. Now the *Dalgonar* . . . was a big full-rigged carrier of 2665 tons, and though she had a very experienced commander in Captain Isbister, she was a difficult vessel to ballast properly. This was specially the case with a ballast which was liable to shift like shingle. The general instructions given to sailing ship masters when using shingle as stiffening were as follows:—The ballast must not be carried too low: the ballast box must be very strong at the fore and after ends: the surface of the ballast should be smoothed off, covered with timber and tommed down from the 'tween deck beams. Whether the ballast should be carried centrally and high up on the ship's sides, or extended more fore and aft with less depth, depended entirely on the particular qualities of the ship herself.

The *Dalgonar* was given the usual ballast box of shifting boards, lashed together with chains, but it was contended afterwards that she should have had a third row of shifting boards down the centre as a further safeguard.

Probably all would have been well if the ship had not been unfortunate enough to run into a hurricane, which produced abnormal conditions. I therefore do not think it would be fair to blame Captain Isbister or his mate, Mr Mull, for her loss.

On October 9 the *Dalgonar* was struck by a heavy squall which forced her over on to her beam ends and set the ballast over to leeward. For the next eight hours it blew a hurricane, whilst the ship lay on her side with her port lower yardarms dragging in the water. The position of the *Dalgonar* was so serious that Captain Isbister gave the order to cut away the masts. Somehow, in spite of sloping decks, flying sprays, bursting seas and a shrieking wind this desperate task was accomplished. But the vessel, though slightly relieved, remained on her beam ends, held down by the shifted ballast and by the raffle of spars and gear to leeward, which could not be cut away owing to the maelstrom of white water which surged over her port topgallant rail.

Captain Isbister and his officers evidently expected the ship to go down under their feet at any moment. Mountainous seas were making a clear breach over her, and it seemed that her end was come. But they evidently failed to take into consideration the pent up air confined in her empty holds, which was undoubtedly keeping the ship afloat.

An effort was now made to launch the life-boats. The boat to leeward was smashed up by the seas whilst still in the davits, but the starboard life-boat was dropped into the water with ten men in her. But she could not live in the fury of broken water alongside and before they could push off she was swamped. Seven of the men managed to scramble aboard again but three were drowned.

It was at this moment of indescribable stress that Captain Isbister lost his life. In a vain endeavour to save his men he had clambered into the main starboard rigging with a coil of rope. A big sea caught him and hurled him to the deck, where he landed on his head, badly hurt, and before anyone could get hold of him the roaring flood carried him over the lee rail and he was never seen again.

After this final tragedy there was no more thought of launching boats and the remaining members of the ship's company took refuge in the 'tween decks. Here they subsisted for three days on ship's biscuit and water, whilst the seas thundered overhead.

On October 10, the French four-mast barque *Loire* hove in sight, but she had to stand by the wreck until October 13 before it became safe to launch a boat and rescue the crew of the *Dalgonar*. The latter was abandoned in lat. 26 deg. S., long. 130 deg. W. It was, of course, expected that she would shortly fill and go to the bottom. But nothing of the sort happened. Before her crew left they cut away all the gear and, relieved of this, the hull began to drift out into the Pacific under the influence of the equatorial current.

On December 10 she was reported by the French barque *Marie*. On February 4, 1914, she had drifted to 26 deg. 33 min. S., 122 deg. 41 min. W., where she was boarded by a boat from the schooner *Inca*. The weather was fine and the sea smooth so that the captain of the *Inca* was not only able to photograph the derelict but to make a complete examination of her, during which he retrieved a compass and binnacle, two chronometers, Captain Isbister's sextant and a few other portable articles. He reported that though she had a heavy list to port, it would be quite possible for a steamer to tow her into the nearest harbour. However,

223, 224 and 225 The last of a famous windjammer. The *Preussen*, 5,081 tons, probably the largest sailing ship ever built, another ship of the P-Line of Hamburg, *above* being towed out of harbour, *top right* wrecked off the White Cliffs of Dover, to become a total loss (*lower right*).

Plate 38 The Return of the Terre Neuvier, by Eugène Boudin (1824–98). Coasting craft would often beach in places that did not have harbour facilities and discharge their cargo over the side at low tide. They then floated off on the next high tide.

nothing was done in the matter. The derelict continued to drift in a westerly direction at about 1 to 2 knots an hour. She was carried past Pitcairn into the vicinity of the Society group. Finally, after a drift which, allowing for twists and turns, must have been in the neighbourhood of 5000 miles, she was brought up by a coral reef off Mopihaa Island in 16 deg. 30 min. S., 154 deg. W., where she stuck fast.

Weed and Barnacles

Green's three-skysail-yard Blackwaller, the *Carlisle Castle*, had a very unpleasant experience of a foul bottom on her first homeward passage in 1869. She took in the usual Calcutta cargo of jute, with invalids in her 'tween decks and army officers in her cabin. Before she sailed from her mooring off the Maidan her passengers had begun to debate the question of weed on iron hulls. Most of them pinned their faith to the quality of the paint on her bottom, and some who were extra sanguine talked of the possibility

of logging 18 knots should they get the wind. But there was one wise dissentient.

He declared:—'The weeds will gather from the time you leave the Sandheads. If Captain Cooper attempts to drive her to make up for lost time, she will take three plunges and under; then you will come up with flooded cuddy, cabins, etc. With her iron sides she will be as hot as an oven, and she will never in her life do the 18 knots you talk about.'

This knowing one advised the passengers to exchange into the copper-bottomed, fast-sailing *Windsor Castle*, in spite of the fact that she was not sailing for another month. 'You will get home sooner,' he prophesied; and he was right, for the *Windsor Castle* got home a month ahead of the *Carlisle Castle*.

However, as usual with most of us, the prospective passengers stuck by their own opinions and sailed in the *Carlisle Castle*. And they had hardly got out into the Bay of Bengal when they found out what they were in for.

Plate 39 *top left* The barque *Fanny*, 1832. One of the earliest steam ships can be seen in the background. Watercolour by Mathieu Antoine Roux (1799–1872).

Plate 40 *top right* A Close Call entering Le Havre. The *Queen Victoria*, a small merchant ship. The single sail–a reefed fore topsail–is so that she could carry her head to the prevailing wind, and is just enough to give her steerage way. Oil by Smartly, 1843.

Plate 41 *bottom left* The *New England* of Bath, built 1849. An American transatlantic passenger ship losing her main and fore topmasts in a gale. Watercolour by Giovanni Luzro.

Plate 42 *bottom right* The *Mount Vernon* of Salem, built 1798. An early American frigate in full sail outrunning a French fleet. Gouache by M. F. Cornè (*c.* 1752–1845).

226 Landing at Madras, as in the hey-day of the East India Company, aquatint after J. B. East, 1837. Double-ended surf boats were used to bring in passengers and goods from ships lying in the offing. Some passengers, like the portly lady in the picture, were able to come ashore dry-shod; others, like the gentleman, comparatively so.

The pilot brig at the Sandheads was riding to two long scopes of hemp cable, as if expecting a cyclone. However, a light breeze carried the Blackwaller clear of the disturbance, though the heavy swell showed that it was not far away. The breeze very soon petered out, and for about a fortnight the *Carlisle Castle* rolled wearily under a blazing sun, which was reflected off the sluggish swell in a way which hurt the eyes.

The *Carlisle Castle* was painted the regulation black of those days, and this so absorbed the heat that the interior of the ship became like a furnace and no one could stay below. On deck, even at night,

it was little better. Anything of metal was blistering to the touch. The pitch bubbled in the deck seams and ran down the planking at every roll of the ship. And then it was noticed that the weed on her sides was visibly growing. Within a month the ship had become so sluggish that she could only be tacked in smooth water. As she slowly neared the Equator, and one calm after another had to be contended with, her company had every opportunity of examining the weed which was plainly visible in the clear water, spreading out from her sides and bottom in long wavy tendrils.

It was mostly ribbon-weed, growing from 3 to 4 feet in length

and from $\frac{3}{8}$ to half an inch wide. Whenever a breeze ruffled the water and the sails filled, this weed trailed out at an angle from the ship's side and effectually prevented her sailing.

At last a sea Samaritan—who happened to be becalmed in the neighbourhood of the *Carlisle Castle*—sent his first mate aboard to enquire if there was anything wrong, for he had noticed that whenever a puff of wind came along it had little or no effect upon the Blackwaller, which appeared to him as if she was at anchor.

On Captain Cooper stating his woes, that mate went back to his ship and returned with a diagram and directions for making an infallible weed scrubber. The carpenter was at once set to work.

The scrubber was simple enough. It consisted of a block of wood, 1 foot wide by 3 feet long, on to which a stout piece of sheet iron was fitted at each end. In the centre of the block a long pole was fitted to keep it down whilst at either end eye-bolts were fixed to which drag-ropes were bent . . .

It was soon found to be useless, for there was no way of keeping it pressed hard against the ship's side, and it would only touch the weed along the water line.

The passengers ever ready with suggestions, proposed keel-hauling it, but this was not possible owing to the overlapping of the iron plates. And when they unshipped the pole and managed to get the scrubber well under the ship's bottom, the weed proved too strong for it and no amount of pulley-hauley could get it to move through the thick foliage of deep sea vegetation on the *Carlisle Castle's* keel.

So at last the scrubber was put away and the ship jogged on as best she could. She had left Calcutta on March 20. When she was about $2\frac{1}{2}$ months out she was passed by the jaunty *Windsor Castle*, to the mortification of those passengers who had refused to listen to the sage's advice.

The Cape of Good Hope was passed on June 6, 78 days out. St. Helena on June 21, Ascension on June 25, the Equator on June 30, Flores on August 2, and the Lizard on August 23. Finally the *Carlisle Castle* docked in Blackwall Dock on September 5, 169 days out from Calcutta, having been posted at Lloyd's for about a month.

This is a very good example of the effect of ribbon-weed. Though bad enough it was not as bad as barnacles. The big oil sailer *Daylight*, on her arrival at Philadelphia in 1908, after a passage of 145 days from Vizagapatam, had 40 tons of barnacles scraped off her bottom. Each of these barnacles was about $4\frac{1}{2}$ inches long with a base the size of a Mexican dollar.

from *The Last of the Windjammers*, by Basil Lubbock, 1927.

227 The Ostend Packet in a Squall, by George Cruikshank, 1824, showing the cramped and sordid quarters endured by passengers on the cross-channel voyage. Berths could be reserved in advance, but were usually over-crowded and sold twice.

228 The *Carlisle Castle*: 'Green's three-skysail-yard Blackwaller, the *Carlisle Castle*, had a very unpleasant experience of a foul bottom . . .'

Merchant schooners

The declining years of the trading sailing ship. With its final departure from the scene a thing of beauty died. But descriptions of the difficulties and dangers of navigation at the mercy of wind and tide made clear the inevitability of the change-over to steam when it became available. This autobiographical note by Captain R. Robinson is published by Basil Greenhill in *The Merchant Schooners*.

Autobiographical note by Captain R. Robinson

I was born at Newhaven in 1873. Both my grandfathers were captains of ships; Sargeant was captain of the *Henry Bennis*, and Robinson captain of the *Topsy*. My father, after serving his time as a sailmaker, made two voyages round the world, then started a business as a sailmaker and ship chandler at Newhaven. He owned at various times four ships: the *Henry Beniss*, which he sold; the *Warblington*, which sprang a leak and went down on the Kent. The *Sussex Maid* he bought when she was towed into this port dismasted. She had been a brig, but he refitted her as a brigantine, which was the usual thing to do at that time as a brigantine was cheaper to work. He also owned the *Amanda*. Both the last two ships I sold after he died in March, 1903. After his death, when these ships arrived in the port, both of them had their quarter boards and ribbon round their sides painted blue as a sign of mourning, a practice usual at that time. My father had four brothers; one a shipwright at Portsmouth; one a captain of a foreign-going barque belonging to Littlehampton; one a captain of various coasting ships; and the youngest one went on a coasting ship to the Tyne and had such a terrible time that he hid himself on a keel that came alongside. The keelman took him up the river to his home and he eventually married the keelman's daughter and did not return to his home in the south until he was a middle-aged man with a family.

I had five brothers and four sisters and my first school was the National School where we had to take 3d a week to pay for our schooling. Afterwards we went to Mr Leaver's grammar school, and when I left school I went in my father's sail loft for about a year. The whole atmosphere of my life had been sails, ships and the sea, so when I expressed a wish to go to sea my father thought I had better go into steam, as sail was dying out. I went on a steamer from Sunderland with a cargo of coals to Savona in Italy, then light to Odessa in Russia, where we loaded grain for Hull then back to Sunderland. The *Sussex Maid* was lying there and as I hated steamers—it wasn't the sort of life I had heard so much of—I got my father to let me go aboard the *Sussex Maid*, where I stopped for about four years. Then I went mate in the *Amanda*

for about two years and became master of her at the age of 22. After two years as master, a vacancy occurred in the pilotage. I got it at the age of 24 and held that appointment for about 39 years, when I had to retire owing to ill-health. When I started going to sea the coasting sailing ships were beginning to feel the competition of the steamers; not that they carried the coals to many of the Channel ports as those small ports could not give them a quick discharge, but they traded to London and other large ports which trade had been done by the sailing brigs, etc., hundreds of which were trading to London alone. That made a great competition which brought down the freights, but it was the war in 1914 that killed the sailing coasters. It is impossible for me to describe what the coasting trade was like, for like everything else, no two things were alike. There was a different way of discharging in most ports. Even at Newhaven I have discharged with the dolly winch, the jump, and steam cranes, into barges and on the shore. Every captain had his own ideas about things and soon told anyone who interfered that he sailed by his own compass, so I will only try and describe what I experienced.

Our voyage started and finished in the south of England. We had Articles of Agreement which had to be read out before the men; they had to sign it before the master and it was witnessed by one other person. It required a 24-hour notice on either side to termi-

229 Fishing upon the Blythe Sand by J. M. W. Turner (1775–1851).

230 *above* The forest of masts and drying sails round the old customs house at Hamburg in this painting by Louis Mecklenburg in 1850, gives a good idea of what a busy port looked like in the days of sail.

231 *right* The *H. H. Cole*, an American topsail schooner built 1843. This rig was an advantage in a following wind while retaining to a large extent the schooner's good performance to windward. Oil by Clement Drew (1806–89).

nate the agreement at the final discharge of the cargo in the south. The food would be sufficient without waste; nothing was weighed out to them, with the exception of meat, of which 1 lb. a day was always allowed, and 1 lb. of sugar a week. If you didn't feed them well, it was a job to get men as it soon became known. The work was heavy and it paid to feed them well. The men signed on to be paid at so much a voyage or so much a month. These Articles had to be taken every six months to the Custom House when a C.C. would be given you which had to be shown at the Custom House every time you required your transire, also your receipt for light dues.

As soon as the last basket of coals were out we ran up our burgee to the masthead so as to claim our turn for the ballast tip. You might be lucky and get it next day, or you might have to wait for days. If the ship was coming back to the same port, you would put all the working gear ashore, derrick, jump or dolly winch, and weights and scales. If not, you would keep it on board, with the exception of weights and scales. You would shift the vessel to the ballast tip, when the chalk ballast would be shot into the main

hold and the crew were required to trim it; that is, throw it as far forrard and aft as possible. When the ballast was in, the ship had to be got ready for sea, the hatches put on and covered, the life-boat put on top and griped down. The mainstay was got into position and secured, cover off the mainsail, the jibboom run out, and anchor got up on the rail. In all harbours, ships on entering had to get in their jibbooms, brace yards sharp up and the anchor must be at the hawse pipe or inboard, and not at the cathead . . .

The coasters in my time were not insured for total loss, only for third-party risks, but they used to insure for the freight. They couldn't afford to insure for total loss, as the freights were so low, and they never had a fair deal in the loading ports as far as the steamers were concerned. There was a known amount of coal that came out of the pits every day, that had to be cleared out of the trucks, and all the time a steamer was there she got it, and the sailing craft were kept in reserve. In case of fog or heavy gales the steamers couldn't arrive, then the sailing coasters would get their turn. I have seen a steamer load and go to London and back three times while I have been waiting my turn.

232 Dutch fishing boats landing fish at Egmont, after E. W. Cooke, mid nineteenth century.

The wages paid in the Newhaven coasters were:

	For the voyage	or	For the month
Master	£9		£5
Mate	£6		£4 5s
A.B.	£4		£3 5s
O.S.	£2 10s		£1 15s
Boy	£1		£1

What amazed me with a ship was the flimsy way the ratlines were made fast to the rigging with only about three turns of marlin, and they were always giving way. I suggested something stronger but was told that sailors must learn to trust to their hands and not their feet. Some sailors were very clever in picking out and naming the various ships even when they were hull down. It was done by noticing the cut of the various sails, as no two ships' sails were exactly alike. The big ships of Newhaven, belonging to the Bull Line, always traded to the Tyne. They were ships of from 400 to 500 tons, and brought the gas coal to Newhaven for Eastbourne, Lewes and other small towns. The house coal was brought by the smaller ships of about 300 tons, and they always traded to Hartlepool, Sunderland and Seaham Harbour. I, being in a small ship, never once went into the Tyne, but always hearing and seeing in the papers about the loss of so many ships and lives at the Tyne, and knowing that I might have to go there sometime, I went over to South Shields to see the place for myself and had a talk to the pilots about it. I asked them why so many were lost, and their explanation was this: that owing to the great strength of the tide on the ebb meeting a hurricane of wind from the east, this made the seas so short and steep that there was no control of the ships, and a lot of them were carried on to the Black Midden rocks which were inside the breakwater, and others were knocked right under. As one pilot told me, 'I stood here and saw one brig coming in. She was loaded, and she came in the entrance all right, then a big sea ran right over her before she could lift and after the sea had passed all I could see of the ship was the top of her galley and knightheads. Another big sea quickly followed and then she disappeared.'

In these heavy gales thousands of people used to assemble at both South and North Shields to watch the ships coming in, and they were helpless to do anything to avoid disasters, but did what they could by forming volunteer rocket apparatus brigades, which were the means of saving a lot of lives after the vessels were ashore, and I believe that North Shields was the birthplace of the first lifeboat. Sunderland was the next port, but the entrance was narrow and the tides were not so strong, and it was not very good in a gale of wind. Seaham Harbour was an artificial one built by Lord Londonderry, and owned by him. It was composed of several breakwaters built out from the land, with inner and outer docks, but when easterly gales were blowing it was closed to trade by putting booms across the entrance. Hartlepool, in my opinion, was the best harbour to run into as there were no tides to contend with because it is composed of an open basin inside with docks at either side.

If you could make nine voyages in one year you were very lucky, for there always seemed to be something to delay you. In winter time it was gales, and in summer time calms and other causes, but in summer time with the long days and short nights, and a fair wind, what could be more delightful for a holiday in ideal surroundings? . . .

I never was in a ship that went ashore but, like everyone else who goes to sea, I had some narrow misses. We were bound to Littlehampton one night. The wind was off the land, but it was hazy. Along that bit of coast from Worthing to Littlehampton the sea runs very shallow a long way off; so shallow that in the summer time, after several weeks of quiet weather, I have gone along there and have been able to see the vegetation growing on the bottom. It was turned high water and too late to get in that tide, so I let go the anchor and stowed the sails in what I thought was a safe berth. When I turned out in the morning it was low water. I

she had been run into by a steamer in the Channel, and the crew had gone aboard and left their ship, thinking she was sinking. She must then have blown into the position in which I saw her afterwards.

Every gale of wind into which we got, we always said was the worst which we had experienced, and if we got home safely we never would come to sea again, but after a few hours of fine weather, and a fair wind, we forgot all about it and the joy there was in having a quick passage with a fine, fair wind is only known to those who have gone through it . . .

I think the worst job was pumping in the *Sussex Maid*. We had the old-fashioned wooden handle that it took three men to work, and it worked with a jerk. In the *Amanda*, we had the flywheel pump which was more easy and all hands could work at it and you could keep on longer. Afterwards a new pump came out by which one man could work it, and throw more water . . .

The mainsail was the worst sail to handle. In fine weather it took six men, and in bad weather at times we had to use the winch to do so. If it wasn't for that we could have worked the ship with six men instead of seven. For that reason, the West Country ships were turned into barquentines. The *Ibis* of Faversham was registered in 1898, when I knew her, as a brigantine. She was afterwards sold down west and in the 1919 Register she was classed as a barquentine; but it didn't pay us to convert as it required six men to work the cargo out, three men in the hold, three men on the winch, and the mate to run the plank, so that already it cost us £2 to employ one man to help work out the cargo which took about a week, and we could get a man for the voyage for £4 plus food. The main boom was a long, heavy pitch-pine spar which required two topping lifts to carry it. In harbour, we used to let it rest in a crutch, and at sea, when not in use, with the wind dead aft and blowing a gale, we lowered it onto the rail aft. The mainsheet block (three fold) was fitted in the centre of the ship, and the falls on either side. It had reefing tackle fitted along it to pull out the sheet or the reefing clew-lines. It also had a boom guy tackle, from the end of the boom to the sampson post. That kept the boom tight against the mainsheet when she was on the wind, for with a light wind and nasty sea it was always swinging about. With a fair wind, this tackle was taken off the sampson post and put on to a wire runner that led outside the main rigging to the midships. It was then hauled tight and the mainsheet slacked away, and held the main boom out tight in case she gybed over. This main boom guy tackle was also used when the ship wouldn't stay in bad weather, and we had to wear her round. Then we slacked away from the sampson post and hauled in the mainsheet until it was tight, then shifted the tackle over to the other sampson post.

dropped the lead over the side and found she only had several inches of water under her, so I hove the anchor up and sheeted home the lower topsail to sail off in deeper water. We had been doing so for about quarter-hour when she touched the bottom; nothing to hurt, but I was surprised at the vibration it caused in the masts and rigging. I said to the men, 'What must it be like to go ashore on rocks in a heavy gale?' . . .

I suppose I've seen some dozens of ships ashore, but I've only seen two sink. It was summer time, and a small fleet had been brought up in the Downs, but the wind having moderated, we all got under way at tide time, started beating round the South Foreland and had got abreast of Dover. Some were beating in towards the land on the port tack and others going off on the starboard tack, the wind being westerly, when I saw two ships approaching one another very close. It was the duty of the ship on the port tack to keep clear of the other, but he didn't make any attempt to do so and the other ship, to avoid a collision, had to do so. I passed the comment that he would do that trick once too often. They made the two tacks and then were in the same position as I had seen them in before, and this time the ship on the starboard tack ran into the other in the midships. She sank in less than half an hour, and the other, minus her bowsprit and jibboom, went into Dover with the assistance of a tug.

The other ship I saw go down was a brigantine, just to the west of Newhaven breakwater. It was daybreak when I saw her with all her sails set, and looking at her with the glass I couldn't see anyone aboard her. Her decks were awash and she went down quietly just afterwards, before anything could be done. It was presumed that

233 A bark and three schooners icebound on the New England coast in the severe winter of 1875, by Wesley Webber (1841–1914).

The gaff of the mainsail is a heavy pitchpine spar, and with the weight of that and the heavy sail, it is a big thing to hoist. On the outer end of the gaff is a small block through which a small manilla rope is rove, both parts being made fast to the boom end. This is used to guide the gaff clear of the topping lifts and also as a downhaul for the end of the gaff. The gaff topsail sheet is made fast to the same ring bolt as the throat halyard block. It then goes to the gaff end, through a block and back to another block under the throat of the gaff and then down to the deck. This is also used as a downhaul for the throat of the gaff, and at times we have had to take it to the winch to heave it down. When you set the gaff topsail a man goes aloft, takes the gasket off the sail, unhooks the sheet of the sail which is then ready to set by those on deck. The downhaul is made fast at the head of the sail, then through a block at the sheet, then to another block at the masthead, and then down to the deck. When you take the sail in, you let go the halyard, slack away the sheet and haul on the downhaul. That brings the sail close to the masthead and it is easy for one man to stow it, by riding it down, putting his legs around it and passing the gasket at the same time around the rigging. When he has done that he unhooks the clip hooks off the sheet and hooks it on to the gaff. The worst of a gaff topsail is that, when you tack, a man has to go aloft and shift the tack over the peak halyards so as to keep the sail leeward of them. The tack is then hauled tight on deck.

All the staysails are easy to handle. The main staysail works on a wire horse itself, and then the sheet is pulled down tight by a tackle, so that in going about you let go the tackle and haul it down when she is on the other tack. One man can handle the three other sheets of the staysails. He lets go all three when she is head to wind and hauls down on the other side. It is only a matter of pulling them over the stays.

Having had experience with both a Bentinck boom and a tack and sheet foresail, I've no hesitation in saying that a boom foresail is best in all ways. It is easy to set and to stow, and in going about it is very little trouble. A short chain in the middle of the boom down to the deck holds it in place, and a short rope at either end to hold it, a tackle at either end to pull it up with, the fore bowline on the leech at both sides is all the gear attached to it.

The lower topsail is the strongest sail in the ship and well secured, having chain sheets that lead through the end of the foreyard, back to the centre of the yard, through iron blocks and down to and through iron eyes on the deck, and made fast to iron belaying pins at the mast. The upper topsail was very rarely reefed, but when it was, I always used to get to the weather earing as you sit astride the yard-arm and have to make the weather earing fast. When you have done so, you call out for them to haul out to leeward, and

234 *top* The three-masted schooner *John R. Halladay*. A type of rigging largely developed by the Americans. Oil by S. F. M. Badger, 1898.

235 Smith's Wharf, Charlestown, Massachusetts, by an unknown artist.

while the men were tying the reef points, etc., I used to sit and admire the ship from that angle—a fine place to admire a ship in a gale of wind. The three lower squaresails required all six men to handle them, but the topgallant sail only required two men.

Going in and out harbour, getting under way, going about reefing, etc., the captain always took the wheel himself. The forestaysail was only set when the foresail was stowed. In harbour it

was stowed and the halyards were hooked into the sheet and pulled up tight. At sea it was stowed on the fife rail or laid across the windlass ready for use. The foretopmast staysail was a small sail and was always set, but the jib was a larger sail and in fine weather was a most helpful sail, though in a strong wind and with the ship lying over to it, I always found it plunged the bows into a head sea and stopped the ship's bows from lifting, and I would always sooner stow the jib and keep the upper topsail up than I would do the reverse. In theory, the jib is supposed to keep the ship's head from griping into the wind, but in practice it doesn't.

Our provisions were taken on board at our home port, and we used to take enough to last the voyage, if possible, but if we were delayed we used to take more on board at the northern ports. We had a freshwater tank made of galvanized iron which was well bolted to the deck, close to the after hatch. It held about 200 gallons, and access to it was only by a copper dipper through a small hole in the centre of the manhole on the top of the tank. Water was easy to get at Newhaven, as the mains ran out to the end of all the jetties, but at the north, at the Weir or Tyne, the water boat used to come alongside and pump it in.

When in harbour at the south we had fresh meat every day, and then we had sufficient sent on board to last the voyage, which we used to salt down and put in the harness cask, which was well bolted down to the deck, close to the after hatch. The butcher always cut the joints into 7-lb. pieces, allowing us 1 lb. per man per day. Our method of salting was to rub bar salt into the meat, stand it in the harness cask for twenty-four hours to let the blood drain out, then take it out and clean the cask, then put it back and pour the brine over it. To make the brine, we used to fill a bucket

236 *top* American sloop-rigged fishing boat. Man spearing fish with a trident over the bows. Watercolour attributed to M. F. Cornè (*c.* 1752–1845).

237 *bottom* Fishing schooners in the Gulf of Saint Lawrence. Crayon by Paul E. Collins, 1925.

Plate 43 Valparaiso – Crepuscule in Flesh Colour and Green, by the great American artist J. A. M. Whistler (1834–1903). The sailing ship throughout the age of sail was an inspiration to some of the greatest painters. Accuracy was sometimes, but not always, a major preoccupation of the artist. Valparaiso was the loading port for sailing ships of many nations for nitrates, the vital fertilizers.

with fresh water and keep putting salt in it, stirring all the time, until a potato would float on the top, then pour it over the meat. In addition, we always carried on board a good bit of pressed beef in tins of about 7 lb., in case of us running short, or in bad weather, when we couldn't cook on the galley stove, and often found it most useful. We used to take a great many half-gallon loaves of bread to last as long as possible. After they were used, we had the hard biscuits to eat. The food in the cabin and fo'castle was the same. We always had to use margarine as we found that butter would not keep in the close, stuffy air of the cabin. When working coals in the south, we always had green vegetables or swedes, etc., and took a small stock with us, putting the same on the ballast to keep them fresh. The nature of the work was such that the men had to live well, and we did, but now and again you would hear of exceptions. I knew one captain whom the men called 'Old Bullock's Head', because he bought a bullock's head, cut off enough meat to make a beef pudding one day, made the meat that was left into a sea pie the next day, and on the third day he boiled all the remains up and made a soup of it.

from *The Merchant Schooners,* by Basil Greenhill, 1951.

Initiation

Joseph Conrad (1857–1924) was a Polish émigré who became a British master mariner before leaving the sea to become one of the greatest novelists in the English language. In this chapter, called *Initiation,* from *The Mirror of the Sea,* a book of reminiscences, he demolishes the oft-sung, land-inspired conception of love of the sea, that implacable enemy of man; but acknowledges the seaman's irresistible love of ships. The whole inner experience of the sailing ship adventure is made conscious by Conrad's genius, when he depicts the face-to-face confrontation of men with 'immensity, the inseparable companion of a ship's life'.

'Ships!' exclaimed an elderly seaman in clean shore togs. 'Ships'—and his keen glance, turning away from my face, ran along the vista of magnificent figureheads that in the late seventies used to overhang in a serried rank the muddy pavement by the side of the New South Dock—'ships are all right; it's the men in 'em . . .'

Fifty hulls, at least, moulded on lines of beauty and speed—hulls of wood, of iron, expressing in their forms the highest achievement of modern ship-building—lay moored all in a row, stem to quay, as if assembled there for an exhibition, not of a great industry, but of a great art. Their colours were grey, black, dark green, with a narrow strip of yellow moulding defining their sheer, or with a row of painted ports decking in warlike decoration their robust flanks of cargo-carriers that would know no triumph but of speed in carrying a burden, no glory other than of a long service, no victory but that of an endless, obscure contest with the sea. The great empty hulls with swept holds, just out of dry-dock with their paint glistening freshly, sat high-sided with ponderous dignity alongside the wooden jetties, looking more like unmovable buildings than things meant to go afloat; others, half loaded, far on the way to recover the true sea-physiognomy of a ship brought down to her load-line, looked more accessible. Their less steeply slanting gangways seemed to invite the strolling sailors in search of a berth to walk on board and try 'for a chance' with the chief mate, the guardian of a ship's efficiency. As if anxious to remain unperceived amongst their overtopping sisters, two or three 'finished' ships floated low, with an air of straining at the leash of their level headfasts, exposing to view their cleared decks and covered hatches, prepared to drop stern first out of the labouring ranks, displaying the true comeliness of form which only her proper sea-trim gives to a ship. And for a good quarter of a mile, from the dockyard-gate to the farthest corner, where the old housed-in hulk, the *President* (drill-ship, then, of the Naval Reserve), used to lie with her frigate side rubbing against the stone of the quay, above all these hulls, ready and unready, a hundred and fifty lofty masts, more or less, held out the web of their rigging

Passenger shipping in the mid nineteenth century varied from the uncomfortable to the infernal. Two events which made the passenger trade especially profitable to more or less scrupulous ship-owners were the California gold rush of 1849 and the mass immigration of the poor and dispossessed to the USA and Canada. To reach California from the east coast of America, ships had to round Cape Horn, the route described by Richard Dana (the Panama Canal was not completed until 1921).

239 On the gold rush speed was vital and famous clippers like the *Flying Cloud*, here seen advertising for passengers, could make the maximum number of voyages in the shortest possible time. Pen and wash by J. C. Wade (*c.* 1827–60).

240 *below* Immigrant ships for poor passengers were notorious for their insanitary overcrowding and starvation conditions; passengers were expected to supplement the diet by bringing their own food, and if the passage proved a long one the inadequate supplies of these poverty-stricken people would run out. Epidemics and deaths were frequent. This advertisement for the immigrant ship *Margaret,* claiming that 'no imposition of any kind is allowed to be practised on the passengers', reflects the reputation these ships had.

241 *top right* This print of the interior of a cross-channel packet is a scene of luxury compared with the immigrant ships.

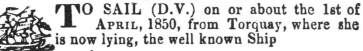

EMIGRATION TO QUEBEC AND THE UNITED STATES.

To SAIL (D.V.) on or about the 1st of APRIL, 1850, from Torquay, where she is now lying, the well known Ship

'MARGARET,'

400 Tons Burthen, W. FIELD, Master.

Few Vessels from the West of England have been more successful in their trips to America, than the MARGARET, hence she has become a decided favourite with persons desirous of emigrating. Those who wish to secure Berths, are therefore recommended to make an early application. The Owners themselves superintend the sailing of the Vessel, and no imposition of any kind is allowed to be practised on the Passengers.

Full particulars as to passage money, &c., may be obtained by applying to Mr. THOMAS STEEL, Edgeley House, Torquay, or to

Mr. THOS. BIDEN, JUN., at Mr. Terrell's,
Saint Martin's Lane, Exeter.

Dated February 6th, 1850.

like an immense net, in whose close mesh, black against the sky, the heavy yards seemed to be entangled and suspended.

It was a sight. The humblest craft that floats makes its appeal to a seaman by the faithfulness of her life; and this was the place where one beheld the aristocracy of ships. It was a noble gathering of the fairest and swiftest, each bearing at the bow the carved emblem of her name as in a gallery of plaster-casts, figures of women with mural crowns, women with flowing robes, with gold fillets on their hair or blue scarves round their waists, stretching out rounded arms as if to point the way; heads of men helmeted or bare; full lengths of warriors, of kings, of statesmen, of lords and princesses, all white from top to toe; with here and there a dusky turbaned figure, bedizened in many colours of some Eastern sultan or hero, all inclined forward under the slant of mighty bowsprits as if eager to begin another run of 11,000 miles in their leaning attitudes. These were the fine figure-heads of the finest ships afloat. But why, unless for the love of the life those effigies shared with us in their wandering impassivity, should one try to reproduce in words an impression of whose fidelity there can be no critic and no judge, since such an exhibition of the art of ship-building and the art of figure-head carving as was seen from year's end to year's end in the open-air gallery of the New South Dock no man's eye shall behold again? All that patient pale company of queens and princesses, of kings and warriors, of allegorical women, of heroines and statesmen and heathen gods, crowned, helmeted, bare-headed, has run for good off the sea stretching to the last above the tumbling foam their fair, rounded arms; holding out their spears, swords, shields, tridents in the same unwearied, striving forward pose. And nothing remains but lingering perhaps in the memory of a few men, the sound of their names, vanished a long time ago from the first page of the great London dailies; from big posters in railway-stations and the doors of shipping offices; from the minds of sailors, dock-masters, pilots, and tug-men; from the hail of gruff voices and the flutter of signal flags exchanged between ships closing upon each other and drawing apart in the open immensity of the sea.

The elderly, respectable seaman, withdrawing his gaze from that multitude of spars, gave me a glance to make sure of our fellowship in the craft and mystery of the sea. We had met casually, and had got into contact as I had stopped near him, my attention being caught by the same peculiarity he was looking at in the rigging of an obviously new ship, a ship with her reputation all to make yet in the talk of the seamen who were to share their life with her. Her name was already on their lips. I had heard it uttered between two thick, red-necked fellows of the semi-nautical type at the Fenchurch Street railway station, where, in those days, the everyday male crowd was attired in jerseys and pilot-cloth mostly, and had the air of being more conversant with the times of high-water than with the times of the trains. I had noticed that new ship's name on the first page of my morning paper. I had stared at the unfamiliar grouping of its letters, blue on white ground, on the advertisement-boards, whenever the train came to a standstill alongside one of the shabby, wooden, wharf-like platforms of the dock railway-line. She had been named, with proper observances, on the day she came off the stocks, no doubt, but she was very far yet from 'having a name'. Untried, ignorant of the ways of the sea, she had been thrust amongst that renowned company of ships to load for her maiden voyage. There was nothing to vouch for her soundness and the worth of her character, but the reputation of the building-yard whence she was launched headlong into the world of waters. She looked modest to me. I imagined her diffident, lying very quiet, with her side nestling shyly against the wharf to which she was made fast with very new lines, intimidated by the company of her tried and experienced sisters already familiar with all the violences of the ocean and the exacting love of men. They had had more long voyages to make their names in than she had known weeks of carefully tended life, for a new ship receives as much attention as if she were a young bride. Even crabbed old dock-masters look at her with benevolent eyes. In her shyness at the threshold of a laborious and uncertain life, where so much is expected of a ship, she could not have been better heartened and comforted, had she only been able to hear and understand, than by the tone of deep conviction in which my elderly, respectable seaman repeated the first part of his saying, 'Ships are all right . . .'

His civility prevented him from repeating the other, the bitter part. It had occurred to him that it was perhaps indelicate to insist. He had recognized in me a ship's officer, very possibly looking for a berth like himself, and so far a comrade, but still a man belonging to that sparsely peopled after-end of a ship, where a great part of her reputation as a 'good ship', in seaman's parlance, is made or marred.

'Can you say that of all ships without exception?' I asked, being in an idle mood, because, if an obvious ship's officer, I was not, as a matter of fact, down at the docks to 'look for a berth', an occupation as engrossing as gambling, and as little favourable to the free exchange of ideas, besides being destructive of the kindly temper needed for casual intercourse with one's fellow-creatures.

'You can always put up with 'em,' opined the respectable seaman, judicially.

He was not averse from talking, either. If he had come down to the dock to look for a berth, he did not seem oppressed by anxiety as to his chances. He had the serenity of a man whose estimable character is fortunately expressed by his personal appearance in an unobtrusive, yet convincing, manner which no chief officer in want of hands could resist. And, true enough, I learned presently that the mate of the *Hyperion* had 'taken down' his name for quartermaster. 'We sign on Friday, and join next day for the morning tide,' he remarked, in a deliberate, careless tone, which contrasted strongly with his evident readiness to stand

242 *above* The figure-head of the *Seringapatam*, one of the famous Blackwall frigates, which reached Bombay from England in 85 days.

243 The prow of Marie Antoinette's skiff, 1777.

227

there yarning for an hour or so with an utter stranger.

'*Hyperion*,' I said. 'I don't remember ever seeing that ship anywhere. What sort of a name has she got?'

It appeared from his discursive answer that she had not much of a name one way or another. She was not very fast. It took no fool, though, to steer her straight, he believed. Some years ago he had seen her in Calcutta, and he remembered being told by somebody then that on her passage up the river she had carried away both her hawse-pipes. But that might have been the pilot's fault. Just now, yarning with the apprentices on board, he had heard that this very voyage, brought up in the Downs, outward bound, she broke her sheer, struck adrift, and lost an anchor and chain. But that might have occurred through want of careful tending in a tideway. All the same, this looked as though she were pretty hard on her ground-tackle. Didn't it? She seemed a heavy ship to handle, anyway. For the rest, as she had a new captain and a new mate this voyage, he understood, one couldn't say how she would turn out . . .

In such marine shore-talk as this is the name of a ship slowly established, her fame made for her, the tale of her qualities and of her defects kept, her idiosyncrasies commented upon with the zest of personal gossip, her achievements made much of, her faults glossed over as things that, being without remedy in our imperfect world, should not be dwelt upon too much by men who, with the help of ships, wrest out a bitter living from the rough grasp of the sea. All that talk makes up her 'name', which is handed

Figure-heads were thought by sailors to personify the ship's character and pride and bring good luck.

244 *above* An Eastern warrior.

245 *bottom, centre* A figure-head design by Alexander Elder (*d. c.* 1855) from a book of designs.

246 *top, centre* Figure-head of the *Jester*.

247 *top, right* Figure-head of the *Ajax*

248 *bottom, right* A Norwegian figure-head.

over from one crew to another without bitterness, without animosity, with the indulgence of mutual dependence, and with the feeling of close association in the exercise of her perfections and in the danger of her defects.

This feeling explains men's pride in ships. 'Ships are all right,' as my middle-aged, respectable quartermaster said with much conviction and some irony; but they are not exactly what men make them. They have their own nature; they can of themselves minister to our self-esteem by the demand their qualities make upon our skill and their shortcomings upon our hardiness and endurance. Which is the more flattering exaction it is hard to say; but there is the fact that in listening for upwards of twenty years to the sea-talk that goes on afloat and ashore I have never detected the true note of animosity. I won't deny that at sea, sometimes, the note of profanity was audible enough in those chiding interpellations a wet, cold, weary seaman addresses to his ship, and in moments of exasperation is disposed to extend to all ships that ever were launched—to the whole everlastingly exacting brood

that swims in deep waters. And I have heard curses launched at the unstable element itself, whose fascination, outlasting the accumulated experience of ages, had captured him as it had captured the generations of his forbears.

For all that has been said of the love that certain natures (on shore) have professed to feel for it, for all the celebrations it had been the object of in prose and song, the sea has never been friendly to man. At most it has been the accomplice of human restlessness, and playing the part of dangerous abettor of world-wide ambitions. Faithful to no race after the manner of the kindly earth, receiving no impress from valour and toil and self-sacrifice, recognizing no finality of dominion, the sea has never adopted the cause of its masters like those lands where the victorious nations of mankind have taken root, rocking their cradles and setting up their gravestones. He—man or people—who, putting his trust in the friendship of the sea, neglects the strength and cunning of his right hand, is a fool! As if it were too great, too mighty for common virtues, the ocean has no compassion, no faith, no law,

249 A scene of maritime London. Blackwall Yard, oil painting by F. Holman (d. 1790).

229

and the love of ships—the untiring servants of our hopes and our self-esteem—for the best and most genuine part. For the hundreds who have reviled the sea, beginning with Shakespeare in the line—

'More fell than hunger, anguish, or the sea.'

down to the last obscure sea-dog of the 'old mode', having but few words and still fewer thoughts, there could not be found, I believe, one sailor who has ever coupled a curse with the good or bad name of a ship. If ever his profanity, provoked by the hardships of the sea, went so far as to touch his ship, it would be lightly, as a hand may, without sin, be laid in the way of kindness on a woman.

The love that is given to ships is profoundly different from the love men feel for every other work of their hands—the love they bear to their houses, for instance—because it is untainted by the pride of possession. The pride of skill, the pride of responsibility, the pride of endurance there may be, but otherwise it is a disinterested sentiment. No seaman ever cherished a ship, even if she belonged to him, merely because of the profit she put in his pocket. No one, I think, ever did; for a ship-owner, even of the best, has always been outside the pale of that sentiment embracing in a feeling of intimate, equal fellowship the ship and the man, backing each other against the implacable, if sometimes dissembled, hostility of their world of waters. The sea—this truth must be confessed—has no generosity. No display of manly qualities—courage, hardihood, endurance, faithfulness—has ever been known to touch its irresponsible consciousness of power. The ocean has the conscienceless temper of a savage autocrat spoiled by much adulation. He cannot brook the slightest appearance of defiance, and has remained the irreconcilable enemy of ships and men ever since ships and men had the unheard-of audacity to go afloat together in the face of his frown. From that day he has gone on swallowing up fleets and men without his resentment being glutted by the number of victims—by so many wrecked ships and wrecked lives. To-day, as ever, he is ready to beguile and betray, to smash and to drown the incorrigible optimism of men who, backed by the fidelity of ships, are trying to wrest from him the fortune of their house, the dominion of their world, or only a dole of food for their hunger. If not always in the hot mood to smash, he is always stealthily ready for a drowning. The most amazing wonder of the deep is its unfathomable cruelty.

I felt its dread for the first time in mid-Atlantic one day, many years ago, when we took off the crew of a Danish brig homeward bound from the West Indies. A thin, silvery mist softened the calm

no memory. Its fickleness is to be held true to men's purposes only by an undaunted resolution and by a sleepless, armed, jealous vigilance, in which, perhaps, there has always been more hate than love. *Odi et amo* may well be the confession of those who consciously or blindly have surrendered their existence to the fascination of the sea. All the tempestuous passions of mankind's young days, the love of loot and the love of glory, the love of adventure and the love of danger, with the great love of the unknown and vast dreams of dominion and power, have passed like images reflected from a mirror, leaving no record upon the mysterious face of the sea. Impenetrable and heartless, the sea has given nothing of itself to the suitors for its precarious favours. Unlike the earth, it cannot be subjugated at any cost of patience and toil. For all its fascination that has lured so many to a violent death, its immensity has never been loved as the mountains, the plains, the desert itself, have been loved. Indeed, I suspect that, leaving aside the protestations and tributes of writers who, one is safe in saying, care for little else in the world than the rhythm of their lines and the cadence of their phrase, the love of the sea, to which some men and nations confess so readily, is a complex sentiment wherein pride enters for much, necessity for not a little,

250 The ship Koh-i-Noor off the Cape of Good Hope, by J. Scott, mid nineteenth century.

forward screamed out, 'There's people on board of her, sir!
I see them!' in a most extraordinary voice—a voice never heard
before in our ship; the amazing voice of a stranger. It gave the
signal for a sudden tumult of shouts. The watch below ran up the
forecastle head in a body, the cook dashed out of the galley.
Everybody saw the poor fellows now. They were there! And all at
once our ship, which had the well-earned name of being without
a rival for speed in light winds, seemed to us to have lost the power
of motion, as if the sea, becoming viscous, had clung to her sides.
And yet she moved. Immensity, the inseparable companion of a
ship's life, chose that day to breathe upon her as gently as a sleeping
child. The clamour of our excitement had died out, and our living
ship, famous for never losing steerage way as long as there was air
enough to float a feather, stole, without a ripple, silent and white
as a ghost, towards her mutilated and wounded sister, come upon
at the point of death in the sunlit haze of a calm day at sea.

With the binoculars glued to his eyes, the captain said in a
quavering tone: 'They are waving to us with something aft there.'
He put down the glasses on the skylight brusquely, and began to
walk about the poop. 'A shirt or a flag,' he ejaculated, irritably.
'Can't make it out . . . Some damn rag or other!' He took a few
more turns on the poop, glancing down over the rail now and
then to see how fast we were moving. His nervous footsteps rang
sharply in the quiet of the ship, where the other men, all looking
the same way, had forgotten themselves in a staring immobility.
'This will never do!' he cried out, suddenly. 'Lower the boats at
once! Down with them!'

Before I jumped into mine he took me aside, as being an
experienced junior, for a word of warning:

'You look out as you come alongside that she doesn't take you
down with her. You understand?'

He murmured this confidentially, so that none of the men at
the falls should overhear, and I was shocked. 'Heavens! as if in
such an emergency one stopped to think of danger!' I exclaimed
to myself mentally, in scorn of such cold-blooded caution.

It takes many lessons to make a real seaman, and I got my
rebuke at once. My experienced commander seemed in one
searching glance to read my thoughts on my ingenuous face.

'What you're going for is to save life, not to drown your boat's
crew for nothing,' he growled, severely, in my ear. But as we
shoved off he leaned over and cried out: 'It all rests on the power
of your arms, men. Give way for life!'

We made a race of it, and I would never have believed that a
common boat's crew of a merchantman could keep up so much
determined fierceness in the regular swing of their stroke. What
our captain had clearly perceived before we left had become plain

and majestic splendour of light without shadows—seemed to
render the sky less remote and the ocean less immense. It was one
of the days, when the might of the sea appears indeed lovable,
like the nature of a strong man in moments of quiet intimacy.
At sunrise we had made out a black speck to the westward,
apparently suspended high up in the void behind a stirring,
shimmering veil of silvery blue gauze that seemed at times to stir
and float in the breeze which fanned us slowly along. The peace
of that enchanting forenoon was so profound, so untroubled,
that it seemed that every word pronounced loudly on our deck
would penetrate to the very heart of that infinite mystery born
from the conjunction of water and sky. We did not raise our
voices. 'A water-logged derelict, I think, sir,' said the second officer,
quietly, coming down from aloft with the binoculars in their case
slung across his shoulders; and our captain, without a word,
signed to the helmsman to steer for the black speck. Presently we
made out a low, jagged stump sticking up forward—all that
remained of her departed masts.

The captain was expatiating in a low conversational tone to
the chief mate upon the danger of these derelicts, and upon his
dread of coming upon them at night, when suddenly a man

to all of us since. The issue of our enterprise hung on a hair above that abyss of waters which will not give up its dead till the Day of Judgment. It was a race of two ship's boats matched against Death for a prize of nine men's lives, and Death had a long start. We saw the crew of the brig from afar working at the pumps—still pumping on that wreck, which already had settled so far down that the gentle, low swell, over which our boats rose and fell easily without a check to their speed, welling up almost level with her head-rails, plucked at the ends of broken gear swinging desolately under her naked bowsprit.

We could not, in all conscience, have picked out a better day for our regatta had we had the free choice of all the days that ever dawned upon the lonely struggles and solitary agonies of ships since the Norse rovers first steered to the westward against the run of Atlantic waves. It was a very good race. At the finish there was not an oar's length between the first and second boat, with Death coming in a good third on the top of the very next smooth swell, for all one knew to the contrary. The scuppers of the brig gurgled softly all together when the water rising against her sides subsided sleepily with a low wash, as if playing about an immovable rock. Her bulwarks were gone fore and aft, and one saw her bare deck low-lying like a raft and swept clean of boats, spars, houses—of everything except the ringbolts and the heads of the pumps. I had one dismal glimpse of it as I braced myself up to receive upon my breast the last man to leave her, the captain, who literally let himself fall into my arms.

of mankind with the sea. On that exquisite day of gentle breathing peace and veiled sunshine perished my romantic love to what men's imagination had proclaimed the most august aspect of Nature. The cynical indifference of the sea to the merits of human suffering and courage, laid bare in this ridiculous, panic-tainted performance extorted from the dire extremity of nine good and honourable seamen, revolted me. I saw the duplicity of the sea's most tender mood. It was so because it could not help itself, but the awed respect of the early days was gone. I felt ready to smile bitterly at its enchanting charm and glare viciously at its furies. In a moment, before we shoved off, I had looked coolly at the life of my choice. Its illusions were gone, but its fascination remained. I had become a seaman at last.

We pulled hard for a quarter of an hour, then laid on our oars waiting for our ship. She was coming down on us with swelling sails, looking delicately tall and exquisitely noble through the mist. The captain of the brig, who sat in the stern sheets by my side with his face in his hands, raised his head and began to speak with a sort of sombre volubility. They had lost their masts and sprung a leak in a hurricane; drifted for weeks, always at the pumps, met more bad weather; the ships they sighted failed to make them out, the leak gained upon them slowly, and the seas had left them nothing to make a raft of. It was very hard to see ship after ship pass by at a distance, 'as if everybody had agreed that we must be left to drown', he added. But they went on trying to keep the brig afloat as long as possible, and working the pumps constantly on insufficient food, mostly raw, till 'yesterday evening,' he continued, monotonously, 'just as the sun went down, the men's hearts broke.'

He made an almost imperceptible pause here, and went on again with exactly the same intonation:

'They told me the brig could not be saved, and they thought they had done enough for themselves. I said nothing to that. It was true. It was no mutiny. I had nothing to say to them. They lay about aft all night, as still as so many dead men. I did not lie down. I kept a look-out. When the first light came I saw your ship at once. I waited for more light; the breeze began to fail on my face. Then I shouted out as loud as I was able, "Look at that ship!" but only two men got up very slowly and came to me. At first only we three stood alone, for a long time, watching you coming down to us, and feeling the breeze drop to a calm almost; but afterwards others, too, rose, one after another, and by and by I had all my crew behind me. I turned round and said to them that they could see the ship was coming our way, but in this small breeze she might come too late after all, unless we turned to and tried to keep the brig afloat long enough to give you time to save us all. I spoke

252, 253 and 254 *opposite Top left:* The Blackwall frigate *Seringapatam* backing her main topsail and topgallant, lithograph by T. G. Dutton (d. 1891). *Bottom left:* The American *Flying Cloud*, one of the most beautiful of the clippers, built by Donald McKay at Boston in 1851. *Bottom right:* the American clipper *Dreadnought* off Sandy Hook 23 February 1854, nineteen days out from Liverpool; built by Currier and Townsend at Newburyport, Massachusetts in 1853, she is here seen in a strong breeze with her main course reefed and her topgallants and mizen course furled.

255 *above* The ship *Benares* (built Boston 1856) losing her masts in a hurricane. Oil by Marshall Johnson (1846–1921).

It had been a weirdly silent rescue—a rescue without a hail, without a single uttered word, without a gesture or a sign, without a conscious exchange of glances. Up to the very last moment those on board stuck to their pumps, which spouted two clear streams of water upon their bare feet. Their brown skin showed through the rents of their shirts; and the two small bunches of half-naked, tattered men went on bowing from the waist to each other in their back-breaking labour, up and down, absorbed, with no time for a glance over the shoulder at the help that was coming to them. As we dashed, unregarded, alongside a voice let out one, only one hoarse howl of command, and then, just as they stood, without caps, with the salt drying grey in the wrinkles and folds of their hairy, haggard faces, blinking stupidly at us their red eyelids, they made a bolt away from the handles, tottering and jostling against each other, and positively flung themselves over upon our very heads. The clatter they made tumbling into the boats had an extraordinarily destructive effect upon the illusion of tragic dignity our self-esteem had thrown over the contests

233

They had lost the date. When I told him it was Sunday, the 22nd, he frowned, making some mental calculation, then nodded twice sadly to himself, staring at nothing.

His aspect was miserably unkempt and wildly sorrowful. Had it not been for the unquenchable candour of his blue eyes, whose unhappy, tired glance every moment sought his abandoned, sinking brig, as if it could find rest nowhere else, he would have appeared mad. But he was too simple to go mad, too simple with that manly simplicity which alone can bear men unscathed in mind and body through an encounter with the deadly playfulness of the sea or with its less abominable fury.

Neither angry, nor playful, nor smiling, it enveloped our distant ship growing bigger as she neared us, our boats with the rescued men and the dismantled hull of the brig we were leaving behind, in the large and placid embrace of its quietness, half lost in the fair haze, as if in a dream of infinite and tender clemency. There was no frown, no wrinkle on its face, not a ripple. And the run of the slight swell was so smooth that it resembled the graceful undulation of a piece of shimmering grey silk shot with gleams of green. We pulled an easy stroke; but when the master of the brig, after a glance over his shoulder, stood up with a low exclamation, my men feathered their oars instinctively, without an order, and the boat lost her way.

He was steadying himself on my shoulder with a strong grip, while his other arm, flung up rigidly, pointed a denunciatory finger at the immense tranquillity of the ocean. After his first exclamation, which stopped the swing of our oars, he made no sound, but his whole attitude seemed to cry out an indignant 'Behold!' . . . I could not imagine what vision of evil had come to him. I was startled, and the amazing energy of his immobilized gesture made my heart beat faster with the anticipation of something monstrous and unsuspected. The stillness around us became crushing.

For a moment the succession of silky undulations ran on innocently. I saw each of them swell up the misty line of the horizon, far, far away beyond the derelict brig, and the next moment, with a slight friendly toss of our boat, it had passed under us and was gone. The lulling cadence of the rise and fall, the invariable gentleness of this irresistible force, the great charm of the deep waters, warmed my breast deliciously, like the subtle poison of a love-potion. But all this lasted only a few soothing seconds before I jumped up, too, making the boat roll like the veriest land-lubber.

Something startling, mysterious, hastily confused was taking place. I watched it with incredulous and fascinated awe, as one watches the confused, swift movements of some deed of violence done in the dark. As if at a given signal, the run of the smooth

like that to them, and then I gave the command to man the pumps.'

He gave the command, and gave the example, too, by going himself to the handles, but it seems that these men did actually hang back for a moment, looking at each other dubiously before they followed him. 'He! he! he!' He broke out into a most unexpected, imbecile, pathetic, nervous little giggle. 'Their hearts were broken so! They had been played with too long,' he explained, apologetically, lowering his eyes, and became silent.

Twenty-five years is a long time—a quarter of a century is a dim and distant past; but to this day I remember the dark-brown feet, hands, and faces of two of these men whose hearts had been broken by the sea. They were lying very still on their sides on the bottom boards between the thwarts, curled up like dogs. My boat's crew, leaning over the looms of their oars, stared and listened as if at the play. The master of the brig looked up suddenly to ask me what day it was.

256 *above* A clipper ship of the Black Ball line entering Boston Harbour.

257 *opposite, top* The Clipper ship *Clarence*, 1858, by T. G. Dutton (*d.* 1891).

258 *opposite, bottom* The *Charlemagne*, an American full-rigged ship, partly dismasted in a storm in the roaring forties, January 1838. Watercolour by Frederic Roux (1805–70).

undulations seemed checked suddenly around the brig. By a strange optical delusion the whole sea appeared to rise upon her in one overwhelming heave of its silky surface where in one spot a smother of foam broke out ferociously. And then the effort subsided. It was all over, and the smooth swell ran on as before from the horizon in uninterrupted cadence of motion, passing under us with a slight friendly toss of our boat. Far away, where the brig had been, an angry white stain undulating on the surface of steely-grey waters, shot with gleams of green, diminished swiftly without a hiss, like a patch of pure snow melting in the sun. And the great stillness after this initiation into the sea's implacable hate seemed full of dread thoughts and shadows of disaster.

'Gone!' ejaculated from the depths of his chest my bowman in a final tone. He spat in his hands, and took a better grip on his oar. The captain of the brig lowered his rigid arm slowly, and looked at our faces in a solemnly conscious silence, which called upon us to share in his simple-minded, marvelling awe. All at once he sat down by my side, and leaned forward earnestly at my boat's crew, who, swinging together in a long, easy stroke, kept their eyes fixed upon him faithfully.

'No ship could have done so well,' he addressed them, firmly, after a moment of strained silence, during which he seemed with trembling lips to seek for words fit to bear such high testimony. 'She was small, but she was good. I had no anxiety. She was strong. Last voyage I had my wife and two children in her. No other ship could have stood so long the weather she had to live through for days and days before we got dismasted a fortnight ago. She was fairly worn out, and that's all. You may believe me. She lasted under us for days and days, but she could not last for ever. It was long enough. I am glad it is over. No better ship was ever left to sink at sea on such a day as this.'

He was competent to pronounce the funereal oration of a ship, this son of ancient sea-folk, whose national existence, so little stained by the excesses of manly virtues, had demanded nothing but the merest foothold from the earth. By the merits of his sea-wise forefathers and by the artlessness of his heart, he was made fit to deliver this excellent discourse. There was nothing wanting in its orderly arrangement—neither piety nor faith, nor the tribute of praise due to the worthy dead, with the edifying recital of their achievement. She had lived, he had loved her; she had suffered, and he was glad she was at rest. It was an excellent discourse. And it was orthodox, too, in its fidelity to the cardinal article of a seaman's faith, of which it was a single-minded confession. 'Ships are all right.' They are. They who live with the sea have got to hold by that creed first and last; and it came to me, as I glanced at him sideways, that some men were not altogether unworthy in

honour and conscience to pronounce the funereal eulogium of a ship's constancy in life and death.

After this, sitting by my side with his loosely clasped hands hanging between his knees, he uttered no word, made no movement till the shadow of our ship's sails fell on the boat, when, at the loud cheer greeting the return of the victors with their prize, he lifted up his troubled face with a faint smile of pathetic indulgence. This smile of the worthy descendant of the most ancient sea-folk whose audacity and hardihood had left no trace of greatness and glory upon the waters, completed the cycle of my initiation. There was an infinite depth of hereditary wisdom in its pitying sadness. It made the hearty bursts of cheering sound like a childish noise of triumph. Our crew shouted with immense confidence—honest souls! As if anybody could ever make sure of having prevailed against the sea, which has betrayed so many ships of great 'name', so many proud men, so many towering ambitions of fame, power, wealth, greatness!

As I brought the boat under the falls my captain, in high good-humour, leaned over, spreading his red and freckled elbows on the rail, and called down to me sarcastically out of the depths of his cynic philosopher's beard: 'So you have brought the boat back after all, have you?'

Sarcasm was 'his way', and the most that can be said for it is that it was natural. This did not make it lovable. But it is decorous and expedient to fall in with one's commander's way. 'Yes. I brought the boat back all right, sir,' I answered. And the good man believed me. It was not for him to discern upon me the marks of my recent initiation. And yet I was not exactly the same youngster who had taken the boat away—all impatience for a race against Death, with the prize of nine men's lives at the end.

Already I looked with other eyes upon the sea. I knew it capable of betraying the generous ardour of youth as implacably as, indifferent to evil and good, it would have betrayed the basest greed or the noblest heroism. My conception of its magnanimous greatness was gone. And I looked upon the true sea—the sea that plays with men till their hearts are broken, and wears stout ships to death. Nothing can touch the brooding bitterness of its soul. Open to all and faithful to none, it exercises its fascination for the undoing of the best. To love it is not well. It knows no bond of plighted troth, no fidelity to misfortune, to long companionship, to long devotion. The promise it holds out perpetually is very great; but the only secret of its possession is strength, strength—the jealous, sleepless strength of a man guarding a coveted treasure within his gates.

from *The Mirror of the Sea*, by Joseph Conrad, 1906.

259 *top* Collision between American ships *Tejuca* and *Excelsior* 1856, oil attributed to Thomas Pitman. The ship on the left was evidently proceeding under topsails which have been blown away.

260 The most perilous position for a square-rigged ship with its limited ability to sail into the wind. This clipper is carrying much more sail than usual in the weather, in an effort to 'claw' her way off a lee shore.

Glossary

Sea terminology in the age of sail comprised a language of its own. Sailors used sea terms so constantly in their work and in conversation with their own kind that they came to know no other way of expressing themselves. They were thus often incomprehensible to the land-lubbers they despised. This glossary comes from Richard Dana's *The Seaman's Friend*.

The spars and rigging of a ship (plate 1)

1 Head	48 Mizen topmast cross-trees	96 Main topgallant braces
2 Head-boards	49 Fore yard	97 Main royal lifts
3 Stem	50 Fore topsail yard	98 Main royal braces
4 Bows	51 Fore topgallant yard	99 Main rigging
5 Forecastle	52 Fore royal yard	100 Main topmast rigging
6 Waist	53 Main yard	101 Main topgallant rigging
7 Quarter-deck	54 Main topsail yard	102 Main topmast backstays
8 Gangway	55 Main topgallant yard	103 Main topgallant backstays
9 Counter	56 Main royal yard	
10 Stern	57 Cross jack yard	104 Main royal backstays
11 Tafferel	58 Mizen topsail yard	105 Cross-jack lifts
12 Fore chains	59 Mizen topgallant yard	106 Cross-jack braces
13 Main chains	60 Mizen royal yard	107 Mizen topsail lifts
14 Mizen chains	61 Fore truck	108 Mizen topsail braces
15 Bowsprit	62 Main truck	109 Mizen topgallant lifts
16 Jib-boom	63 Mizen truck	110 Mizen topgall. braces
17 Flying jib-boom	64 Fore stay	111 Mizen royal lifts
18 Spritsail yard	65 Fore topmast stay	112 Mizen royal braces
19 Martingale	66 Jib stay	113 Mizen stay
20 Bowsprit cap	69 Top foregallant stay	114 Mizen topmast stay
21 Foremast	70 Fore skysail stay	115 Mizen topgallant stay
22 Fore topmast	71 Jib guys	116 Mizen royal stay
23 Fore topgall. mast	72 Flying-jib guys	117 Mizen skysail stay
24 Fore royal mast	73 Fore lifts	118 Mizen rigging
25 Fore skysail mast	74 Fore braces	119 Mizen topmast rigging
26 Main mast	75 Fore topsail lifts	120 Mizen topgall. shrouds
27 Main topmast	76 Fore topsail braces	121 Mizen topmast backstays
28 Main topgall. mast	77 Fore topgallant lifts	
29 Main royal mast	78 Fore topgallant braces	122 Mizen topgallant backstays
30 Main skysail mast	79 Fore royal lifts	
31 Mizen mast	80 Fore royal braces	123 Mizen royal backstays
32 Mizen topmast	81 Fore rigging	124 Fore spencer vangs
33 Mizen topgall. mast	82 Fore topmast rigging	125 Main spencer vangs
34 Mizen royal mast	83 Fore topgallant shrouds	126 Spanker vangs
35 Mizen skysail mast	84 Fore topmast backstays	127 Ensign halyards
36 Fore spencer gaff	85 Fore topgall. backstays	128 Spanker peak halyards
37 Main spencer gaff	86 Fore royal backstays	129 Foot-rope to fore yard
38 Spanker gaff	87 Main stay	130 Foot-rope to main yard
39 Spanker boom	88 Main topmast stay	131 Foot-rope to cross-jack yard
40 Fore top	89 Main topgallant stay	
41 Foremast cap	90 Main royal stay	
42 Fore topm. cross-tr.	91 Main lifts	
43 Main top	92 Main braces	
44 Mainmast cap	93 Main topsail lifts	
45 Main topm. cross-tr.	94 Main topsail braces	
46 Mizen top	95 Main topgallant lifts	
47 Mizenmast cap		

A ship's sails (plate II)

1	Fore topmast staysail	25	Main topmast studdingsail
2	Jib	25a	Lee ditto
3	Flying jib	26	Main topgallant studdingsail
4	Fore spencer		
5	Main spencer	26a	Lee ditto
6	Spanker	27	Main royal studdingsail
7	Foresail		
8	Fore topsail	27a	Lee ditto
9	Fore topgallant sail		
10	Fore royal		
11	Fore skysail		
12	Mainsail		
13	Main topsail		
14	Main topgallant sail		
15	Main royal		
16	Main skysail		
17	Main topsail		
18	Mizen topgallant sail		
19	Mizen royal		
20	Mizen skysail		
21	Lower studdingsail		
21a	Lee ditto		
22	Fore topmast studdingsail		
22a	Lee ditto		
23	Fore topgallant studdingsail		
23a	Lee ditto		
24	Fore royal studdingsail		
24a	Lee ditto		

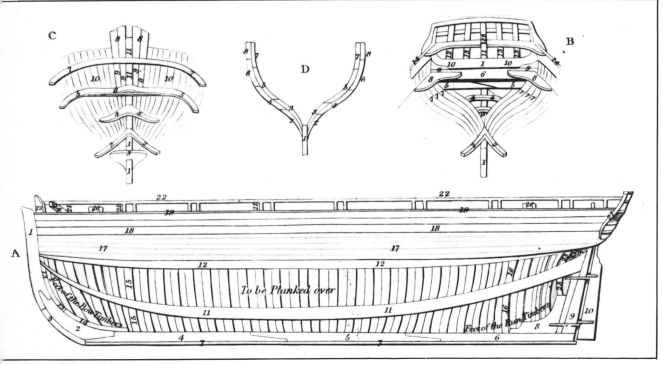

The frame of a ship (plate III)

A. THE OUTSIDE

1 Upper stem-piece
2 Lower stem-piece
3 Gripe
4 Forward keel-piece
5 Middle keel-piece
6 After keel-piece
7 False keel
8 Stern knee
9 Stern post
10 Rudder
11 Bilge streaks
12 First streak under the wales
13 Apron
14 Lower apron
15 Fore frame
16 After frame
17 Wales
18 Waist
19 Plank-shear
20 Timber-heads
21 Stanchions
22 Rail
23 Knight-heads
24 Cathead
25 Fashion timbers

26 Transoms
27 Quarter pieces

B. THE INSIDE OF THE STERN

1 Keelson
2 Pointers
3 Chock
4 Transoms
5 Half transoms
6 Main transoms
7 Quarter timbers
8 Transom knees
9 Horn timbers
10 Counter-timber knee
11 Stern-post
12 Rudder-head
13 Counter timbers
14 Upper-deck clamp

C. THE INSIDE OF THE BOWS

1 Keelson
2 Pointers
3 Step for the mast
4 Breast-hook
5 Lower-deck breast-hook
6 Forward beam

7 Upper-deck clamp
8 Knight-heads
9 Hawse-timbers
10 Bow timbers
11 Apron of the stem

D. THE TIMBERS

1 Keelson
2 Floor timbers
3 Naval timbers or ground futtocks
4 Lower futtocks
5 Middle futtocks
6 Upper futtocks
7 Top timbers
8 Half timbers, or half top-timbers

Ship

Bark

Full-rigged Brig

Hermaphrodite Brig

Top-sail Schooner

Fore & aft Schooner

Sloop

Types of sailing ship (plate IV)

SHIP. A ship is square-rigged throughout; that is, she has tops, and carries square sails on all three of her masts.

BARK. A bark is square-rigged at her fore and main masts, and differs from a ship in having no top, and carrying only fore-and-aft sails at her mizen mast.

BRIG. A full-rigged brig is square-rigged at both her masts.

HERMAPHRODITE BRIG. An hermaphrodite brig is square-rigged at her foremast; but has no top, and only fore-and-aft sails at her main mast.

TOPSAIL SCHOONER. A topsail schooner has no tops at her foremast, and is fore-and-aft rigged at her mainmast. She differs from an hermaphrodite brig in that she is not properly square-rigged at her foremast, having no top, and carrying a fore-and-aft foresail, instead of a square foresail and a spencer.

FORE-AND-AFT SCHOONER. A fore-and-aft schooner is fore-and-aft rigged throughout, differing from a topsail schooner in that the latter carries small square sails aloft at the fore.

SLOOP. A sloop has one mast, fore-and-aft rigged.

HERMAPHRODITE BRIGS sometimes carry small square sails aloft at the main; in which case they are called BRIGANTINES, and differ from a FULL-RIGGED BRIG in that they have no top at the mainmast, and carry a fore-and-aft mainsail instead of a square mainsail and trysail. Some TOPSAIL SCHOONERS carry small square sails aloft at the main as well as the fore; being in other respects fore-and-aft rigged. They are then called MAIN TOPSAIL SCHOONERS.

Dictionary of sea terms

ABACK. The situation of the sails when the wind presses their surfaces against the mast, and tends to force the vessel astern.

ABAFT. Toward the stern of a vessel.

ABOARD. Within a vessel.

ABOUT. On the other tack.

ABREAST. Alongside of. Side by side.

ACCOMMODATION. (See LADDER).

A-COCK-BILL. The situation of the yards when they are topped up at an angle with the deck. The situation of an anchor when it hangs to the cathead by the ring only.

ADRIFT. Broken from moorings or fasts. Without fasts.

AFLOAT. Resting on the surface of the water.

AFORE. Forward. The opposite of abaft.

AFT—AFTER. Near the stern.

AGROUND. Touching the bottom.

AHEAD. In the direction of the vessel's head. *Wind ahead* is from the direction toward which the vessel's head points.

A-HULL. The situation of a vessel when she lies with all her sails furled and her helm lashed a-lee.

A-LEE. The situation of the helm when it is put in the opposite direction from that in which the wind blows.

ALL-ABACK. When all the sails are aback.

ALL HANDS. The whole crew.

ALL IN THE WIND. When all the sails are shaking.

ALOFT. Above the deck.

ALOOF. At a distance.

AMAIN. Suddenly. At once.

AMIDSHIPS. In the centre of the vessel; either with reference to her length or to her breadth.

ANCHOR. The machine by which, when dropped to the bottom, the vessel is held fast.

ANCHOR-WATCH. (See WATCH.)

AN-END. When a mast is perpendicular to the deck.

A-PEEK. When the cable is hove taut so as to bring the vessel nearly over her anchor. The *yards* are *a-peek* when they are topped up by contrary lifts.

ANCHOR

BEACON

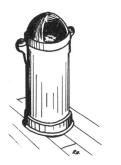

BINNACLE

BITTS

APRON. A piece of timber fixed behind the lower part of the stem, just above the fore end of the keel. A covering to the vent or lock of a cannon.

ARM. YARD-ARM. The extremity of a yard. Also, the lower part of an anchor, crossing the shank and terminating in the flukes.

ARMING. A piece of tallow put in the cavity and over the bottom of a lead-line.

A-STERN. In the direction of the stern. The opposite of a-head.

A-TAUNT. (See TAUNT.)

ATHWART. Across.

Athwart-ships. Across the line of the vessel's keel.

Athwart-hawse. Across the direction of a vessel's head. Across her cable.

ATHWART-SHIPS. Across the length of a vessel. In opposition to fore-and-aft.

A-TRIP. The situation of the anchor when it is raised clear of the ground. The same as a-weigh.

AVAST, or 'VAST. An order to stop; as, 'Avast heaving!'

A-WEATHER. The situation of the helm when it is put in the direction from which the wind blows.

A-WEIGH. The same as a-trip.

AWNING. A covering of canvas over a vessel's deck, or over a boat, to keep off sun or rain.

BACK. *To back an anchor,* is to carry out a smaller one ahead of the one by which the vessel rides, to take off some of the strain.

To back a sail, is to throw it aback.

To back and fill, is alternately to back and fill the sails.

BACKSTAYS. Stays running from a masthead to the vessel's side, slanting a little aft. (See STAYS.)

BAGPIPE. *To bagpipe the mizen,* is to lay it aback by bringing the sheet to the weather mizen rigging.

BALANCE-REEF. A reef in a spanker or fore-and-aft mainsail, which runs from the outer head-earing, diagonally, to the tack. It is the closest reef, and makes the sail triangular, or nearly so.

BALE. *To bale a boat,* is to throw water out of her.

BALLAST. Heavy material, as iron, lead, or stone, placed in the bottom of the hold, to keep a vessel from upsetting.

To freshen ballast, is to shift it. Coarse gravel is called *shingle ballast.*

BANK. *To double bank* an oar, is to have it pulled by two men.

BAR. A bank or shoal at the entrance of a harbour.

Capstan-bars are heavy pieces of wood by which the capstan is hove round.

BARE-POLES. The condition of a ship when she has no sail set.

BARGE. A large double-banked boat, used by the commander of a vessel, in the navy.

BARK, or BARQUE. (See PLATE 4.) A three-masted vessel, having her fore and main masts rigged like a ship's, and her mizen mast like the main mast of a schooner, with no sail upon it but a spanker.

BARNACLE. A shell-fish often found on a vessel's bottom.

BATTENS. Thin strips of wood put around the hatches, to keep the tarpaulin down. Also, put upon rigging to keep it from chafing. A large batten widened at the end, and put upon rigging, is called a *Scotchman.*

BEACON. A post or buoy placed over a shoal or bank to warn vessels off. Also as a signal-mark on land.

BEAMS. Strong pieces of timber stretching across the vessel, to support the decks.

On the weather or lee beam, is in a direction to windward or leeward, at right angles with the keel.

On beam ends. The situation of a vessel when turned over so that her beams are inclined toward the vertical.

BEAR. An object *bears* so and so, when it is in such a direction from the person looking.

To bear down upon a vessel, is to approach her from the windward.

To bear up, is to put the helm up and keep a vessel off from her course, and move her to leeward.

To bear away, is the same as to *bear up;* being applied to the vessel instead of to the tiller.

To bear-a-hand. To make haste.

BEARING. The direction of an object from the person looking. The *bearings* of a vessel are the widest part of her below the plank-shear. That part of her hull which is on the waterline when she is at anchor and in her proper trim.

BEATING. Going toward the direction of the wind, by alternate tacks.

BECALM. To intercept the wind. A vessel or highland to windward is said to *becalm* another. So one sail *becalms* another.

BECKET. A piece of rope placed so as to confine a spar or another rope. A handle made of rope, in the form of a circle (as the handle of a chest,) is called a *becket.*

BEES. Pieces of plank bolted to the outer end of the bowsprit, to reeve the foretopmast stays through.

BELAY. To make a rope fast by turns round a pin or coil, without hitching or seizing it.

BEND. To make fast.

To bend a sail, is to make it fast to the yard.

To bend a cable, is to make it fast to the anchor.

A bend, is a knot by which one rope is made fast to another.

BENDS. (See PLATE 3.) The strongest part of a vessel's side, to which the beams, knees, and foot-hooks are bolted. The part between the water's edge and the bulwarks.

BENEAPED. (See NEAPED.)

BENTICK SHROUDS. Formerly used, and extending from the futtock-staves to the opposite channels.

BERTH. The place where a vessel lies. The place in which a man sleeps.

BETWEEN-DECKS. The space between any two decks of a ship.

BIBBS. Pieces of timber bolted to the hounds of a mast, to support the trestle trees.

BIGHT. The double part of a rope when it is folded; in contra-distinction from the ends. Any part of a rope may be called the bight, except the ends. Also, a bend in the shore, making a small bay or inlet.

BILGE. That part of the floor of a ship upon which she would rest if aground; being the part near the keel which is more in a horizontal than a perpendicular line.

Bilge-ways. Pieces of timber bolted together and placed under the bilge in launching.

Bilged. When the bilge is broken in.

Bilge water. Water which settles in the bilge.

Bilge. The largest circumference of a cask.

BILL. The point at the extremity of the fluke of an anchor.

BILLET-HEAD. (See HEAD.)

BINNACLE. A box near the helm, containing the compass.

BITTS. Perpendicular pieces of timber going through the deck, placed to secure anything to. The cables are fastened to them, if there is no windlass. There are also *bitts* to secure the windlass, and on each side of the heel of the bowsprit.

BITTER, or BITTER-END. That part of the cable which is abaft the bitts.

BLADE. The flat part of an oar which goes into the water.

BLOCK. A piece of wood, with sheaves or wheels in it, through which the ropes are rove.

BLUFF. A *bluff-bowed* or *bluff-headed* vessel is one which is full and square forward.

BOARD. The stretch a vessel makes upon one tack, when she is beating.

Stern-board. When a vessel goes stern foremost.

By the board. Said of masts when they fall over the side.

BOAT-HOOK. An iron hook with a long staff, held in the hand, by which a boat is kept fast to a wharf, or vessel.

BOATSWAIN. (Pronounced *bo-s'n.*) A warrant officer in the navy, who has charge of the rigging, and calls the crew to duty.

BOBSTAYS. Used to confine the bowsprit down to the stem or cutwater.

BOLSTERS. Pieces of soft wood, covered with canvas, placed on the trestle-trees, for the eyes of the rigging to rest upon.

BOLTS. Long cylindrical bars of iron or copper, used to secure or unite the different parts of a vessel.

BOLT-ROPE. The rope which goes round a sail, and to which the canvas is sewed.

BONNET. An additional piece of canvas attached to the foot of a jib, or a schooner's foresail, by lacings. Taken off in bad weather.

BOOM. A spar used to extend the foot of a fore-and-aft or studding-sail.

Boom-irons. Iron rings on the yards, through which the studding-sail booms traverse.

BOOT-TOPPING. Scraping off the grass, or other matter, which may be on a vessel's bottom, and daubing it over with tallow, or some mixture.

BOUND. *Wind-bound.* When a vessel is kept in port by a head wind.

BOW. The rounded part of a vessel, forward.

BOWER. A working anchor, the cable of which is bent and reeved through the hawse-hole.

Best bower is the larger of the two bowers.

BOW-GRACE. A frame of old rope or junk, placed round the bows and sides of a vessel, to prevent the ice from injuring her.

BOWLINE. (Pronounced *bo-lin.*) A rope leading forward from the leach of a square sail, to keep the leach well out when sailing close-hauled. A vessel is said to be *on a bowline,* or *on a taut bowline,* when she is close-hauled.

Bowline-bridle. The span on the leach of the sail to which the bowline is toggled.

BOWSE. To pull upon a tackle.

BOWSPRIT. (Pronounced *bo-sprit.*) A large and strong spar, standing from the bows of a vessel. (See PLATE I.)

BOX-HAULING. Wearing a vessel by backing the head sails.

BLOCK

CAT-HEAD

CAT

CHAIN-PLATES

CLEAT

BOX. *To box the compass,* is to repeat the thirty-two points of the compass in order.

BRACE. A rope by which a yard is turned about.

To brace a yard, is to turn it about horizontally.

To brace up, is to lay the yard more fore and aft.

To brace in, is to lay it nearer square.

To brace aback. (See ABACK.)

To brace to, is to brace the head yards a little aback, in tacking or wearing.

BRAILS. Ropes by which the foot or lower corners of fore-and-aft sails are hauled up.

BRAKE. The handle of a ship's pump.

BREAK. *To break bulk,* is to begin to unload.

To break ground, is to lift the anchor from the bottom.

To break shear, is when a vessel, at anchor, in tending, is forced the wrong way by the wind or current, so that she does not lie so well for keeping herself clear of her anchor.

BREAKER. A small cask containing water.

BREAMING. Cleaning a ship's bottom by burning.

BREAST-FAST. A rope used to confine a vessel sideways to a wharf, or to some other vessel.

BREAST-HOOKS. Knees placed in the forward part of a vessel, across the stem, to unite the bows on each side. (See PLATE III.)

BREAST-ROPE. A rope passed round a man in the chains, while sounding.

BREECH. The outside angle of a knee-timber.

BREECHING. A strong rope used to secure the breech of a gun to the ship's side.

BRIDLE. Spans of rope attached to the leaches of square sails, to which bowlines are made fast.

Bridle-port. The foremost port, used for stowing the anchors.

BRIG. A square-rigged vessel, with two masts. An *hermaphrodite brig* has a brig's foremast, and a schooner's mainmast. (See PLATE IV.)

BROACH-TO. To fall off so much, when going free, as to bring the wind round on the other quarter, and take the sails aback.

BROADSIDE. The whole side of a vessel.

BROKEN-BACKED. The state of a vessel when she is so loosened as to droop at each end.

BUCKLERS. Blocks of wood made to fit in the hawse-holes, or holes in the half-ports, when at sea. Those in the hawse-holes are sometimes called *hawse-blocks.*

BULGE. (See BILGE.)

BULK. The whole cargo, when stowed.

Stowed in bulk, is when goods are stowed loose, instead of being stowed in casks of bags. (See BREAK-BULK.)

BULK-HEAD. Temporary partitions of boards to separate different parts of a vessel.

BULL. A sailor's term for a small keg, holding a gallon or two.

BULL'S-EYE. A small piece of stout wood with a hole through the centre for a stay rope to reeve through, without any sheave, and with a groove round it for the strap, which is usually of iron. Also a piece of thick glass inserted in the deck, to let light below.

BULWARKS. The wood-work round a vessel, above her deck, consisting of boards fastened to stanchions and timber-heads.

BUM-BOATS. Boats which lie alongside a vessel in port with provisions and fruit to sell.

BUMPKIN. Pieces of timber projecting from the vessel to board the fore tack to; and from each quarter for the main brace-blocks.

BUNT. The middle of a sail.

BUNTING. (Pronounced *buntin.*) Thin woollen stuff of which a ship's colours are made.

BUNTLINES. Ropes used for hauling up the body of a sail.

BUOY. A floating cask, or piece of wood, attached by a rope to an anchor, to show its position. Also floated over a shoal, or other dangerous place, as a beacon.

To stream a buoy, is to drop it into the water before letting go the anchor.

A buoy is said to *watch,* when it floats upon the surface of the water.

BURTON. A tackle, rove in a particular manner.

A single Spanish burton has three single blocks, or two single blocks and a hook in the bight of one of the running parts.

A double Spanish burton has three double blocks.

BUTT. The end of a plank where it unites with the end of another.

Scuttle-butt. A cask with a hole cut in its bilge, and kept on deck to hold water for daily use.

BUTTOCK. That part of the convexity of a vessel abaft, under the stern, contained between the counter above and the after part of the bilge below, and between the quarter on the side and the stern-post. (See PLATE III.)

BY. *By the head.* Said of a vessel when her head is lower in the water than her stern. If her stern is lower, she is *by the stern.*

By the lee. (See LEE. See RUN.)

CABIN. The after part of a vessel, in which the officers live.

CABLE. A large, strong rope, made fast to the anchor, by which the vessel is secured. It is usually 120 fathoms in length.

CABLE-TIER. (See TIER.)

CABOOSE. A house on deck, where the cooking is done. Commonly called the *Galley.*

CALK. (see CAULK.)

CAMBERED. When the floor of a vessel is higher at the middle than towards the stem and stern.

CAMEL. A machine used for lifting vessels over a shoal or bar.

CAMFERING. Taking off an angle or edge of a timber.

CAN-HOOKS. Slings with flat hooks at each end, used for hoisting barrels or light casks, the hooks being placed round the chimes, and the purchase hooked to the centre of the slings. Small ones are usually wholly of iron.

CANT-PIECES. Pieces of timber fastened to the angles of fishes and side-trees, to supply any part that may prove rotten.

CANT-TIMBERS. Timbers at the two ends of a vessel, raised obliquely from the keel.

Lower Half Cants. Those parts of frames situated forward and abaft the square frames, or the floor-timbers which cross the keel.

CANVAS. The cloth of which sails are made. No. 1 is the coarsest and strongest.

CAP. A thick, strong block of wood with two holes through it, one square and the other round, used to confine together the head of one mast and the lower part of the mast next above it. (See PLATE I.)

CAPSIZE. To overturn.

CAPSTAN. A machine placed perpendicularly in the deck, and used for a strong purchase in heaving or hoisting. Men-of-war weigh their anchors by capstans. Merchant-vessels use a windlass. (See BAR.)

CAREEN. To heave a vessel down upon her side by purchases upon the masts. To lie over, when sailing on the wind.

CARLINGS. Short and small pieces of timber running between the beams.

CARRICK-BEND. A kind of knot.

Carrick-bitts are the windlass bitts.

CARRY-AWAY. To break a spar, or part a rope.

CAST. To pay a vessel's head off, in getting under way, on the tack she is to sail upon.

CAT. The tackle used to hoist the anchor up to the cat-head.

Cat-block, the block of this tackle.

CAT-HAIRPIN. An iron leg used to confine the upper part of the rigging to the mast.

CAT-HEAD. Large timbers projecting from the vessel's side, to which the anchor is raised and secured.

CAT'S-PAW. A kind of hitch made in a rope. A light current of air seen on the surface of the water during a calm.

CAULK. To fill the seams of a vessel with oakum.

CAVIL. (See KEVEL.)

CEILING. The inside planking of a vessel.

CHAFE. To rub the surface of a rope or spar.

Chafing-gear is the stuff put upon the rigging and spars to prevent their chafing.

CHAINS. (See PLATE I.) Strong links or plates of iron, the lower ends of which are bolted through the ship's side to the timbers. Their upper ends are secured to the bottom of the dead-eyes in the channels. Also, used familiarly for the CHANNELS, which see. The chain-cable of a vessel is called familiarly her *chain.*

Rudder-chains lead from the outer and upper end of the rudder to the quarters. They are hung slack.

CHAIN-PLATES. Plates of iron bolted to the side of a ship, to which the chains and dead-eyes of the lower rigging are connected.

CHANNELS. Broad pieces of plank bolted edgewise to the outside of a vessel. Used for spreading the lower rigging. (See CHAINS.)

CHAPELLING. Wearing a ship round, when taken aback, without bracing the head-yards.

CHECK. A term sometimes used for slacking off a little on a brace, and then belaying it.

CHEEKS. The projections on each side of a mast, upon which the trestle-trees rest. The sides of the shell of a block.

CHEERLY! Quickly, with a will.

CHESS-TREES. Pieces of oak, fitted to the sides of a vessel, abaft the fore chains, with a sheave in them, to board the main tack to. Now out of use.

CHIMES. The ends of the staves of a cask, where they come out beyond the head of the cask.

CHINSE. To thrust oakum into seams with a small iron.

CHOCK. A wedge used to secure anything with, or for anything to rest upon. The long-boat rests upon two large *chocks,* when it is stowed.

Chock-a-block. When the lower block of a tackle is run close up to the upper one, so that you can hoist no higher. This is also called

CAPSTAN

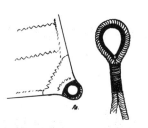

CRINGLES

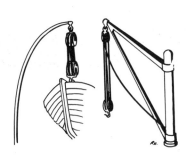

DAVIT (BOAT)   DAVIT (ANCHOR)

DEAD EYE

CISTERN. An apartment in the hold of a vessel, having a pipe leading out through the side, with a cock, by which water may be let into her.

CLAMPS. Thick planks on the inside of vessels, to support the ends of beams. Also, crooked plates of iron fore-locked upon the trunnions of cannon. Any plate of iron made to turn, open, and shut so as to confine a spar or boom, as, a studdingsail boom, or a boat's mast.

CLASP-HOOK. (See CLOVE-HOOK.)

CLEAT. A piece of wood used in different parts of a vessel to belay ropes to.

CLEW. The lower corner of square sails, and the after corner of a fore-and-aft sail.

To clew up, is to haul up the clew of a sail.

CLEW-GARNET. A rope that hauls up the clew of a foresail or mainsail in a square-rigged vessel.

CLEWLINE. A rope that hauls up the clew of a square-sail. The *clew-garnet* is the clewline of a course.

CLINCH. A half-hitch, stopped to its own part.

CLOSE-HAULED. Applied to a vessel which is sailing with her yards braces up so as to get as much as possible to windward. The same as *on a taut bowline, full and by, on the wind,* &c.

CLOVE-HITCH. Two half-hitches round a spar or other rope.

CLOVE-HOOK. An iron clasp, in two parts, moving upon the same pivot, and overlapping one another. Used for bending chain-sheets to the clews of sails.

CLUB-HAUL. To bring a vessel's head round on the other tack, by letting go the lee anchor, and cutting or slipping the cable.

CLUBBING. Drifting down a current with an anchor out.

COAKING. Uniting pieces of spar by means of tabular projections, formed by cutting away the solid of one piece into a hollow, so as to make a projection in the other, in such a manner that they may correctly fit, the butts preventing the pieces from drawing assunder.

Coaks are fitted into the beams and knees of vessels to prevent their drawing.

COAL TAR. Tar made from bituminous coal.

COAMINGS. Raised work round the hatches, to prevent water going down into the hold.

COAT. *Mast-coat* is a piece of canvas, tarred or painted, placed round a mast or bowsprit, where it enters the deck.

COCK-BILL. To cock-bill a yard or anchor. (See A-COCK-BILL.)

COCK-PIT. An apartment in a vessel of war, used by the surgeon during an action.

CODLINE. An eighteen thread line.

COXWAIN. (Pronounced *cox'n.*) The person who steers a boat and has charge of her.

COIL. To lay a rope up in a ring, with one turn or fake over another.

A coil is a quantity of rope laid up in that manner.

COLLAR. An eye in the end of bight of a shroud or stay, to go over the mast head.

COME. *Come home,* said of an anchor when it is broken from the ground and drags.

To come up a rope of tackle, is to slack it off.

COMPANION. A wooden covering over the staircase to a cabin.

Companion-way, the staircase to the cabin.

Companion-ladder. The ladder leading from the poop to the main deck.

COMPASS. The instrument which tells the course of a vessel.

Compass-timbers are such as are curved or arched.

CONCLUDING-LINE. A small line leading through the centre of the steps of a rope or Jacob's ladder.

CONNING, or CUNNING. Directing the helmsman in steering a vessel.

COUNTER. (See PLATE III.) That part of a vessel between the bottom of the stern and the wing-transom and buttock.

counter-timbers are short timbers put in to strengthen the counter.

To counter-brace yards, is to brace the head-yards one way and the after-yards another.

COURSES. The common term for the sails that hang from a ship's lower yards. The foresail is called the *fore course* and the mainsail the *main course.*

CRANES. Pieces of iron or timber at the vessel's sides, used to stow boats or spars upon. A machine used at a wharf for hoisting.

CRANK. The condition of a vessel when she is inclined to lean over a great deal and cannot bear much sail. This may be owing to her construction or to her stowage.

CREEPER. An iron instrument, like a grapnell, with four claws, used for dragging the bottom of a harbour or river, to find anything lost.

CRINGLE. A short piece of rope with each end spliced into the bolt-rope of a sail, confining an iron ring or thimble.

CROSS-BARS. Round bars of iron, bent at each end, used as levers to turn the shank of an anchor.

CROSS-CHOCKS. Pieces of timber fayed across the dead-wood amidships, to make good the deficiency of the heels of the lower futtocks.

CROSS-JACK. (Pronounced *croj-jack.*) The cross-jack yard is the lower yard on the mizen mast. (See PLATE I.)

CROSS-PAWLS. Pieces of timber that keep a vessel together while in her frames.

CROSS-PIECE. A piece of timber connecting two bitts.

CROSS-SPALES. Pieces of timber placed across a vessel, and nailed to the frames, to keep the sides together until the knees are bolted.

CROSS-TREES. (See PLATE I.) Pieces of oak supported by the cheeks and trestle-trees, at the mast heads, to sustain the tops on the lower mast, and to spread the topgallant rigging at the topmast head.

CROW-FOOT. A number of small lines rove through the uvrou to suspend an awning by.

CROWN of an anchor, is the place where the arms are joined to the shank.

To crown a knot, is to pass the strands over and under each other above the knot.

CRUTCH. A knee or piece of knee timber, placed inside of a vessel to secure the heels of the cant-timbers abaft. Also, the chock upon which the spanker-boom rests when the sail is not set.

CUCKOLD'S NECK. A knot by which a rope is secured to a spar, the two parts of the rope crossing each other, and seized together.

CUDDY. A cabin in the fore part of a boat.

CUNTLINE. The space between the bilges of two casks, stowed side by side. Where one cask is set upon the cuntline between two others, they are stowed *bilge and cuntline.*

CUT-WATER. The foremost part of a vessel's prow, which projects forward of the bows.

CUTTER. A small boat. Also, a kind of sloop.

DAGGER. A piece of timber crossing all the puppets of the bilgeways to keep them together.

Dagger-knees. Knees placed obliquely, to avoid a port.

DAVITS. Pieces of timber or iron, with sheaves or blocks at their ends, projecting over a vessel's side or stern, to hoist boats up to. Also, a spar with a roller or sheave at its end, used for fishing the anchor, called a *fish-davit.*

DEAD-EYE. A circular block of wood, with three holes through it, for the lanyards of rigging to reeve through, without sheaves, and with a groove round it for an iron strap.

DEAD-FLAT. One of the bends amidships.

DEAD-LIGHT. Ports placed in the cabin windows in bad weather.

DEAD RECKONING. A reckoning kept by observing a vessel's courses and distances by the log, to ascertain her position.

DEAD-RISING, or RISING-LINE. Those parts of a vessel's floor, throughout her whole length, where the floor timber is terminated upon the lower futtock.

DEAD-WATER. The eddy under a vessel's counter.

DEAD-WOOD. Blocks of timber, laid upon each end of the keel where the vessel narrows.

DECK. The planked floor of a vessel, resting upon her beams.

DECK-STOPPER. A stopper used for securing the cable forward of the windlass or capstan, while it is overhauled. (See STOPPER.)

DEEP-SEA-LEAD. (Pronounced *dipsey.*) The lead used in sounding at great depths.

DEPARTURE. The easting or westing made by a vessel. The bearing of an object on the coast from which a vessel commenced her dead reckoning.

DERRICK. A single spar, supported by stays and guys, to which a purchase is attached, used to unload vessels, and for hoisting.

DOG. A short iron bar, with a fang or teeth at one end, and a ring at the other. Used for a purchase, the fang being placed against a beam or knee, and the block of a tackle hooked to the ring.

DOG-VANE. A small vane, made of feathers or buntin, to show the direction of the wind.

DOG-WATCHES. Half watches of two hours each, from 4 to 6 and from 6 to 8 p.m. (See WATCH.)

DOLPHIN. A rope or strap round a mast to support the puddening, where the lower yards rest in the slings. Also, a spar or buoy with a large ring in it, secured to an anchor, to which vessels may bend their cables.

DOLPHIN-STRIKER. The martingale. (See PLATE I.)

DOUSE. To lower suddenly.

DOWELLING. A method of coaking, by letting pieces into the solid, or uniting two pieces together by tenons.

DOWNHAUL. A rope used to haul down jibs, staysails, and studdingsails.

DRABLER. A piece of canvas laced to the bonnet of a sail, to give it more drop.

DRAG. A machine with a bag net, used for dragging on the bottom for anything lost.

DRAUGHT. The depth of water which a vessel requires to float her.

DRAW. A sail *draws* when it is filled by the wind.

To draw a jib, is to shift it over the stay to leeward, when it is aback.

DRIFTS. Those pieces in the sheer-draught where the rails are cut off.

DRIVE. To scud before a gale, or to drift in a current.

DRIVER. A spanker.

DROP. The depth of a sail, from head to foot, amidships.

DEAD-WOOD

EYE-BOLT

FENDER

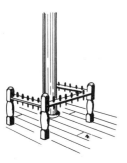

FIFE-RAIL

DRUM-HEAD. The top of the capstan.

DUB. To reduce the end of a timber.

DUCK. A kind of cloth, lighter and finer than canvas; used for small sails.

DUNNAGE. Loose wood or other matters, placed on the bottom of the hold, above the ballast, to stow cargo upon.

EARING. A rope attached to the cringle of a sail; by which it is bent or reefed.

EIKING. A piece of wood fitted to make good a deficiency in length.

ELBOW. Two crosses in a hawse.

ESCUTCHEON. The part of a vessel's stern where her name is written.

EVEN-KEEL. The situation of a vessel when she is so trimmed that she sits evenly upon the water, neither end being down more than the other.

EUPLUVE. A piece of wood, by which the legs of the crow-feet to an awning are extended. (See UNION.)

EYE. The circular part of a shroud or stay, where it goes over a mast.

Eye-bolt. A long iron bar, having an eye at one end, driven through a vessel's deck or side into a timber or beam, with the eye remaining out, to hook a tackle to. If there is a ring through this eye, it is called a *ring-bolt.*

An eye-splice is a certain kind of splice made with the end of a rope.

Eyelet-hole. A hole made in a sail for cringle or roband to go through.

The Eyes of a vessel. A familiar phrase for the forward part.

FACE-PIECES. Pieces of wood wrought on the fore part of the knee of the head.

FACING. Letting one piece of timber into another, with a rabbet.

FAG. A rope is *fagged* when the end is untwisted.

FAIR-LEADER. A strip of board or plank, with holes in it, for running rigging, to lead through. Also, a block or thimble used for the same purpose.

FAKE. One of the circles or rings made in coiling a rope.

FALL. That part of a tackle to which the power is applied in hoisting.

FALSE-KEEL. Pieces of timber under the main keel of vessels.

FANCY-LINE. A line rove through a block at the jaws of a gaff, used as a downhaul. Also, a line used for cross-hauling the lee topping-lift.

FASHION-PIECES. The aftermost timbers, terminating the breadth and forming the shape of the stern.

FAST. A rope by which a vessel is secured to a wharf. There are *bow* or *head, breast, quarter,* and *stern* fasts.

FATHOM. Six feet.

FEATHER. *To feather an oar* in rowing, is to turn the blade horizontally with the top aft as it comes out of the water.

FEATHER-EDGED. Planks which have one side thicker than another.

FENDERS. Pieces of rope or wood hung over the side of a vessel or boat, to protect it from chafing. The fenders of a neat boat are usually made of canvas and stuffed.

FID. A block of wood or iron, placed through the hole in the heel of a mast, and resting on the trestle-trees of the mast below. This supports the mast. Also, a wooden pin, tapered, used in splicing large ropes, in opening eyes, &c.

FIDDLE-BLOCK. A long shell, having one sheave over the other, and the lower smaller than the upper.

FIDDLE-HEAD. (See HEAD.)

FIFE-RAIL. The rail going round a mast.

FIGURE-HEAD. A carved head or full-length figure, over the cutwater.

FILLINGS. Pieces of timber used to make the curve fair for the mouldings, between the edges of the fish-front and the sides of the mast.

FILLER. (See MADE MAST.)

FINISHING. Carved ornaments of the quarter-galley, below the second counter, and above the upper lights.

FISH. To raise the flukes of an anchor upon the gunwale. Also, to strengthen a spar when sprung or weakened, by putting in or fastening on another piece.

Fish-front. Fishes-sides. (See MADE MAST.)

FISH-DAVIT. The davit used for fishing an anchor.

FISH-HOOK. A hook with a pennant, to the end of which the fish-tackle is hooked.

FISH-TACKLE. The tackle used for fishing an anchor.

FLARE. When the vessel's sides go out from the perpendicular. In opposition to *falling-home* or *tumbling-in.*

FLAT. A sheet is said to be hauled *flat,* when it is hauled down close.

Flat-aback, when a sail is blown with its after surface against the mast.

FLEET. To come up a tackle and draw the blocks apart, for another pull, after they have been hauled *two-blocks.*

Fleet Ho! The order given at such times. Also, to shift the position of a block or fall, so as to haul to more advantage.

FLEMISH COIL. (See FRENCH-FAKE.)

FLEMISH-EYE. A kind of eye-splice.

FLEMISH-HORSE. An additional foot-rope at the end of topsail yards.

FLOOR. The bottom of a vessel, on each side of the keelson.

FLOOR TIMBERS. Those timbers of a vessel which are placed across the keel. (See PLATE III.)

FLOWING SHEET. When a vessel has the wind free, and the lee clews eased off.

FLUKES. The broad triangular plates at the extremity of the arms of an anchor, terminating in a point called the *bill.*

FLY. That part of a flag which extends from the Union to the extreme end. (See UNION.)

FOOT. The lower end of a mast or sail. (See FORE-FOOT.)

FOOT-ROPE. The rope stretching along a yard, upon which men stand when reefing or furling, formerly called *horses.*

FOOT WALING. The inside planks or lining of a vessel, over the floor-timbers.

FORE. Used to distinguish the forward part of a vessel, or things in that direction; as, *fore mast, fore hatch,* in opposition to *aft* or *after.*

FORE-AND-AFT. Lengthwise with the vessel. In opposition to *athwart ships.* (See SAILS.)

FORECASTLE. That part of the upper deck forward of the foremast; or, as some say, forward of the after part of the fore channels. (See PLATE I.) Also, the forward part of the vessel, under the deck, where the sailors live, in merchant vessels.

FORE-FOOT. A piece of timber at the forward extremity of the keel, upon which the lower end of the stem rests. (See PLATE III.)

FORE-GANGER. A short piece of rope grafted on a harpoon, to which the line is bent.

FORE LOCK. A flat piece of iron, driven through the end of a bolt, to prevent its drawing.

FORE MAST. The forward mast of all vessels. (See PLATE I.)

FORE-REACH. To shoot ahead, especially when going in stays.

FORE-RUNNER. A piece of rag, terminating the stray-line of the log-line.

FORGE. *To forge ahead,* to shoot ahead; as, in coming to anchor, after the sails are furled. (See FORE-REACH.)

FORMERS. Pieces of wood used for shaping cartridges or wads.

FOTHER, or FODDER. To draw a sail, filled with oakum, under a vessel's bottom, in order to stop a leak.

FOUL. The term for the opposite of clear.

FOUL ANCHOR. When the cable has a turn round the anchor.

FOUL HAWSE. When the two cables are crossed or twisted outside the stem.

FOUNDER. A vessel *founders* when she fills with water and sinks.

FOX. Made by twisting together two or more rope-yarns.

A Spanish fox is made by untwisting a single yarn and laying it up the contrary way.

FRAP. To pass ropes round a sail to keep it from blowing loose. Also, to draw ropes round a vessel which is weakened, to keep her together.

FREE. A vessel is going *free,* when she has a fair wind and her yards braced in. A vessel is said to be *free,* when the water has been pumped out of her.

FRESHEN. To relieve a rope, by moving its place; as, to *freshen the nip* of a stay, is to shift it, so as to prevent its chafing through.

To freshen ballast, is to alter its position.

FRENCH-FAKE. To coil a rope with each fake outside of the other, beginning in the middle. If there are to be riding fakes, they begin outside and go in; and so on. This is called a *Flemish coil.*

FULL-AND-BY. Sailing close-hauled on a wind.

Full-and-by! The order given to the man at the helm to keep the sails full and at the same time close to the wind.

FURL. To roll a sail up snugly on a yard or boom, and secure it.

FUTTOCK-PLATES. Iron plates crossing the sides of the top-rim perpendicularly. The dead eyes of the topmast rigging are fitted to their upper ends, and the futtock-shrouds to their lower ends.

FUTTOCK-SHROUDS. Short shrouds, leading from the lower ends of the futtock-plates to a bend round the lower mast, just below the top.

FUTTOCK-STAFF. A short piece of wood or iron, seized across the upper part of the rigging, to which the catharpin legs are secured.

FUTTOCK-TIMBERS. (See PLATE III.) Those timbers between the floor and naval timbers, and the top-timbers. There are two—the *lower,* which is over the floor, and the *middle,* which is over the naval timber. The naval timber is sometimes called the *ground futtock.*

GAFF. A spar, to which the head of a fore-and-aft sail is bent. (See PLATE I.)

GAFF-TOPSAIL. A light sail set over a gaff, the foot being spread by it.

GAGE. The depth of water of a vessel. Also, her position as to another vessel, as having the *weather* or *lee gage.*

FOOT-ROPE

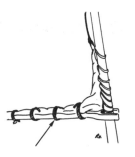

GASKETS

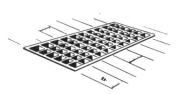

GRATING

GALLEY. The place where the cooking is done.

GALLOW-BITTS. A strong frame raised amidships, to support spare spars, &c., in port.

GAMMONING. (See PLATE I.) The lashing by which the bowsprit is secured to the cut-water.

GANG-CASKS. Small casks, used for bringing water on board in boats.

GANGWAY. (See PLATE I.) That part of a vessel's side, amidships, where people pass in and out of the vessel.

GANTLINE. (See GIRTLINE.)

GARBOARD-STREAK. (See PLATE III.) The range of planks next to the keel, one each side.

GARLAND. A large rope, strap or grommet, lashed to a spar when hoisting it on board.

GARNET. A purchase on the main stay, for hoisting cargo.

GASKETS. Ropes or pieces of plaited stuff, used to secure a sail to the yard or boom when it is furled. They are called a *bunt, quarter,* or *yard-arm gasket,* according to their position on the yard.

GIMBLET. To turn an anchor round by its stock. To turn anything round on its end.

GIRT. The situation of a vessel when her cables are too taut.

GIRTLINE. A rope rove through a single block aloft, making a whip purchase. Commonly used to hoist rigging by, in fitting it.

GIVE WAY! An order to men in a boat to pull with more force, or to begin pulling. The same as, *Lay out on your oars!* or, *Lay out!*

GLUT. A piece of canvas sewed into the centre of a sail, near the head. It has an eyelet-hole in the middle for the bunt-jigger or becket to go through.

GOB-LINE, or GAUB-LINE. A rope leading from the martingale inboard. The same as *back-rope.*

GOODGEON. (See GUDGEON.)

GOOSE-NECK. An iron ring fitted to the end of a yard or boom, for various purposes.

GOOSE-WINGED. The situation of a course when the buntlines and lee clew are hauled up, and the weather clew down.

GORES. The angles at one or both ends of such cloths as increase the breadth or depth of a sail.

GORING-CLOTHS. Pieces cut obliquely and put in to add to the breadth of a sail.

GRAFTING. A manner of covering a rope by weaving together yarns.

GRAINS. An iron, with four or more barbed points to it, used for striking small fish.

GRAPNEL. A small anchor, with several claws, used to secure boats.

GRAPPLING IRONS. Crooked irons, used to seize and hold fast another vessel.

GRATING. Open lattice work of wood. Used principally to cover hatches in good weather.

GREAVE. To clean a ship's bottom by burning.

GRIPE. The outside timber of the forefoot, under water, fastened to the lower stem-piece. (See PLATE III.) A vessel *gripes* when she tends to come up into the winds.

GRIPES. Bars of iron, with lanyards, rings, and clews, by which a large boat is lashed to the ring-bolts of the deck. Those for a quarter-boat are made of long strips of matting, going round her and set taut by a lanyard.

GROMMET. A ring formed of rope, by laying round a single strand.

GROUND TACKLE. General term for anchors, cables, warps, springs, &c.; everything used in securing a vessel at anchor.

GROUND-TIER. The lowest tier of casks in a vessel's hold.

GUESS-WARP, or GUESS-ROPE. A rope fastened to a vessel or wharf, and used to tow a boat by; or to haul it out to the swinging boom-end, when in port.

GUN-TACKLE PURCHASE. A purchase made by two single blocks.

GUNWALE. (Pronounced *gun-nel.*) The upper rail of a boat or vessel.

GUY. A rope attaching to anything to steady it, and bear it one way and another in hoisting.

GYBE. (Pronounced *jibe.*) To shift over the boom of a fore-and-aft sail.

HAIL. To speak or call to another vessel, or to men in a different part of a ship.

HALYARDS. Ropes or tackles used for hoisting and lowering yards, gaffs, and sails.

HAMMOCK. A piece of canvas, hung at each end, in which seamen sleep.

HAND. To *hand* a sail is to *furl* it.

Bear a hand: make haste.

Lend a hand: assist.

Hand-over-hand: hauling rapidly on a rope, by putting one hand before the other alternately.

HAND-LEAD. A small lead, used for sounding in rivers and harbours.

HANDSOMELY. Slowly, carefully. Used for an order, as, 'Lower handsomely!'

HANDSPIKE. A long wooden bar, used for heaving at the windlass.

HANDY BILLY. A watch-tackle.

HANKS. Rings or hoops of wood, rope, or iron, round a stay, and seized to the luff of a fore-and-aft sail.

HARPINGS. The fore part of the wales, which encompass the bows of a vessel, and are fastened to the stem. (See PLATE 3.)

HARPOON. A spear used for striking whales and other fish.

HATCH, or HATCHWAY. An opening in the deck to afford a passage up and down. The coverings over these openings are also called *hatches.*

Hatch-bar is an iron bar going across the hatches to keep them down.

HAUL. *Haul her wind,* said of a vessel when she comes up close upon the wind.

HAWSE. The situation of the cables before a vessel's stem when moored. Also the distance upon the water a little in advance of the stem; as, a vessel sails *athwart the hawse,* or anchors *in the hawse* of another.

Open hawse. When a vessel rides by two anchors, without any cross in her cables.

HAWSE-HOLE. The hole in the bows through which the cable runs.

HAWSE-PIECES. Timbers through which the hawse-holes are cut.

HAWSE-BLOCK. A block of wood fitted into a hawse-hole at sea.

HAWSER. A large rope used for various purposes, as warping, for a spring, &c.

HAWSER-LAID, or CABLE-LAID rope, is rope laid with nine strands against the sun.

HAZE A term for punishing a man by keeping him unnecessarily at work upon a disagreeable or difficult duty.

HEAD. The work at the prow of a vessel. If it is a carved figure, it is called a *figure-head;* if simple carved work, bending over and out, a *billet-head;* and if bending in, like the handle of a violin, a *fiddle-head.* Also, the upper end of a mast, called a *mast-head.* (See BY-THE-HEAD. See FAST.)

HEAD-LEDGES. Thwarting pieces that frame the hatchways.

HEAD-SAILS. A general name given to all sails that set forward of the fore-mast.

HEART. A block of wood in the shape of a heart, for stays to reeve through.

HEART-YARNS. The centre yarns of a strand.

HEAVE SHORT. To heave in on the cable until the vessel is nearly over her anchor.

HEAVE-TO. To put a vessel in the position of lying to. (See LIE-TO.)

HEAVE IN STAYS. To go about in tacking.

HEAVER. A short wooden bar, tapering at each end. Used as a purchase.

HEEL. The after part of the keel. Also the lower end of a mast or boom. Also the lower end of the stern post.

To heel, is to lie over on one side.

HEELING. The square part of the lower end of a mast, through which the fid-hole is made.

HELM. The machinery by which a vessel is steered, including the rudder, tiller, wheel, &c. Applied more particularly, perhaps, to the tiller.

HELM-PORT. The hole in the counter through which the rudderhead passes.

HELM-PORT TRANSOM. A piece of timber placed across the lower counter, inside at the height of the helm-port, and bolted through every timber, for the security of that port. (See PLATE III.)

HIGH AND DRY. The situation of a vessel when she is aground, above water mark.

HITCH. A peculiar manner of fastening ropes.

HOG. A flat, rough broom, used for scrubbing the bottom of a vessel.

HOGGED. The state of a vessel when by any strain she is made to droop at each end, bringing her centre up.

HOLD. The interior of a vessel where the cargo is stowed.

HOLD-WATER. To stop the progress of a boat by keeping the oar-blades in the water.

HOLY-STONE. A large stone, used for cleaning a ship's decks.

HOME. The sheets of a sail are said to be *home,* when the clews are hauled chock out to the sheave-holes. An anchor *comes home* when it is loosened from the ground, and is hove in toward the vessel.

HOOD. A covering for a companion hatch.

HOOD-ENDS, or HOODING-ENDS, or WHOODEN-ENDS. Those ends of the planks which fit into the rabbets of the stem or stern-post.

HOOK-AND-BUTT. The scarfing, or laying the ends of timbers over each other.

HORNS. The jaws of booms. Also the ends of cross-trees.

HORSE. (See FOOT-ROPE.)

HOUNDS. Those projections at the mast-head serving as shoulders for the top or trestle-trees to rest upon.

HOUSE. To *house* a mast, is to lower it about half its length, and secure it by lashing its heel to the mast below.

To house a gun, is to run it in clear of the port and secure it.

HOUSING, or HOUSE-LINE. (Pronounced *houze-lin.*) A small cord made of three small yarns, and used for seizings.

HULL. The body of a vessel. (See A-HULL.)

IN-AND-OUT. A term sometimes used for the scantline of the timbers, the moulding way, and particularly for those bolts that are driven into the hanging and lodging knees, through the sides, which are called *in-and-out bolts.*

INNER-POST. A piece brought on at the fore side of the main-post, and generally continued as high as the wing-transom, to seat the other transoms upon.

IRONS. A ship is said to be in *irons* when, in working, she will not cast one way or the other.

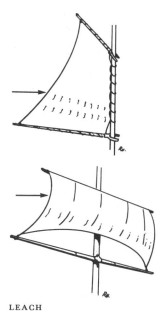

JACK. A common term for the *jack-cross-trees*. (See UNION.)

JACK-BLOCK. A block used in sending topgallant masts up and down.

JACK-CROSS-TREES. (See PLATE I.) Iron cross-trees at the head of long topgallant masts.

JACK-STAFF. A short staff, raised at the bowsprit cap, upon which the Union Jack is hoisted.

JACK-STAYS. Ropes stretched taut along a yard to bend the head of the sail to. Also long strips of wood or iron, used now for the same purpose.

JACK-SCREW. A purchase, used for stowing cotton.

JACOB'S LADDER. A ladder made of rope, with wooden steps.

JAWS. The inner ends of booms or gaffs, hollowed in.

JEERS. Tackles for hoisting the lower yards.

JEWEL-BLOCKS. Single blocks at the yard-arms, through which the studdingsail halyards lead.

JIB. (See PLATE II.) A triangular sail, set on a stay, forward.

Flying-jib sets outside of the jib; and the *jib-o'-jib* outside of that.

JIB-BOOM. (See PLATE I.) The boom rigged out beyond the bowsprit, to which the tack of the jib is lashed.

JIGGER. A small tackle used about decks or aloft.

JOLLY-BOAT. A small boat, usually hoisted at the stern.

JUNK. Condemned rope, cut up and used for making mats, swabs, oakum, &c.

JURY-MAST. A temporary mast, rigged at sea, in place of one lost.

LEACH

KECKLING. Old rope wound round cables, to keep them from chafing. (See ROUNDING.)

KEDGE. A small anchor, with an iron stock, used for warping.

To kedge, is to warp a vessel ahead by a kedge and hawser.

KEEL. (See PLATE III.) The lowest and principal timber of a vessel, running fore-and-aft its whole length, and supporting the whole frame. It is composed of several pieces, placed lengthwise, and scarfed and bolted together. (See FALSE KEEL.)

KEEL-HAUL. To haul a man under a vessel's bottom, by ropes at the yard-arms on each side. Formerly practised as a punishment in ships of war.

KEELSON. (See PLATE III.) A timber placed over the keel on the floor timbers, and running parallel with it.

KENTLEDGE. Pig-iron ballast, laid each side of the keelson.

KEVEL, or CAVIL. A strong piece of wood, bolted to some timber or stanchion, used for belaying large ropes to.

KEVEL-HEADS. Timber-heads used as kevels.

KINK. A twist in a rope.

KNEES. (See PLATE III.) Crooked pieces of timber, having two arms, used to connect the beams of a vessel with her timbers. (See DAGGER.)

Lodging-knees, are placed horizontally, having one arm bolted to a beam, and the other across two of the timbers.

Knee of the head, is placed forward of the stem, and supports the figure-head.

KNIGHT-HEADS, or BOLLARD-TIMBERS. The timbers next the stem on each side, and continued high enough to form a support for the bowsprit. (See PLATE III.)

KNITTLES, or NETTLES. The halves of two adjoining yarns in a rope, twisted up together, for pointing or grafting. Also, small line used for seizings and for hammock-clews.

KNOCK-OFF! An order to leave off work.

KNOT. A division on the log-line, answering to a mile of distance.

LEAD

LABOUR. A vessel is said to labour when she rolls or pitches heavily.

LACING. Rope used to lash a sail to a gaff, or a bonnet to a sail. Also, a piece of compass or knee timber, fayed to the back of the figure-head and the knee of the head, and bolted to each.

LAND-FALL. The making land after being at sea.

A good land-fall, is when a vessel makes the land as intended.

LAND HO! The cry used when land is first seen.

LANYARDS. Ropes rove through dead-eyes for setting up rigging. Also, a rope made fast to anything to secure it, or as a handle, is called a *lanyard.*

LARBOARD. The left side of a vessel, looking forward.

LARBOWLINES. The familiar term for the men in the larboard watch.

LARGE. A vessel is said to be going *large,* when she has the wind free.

LATCHINGS. Loops on the head-rope of a bonnet, by which it is laced to the foot of the sail.

LAUNCH. A large boat. The LONG-BOAT.

LEE-BOARD

LAUNCH HO! High enough!

LAY. To come or to go; as, Lay aloft! Lay forward! Lay aft! Also the direction in which the strands of a rope are twisted; as, from left to right, or from right to left.

LEACH. The border or edge of a sail, at the sides.

LEACHLINE. A rope used for hauling up the leach of a sail.

LEAD. A piece of lead, in the shape of a cone or pyramid, with a small hole at the base, and a line attached to the upper end, used for sounding. (See HAND-LEAD, DEEP-SEA-LEAD.)

LEADING-WIND. A fair wind. More particularly applied to a wind abeam or quartering.

LEAK. A hole or breach in a vessel, at which the water comes in.

LEDGES. Small pieces of timber placed athwart-ships under the decks of a vessel, between the beams.

LEE. The side opposite to that from which the wind blows; as if a vessel has the wind on her starboard side, that will be the *weather,* and the larboard will be the *lee* side.

A lee shore is the shore upon which the wind is blowing.

Under the lee of anything, is when you have that between you and the wind.

By the lee. The situation of a vessel going free, when she has fallen off so much as to bring the wind round her stern, and to take her sails aback on the other side.

LEE-BOARD. A board fitted to the lee side of flat-bottomed boats, to prevent their drifting to leeward.

LEE-GAGE. (See GAGE.)

LEEWAY. What a vessel loses by drifting to leeward. When sailing close-hauled with all sail set, a vessel should make no leeway. If the topgallant sails are furled, it is customary to allow one point; under close-reefed topsails, two points; when under one close-reefed sail, four or five points.

LEEFANGE. An iron bar, upon which the sheets of fore-and-aft sails traverse. Also, a rope rove through the cringle of a sail which has a bonnet to it, for hauling in, so as to lace on the bonnet. Not much used.

LEEWARD. (Pronounced *lu-ard.*) The lee side. In a direction opposite to that from which the wind blows, which is called *windward.* The opposite of *lee* is *weather,* and of *leeward* is *windward;* the first two being adjectives.

LIE-TO, is to stop the progress of a vessel at sea, either by counter-bracing the yards, or by reducing sail so that she will make little or no headway, but will merely come to and fall off by the counteraction of the sails and helm.

LIFE-LINES. Ropes carried along yards, booms, &c., or at any part of the vessel, for men to hold on by.

LIFT. A rope or tackle, going from the yard-arms to the mast-head, to support and move the yard. Also, a term applied to the sails when the wind strikes them on the leaches and raises them slightly.

LIGHT. To move or lift anything along; as, to 'Light out to windward!' that is, haul the sail over to windward. The *light sails* are all above the topsails, also the studdingsails and flying jib.

LIGHTER. A large boat, used in loading and unloading vessels.

LIMBERS, or LIMBER-HOLES. Holes cut in the lower part of the floor-timbers, next the keelson, forming a passage for the water fore-and-aft.

Limber-boards are placed over the limbers, and are moveable.

Limber-rope. A rope rove fore-and-aft through the limbers to clear them if necessary.

Limber-streak. The streak of foot-waling nearest the keelson.

LIST. The inclination of a vessel to one side; as, a *list* to port, or a *list* to starboard.

LIZARD. A piece of rope, sometimes with two legs, and one or more iron thimbles spliced into it. It is used for various purposes. One with two legs, and a thimble to each, is often made fast to the topsail tye, for the buntlines to reeve through. A single one is sometimes used on the swinging-boom topping-lift.

LOCKER. A chest or box to stow anything away in.

Chain-locker. Where the chain cables are kept.

Boatswain's locker. Where tools and small stuff for working upon rigging are kept.

LOG, or LOG-BOOK. A journal kept by the chief officer, in which the situation of the vessel, winds, weather, courses, distances, and everything of importance that occurs, is noted down.

Log. A line with a piece of board, called the *log-ship,* attached to it, wound upon a reel, and used for ascertaining the ship's rate of sailing.

LONG-BOAT. The largest boat in a merchant-vessel. When at sea, it is carried between the fore and main masts.

LONGERS. The longest casks, stowed next the keelson.

LONG-TIMBERS. Timbers in the cant-bodies, reaching from the dead-wood to the head of the second futtock.

LOOF. That part of a vessel where the planks begin to bend as they approach the stern.

MARLING-HITCH

MARLING-SPIKE

MARTINGALE (DOLPHIN-STRIKER)

BOBSTAYS

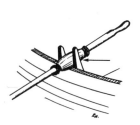

MUFFLE

LOOM. That part of an oar which is within the row-lock. Also, to appear above the surface of the water; to appear larger than nature, as in a fog.

LUBBER'S HOLE. A hole in the top, next the mast.

LUFF. To put the helm so as to bring the ship up nearer to the wind.

Spring-a-luff! Keep your luff! &c. Orders to luff. Also, the roundest part of a vessel's bow. Also the forward leach of fore-and-aft sails.

LUFF-TACKLE. A purchase composed of a double and single block.

Luff-upon-Luff. A luff-tackle applied to the fall of another.

LUGGER. A small vessel carrying lug-sails.

Lug-sail. A sail used in boats and small vessels, bent to a yard which hangs obliquely to the mast.

LURCH. The sudden rolling of a vessel to one side.

LYING-TO. (See LIE-TO.)

MADE. A *made mast* or *block* is one composed of different pieces. A ship's lower mast is a made spar, her topmast is a whole spar.

MALL, or MAUL. (Pronounced *mawl*.) A heavy iron hammer used in driving bolts. (See TOP-MAUL.)

MALLET. A small maul, made of wood; as, *caulking-mallet;* also, *serving-mallet,* used in putting service on a rope.

MANGER. A coaming just within the hawse-hole.

MAN-ROPES. Ropes used in going up and down a vessel's side.

MARL. To wind or twist a small line or rope round another.

MARLINE. (Pronounced *mar-lin.*) Small two-stranded stuff, used for marling. A finer kind of spunyarn.

MARLING-HITCH. A kind of hitch used in marling.

MARLINGSPIKE. An iron pin, sharpened at one end, and having a hole in the other for a lanyard. Used both as a fid and a heaver.

MARRY. To join ropes together by a worming over both.

MARTINGALE. A short, perpendicular spar, under the bowsprit-end, used for guying down the head-stays. (See DOLPHIN-STRIKER.)

MAST. A spar set upright from the deck, to support rigging, yards, and sails. Masts are whole or *made.*

MAT. Made of strands of old rope, and used to prevent chafing.

MATE. An officer under the master.

MAUL. (See MALL.)

MEND. *To mend service,* is to add more to it.

MESHES. The places between the lines of a netting.

MESS. Any number of men who eat or lodge together.

MESSENGER. A rope used for heaving in a cable by the capstan.

MIDSHIPS. The timbers at the broadest part of the vessel. (See AMIDSHIPS.)

MISS-STAYS. To fail of going about from one tack to another.

MIZEN-MAST. The aftermost mast of a ship. (See PLATE I.) The spanker is sometimes called the *mizen.*

MONKEY BLOCK. A small single block strapped with a swivel.

MOON-SAIL. A small sail sometimes carried in light winds, above a skysail.

MOOR. To secure by two anchors.

MORTICE. A *morticed block* is one made out of a whole block of wood with a hole cut in it for the sheave; in distinction from a *made block.*

MOULDS. The patterns by which the frames of a vessel are worked out.

MOUSE. To put turns of rope yarn or spun yarn round the end of a hook and its standing part, when it is hooked to anything, so as to prevent its slipping out.

MOUSING. A knot or puddening, made of yarns, and placed on the outside of a rope.

MUFFLE. Oars are muffled by putting mats or canvas round their looms in the row-locks.

MUNIONS. The pieces that separate the lights in the galleries.

NAVAL HOODS, OR HAWSE BOLSTERS. Plank above and below the hawse-holes.

NEAP TIDES. Low tides, coming at the middle of the moon's second and fourth quarters. (See SPRING TIDES.)

NEAPED, OR BENEAPED. The situation of a vessel when she is aground at the height of the spring tides.

NEAR. Close to wind. 'Near!' the order to the helmsman when he is too near the wind.

NETTING. Network or rope or small lines. Used for stowing away sails or hammocks.

NETTLES. (See KNITTLES.)

NINEPIN BLOCK. A block in the form of a ninepin, used for a *fair leader* in the rail.

NIP. A short turn in a rope.

NIPPERS. A number of yarns marled together, used to secure a cable to the messenger.

NOCK. The forward upper end of a sail that sets with a boom.

NUN-BUOY. A buoy tapering at each end.

NUT. Projections on each side of the shank of an anchor, to secure the stock to its place.

OAKUM. Stuff made by picking rope-yarns to pieces. Used for caulking, and other purposes.

OAR. A long wooden instrument with a flat blade at one end, used for propelling boats.

OFF-AND-ON. To stand on different tacks towards and from the land.

OFFING. Distance from the shore.

ORLOP. The deck beneath the lower deck of a ship of the line on which the cables are stowed.

OUT-HAUL. A rope used for hauling out the clew of a boom sail.

OUT-RIGGER. A spar rigged out to windward from the tops or cross-trees, to spread the breast-backstays.

OVERHAUL. To *overhaul a tackle,* is to let go the fall and pull on the leading parts so as to separate the blocks.

To overhaul a rope, is generally to pull a part through a block so as to make slack.

To overhaul rigging, is to examine it.

OVER-RAKE. Said of heavy seas which come over a vessel's head when she is at anchor, head to the sea.

PAINTER. A rope attached to the bows of a boat, used for making her fast.

PALM. A piece of leather fitted over the hand, with an iron for the head of a needle to press against in sewing upon canvas. Also, the fluke of an anchor.

PANCH. (See PAUNCH.)

PARBUCKLE. To hoist or lower a spar or cask by single ropes passed round it.

PARCEL. To wind tarred canvas (called *parcelling*) round a rope.

PARCELLING. (See PARCEL.)

PARLIAMENT-HEEL. The situation of a vessel when she is careened.

PARRAL. The rope by which a yard is confined to a mast at its centre.

PART. To break a rope.

PARTNERS. A framework of short timber fitted to the hole in a deck, to receive the heel of a mast or pump, &c.

PAZAREE. A rope attached to the clew of the foresail and rove through a block on the swinging boom. Used for guying the clews out when before the wind.

PAUNCH MAT. A thick mat, placed at the slings of a yard or elsewhere.

PAWL. A short bar of iron, which prevents the capstan or windlass from turning back.

To pawl, is to drop a pawl and secure the windlass or capstan.

PAY-OFF. When a vessel's head falls off from the wind.

To pay, to cover over with tar or pitch.

To pay out. To slack up on a cable and let it run out.

PEAK. The upper outer corner of a gaff-sail.

PEAK. (See A-PEAK.)

A *stay-peak* is when the cable and forestay form a line.

A *short stay-peak* is when the cable is too much in to form this line.

PENDANT, OR PENNANT. A long narrow piece of bunting, carried at the mast-head.

Broad pennant, is a swallow-tailed piece, carried in the same way, in a commodore's vessel.

Pennant. A rope to which a purchase is hooked. A long strap fitted at one end to a yard or mast-head, with a hook or block at the other end, for a brace to reeve through, or to hook a tackle to.

PILLOW. A block which supports the inner end of the bowsprit.

PIN. The axis on which a sheave turns. Also, a short piece of wood or iron to belay ropes to.

PINK-STERN. A high, narrow stern.

PINNACE. A boat, in size between the launch and a cutter.

PINTLE. A metal bolt used for hanging a rudder.

PITCH. A resin taken from pine, and used for filling up the seams of a vessel.

PLANKS. Thick, strong boards, used for covering the sides and decks of vessels.

PLAT. A braid of foxes. (See FOX.)

PLATE. (See CHAIN-PLATE.)

PLUG. A piece of wood, fitted into a hole in a vessel or boat, so as to let in or keep out water.

POINT. To take the end of a rope and work it over with knittles. (See REEF-POINTS.)

POLE. Applied to the highest mast of a ship, usually painted; as, *sky-sail pole.*

POOP. A deck raised over the after part of the spar deck. A vessel is *pooped* when the sea breaks over her stern.

POPPETS. Perpendicular pieces of timber fixed to the fore-and-aft part of the bilge-ways in launching.

PORT. Used instead of larboard.

To port the helm, is to put it to the larboard.

PORT, OR PORT-HOLE. Holes in the side of a vessel, to point cannon out of. (See BRIDLE.)

NUN-BUOY

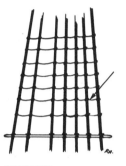

RATLINES

PORTOISE. The gunwale. The yards are *a-portoise* when they rest on the gunwale.

PORT-SILLS. (See SILLS.)

PREVENTER. An additional rope or spar, used as a support.

PRICK. A quantity of spunyarn or rope laid close up together.

PRICKER. A small marlinspike, used in sail-making. It generally has a wooden handle.

PUDDENING. A quantity of yarns, matting, or oakum, used to prevent chafing.

PUMP-BRAKE. The handle to the pump.

PURCHASE. A mechanical power which increases the force applied.

To purchase, is to raise by a purchase.

QUARTER. The part of a vessel's side between the after part of the main chains and the stern. The *quarter* of a yard is between the slings and the yard-arm.

The wind is said to be *quartering*, when it blows in a line between that of the keel and the beam, and abaft the latter.

QUARTER-BLOCK. A block fitted under the quarters of a yard on each side the slings, for the clewlines and sheets to reeve through.

QUARTER-DECK. That part of the upper deck abaft the main-mast.

QUARTER-MASTER. A petty officer in a man-of-war, who attends the helm and binnacle at sea, and watches for signals, &c., when in port.

QUICK-WORK. That part of a vessel's side which is above the chain-wales and decks. So called in ship-building.

QUILTING. A coating about a vessel, outside, formed of ropes woven together.

QUOIN. A wooden wedge for the breech of a gun to rest upon.

RACE. A strong rippling tide.

RACK. To seize two ropes together, with cross-turns. Also, a *fair-leader* for running rigging.

RACK-BLOCK. A course of blocks made from one piece of wood, for fair-leaders.

RAKE. The inclination of a mast from the perpendicular.

RAMLINE. A line used in mast-making to get a straight middle line on a spar.

RANGE OF CABLE. A quantity of cable, more or less, placed in order for letting go the anchor or paying out.

RATLINES. (Pronounced *rat-lins*.) Lines running across the shrouds, horizontally, like the rounds of a ladder, and used to step upon in going aloft.

RATTLE DOWN RIGGING. To put ratlines upon rigging. It is still called rattling *down*, though they are now rattled *up*; beginning at the lowest.

RAZEE. A vessel of war which has one deck cut down.

REEF. To reduce a sail by taking in upon its head, if a square sail, and its foot, if a fore-and-aft sail.

REEF-BAND. A band of stout canvas sewed on the sail across, with points in it, and earings at each end for reefing.

A *reef* is all of the sail that is comprehended between the head of the sail and the first reef-band, or between two reef-bands.

REEF-TACKLE. A tackle used to haul the middle of each leach up toward the yard, so that the sail may be easily reefed.

REEVE. To pass the end of a rope through a block, or any aperture.

RELIEVING TACKLE. A tackle hooked to the tiller in a gale of wind, to steer by, in case anything should happen to the wheel or tiller-ropes.

RENDER. To pass a rope through a place. A rope is said to *render* or not, according as it goes freely through any place.

RIB-BANDS. Long, narrow, flexible pieces of timber nailed to the outside of the ribs, so as to encompass the vessel lengthwise.

RIBS. A figurative term for a vessel's timbers.

RIDE AT ANCHOR. To lie at anchor. Also, to bend or bear down by main strength and weight; as, to ride down the main tack.

RIDERS. Interior timbers placed occasionally opposite the principal ones, to which they are bolted, reaching from the keelson to the beams of the lower deck. Also, casks forming the second tier in a vessel's hold.

RIGGING. The general term for all the ropes of a vessel. (See RUNNING, STANDING.) Also the common term for the shrouds with their ratlines; as, the main *rigging, mizen rigging,* &c.

RIGHT. To *right* the helm, is to put it amidships.

RIM. The edge of a top.

RING. The iron ring at the upper end of an anchor, to which the cable is bent.

RING-BOLT. An eye-bolt with a ring through the eye. (See EYE-BOLT.)

RING-TAIL. A small sail, shaped like a jib, set abaft the spanker in light winds.

ROACH. A curve in the foot of a square sail, by which the clews are brought below the middle of the foot. The *roach* of a fore-and-aft sail is in its forward leach.

ROAD, or ROADSTEAD. An anchorage at some distance from the shore.

ROBANDS. (See ROPE-BANDS.)

ROLLING-TACKLE. Tackles used to steady the yards in a heavy sea.

ROMBOWLINE. Condemned canvas, rope, &c.

ROPE-BANDS, or ROBANDS. Small pieces of two or three yarn, spunyarn, or marline, used to confine the head of the sail to the yard or gaff.

ROPE-YARN. A thread of hemp, or other stuff, of which a rope is made.

ROUGH-TREE. An unfinished spar.

ROUND IN. To haul in on a rope, especially a weather-brace.

ROUND UP. To haul up on a tackle.

ROUNDING. A service of rope, hove round a spar or larger rope.

ROWLOCKS, or ROLLOCKS. Places cut in the gunwale of a boat for the oar to rest in while pulling.

ROYAL. A light sail next above a topgallant sail. (See PLATE II.)

ROYAL YARD. The yard from which the royal is set. The fourth from the deck. (See PLATE I.)

RUBBER. A small instrument used to rub down or flatten down the seams of a sail in sail-making.

RUDDER. The machine by which a vessel or boat is steered.

RUN. The after part of a vessel's bottom, which rises and narrows in approaching the stern-post.

By the run. To let go *by the run,* is to let go altogether instead of slacking off.

RUNG-HEADS. The upper ends of the floor timbers.

RUNNER. A rope used to increase the power of a tackle. It is rove through a single block which you wish to bring down, and a tackle is hooked to each end, or to one end, the other being made fast.

RUNNING RIGGING. The ropes that reeve through blocks, and are pulled and hauled, such as braces, halyards, &c.; in opposition to the *standing rigging,* the ends of which are securely seized, such as stays, shrouds, &c.

SADDLES. Pieces of wood hollowed out to fit on the yards, to which they are nailed, having a hollow in the upper part for the boom to rest in.

SAG. To *sag to leeward,* is to drift off bodily to leeward.

SAILS are of two kinds: *square sails,* which hang from yards, their foot lying across the line of the keel, as the courses, topsails, &c.; and *fore-and-aft sails,* which set upon gaffs, or on stays, their foot running with the line of the keel, as jib spanker, &c.

SAIL HO! The cry used when a sail is first discovered at sea.

SAVE-ALL. A small sail sometimes set under the foot of a lower studdingsail. (See WATER SAIL.)

SCANTLING. A term applied to any piece of timber, with regard to its breadth and thickness, when reduced to the standard size.

SCARF. To join two pieces of timber at their ends by shaving them down and placing them over-lapping.

SCHOONER. (See PLATE IV.) A small vessel with two masts and no tops.

A *fore-and-aft schooner* has only fore-and-aft sails.

A *topsail schooner* carries a square fore topsail, and frequently, also, topgallant sail and royal. There are some schooners with three masts. They also have no tops.

A *maintopsail schooner* is one that carries square topsails, fore and aft.

SCORE. A groove in a block or dead-eye.

SCOTCHMAN. A large batten placed over the turnings-in of rigging. (See BATTEN.)

SCRAPER. A small, triangular iron instrument, with a handle fitted to its centre, and used for scraping decks and masts.

SCROWL. A piece of timber bolted to the knees of the head, in place of a figure-head.

SCUD. To drive before a gale, with no sail, or only enough to keep the vessel ahead of the sea. Also, low, thin clouds that fly swiftly before the wind.

SCULL. A short oar.

To scull, is to impel a boat by one oar at the stern.

SCUPPERS. Holes cut in the water-ways for the water to run from the decks.

SCUTTLE. A hole cut in a vessel's deck, as, a hatchway. Also, a hole cut in any part of a vessel. *To scuttle,* is to cut or bore holes in a vessel to make her sink.

SCUTTLE-BUTT. (See BUTT.)

SEAMS. The intervals between planks in a vessel's deck or side.

SEIZE. To fasten ropes together by turns of small stuff.

SEIZINGS. The fastenings of ropes that are seized together.

SELVAGEE. A skein of rope-yarns or spun yarn, marled together. Used as a neat strap.

SEND. When a ship's head or stern pitches suddenly and violently into the trough of the sea.

SENNIT, or SINNIT. A braid, formed by plaiting rope-yarns or spunyarn together. Straw, plaited in the same way for hats, is called sennit.

SERVE. To wind small stuff, as rope-yarns, spun-yarn, &c., round a rope, to keep it from

TAFRAIL

chafing. It is wound and hove round taut by a serving-board or mallet.

SERVICE, is the stuff so wound round.

SET. To *set up rigging*, is to tauten it by tackles. The seizings are then put on afresh.

SHACKLES. Links in a chain cable which are fitted with a moveable bolt, so that the chain can be separated.

SHAKES. The staves of hogsheads taken apart.

SHANK. The main piece in an anchor, at one end of which the stock is made fast, and at the other the arms.

SHANK-PAINTER. A strong rope by which the lower part of the shank of an anchor is secured to the ship's side.

SHARP UP. Said of yards when braced as near fore-and-aft as possible.

SHEATHING. A casing or covering on a vessel's bottom.

SHEARS. Two or more spars, raised at angles and lashed together near their upper ends, used for taking in masts.

SHEAR HULK. An old vessel fitted with shears, &c., and used for taking out and putting in the masts of other vessels.

SHEAVE. The wheel in a block upon which the rope works.

Sheave-hole, the place cut in a block for the rope to reeve through.

SHEEP-SHANK. A kind of hitch or bend, used to shorten a rope temporarily.

SHEER, or SHEER-STRAKE. The line of plank on a vessel's side, running fore-and-aft under the gunwhale. Also, a vessel's position when riding by a single anchor.

SHEET. A rope used in setting a sail, to keep the clew down to its place. With square sails, the sheets run through each yard-arm. With boom sails, they haul the boom over one way and another. They keep down the inner clew of a studdingsail and the after clew of a jib. (See HOME.)

SHEET ANCHOR. A vessel's largest anchor: not carried at the bow.

SHELL. The case of a block.

SHINGLE. (See BALLAST.)

SHIP. A vessel with three masts, with tops and yards to each. (See PLATE IV.) To enter on board a vessel. To fix anything in its place.

SHIVER. To shake the wind out of a sail by bracing it so that the wind strikes upon the leach.

SHOE. A piece of wood used for the bill of an anchor to rest upon, to save the vessel's side. Also, for the heels of shears, &c.

SHOE-BLOCK. A block with two sheaves, one above the other, the one horizontal and the other perpendicular.

SHORE. A prop or stanchion, placed under a beam. To *shore,* to prop up.

SHROUDS. A set of ropes reaching from the mast-heads to the vessel's sides, to support the masts.

SILLS. Pieces of timber put in horizontally between the frames to form and secure any opening; as, for ports.

SISTER BLOCK. A long piece of wood with two sheaves in it, one above the other, with a score between them for a seizing, and a groove around the block, lengthwise.

SKIDS. Pieces of timber placed up and down a vessel's side, to bear any articles off clear that are hoisted in.

SKIN. The part of a sail which is outside and covers the rest when it is furled. Also, familiarly, the sides of the hold; as, an article is said to be stowed *next the skin.*

SKYSAIL. A light sail next above the royal. (See PLATE II.)

SKY-SCRAPER. A name given to a skysail when it is triangular.

SLABLINE. A small line used to haul up the foot of a course.

SLACK. The part of a rope or sail that hangs down loose.

Slack in stays, said of a vessel when she works slowly in tacking.

SLEEPERS. The knees that connect the transoms to the after timbers of the ship's quarter.

SLING. To set a cask, spar, gun, or other article, in ropes, so as to put on a tackle and hoist or lower it.

SLINGS. The ropes used for securing the centre of a yard to the mast.

Yard-slings are now made of iron. Also, a large rope fitted so as to go round any article which is to be hoisted or lowered.

SLIP. To let a cable go and stand out to sea.

SLIP-ROPE. A rope bent to the cable just outside the hawse-hole, and brought in on the weather quarter, for slipping.

SLOOP. A small vessel with one mast. (See PLATE IV.)

SLOOP OF WAR. A vessel of any rig, commanded by a commander in the navy.

SLUE. To turn anything round or over.

SMALL STUFF. The term for spunyarn, marline, and the smallest kinds of rope, such as ratline-stuff, &c.

SNAKE. To pass small stuff across a seizing, with marling hitches at the outer turns.

SNATCH-BLOCK. A single block, with an opening in its side below the sheave, or at the bottom to receive the bight of a rope.

SNOTTER. A rope going over a yard-arm, with an eye, used to bend a tripping-line to in sending down topgallant and royal yards in vessels of war.

SNOW. A kind of brig, formerly used.

SNUB. To check a rope suddenly.

SNYING. A term for a circular plank, edgewise, to work in the bows of a vessel.

SO! An order to 'vast hauling upon anything when it has come to its right position.

SOLE. A piece of timber fastened to the foot of the rudder, to make it level with the false keel.

SOUND. To get the depth of water by a lead and line. The pumps are *sounded* by an iron *sounding rod,* marked with a scale of feet and inches.

SPAN. A rope with both ends made fast, for a purchase to be hooked to its bight.

SPANKER. The after sail of a ship or bark. It is a fore-and-aft sail, setting with a boom and gaff. (See PLATE II.)

SPAR. The general term for all masts, yards, booms, gaffs, &c.

SPELL. The common term for a portion of time given to any work.

To spell, is to relieve another at his work.

Spell ho! An exclamation used as an order or request to be relieved at work by another.

SPENCER. A fore-and-aft sail, set with a gaff and no boom, and hoisting from a small mast called a *spencer-mast,* just abaft the fore and main masts. (See PLATES II and IV.)

SPILL. To shake the wind out of a sail by bracing it so that the wind may strike its leach and shiver it.

SPILLING LINE. A rope used for spilling a sail. Rove in bad weather.

SPINDLE. An iron pin upon which the capstan moves. Also, a piece of timber forming the diameter of a made mast. Also, any long pin or bar upon which anything revolves.

SPIRKETING. The planks from the water-ways to the port-sills.

SPLICE. To join two ropes together by interweaving their strands.

SPOON-DRIFT. Water swept from the tops of the waves by the violence of the wind in a tempest, and driven along before it, covering the surface of the sea.

SPRAY. An occasional sprinkling dashed from the top of a wave by the wind, or by striking an object.

SPRING. To crack or split a mast.

To spring a leak, is to begin to leak.

To spring a luff, is to force a vessel close to the wind, in sailing.

SPRING-STAY. A preventer-stay, to assist the regular one. (See STAY.)

SPRING TIDES. The highest and lowest course of tides, occurring every new and full moon.

SPRIT. A small boom or gaff, used with some sails in small boats. The lower end rests in a becket or snotter by the foot of the mast, and the other end spreads and raises the outer upper corner of the sail, crossing it diagonally. A sail so rigged in a boat is called a *sprit-sail.*

SPRIT-SAIL YARD. (See PLATE I.) A yard lashed across the bow-sprit or knight-heads, and used to spread the guys of the jib and flying jib-boom. There was formerly a sail bent to it called a *sprit-sail.*

SPUNYARN. A cord formed by twisting together two or three rope-yarns.

SPURLING-LINE. A line communicating between the tiller and tell-tale.

SPURS. Pieces of timber fixed on the bilge-ways, their upper ends being bolted to the vessel's sides above the water. Also, curved pieces of timber, serving as half beams, to support the decks where whole beams cannot be placed.

SPUR-SHOES. Large pieces of timber that come abaft the pump-well.

SQUARE. Yards are *squared* when they are horizontal and at right angles with the keel. squaring by the lifts makes them horizontal; and by the braces, makes them at right angles with the vessel's line. Also, the proper term for the length of yards. A vessel has square yards when her yards are unusually long. A sail is said to be very *square* in the head when it is long on the head.

To square a yard, in working a ship, means to bring it in square by the braces.

SQUARE-SAIL. A temporary sail set at the fore-mast of a schooner or sloop when going before the wind. (See SAIL.)

STABBER. A PRICKER.

STAFF. A pole or mast used to hoist flags upon.

STANCHIONS. (See PLATE III.) Upright posts of wood or iron, placed so as to support the beams of a vessel. Also, upright pieces of timber, placed at intervals along the sides of a vessel, to support the bulwarks and rail, and reaching down to the bends, by the side of the timbers, to which they are bolted. Also, any fixed upright support; as to an awning, or for the man-ropes.

STAND BY! An order to be prepared.

STANDARD. An inverted knee, placed above the deck, instead of beneath it; as, bitt-standard, &c.

STANDING. The *standing part* of a rope is that which is fast, in opposition to the part that

248

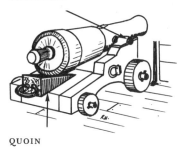

TRUNNIONS

QUOIN

is hauled upon; or the main part, in opposition to the end.

The *standing part* of a tackle is that part which is made fast to the blocks, and between that and the next sheave, in opposition to the hauling and leading parts.

STANDING RIGGING. That part of a vessel's rigging which is made fast and not hauled upon. (See RUNNING.)

STARBOARD. The right side of a vessel, looking forward.

STARBOWLINES. The familiar term for the men in the starboard watch.

START. To *start a cask*, is to open it.

STAY. To tack a vessel, or put her about, so that the wind, from being on one side, is brought upon the other, round the vessel's head. (See TACK, WEAR.)

To stay a mast, is to incline it forward or aft, or to one side or the other, by the stays and backstays. Thus, a mast is said to be *stayed* too much forward or aft, or too much to port, &c.

STAYS. Large ropes, used to support masts, and leading from the head of some mast down to some other mast, or to some part of the vessel. Those which lead forward are called *fore-and-aft stays;* and those which lead down to the vessel's sides, *backstays.* (See BACK-STAYS.)

In stays, or *hove in stays*, the situation of a vessel when she is *staying*, or going about from one tack to the other.

STAYSAIL. A sail which hoists upon a stay.

STEADY! An order to keep the helm as it is.

STEERAGE. That part of the between-decks which is just forward of the cabin.

STEEVES. A bowsprit *steeves* more or less, according as it is raised more or less from the horizontal.

The *steeve* is the angle it makes with the horizon. Also, a long heavy spar, with a place to fit a block at one end, and used in stowing certain kinds of cargo, which need be driven in close.

STEM. (See PLATE III.) A piece of timber reaching from the forward end to the keel, to which is is scarfed, up to the bowsprit, and to which the two sides of the vessel are united.

STEMSON. A piece of compass timber, fixed on the after part of the apron inside. The lower end is scarfed to the keelson, and receives the scarf of the stem, through which it is bolted.

STEP. A block of wood secured to the keel, into which the heel of the mast is placed.

To step a mast, is to put it in its step.

STERN. (See PLATE III.) The after end of a vessel. (See BY THE STERN.)

STERN-BOARD. The motion of a vessel when going stern foremost.

STERN-FRAME. The frame composed of the stern-post transom and the fashion-pieces.

STERN-POST. (See PLATE III.) The aftermost timber in a ship, reaching from the after end of the keel to the deck. The stem and stern-post are the two extremes of a vessel's frame.

Inner stern-post. A post on the inside, corresponding to the *stern-post.*

STERN-SHEETS. The after part of a boat, abaft the rowers, where the passengers sit.

STIFF. The quality of a vessel which enables it to carry a great deal of sail without lying over much on her side. The opposite to *crank.*

STIRRUPS. Ropes with thimbles at their ends, through which the foot-ropes are rove, and by which they are kept up towards the yards.

STOCK. A beam of wood, or a bar of iron, secured to the upper end of the shank of an anchor, at right angles with the arms. An iron stock usually goes with the key, and unships.

STOCKS. The frame upon which a vessel is built.

STOOLS. Small channels for the dead eyes of the backstays.

STOPPER. A stout rope with a knot at one end and sometimes a hook at the other, used for various purposes about decks; as, making fast a cable, so as to overhaul. (See CAT STOPPER, DECK STOPPER.)

STOPPER BOLTS. Ring-bolts to which the deck stoppers are secured.

STOP. A fastening of small stuff. Also, small projections on the outside of the cheeks of a lower mast, at the upper parts of the hounds.

STRAND. A number of rope-yarns twisted together. Three, four, or nine strands twisted together form a rope.

A rope is *stranded* when one of its strands is parted or broken by chafing or by a strain.

A vessel is *stranded* when she is driven on shore.

STRAP. A piece of rope spliced round a block to keep its parts well together. Some blocks have iron straps, in which case they are called *iron-bound.*

STREAK, or STRAKE. A range of planks running fore and aft on a vessel's side.

STREAM. The *stream anchor* is one used for warping, &c., and sometimes as a lighter anchor to moor by, with a hawser. It is smaller than the *bowers*, and larger than the *kedges.*

To stream a buoy, is to drop it into the water.

STRETCHERS. Pieces of wood placed across a boat's bottom, inside, for the oarsmen to place their feet against, in rowing. Also, cross pieces placed between a boat's sides to keep them apart when hoisted up and griped.

STRIKE. To lower a sail or colours.

STUDDINGSAILS. (See PLATE II.) Light sails set outside the square sails on booms rigged out for that purpose. They are only carried with a fair wind and in moderate weather.

SUED or SEWED. The condition of a ship when she is high and dry on shore. If the water leaves her two feet, she sues, or is sued, two feet.

SUPPORTERS. The knee-timbers under the cat-heads.

SURF. The breaking of the sea upon the shore.

SURGE. A large, swelling wave.

To *surge* a rope or cable, is to slack it up suddenly where it renders round a pin, or round the windlass or capstan.

Surge ho! The notice given when a cable is to be *surged.*

SWAB. A mop, formed of old rope, used for cleaning and drying decks.

SWEEP. To drag the bottom for an anchor. Also, large oars, used in small vessels to force them ahead.

SWIFT. To bring two shrouds or stays close together by ropes.

SWIFTER. The forward shroud to a lower mast. Also, ropes used to confine the capstan bars to their places when shipped.

SWIG. A term used by sailors for the mode of hauling off upon the bight of a rope when its lower end is fast.

SWIVEL. A long link of iron, used in chain cables, made so as to turn upon an axis and keep the turns out of a chain.

SYPHERING. Lapping the edges of planks over each other for a bulk-head.

TABLING. Letting one beam-piece into another. (See SCARFING.) Also, the broad hem on the borders of sails, to which the bolt-rope is sewed.

TACK. To put a ship about, so that from having the wind on one side, you bring it round on the other by the way of her head. The opposite of *wearing.*

A vessel is on the *starboard tack*, or has her *starboard tacks on board*, when she has the wind on her starboard side.

The rope or tackle by which the weather clew of a course is hauled forward and down to the deck.

The *tack* of a fore-and-aft sail is the rope that keeps down the lower forward clew; and of a studding sail, the lower outer clew. The tack of the lower studding sail is called the *out-haul.* Also, that part of a sail to which the tack is attached.

TACKLE. (Pronounced *tay-cle.*) A purchase formed by a rope rove through one or more blocks.

TAFFRAIL, or TAFFEREL. The rail round a ship's stern.

TAIL. A rope spliced into the end of a block, and used for making it fast to rigging or spars. Such a block is called a *tail-block.*

A ship is said to *tail* up or down stream, when at anchor, according as her stern swings up or down with the tide; in opposition to *heading* one way or another, which is said of a vessel when under way.

TAIL-TACKLE. A watch-tackle.

TAIL-ON! or TALLY ON! An order given to take hold of a rope and pull.

TANK. An iron vessel placed in the hold to contain the vessel's water.

TAR. A liquid gum, taken from pine and fir trees, and used for caulking, and to put upon yarns in rope-making, and upon standing rigging, to protect it from the weather.

TARPAULIN. A piece of canvas, covered with tar, used for covering hatches, boats, &c. Also the name commonly given to a sailor's hat when made of tarred or painted cloth.

TAUNT. High or tall. Commonly applied to a vessel's masts.

All-a-taunt-o. Said of a vessel when she has all her light and tall masts and spars aloft.

TAUT. Tight.

TELL-TALE. A compass hanging from the beams of the cabin, by which the heading of a vessel may be known at any time. Also, an instrument connected with the barrel of the wheel, and traversing so that the officer may see the position of the wheel.

TEND. To watch a vessel at anchor at the turn of tides, and cast her by the helm, and some sail if necessary, so as to keep turns out of her cables.

TENON. The heel of a mast, made to fit into the step.

THICK-AND-THIN BLOCK. A block having one sheave larger than the other. Sometimes used for quarter-blocks.

THIMBLE. An iron ring, having its rim concave on the outside for a rope or strap to fit snugly round.

THOLE-PINS. Pins in the gunwale of a boat, between which an oar rests when pulling, instead of a rowlock.

THROAT. The inner end of a gaff, where it widens and hollows in to fit the mast. (See JAWS.) Also, the hollow part of a knee.

The *throat* brails, halyards, &c., are those that hoist or haul up the gaff or sail near the throat. Also, the angle where the arm of an anchor is joined to the shank.

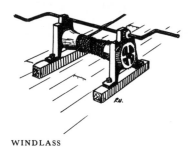

WINDLASS

THRUM. To stick short strands of yarn through a mat or piece of canvas, to make a rough surface.

THWARTS. The seats going across a boat, upon which the oarsmen sit.

THWARTSHIPS. (See ATHWARTSHIPS.)

TIDE. To *tide up or down* a river or harbour, is to work up or down with a fair tide and head wind or calm, coming to anchor when the tide turns.

TIDE-RODE. The situation of a vessel, at anchor, when she swings by the force of the tide. In opposition to *wind-rode*.

TIER. A range of casks. Also, the range of the fakes of a cable or hawser.

The *cable tier* is the place in a hold or between decks where the cables are stowed.

TILLER. A bar of wood or iron, put into the head of the rudder, by which the rudder is moved.

TILLER-ROPES. Ropes leading from the tiller-head round the barrel of the wheel, by which a vessel is steered.

TIMBER. A general term for all large pieces of wood used in ship-building. Also, more particularly, long pieces of wood in a curved form, bending outward, and running from the keel up, on each side, forming the *ribs* of a vessel. The keel, stem, sternposts, and timbers form a vessel's outer frame. (See PLATE III.)

TIMBER-HEADS. (See PLATE III.) The ends of the timbers that come above the decks. Used for belaying hawsers and large ropes.

TIMENOGUY. A rope carried taut between different parts of the vessel, to prevent the sheet or tack of a course from getting foul, in working ship.

TOGGLE. A pin placed through the bight or eye of a rope, block-strap, or bolt, to keep it in its place, or to put the bight or eye of another rope upon, and thus to secure them both together.

TOMPION. A bung or plug placed in the mouth of a cannon.

TOP. A platform placed over the head of a lower mast, resting on the trestle-trees, to spread the rigging, and for the convenience of men aloft. (See PLATE I.)

To *top* up a yard or boom, is to raise up one end of it by hoisting on the lift.

TOP-BLOCK. A large iron-bound block, hooked into a bolt under the lower cap, and used for the top-rope to reeve through in sending up and down topmasts.

TOP-LIGHT. A signal-lantern carried in the top.

TOP-LINING. A lining on the after part of sails, to prevent them from chafing against the top-rim.

TOPMAST. (See PLATE I.) The second mast above the deck. Next above the lower mast.

TOPGALLANT MAST. (See PLATE I.) The third mast above the deck.

TOP-ROPE. The rope used for sending topmasts up and down.

TOPSAIL. (See PLATE II.) The second sail above the deck.

TOPGALLANT SAIL. (See PLATE II.) The third sail above the deck.

TOPPING-LIFT. (See PLATE I.) A lift used for topping up the end of a boom.

TOP TIMBERS. The highest timbers on a vessel's side, being above the futtocks. (See PLATE III.)

TOSS. To throw an oar out of the rowlock, and raise it perpendicularly on its end, and lay it down in the boat, with its blade forward.

TOUCH. A sail is said to *touch*, when the wind strikes the leach so as to shake it a little.

Luff and touch her! The order to bring the vessel up and see how near she will go to the wind.

TOW. To draw a vessel along by means of a rope.

TRAIN-TACKLE. The tackle used for running guns in and out.

TRANSOMS. (See PLATE III.) Pieces of timber going across the stern-post, to which they are bolted.

TRANSOM-KNEES. Knees bolted to the transoms and after timbers.

TRAVELLER. An iron ring, fitted so as to slip up and down a rope.

TREENAILS, or TRUNNELS. Long wooden pins, used for nailing a plank to a timber.

TREND. The lower end of the shank of an anchor, being the same distance on the shank from the throat that the arm measures from the throat to the bill.

TRESTLE-TREES. Two strong pieces of timber, placed horizontally and fore-and-aft on opposite sides of a mast-head, to support the cross-trees and top, and for the fid of the mast above to rest upon.

TRIATIC STAY. A rope secured at each end to the heads of the fore and main masts, with thimbles spliced into its bight, to hook the stay tackles to.

TRICE. To haul up by means of a rope.

TRICK. The time allotted to a man to stand at the helm.

TRIM. The condition of a vessel, with reference to her cargo and ballast. A vessel is *trimmed* by the head or by the stern.

In ballast trim, is when she has only ballast on board.

Also, to arrange the sails by the braces with reference to the wind.

TRIP. To raise an anchor clear of the bottom.

TRIPPING LINE. A line used for tripping a topgallant or royal yard in sending it down.

TRUCK. A circular piece of wood, placed at the head of the highest mast on a ship. It has small holes or sheaves in it for signal halyards to be rove through. Also, the wheel of a gun-carriage.

TRUNNIONS. The arms on each side of a cannon by which it rests upon the carriage, and on which, as an axis, it is elevated or depressed.

TRUSS. The rope by which the centre of a lower yard is kept in toward the mast.

TRYSAIL. A fore-and-aft sail, set with a boom and gaff, and hoisting on a small mast abaft the lower mast, calling a *trysail-mast*. This name is generally confined to the sail so carried at the mainmast of a full-rigged brig; those carried at the foremast and at the mainmast of a ship or bark being called *spencers,* and those that are at the mizenmast of a ship or bark, *spankers.*

TUMBLING HOME. Said of a ship's sides when they fall in above the bends. The opposite of *wall-sided.*

TURN. Passing a rope once or twice round a pin or kevel, to keep it fast. Also, two crosses in a cable.

To turn in or *turn out,* nautical terms for going to rest in a berth or hammock, and getting up from them.

Turn up! The order given to send the men up from between decks.

TYE. A rope connected with a yard, to the other end of which a tackle is attached for hoisting.

UNBEND. To cast off or untie. (See BEND.)

UNION. The upper inner corner of an ensign. The rest of the flag is called the *fly.* The *union* of the U.S. ensign is a blue field with white stars, and the *fly* is composed of alternate white and red stripes.

Union-down. The situation of a flag when it is hoisted upside down, bringing the union down instead of up. Used as a signal of distress.

Union-jack. A small flag, containing only the union without the fly, usually hoisted at the bowsprit-cap.

UNMOOR. To heave up one anchor so that the vessel may ride at a single anchor. (See MOOR.)

UNSHIP. (See SHIP.)

UVROE. (See EUVROU.)

VANE. A fly worn at the mast-head, made of feathers or buntine, traversing on a spindle, to show the direction of the wind. (See DOG VANE.)

VANG. (See PLATE I.) A rope leading from the peak of the gaff of a fore-and-aft sail to the rail on each side, and used for steadying the gaff.

'VAST. (See AVAST.)

VEER. Said of the wind when it changes. Also to slack a cable and let it run out. (See PAY.)

To veer and haul, is to haul and slack alternately on a rope, as in warping, until the vessel or boat gets headway.

VIOL, or VOYAL. A larger messenger sometimes used in weighing an anchor by a capstan. Also the block through which the messenger passes.

WAIST. That part of the upper deck between the quarter-deck and forecastle.

Waisters. Green hands, or broken-down seamen, placed in the waist of a man-of-war.

WAKE. The track or path a ship leaves behind her in the water.

WALES. Strong planks in a vessel's sides running her whole length fore and aft.

WALL. A knot put on the end of a rope.

WALL-SIDED. A vessel is *wall-sided* when her sides run up perpendicularly from the bends. In opposition to *tumbling home* or *flaring out.*

WARD-ROOM. The room in a vessel of war in which the commissioned officers live.

WARE, OR WEAR. To turn a vessel round, so that from having the wind one one side, you bring it upon the other, carrying her stern round by the wind. In *tacking,* the same result is produced by carrying a vessel's head round by the wind.

WARP. To move a vessel from one place to another by means of a rope made fast to some fixed object, or to a kedge.

A *warp* is a rope used for warping. If the warp is bent to a kedge which is let go, and the vessel is hove ahead by the capstan or windlass, it would be called *kedging.*

WASH-BOARDS. Light pieces of board placed above the gunwale of a boat.

WATCH. A division of time on board ship. There are seven watches in a day, reckoning from 12 M. round through the 24 hours, five of them being of fours hours each, and the two others, called *dog watches,* of two hours each, viz., from 4 to 6, and from 6 to 8 P.M. (See DOG WATCH.) Also a certain portion of a ship's company, appointed to stand a given length of time. In the merchant service all hands are divided into two watches, larboard and starboard, with a mate to command each.

A *buoy* is said to *watch* when it floats on the surface.

WATCH-AND-WATCH. The arrangement by which the watches are alternated every other four hours. In distinction from keeping all hands during one or more watches.
Anchor watch, a small watch of one or two men, kept while in port.
WATCH-HO! WATCH! The cry of the man that heaves the deep-sea lead.
WATCH-TACKLE. A small luff purchase with a short fall, the double block having a tail to it, and the single one a hook. Used for various purposes about decks.
WATER-SAIL. A *save all,* set under the swinging-boom.
WATER-WAYS. Long pieces of timber, running fore and aft on both sides, connecting the deck with the vessel's sides. The *scuppers* are made through them to let the water off. (See PLATE III.)
WEAR. (See WARE.)
WEATHER. In the direction from which the wind blows. (See WINDWARD, LEE.)
A ship carries a *weather-helm* when she tends to come up into the wind, requiring you to put the helm up.
Weather gage. A vessel has the *weather gage* of another when she is to windward of her.
A *weatherly ship,* is one that works well to windward, making but little leeway.
WEATHER-BITT. To take an additional turn with cable round the windlass-end.
WEATHER ROLL. The roll which a ship makes to windward.
WEIGH. To lift up; as, to weigh an anchor or a mast.
WHEEL. The instrument by which a ship is steered; being a barrel (round which the tiller-ropes go), and a wheel with spokes.
WHIP. A purchase formed by a rope rove through a single block.
To whip, is to hoist by a whip. Also, to secure the end of a rope from fagging by a seizing of twine.
Whip-upon-whip. One whip applied to the fall of another.
WINCH. A purchase formed by a horizontal spindle or shaft with a wheel or crank at the end. A small one with a wheel is used for making ropes or spunyarn.
WINDLASS. The machine used in merchant vessels to weigh the anchor by.
WIND-RODE. The situation of a vessel at anchor, when she swings and rides by the force of the wind, instead of the tide or current. (See TIDE-RODE.)
WING. That part of the hold or between-decks which is next the side.
WINGERS. Casks stowed in the wings of a vessel.
WING-AND-WING. The situation of a fore-and-aft vessel when she is going dead before the wind, with her foresail hauled over on one side and her mainsail on the other.
WITHE, or WYTHE. An iron instrument fitted on the end of a boom or mast, with a ring to it through which another boom or mast is rigged out and secured.
WOOLD. To wind a piece of rope round a spar.
WORK UP. To draw the yarns from old rigging and make them into spunyarn, foxes, sennet, &c. Also, a phrase for keeping a crew constantly at work upon needless matters, and in all weathers, and beyond their usual hours, for punishment.
WORM. To fill up between the lays of a rope with small stuff wound round spirally. Stuff so wound round is called *worming.*
WRING. To bend or strain a mast by setting the rigging up too taut.
WRING-BOLTS. Bolts that secure the planks to the timbers.
WRING-STAVES. Strong pieces of plank used with the ring-bolts.

YACHT. (Pronounced *yot.*) A vessel of pleasure or state.
YARD. (See PLATE I.) A long piece of timber, tapering slightly toward the ends, and hung by the centre to a mast, to spread the square sails upon.
YARD-ARM. The extremities of a yard.
YARD-ARM AND YARD-ARM. The situation of two vessels, lying alongside one another, so near that their yard-arms cross or touch.
YARN. (See ROPEYARN.)
YAW. The motion of a vessel when she goes off from her course.
YEOMAN. A man employed in a vessel of war to take charge of a store-room; as, boatswain's yeoman, the man that has charge of the stores of rigging, &c.
YOKE. A piece of wood placed across the head of a boat's rudder, with a rope attached to each end, by which the boat is steered.

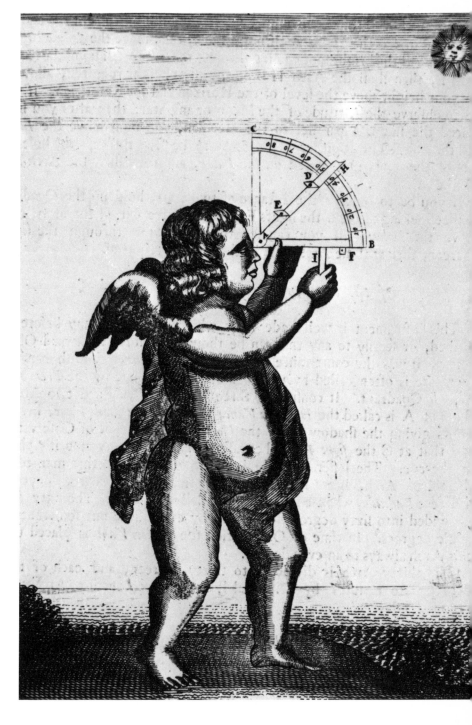

265 Cherub using quadrant, 1681.

List of black and white illustrations